100

CONTEMPORARY ARCHITECTS

100 zeitgenössische Architekten
100 architectes contemporains
Philip Jodidio

J–Z

TASCHEN

CONTENTS

CONTENTS

JAKOB + MACFARLANE

Jakob + MacFarlane SARL d'Architecture
13–15, rue des Petites Écuries
75010 Paris
France

Tel: +33 1 4479 0572
Fax: +33 1 4800 9793
E-mail: info@jakobmacfarlane.com
Web: www.jakobmacfarlane.com

DOMINIQUE JAKOB was born in 1966 and holds a degree in art history from the Université de Paris I (1990) and a degree in architecture from the École d'Architecture Paris-Villemin (1991). She has taught at the École Spéciale d'Architecture (1998–99) and at the École d'Architecture Paris-Villemin (1994–2000). Born in New Zealand in 1961, **BRENDAN MACFARLANE** received his B.Arch. at SCI-Arc, Los Angeles (1984), and his M.Arch. degree at the Harvard Graduate School of Design (1990). He has taught at the Paris La Villette architecture school (1995–96), at the Berlage Institute, Amsterdam (1996), at the Bartlett School of Architecture in London (1996–98) and at the École Spéciale d'Architecture in Paris (1998–99). From 1995 to 1997, MacFarlane was an architectural critic at the Architectural Association (AA) in London. Jakob and MacFarlane founded their own agency in 1992 in Paris. Their main projects include the T House, La-Garenne-Colombes, France (1994–98); the Georges Restaurant at Georges Pompidou Center, Paris (1999–2000); the restructuring of the Maxime Gorki Theater, Petit-Quevilly, France (1999–2000); the Renault International Communication Center, Boulogne (2002–05); the Herold housing complex in Paris (2008); and the transformation of Parisian docks into a city of fashion and design (2008).

DOMINIQUE JAKOB, 1966 in Paris geboren, schloss 1990 ihr Studium der Kunstgeschichte an der Université de Paris 1 ab und machte 1991 ihren Abschluss in Architektur an der École d'Architecture Paris-Villemin. 1998/99 lehrte sie an der École Spéciale d'Architecture und von 1994 bis 2000 an der École d'Architecture Paris-Villemin. Der 1961 in Christ Church in Neuseeland geborene **BRENDAN MACFARLANE** erwarb 1984 seinen Bachelor of Architecture am Southern California Institute of Architecture (SCI-Arc) und 1990 seinen Master of Architecture an der Harvard Graduate School of Design. Er lehrte an der Pariser Architekturhochschule La Villette (1995–1996), am Berlage-Institut in Amsterdam (1996), der Bartlett School of Architecture in London (1996–98) und an der École Spéciale d'Architecture in Paris (1998–99). 1995 bis 1997 war McFarlane Architekturtheoretiker an der Architectural Association (AA) in London. Jakob und MacFarlane gründeten ihr eigenes Architekturbüro 1992 in Paris. Zu ihren wichtigsten Projekten gehören das T-Haus im französischen La-Garenne-Colombes (1994–98), das Restaurant Georges im Pariser Centre Georges Pompidou (1999–2000), die Neugestaltung des Maxime-Gorki-Theaters in Le-Petit-Quévilly in Frankreich (1999–2000) und das Renault International Communication Center in Boulogne (2002–05). Weitere Projekte sind der Herold-Wohnkomplex in Paris (2008) und die Umgestaltung von Docks in Paris in eine Mode- und Designstadt (2008).

DOMINIQUE JAKOB, née à Paris en 1966, est diplômée d'histoire de l'art de l'Université de Paris 1 (1990) puis diplômée d'architecture de l'École d'architecture de Paris-Villemin (1991). Elle a enseigné à l'École Spéciale d'Architecture (1998–99) puis à l'École d'architecture de Paris-Villemin (1994–2000). Né en Nouvelle-Zélande en 1961, **BRENDAN MACFARLANE** est Bachelor of Architecture du Southern California Institute of Architecture (1984) et Master of Architecture de l'Harvard Graduate School of Design (1990). Il a enseigné à l'École nationale supérieure d'architecture de Paris-La Villette (1995–96), à l'Institut Berlage d'Amsterdam (1996), à la Bartlett School of Architecture de Londres (1996–98) et à l'École Spéciale d'Architecture de Paris (1998–99). De 1995 à 1997, MacFarlane a été critique d'architecture à l'Architectural Association (AA) de Londres. Jakob et MacFarlane ont créé leur propre agence à Paris en 1992. Parmi leurs principaux projets : la Maison T (La Garenne-Colombes, France, 1994–98), le restaurant du Centre Georges Pompidou (Paris, France, 1999–2000), la restructuration du Théâtre Maxime Gorki (Le Petit Quevilly, France, 1999–2000) et le Centre de communication Renault (Boulogne-Billancourt, 2002–05). Citons également le complexe d'appartements Herold à Paris (2008) et la transformation des docks parisiens en une cité de la mode et du design (2008).

CENTRE GEORGES POMPIDOU RESTAURANT

Paris, France, 1998–2000

Competition: 1998. Construction: 3/99–1/2000. Client: Costes.
Floor area: 900 m² (restaurant), 450 m² (terrace). Costs: c. € 2.4 million.

Designed in conjunction with the overall renovation of the Centre by Renzo Piano and Jean-François Baudin, the **CENTRE GEORGES POMPIDOU RESTAURANT** occupies a corner with a spectacular view of Paris. The aluminum floor rises up to form four "sky grottoes" that house the kitchen, toilets, a bar and a VIP guestroom. The overall silver color scheme is broken in the interior rooms with bright red, yellow, green and orange rubber coating applied to the aluminum walls. Steel-frame tables, with battery-operated lights that make them appear to glow from within, were designed by the architects to fit into the overall grid, as were the steel and polyurethane chairs. Although the design competition was organized by the Centre before the operators of the restaurant, the well-known Costes brothers, had been selected, they were able to participate in the decision regarding the final details of the concept.

Das **CENTRE GEORGES POMPIDOU RESTAURANT**, das einen fantastischen Ausblick auf Paris bietet, wurde im Rahmen der von Renzo Piano und Jean-François Baudin durchgeführten umfassenden Renovierung des Gebäudes entworfen. Der Aluminiumboden erhebt sich zu vier Volumen, den „Himmelshöhlen", in denen die Küche, Toiletten, eine Bar und ein VIP-Raum untergebracht sind. Die insgesamt vorherrschende silberne Farbgebung wird in den Innenräumen von hellroten, gelben, grünen und orangen Gummibelägen auf den Aluminiumwänden durchbrochen. Stahlrahmentische, die mit batteriebetriebenen Lampen von innen beleuchtet werden, und die Stühle aus Stahl und Polyurethan wurden von den Architekten entworfen. Obwohl der Designwettbewerb vom Centre Pompidou durchgeführt wurde, bevor die bekannten Costes-Brüder als Restaurantbetreiber ausgewählt waren, konnten sie sich an der Entscheidung über das endgültige Baukonzept beteiligen.

Créé dans le cadre de la rénovation d'ensemble du Centre par Renzo Piano et Jean-François Bodin, le **CENTRE GEORGES POMPIDOU RESTAURANT** occupe un angle du bâtiment, au 6ème étage, et bénéficie donc d'une vue spectaculaire sur Paris. Le sol d'aluminium semble se soulever pour former quatre « grottes » qui abritent la cuisine, les toilettes, un bar et un salon VIP. Leur intérieur revêtu de caoutchouc rouge vif, jaune, vert et orange, rompt avec la coloration générale argentée. Des tables à piétement d'acier, dotées d'un éclairage sur batterie qui leur donne l'impression de luire de l'intérieur, ont été dessinées par les architectes pour s'intégrer dans la trame générale, de même que les sièges en acier et polyuréthane. Si le concours a été organisé avant que le concessionnaire – les Frères Costes – n'ait été choisi, celui-ci a pu participer à la mise au point des détails.

The aluminum volumes added to the Centre Pompidou's top floor house bathrooms, kitchens and a bar.

Im Obergeschoss sind von Aluminium-wänden begrenzt Küche, Toiletten und eine Bar untergebracht.

Les volumes d'aluminium du dernier étage abritent la cuisine, un bar et les toilettes.

MICHAEL JANTZEN

Michael Jantzen
27800 N. McBean Parkway, Suite 319
Valencia, California 91354
USA

Tel: +1 310 989 1897
E-mail: mjantzen@me.com
Web: www.humanshelter.org

In 1971, **MICHAEL JANTZEN** received a bachelor's degree with a major in fine arts from Southern Illinois University (Edwardsville, Illinois). In 1973, he received an MFA degree with a major in multimedia from Washington University (St. Louis, Missouri). Jantzen was then hired by Washington University's School of Fine Arts and by the School of Architecture to teach studio courses as a visiting professor. In 1975, one of his first solar houses was featured in numerous national and international magazines. Over the next ten years, he continued to design and build energy-efficient structures with an emphasis on modular high-tech housing systems. In 1997, he was awarded a grant from Art Center College of Design Digital Media Department to develop ideas for an interface between media and architecture. In 1998, Jantzen developed several digital media projects that were published widely. He created a conceptual house called the Malibu Video Beach House, and Elements, an interactive digital media theme park for the next millennium. Early in 1999, he began to design and build the M-House project, a modular, relocatable, environmentally responsive, alternative housing system, which was completed in 2000.

MICHAEL JANTZEN erwarb 1971 seinen Bachelor of Fine Arts (BFA) an der Southern Illinois University in Edwardsville, Illinois und 1973 den Master (MFA) im Hauptfach Multimedia an der Washington University in St. Louis, Missouri. Anschließend war Jantzen an der School of Fine Arts und der School of Architecture der Washington University als Gastprofessor tätig. 1975 wurde eins seiner ersten Solarhäuser in etlichen amerikanischen und internationalen Zeitschriften vorgestellt. Während der nächsten zehn Jahre entwarf und gestaltete er energiesparende Bauten mit dem Schwerpunkt auf modularen Hightech-Wohnbausystemen. 1997 wurde er vom Design Digital Media Department des Art Center College of Design mit einem Stipendium ausgezeichnet, um seine Ideen für ein Interface zwischen elektronischen Medien und Architektur weiterentwickeln zu können. 1998 führte Jantzen mehrere digitale Medienprojekte durch, die große Beachtung fanden. Er entwarf ein Modellhaus namens Malibu Video Beach House sowie einen interaktiven digitalen Medienthemenpark für das neue Jahrtausend namens Elements. Anfang 1999 begann er mit der Planung und Konstruktion des Projekts M-House, bei dem es sich um ein modulares, versetzbares und ökologisch-alternatives Wohnbausystem handelt und das mittlerweile fertiggestellt ist.

MICHAEL JANTZEN est B. A. de la Southern Illinois University (Edwardsville, Illinois) en 1971. En 1973, il est M. A. en Multimédia à Washington University (St. Louis, Missouri) dont il devient immédiatement professeur d'atelier invité par l'École des Beaux-Arts et l'École d'architecture. En 1975, l'une de ses premières maisons solaires est publiée dans de nombreux journaux et magazines internationaux. Au cours des dix années suivantes, il continue à concevoir et réaliser des constructions axées sur les économies d'énergie en étudiant particulièrement des systèmes de logement high-tech modulaires. En 1997, il reçoit une bourse du Art Center College of Design Digital Media Department pour développer ses idées sur une interface médias-architecture. En 1998, il met au point plusieurs projets sur médias numériques amplement publiés. Il a créé une maison conceptuelle, la Malibu Video Beach House, et Elements, un parc thématique en images de synthèse. Dès le début de 1999, il entreprend la conception et la construction de la M-House, un système de logement modulaire, déplaçable et écologique. Ce projet est désormais achevé.

M-HOUSE

Gorman, California, USA, 2000

*Area: 90 m². Structure: painted composite concrete panels hinged onto
a steel-tube frame of seven intersecting cubes.*

"It's not just a funny-looking building," says Michael Jantzen, who describes himself more as an artist than an architect. "I'm rethinking the whole notion of living space," he says. What he calls "Relocatable M-vironments" are made of a "wide variety of manipulatable components that can be connected in many different ways to a matrix of modular support frames." He writes that the **M-HOUSE**, which is made from the M-vironment system, consists of a series of rectangular panels that are attached with hinges to an open space frame grid of seven interlocking cubes. The panels are hinged to the cubes in either a horizontal or a vertical orientation. The hinges allow the panels to fold into, or out of the cube frames to perform various functions." This version of the house was built with nonflammable composite concrete panels hinged to a steel tube frame. Jantzen built this one-bedroom cottage entirely by himself on a site northwest of Los Angeles. The structure is designed to withstand high winds and earthquakes, and can be assembled or disassembled by a crew of four in one week.

„Es ist nicht bloß ein komisch aussehendes Gebäude", sagt Michael Jantzen, der sich eher als Künstler denn als Architekt sieht, über sein M-House: Vielmehr sei es der Versuch, das Konzept Wohnraum von Grund auf neu zu überdenken. Was der Architekt als „umsiedelbare M-vironments" bezeichnet, besteht aus einer Vielzahl veränderbarer Komponenten, die auf unterschiedliche Weise bausteinartig mit einer Matrix wandelbarer Tragrahmen verbunden werden können. Das aus dem M-vironment-System entstandene **M-HOUSE** besteht aus einer Reihe rechteckiger Paneele, die mittels Scharniere entweder horizontal oder vertikal an einer offenen Gitterkonstruktion aus sieben ineinandergreifenden Kuben befestigt sind. Durch die Scharniere können die einzelnen Paneele in den Rahmen hinein oder aus ihm herausgeklappt werden und auf diese Weise unterschiedliche Funktionen erfüllen. Die hier vorgestellte Ein-Zimmer-Version des Hauses, die der Architekt selbst auf einem Grundstück nordwestlich von Los Angeles aufgebaut hat, wurde aus nichtbrennbaren Verbundbetonplatten und einem Stahlrohrrahmen gefertigt. Dieses Cottage ist so konstruiert, dass es sturmfest und erdbebensicher ist und von vier Leuten innerhalb einer Woche auf- oder abgebaut werden kann.

« Ce n'est pas seulement un bâtiment à l'air bizarre », commente Michael Jantzen qui se présente plus comme un artiste qu'un architecte. « Je repense toute la notion d'espace de vie. » Ce qu'il appelle les « Relocatable M-vironments » sont constitués d'une « grande variété de composants manipulables qui peuvent être connectés de multiples façons à une matrice structurelle de soutien modulaire. « La **M-HOUSE**, qui fait appel au M-vironment System, consiste en série de panneaux rectangulaires attachés par des charnières à une trame structurelle ouverte de sept cubes imbriqués. Les panneaux s'articulent verticalement ou horizontalement sur les cubes par des charnières. Celles-ci permettent aux panneaux de se replier vers l'intérieur ou de s'ouvrir vers l'extérieur pour remplir diverses fonctions. » Cette version de la maison a été construite en panneaux de béton composite non feu articulés à une ossature en tube d'acier. Jantzen a réalisé entièrement lui-même cette maisonnette de deux pièces sur un terrain au nord-ouest de Los Angeles. Elle est conçue pour résister aux vents violents et aux tremblements de terre, et peut être montée ou démontée par quatre personnes en une semaine.

Although made up here of seven cubes, the structure is infinitely variable and could conceivably be much larger. Its green color, inside and out, is intended to "immerse" the resident in the design.

Die hier in sieben Kuben ausgeführte Konstruktion ist unendlich variabel und könnte auch sehr viel weiter ausgebaut werden. Die außen und innen angebrachte grüne Farbe soll den Bewohner ganz in das Design hineinziehen.

Bien que composée ici de sept cubes, la structure peut varier à l'infini et pourrait être beaucoup plus importante. Sa couleur verte, à l'intérieur comme à l'extérieur, participe à « l'immersion » de l'habitant dans le projet.

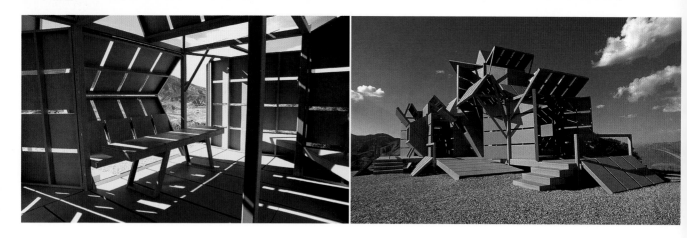

Built-in furniture and a large variety of possible openings make the house both practical and easy to modify.

Einbaumöbel und eine Vielzahl an Öffnungen machen das Haus sowohl praktisch als auch leicht modifizierbar.

Des meubles intégrés et la multiplicité des possibilités d'ouverture rendent la maison à la fois pratique et facile à modifier.

JONES, PARTNERS: ARCHITECTURE

Jones, Partners: Architecture
800 McGarry Street, #436
Los Angeles, California 90021
USA

Tel: +1 213 327 0034
E-mail: info@jonespartners.com
Web: www.jonespartners.com

WES JONES, born in 1958 in Santa Monica, attended the United States Military Academy at West Point, the University of California at Berkeley (B. Arch., 1980), and the Harvard Graduate School of Design, where he received a M.Arch. degree (1983). A recipient of the Rome Prize in Architecture, he has taught at Harvard, Princeton, IIT, Ohio, and Columbia Universities. He presently teaches at the Southern California Institute of Architecture (SCI-Arc). He worked with Eisenman/Robertson, Architects in New York before becoming partner in charge of design at Holt Hinshaw Pfau Jones in San Francisco. He founded his own practice, Jones, Partners: Architecture, in 1993. **DOUG JACKSON**, born in 1970 in Hampton (Virginia), attended Virginia Tech (B.Arch., 1993) and Princeton University (M.Arch., 2000). He has collaborated with Jones, Partners: Architecture on various projects. His projects include duplex residences in Silverlake and Redondo Beach, single-family residences in Manhattan Beach, Hollywood, Agua Dulce (all California), and Phoenix, Arizona; offices in Carson and Culver City, California; the Book Concern Building apartments in San Francisco, California; a telecom co-location facility in Bahrain; and a host of PRO/con (container) projects in Arcata, Venice, and Culver City, California, and on Molokai, Hawaii.

WES JONES, 1958 in Santa Monica geboren, studierte an der United States Military Academy in West Point, der University of California in Berkeley (B. Arch., 1980) und an der Harvard Graduate School of Design, wo er den Master in Architektur erwarb. Er erhielt den Prix de Rome für Architektur und unterrichtete an den Universitäten Harvard, Princeton, IIT, Ohio und Columbia. Derzeit ist er Dozent an der Southern California School of Architecture (SCI-Arc). Wes Jones arbeitete im New Yorker Büro Eisenman/Robertson, Architects, bevor er Partner und Director of Design bei Holt Hinshaw Pfau Jones in San Francisco wurde. 1993 gründete er ein eigenes Büro, Jones, Partners: Architecture. **DOUG JACKSON** wurde 1970 in Hampton (Virginia) geboren und besuchte die Virginia Tech (B. Arch. 1993) sowie die Universität Princeton (M. Arch. 2000). Er hat bei verschiedenen Projekten mit Jones, Partners: Architecture zusammengearbeitet. Zu seinen Projekten in Kalifornien gehören Wohnhäuser in Silverlake und Redondo Beach, Einfamilienhäuser in Manhattan Beach, Hollywood und Agua Dulce; Büros in Carson und Culver City, die Book Concern Building Apartments in San Francisco. Daneben baute er Einfamilienhäuser in Phoenix (Arizona). Eine Kollokationseinrichtung für den Telefonverkehr entstand in Bahrain und PRO/con-Projekte (Container) in Arcata, Venice und Culver City in Kalifornien sowie auf Molokai in Hawaii.

WES JONES, né en 1958 à Santa Monica, étudie à l'école militaire de West Point, à l'Université de Californie à Berkeley (B. Arch. 1980) et à l'Harvard Graduate School of Design dont il est M. Arch. Titulaire du prix de Rome d'architecture, il a enseigné à Harvard, Princeton, IIT, Ohio et Columbia. Actuellement il enseigne à la Southern School of Architecture (SCI-Arc). Il a travaillé avec Eisenman/Robertson, Architects à New York avant de devenir associé et directeur de la conception chez Holt & Hinshaw à San Francisco. En 1993, il fonde sa propre agence, Jones, Partners : Architecture. **DOUG JACKSON**, né à Hampton (Virginie) en 1970, étudie à la Virginia Tech (B. Arch, 1993) et à l'Université de Princeton dont il sort M. Arch. (2000). Il a collaboré sur plusieurs projets avec Jones, Partners : Architectures. Parmi ses réalisations en Californie : des résidences à Silverlake et Redondo Beach, des maisons individuelles à Manhattan Beach, Hollywood, Algua Dulce, et Phoenix, (Arizona) ; des bureaux à Carson et Culver City, les Book Concern Building Apartments à San Francisco. De plus, il a construit des maisons individuelles à Phoenix (Arizona). Une installation de colocation pour télécommunication a vu le jour à Bahrain de même que les projets PRO/con (conteneurs) à Arcata (Venice), à Culver City (Californie) et à Molokai (Hawaii).

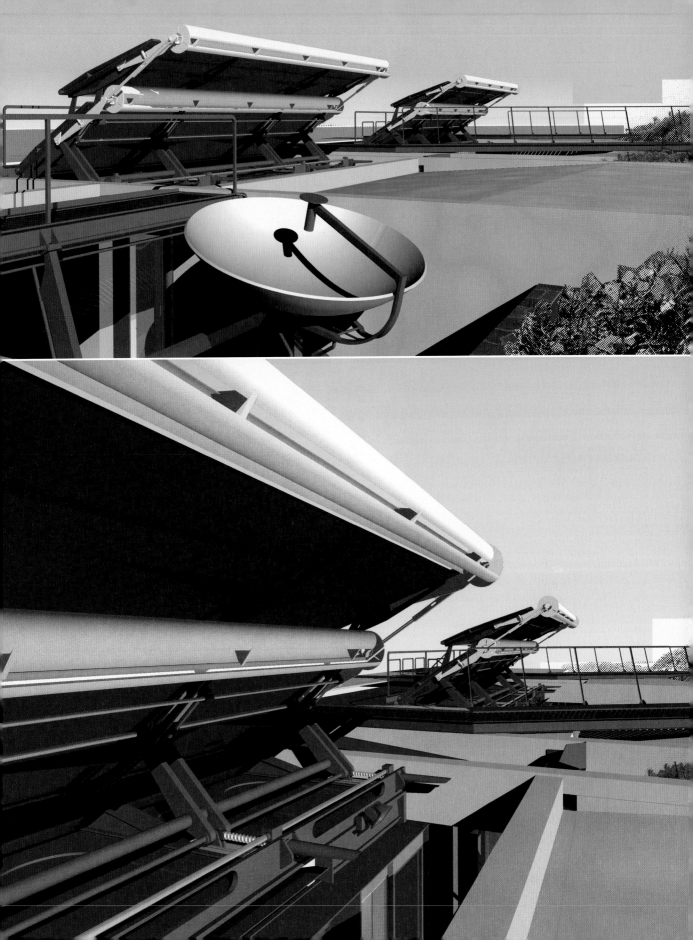

QUEBRADILLAS HOUSE

Quebradillas, Puerto Rico, 2001–02

Client: Eric and Nanette Brill. Structure: cast-in-place reinforced concrete bearing walls and flat slab on concrete footings.
Site area: 1.5 hectares. Area: 190 m².

Set on a 1.5 hectare site on a volcanic cliff overlooking the sea on the northern coast of Puerto Rico, this house for a couple and their three children is specifically designed to resist frequent hurricane-force winds. The **QUEBRADILLAS HOUSE** is approached from the roof side. The architect says that the house is to be seen to a certain extent "as an outpost" and as such has "two adjustable wing-mounted, horizontal-axis wind turbine assemblies projecting from the upper deck" to take advantage of the nearly constant wind from the north. Rainwater is stored in cisterns beneath the living spaces and vents provide for natural ventilation. Emphasizing the fortified aspect of the house, the lower walkways and decks "are hinged to rotate up and act as storm shutters, protecting the glazing as well as locking the house up tight." Made mostly with cast-in-place concrete, the house has got sealed or waxed concrete, local veneer plywoods, stainless steel and plaster for the interior finishes. The floor area of the house is just under 200 m².

Das für eine Familie mit drei Kindern gebaute Wohnhaus mit Meerblick liegt an der Nordküste von Puerto Rico auf einem 1,5 ha großen Grundstück am Abhang eines Vulkans. Das Gebäude wurde so konstruiert, dass es den häufig auftretenden Hurrikans standhält; der Zugang liegt auf der Hangseite. Das **QUEBRADILLAS-HAUS** sei eine Art „Vorposten", so der Architekt, und habe zwei verstellbare, über das Dach auskragende, flügelartige Windräder mit horizontaler Kippachse, um den fast unablässig von Norden her wehenden Wind zu nutzen. Unterhalb der Wohnräume befinden sich Regenwasserspeicher, Abzugsöffnungen sorgen für eine natürliche Be- und Entlüftung. Die unteren Durchgänge und Dachteile haben eine Kippvorrichtung und lassen sich nach oben drehen, um als Windschutz zu fungieren, was den festungsartigen Charakter des Hauses optisch noch verstärkt und sowohl die Verglasungen schützt als auch das Haus fest verschließt. Der Bau ist hauptsächlich aus vor Ort gegossenem Beton gefertigt. Die Innenräume sind mit versiegeltem oder gewachstem Beton, Furnierplatten aus einheimischem Holz, rostfreiem Stahl und Gipsverputz ausgestattet. Der Grundriss des Hauses umfasst knapp 200 m² Nutzfläche.

Implantée sur un terrain de 1,5 hectare en bordure d'une falaise volcanique qui domine l'océan sur la côte nord de Puerto Rico, cette maison destinée à un couple et ses trois enfants a été conçue pour résister aux ouragans. On y accède par le toit. L'architecte explique qu'elle doit être considérée dans une certaine mesure comme un « avant-poste ». Elle possède « deux turbines éoliennes à axe horizontal montées en ailes réglables qui se projettent du pont supérieur » pour tirer parti du vent qui souffle en permanence du nord. L'eau de pluie est conservée dans des citernes sous la maison et le vent assure la ventilation naturelle. Mettant en valeur l'aspect fortifié de la **MAISON QUEBRADILLAS**, les ponts et coursives de la partie inférieure « sont articulés pour se refermer et servir de volet de protection en cas de tempête, protéger les baies vitrées et l'étanchéité de la maison ». La maison est essentiellement réalisée en béton coulé sur place, béton lissé ou ciré, contre-plaqués d'origine locale, acier inoxydable et plâtre pour les finitions intérieures. Sa surface totale ne dépasse pas 200 m².

Located on a cliff, the low-lying house is meant to "break" the force of hurricane winds by facing the ocean at a low angle. This is also the reason that its roof is at the level of the adjacent ground.

Das an einem Abhang liegende Haus ist im flachen Winkel zum Ozean hin ausgerichtet, um die Wucht der Hurrikans zu brechen. Aus demselben Grund wurde das Dach nicht über den Hang hinausgebaut.

Implantée sur une falaise, cette maison basse veut « briser » la force des vents des ouragans par sa position surbaissée face à l'océan. C'est la raison pour laquelle le toit se trouve au niveau du sol.

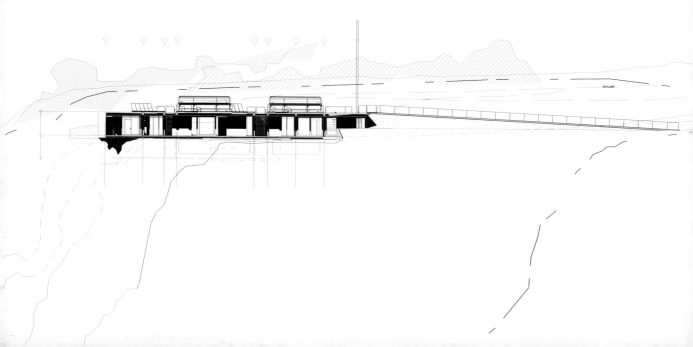

The house is approached from the uphill side, with the visitor coming down toward the roof of the structure. The roof-deck also serves as a platform to observe the ocean.

Der Zugang zum Haus erfolgt von der Hangseite, von wo der Besucher auf das tief liegende Dach zugeht. Die Dachterrasse selbst dient auch als Aussichtsplattform.

Le visiteur accède à la maison par le haut de la colline, et descend donc vers le toit. Celui-ci, qui fait office de terrasse, permet l'observation de l'océan.

As the architect says, "The view is presented directly: as if in deference to its power, the house itself is very simple and straightforward, a linked series of alcoves off the organizing horizon."

Der Architekt über seinen Entwurf: „Der Ausblick präsentiert sich unmittelbar: Wie um Rücksicht auf seine kraftvolle Wirkung zu nehmen, ist das Haus selbst sehr einfach strukturiert – als eine horizontal ausgerichtete Reihe von Nischen."

Pour l'architecte : « La vue est directe, comme si, par déférence envers son pouvoir, la maison elle-même se faisait simple et sans détour, série d'alcôves reliées entre elles, face à l'horizon qui lui donne son sens. »

PATRICK JOUIN

Agence Patrick Jouin
8, passage de la Bonne Graine
75011 Paris
France

Tel: +33 1 5528 8920
Fax: +33 1 5830 6070
E-mail: agence@patrickjouin.com
Web: www.patrickjouin.com

Born in Nantes, France, in 1967, **PATRICK JOUIN** studied at the École Nationale Supérieure de Création Industrielle (ENSCI) in Paris and received his diploma in 1992. He worked in 1992 as a designer at the Compagnie des Wagons-Lits, and for the two following years at Tim Thom, Thomson Multimédia, under Philippe Starck who was then Artistic Director of the brand. From 1995 to 1999, Patrick Jouin was a designer in Philippe Starck's Paris studio. He created his own office in 1998. **SANJIT MANKU**, born in Nairobi, Kenya in 1971, and educated at Carlton University School of Architecture, became a partner in 2006, with the intention of working on architectural projects. Patrick Jouin has designed numerous objects and pieces of furniture. The firm's architectural work includes: Alain Ducasse au Plaza Athénée Restaurant (Paris, 2000); 59 Poincaré Restaurant (Paris, 2000); Plastic Products Factory (Nantes, 2001); Plaza Athénée Bar (Paris, 2001); Spoon Byblos Restaurant (Saint Tropez, 2002); Mix New York Restaurant for Alain Ducasse (2003); Chlösterli Restaurants et Club, Spoon des Neiges Restaurant (Gstaad, Switzerland, 2004); Mix Restaurant Las Vegas (2004); Terrasse Montaigne, Plaza Athénée (Paris, 2005); Gilt Restaurant and Bar (New York, 2005); and a house in Kuala Lumpur (Malaysia, 2004–07). Jouin's Solid collection of furniture for the Belgian firm MGX uses the sophisticated technique of stereo-lithography to create remarkable, unique polymer objects.

Der 1967 in Nantes geborene **PATRICK JOUIN** studierte an der École nationale supérieure de création industrielle (ENSCI) in Paris, wo er 1992 sein Diplom erhielt. Im selben Jahr arbeitete er als Designer bei der Compagnie des Wagons-Lits und in den beiden folgenden Jahren bei Tim Thom, Thomsen Multimédia, für Philippe Starck, der damals Art Director für die Marke war. Von 1995 bis 1999 war Patrick Jouin Designer bei Philippe Starck in Paris. Er gründete 1998 sein eigenes Büro. **SANJIT MANKU**, geboren 1971 in Nairobi, Kenia, studierte an der Carlton University School of Architecture. Er wurde 2006 Partner, um an Architekturprojekten zu arbeiten. Patrick Jouin entwarf zahlreiche Objekte und Möbelstücke, zu den Architekturprojekten der Agentur gehören u. a. folgende: das Restaurant Alain Ducasse im Plaza Athénée (Paris, 2000), das Restaurant 59 Poincaré (Paris, 2000), eine Fabrik für Kunststoffprodukte (Nantes, 2001), Plaza Athénée Bar (Paris, 2001), das Restaurant Spoon Byblos (Saint-Tropez, 2002), das Mix Restaurant für Alain Ducasse (New York, 2003), das Chlösterli mit zwei Restaurants und Club, das Restaurant Spoon des Neiges (beide in Gstaad, Schweiz, 2004), das Mix Restaurant in Las Vegas (2004), die Terrasse Montaigne im Plaza Athénée (Paris, 2005), das Gilt Restaurant mit Bar (New York, 2005) sowie ein Haus in Kuala Lumpur (Malaysia, 2004–07). Seine Möbelkollektion „Solid" für die belgische Firma MGX setzt die anspruchsvolle Technik der Stereo-Lithografie ein, um einzigartige Polymerobjekte herzustellen.

Né à Nantes en 1967, **PATRICK JOUIN** a étudié à l'École nationale supérieure de création industrielle (ENSCI) à Paris dont il est sorti diplômé en 1992. Il a ensuite travaillé pour la Compagnie des Wagons-Lits, puis les deux années suivantes pour Tim Thom, département de design de Thomson Multimédia animé par Philippe Starck, alors directeur artistique de la marque. De 1995 à 1999, il a été designer chez celui-ci. Il a crée son agence en 1998. **SANJIT MANKU**, né à Nairobi au Kenya en 1971, a fait ses études à l'École d'architecture de la Carlton University et a rejoint Patrick Jouin en 2006 pour travailler sur les projets architecturaux. Patrick Jouin a conçu de nombreux objets et meubles. Les interventions architecturales de l'agence comprennent : le restaurant Alain Ducasse du Plaza Athénée, Paris (2000) ; le restaurant 59 Poincaré, Paris (2000) ; une usine de produits en plastique, Nantes (2001) ; le bar du Plaza Athénée, Paris (2001) ; le restaurant Spoon Byblos, Saint-Tropez (2002) ; le restaurant Mix pour Alain Ducasse, New York (2003) ; les restaurants et club Chlösterli et le restaurant Spoon des Neiges à Gstaad, Suisse (2004) ; le restaurant Mix, Las Vegas (2004) ; la Terrasse Montaigne, Plaza Athénée, Paris (2005) ; le Gilt Restaurant and Bar, New York (2005) et une maison à Kuala Lumpur, Malaisie (2004–07). Sa collection de meubles Solid pour le fabricant belge MGX fait appel à des techniques sophistiquées de stéréolithographie pour créer de remarquables objets uniques en polymères.

CHLÖSTERLI

Gstaad, Switzerland, 2003

Floor area: 700 m² (bar, lounge, discotheque, 2 restaurants, 2 kitchens). Client: Michel Pastor.
Costs: not disclosed.

Located outside the town, on the main road leading into Gstaad, **CHLÖSTERLI** was created by Patrick Jouin inside a traditional Swiss chalet, built around 1700 by the monks of the Rougemont Abbey. Although the designer did add a comfortable outside terrace, he essentially left the exterior of the wooden building as it was. Inside, a 6-meter-long wall of glass containing an exceptional wine collection cuts the space in two. The kitchen is on one side of this wall, and two restaurants, a bar and a discotheque on the other. A slate floor with some luminous colored glass inserts marks the disco area, while the architect plays in a clever way on the traditional chalet interiors of the country, using milking pots as champagne chillers for example. In the bar, video screens evoke the chimney and fireplaces that modern regulations and an old wooden building don't allow. Much of the interior furnishing is Jouin's own creation, including the tables, lighting, and dining room seating with the "Mabelle" chair from his 2003 furniture collection of Cassina.

Das traditionelle, außerhalb von Gstaad an der Hauptstraße in die Stadt gelegene Schweizer Chalet wurde um 1700 von Mönchen der Rougemont-Abtei errichtet und beherbergt das von Patrick Jouin umgestaltete Restaurant **CHLÖSTERLI**. Eine komfortable Außenterrasse kam hinzu, ansonsten blieb die Hülle des Holzbaus intakt. Das Innere des Gebäudes wird durch eine 6 m lange Glaswand, die eine außergewöhnliche Weinsammlung aufnimmt, in zwei Teile geteilt. Auf der einen Seite befindet sich die Küche, auf der anderen Seite liegen zwei Restaurants, eine Bar und eine Diskothek. Der Bereich der Diskothek wird durch einen Schieferboden mit einigen farbig leuchtenden Glaseinsätzen gekennzeichnet. Der Architekt spielt geschickt mit der traditionellen Einrichtung eines Chalets und verwendet beispielsweise Milchkannen als Sektkühler. In der Bar werden auf Videobildschirmen Schornstein und Kamin simuliert; aufgrund der heutigen Bauvorschriften war ein echter Kamin in dem alten Gebäude nicht zulässig. Ein großer Teil der Inneneinrichtung stammt von Jouin: Tische, Beleuchtungskörper und die Restaurantbestuhlung mit dem Mabelle-Stuhl sind aus seiner Kollektion 2003 für Cassina.

C'est en dehors de la ville, sur la route principale conduisant à Gstaad, que Patrick Jouin a aménagé le **CHLÖSTERLI** à l'intérieur d'un chalet traditionnel construit vers 1700 par les moines de l'abbaye de Rougemont. Bien qu'il ait ajouté une confortable terrasse, il a laissé quasiment intact l'extérieur du bâtiment en bois. À l'intérieur, un mur de verre de 6 m de long, contenant une exceptionnelle collection de grands crus, coupe le volume en deux avec, d'un côté, la cuisine et de l'autre, deux restaurants, un bar et une discothèque. Le sol en ardoise ponctué d'inserts de verre de couleur rétro-éclairés marque la zone de la discothèque. Ailleurs, l'architecte joue intelligemment sur les aspects traditionnels de la décoration de chalet, utilisant par exemple des pots à lait comme seaux à champagne. Dans le bar, un écran vidéo évoque le feu de bois que les règlements modernes et les constructions anciennes en bois interdisent de nos jours. La plus grande partie du mobilier est signée de Jouin, en particulier les tables, les luminaires et les sièges de la salle à manger qui ne sont autres que les fauteuils « Mabelle » de sa collection 2003 éditée par Cassina.

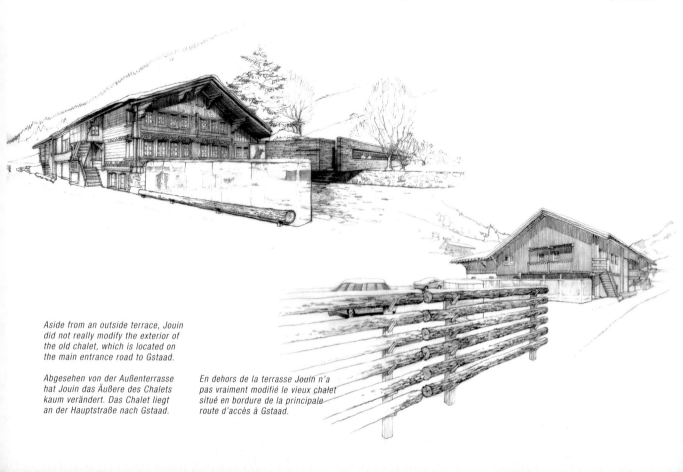

Aside from an outside terrace, Jouin did not really modify the exterior of the old chalet, which is located on the main entrance road to Gstaad.

Abgesehen von der Außenterrasse hat Jouin das Äußere des Chalets kaum verändert. Das Chalet liegt an der Hauptstraße nach Gstaad.

En dehors de la terrasse Jouin n'a pas vraiment modifié le vieux chalet situé en bordure de la principale route d'accès à Gstaad.

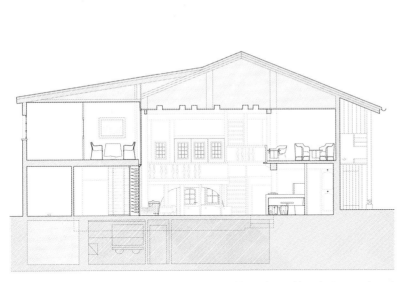

The outside terrace of the restaurant offers an excellent view of the surrounding countryside and mountains without altering the very old feeling of the main building.

Die Außenterrasse bietet einen schönen Blick auf die bergige Landschaft der Umgebung; die Stimmung in dem uralten Chalet verändert sich durch diese Terrasse aber nicht.

La terrasse du restaurant offre une vue remarquable sur la campagne et les montagnes environnantes, sans trahir l'impression de construction très ancienne que donne le chalet.

A discotheque and bar space on the ground floor making use of floor blocks lit from below, and a spectacular wine cellar inserted into a glass wall. A private dining room on the upper floor is visible at the top of the image on this page.

Die Diskothek und die Bar im Erdgeschoss werden durch einzelne Fußbodenfelder von unten beleuchtet. Die spektakuläre Weinsammlung ist in eine Glaswand integriert. Oben im Bild ein Essraum für geschlossene Gesellschaften.

La discothèque, le bar du rez-de-chaussée au sol éclairé et une spectaculaire cave à vin enchâssée dans un mur de verre. À l'étage, une salle à manger privée, visible en haut de la photo de cette page.

Throughout the different areas on the ground and upper floors, Jouin makes clever use of traditional elements in a modern context. For a bar area (left page, bottom, middle) he uses video screens with pictures of cozy fires, in particular because current fire regulations did not allow for a real fireplace. He mixes his own existing furniture designs with newly created chairs, tables and accessories.

In allen Bereichen des Erd- und Obergeschosses mischt Jouin geschickt traditionelle Elemente in den modernen Umbau. Im Barbereich (linke Seite, unten Mitte) lodern auf Bildschirmen Kaminfeuer. Dies ist vor allem den heutigen Brandschutzvorschriften geschuldet, die einen echten Kamin nicht zuließen. Jouin verwendet seine früheren Möbelentwürfe ebenso wie neu entworfene Stühle, Tische und Accessoires.

Au rez-de-chaussée comme à l'étage, Jouin a habilement réutilisé des éléments traditionnels dans un contexte moderne. Ainsi dans le bar (page de gauche, en bas et au centre), des écrans vidéo diffusent des images de feu de bois, la réglementation ne permettant pas d'installer une vraie cheminée. Il a mélangé ses meubles déjà édités à de nouveaux modèles de fauteuils, tables et accessoires.

RICK JOY

Rick Joy Architects
400 South Rubio Avenue
Tucson, Arizona 85701
USA

Tel: +1 520 624 1442
Fax: +1 520 791 0699
E-mail: studio@rickjoy.com
Web: www.rickjoy.com

Tyler Residence ►

RICK JOY's first working experience was not as an architect, but as a musician and a carpenter in Maine. He obtained his degree in architecture in 1990 and spent three years in the office of Will Bruder, working on the design team for the Phoenix Central Library. He then set up his own practice in Tucson, Arizona. Joy received in 1993 the Young Architects Award from *Progressive Architecture* magazine; the 1994 AIA Honor Award for Arizona Home of the Year; The Architectural League of New York Young Architects Forum Award in 1996; a 1997 *Architectural Record* magazine Record Houses Award; *I. D.* magazine's Award for Environments in both 1997 and 2000; The Architectural League of New York Emerging Voices 2000 Award; the 2002 Architectural Award of the American Academy of Arts and Letters; and the 2004 National Design Award of the Cooper-Hewitt Museum. "Bold, modern architecture that is rooted in the context and culture of its place," says Rick Joy, "and that is developed in combination with the basics of proper solar orientation and site protection, and the responsible use of sensible materials and fine craftsmanship, will have the quality to withstand the tests of time."

RICK JOY machte seine ersten Berufserfahrungen nicht als Architekt, sondern als Musiker und Zimmermann in Maine. Nachdem er 1990 sein Architekturstudium abgeschlossen hatte, verbrachte er drei Jahre im Büro von Will Bruder, wo er im Planungsteam für die Phoenix Central Library arbeitete. Danach machte er sich mit einem eigenen Büro in Tucson selbstständig. Rick Joy erhielt etliche Preise und Auszeichnungen: 1993 den Young Architects Award der Zeitschrift *Progressive Architecture*, 1994 und 2000 den AIA Honor Award for Arizona Home of the Year, 1996 den Architectural League of New York Young Architects Forum Award, 1997 den Record Houses Award der Zeitschrift *Architectural Record*, 1997 und 2000 den Award for Environments der Zeitschrift *I. D.*, 2000 den Emerging Voices Award der Architectural League of New York, 2002 den Architekturpreis der American Academy of Arts and Letters und 2004 den National Design Award des Cooper-Hewitt-Museums. Rick Joy über die Ziele seiner Arbeit: „Eine kühne, moderne Architektur, die einerseits im Kontext und in der Kultur ihres Standorts verwurzelt ist und sich andererseits auszeichnet durch eine Kombination von optimaler Nutzung der Sonnenenergie, Standortschutz sowie dem verantwortungsvollen Einsatz ökologisch sinnvoller Materialien und der Handwerkskunst, wird immer eine zeitlose Qualität haben."

RICK JOY débute professionnellement comme musicien et charpentier dans le Maine. Diplômé d'architecture en 1990, il passe trois années dans l'agence de Will Bruder où il travaille dans l'équipe projet de la Phoenix Central Library, avant de créer sa propre agence à Tucson. En 1993, il reçoit le Young Architects Award du magazine *Progressive Architecture* ; en 1994 et en 2000, le AIA Honor Award pour la maison de l'année en Arizona ; en 1996, le Young Architects Forum Award de l'Architectural League of New York ; en 1997, le Record Houses Award du magazine *Architectural Record* ; en 1997 et 2000, le prix de l'environnement du magazine *I. D.* ; en 2000, l'Emerging Voices Award de l'Architectural League of New York ; en 2002, le Prix d'architecture de l'American Academy of Arts and Letters et, en 2004, le National Design Award du Cooper-Hewitt Museum. « Une architecture moderne et audacieuse enracinée dans le contexte et la culture du lieu », commente Rick Joy, « et qui se développe en combinaison avec les fondamentaux de l'orientation solaire et de la protection du site ainsi qu'avec l'usage responsable de matériaux sensibles et un travail d'exécution soigné, résistera au test du temps. »

TYLER RESIDENCE

Tubac, Arizona, USA, 1999–2000

Clients: Warren and Rose Tyler. Area: 230 m² (main house), 140 m² (guest house).
Materials: weathered steel, polished black concrete floors, pale maple, sandblasted glass, stainless steel.

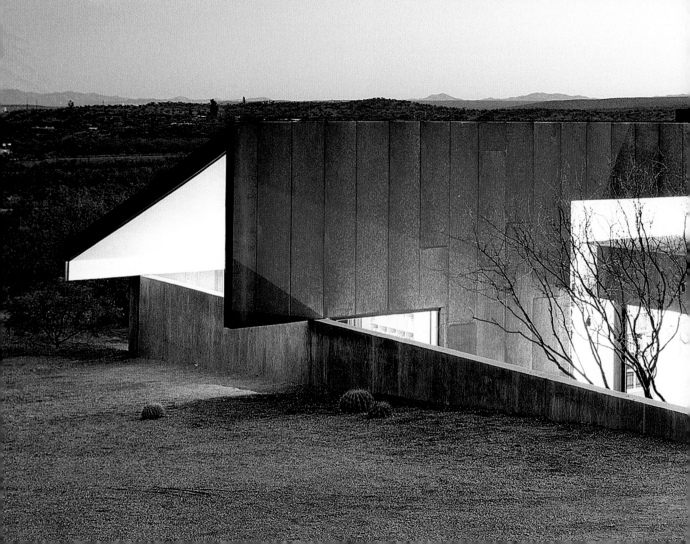

The entrance side of the house seen at nightfall. The use of weathered steel for the exterior cladding gives the geometric forms an appearance not unlike that of some contemporary sculptures.

Die Eingangsseite des Hauses bei Einbruch der Dunkelheit. Der verwitterte Stahl der Außenverkleidung gibt den geometrischen Formen eine gewisse Ähnlichkeit mit modernen Skulpturen.

La façade d'entrée de la maison à la tombée de la nuit. L'habillage externe en acier patiné donne aux formes géométriques un aspect qui n'est pas étranger à celui de certaines sculptures contemporaines.

Set in the Sonoran Desert with views toward the Tumacacori, Santa Rita and San Cayetano mountains, the **TYLER RESIDENCE** is divided into a 240 m^2 main structure containing a master bedroom, living, dining and cooking areas as well as two studies, and a 150 m^2 guest house, with two bedrooms, a workshop and a garage. The architect chose to give the house a low profile in rapport with the 1.5 hectare site located about 20 kilometers north of the Mexican border. Using a naturally weathered steel for the exterior cladding, the architect placed the openings of the house in specific locations to profit from pre-determined views. In this aspect of the house, both client and architect were influenced by houses in Majorca designed by Jørn Utzon. Polished black concrete floors, pale maple, sand-blasted glass, stainless and matte-gray steel are used for the interiors, completing a Modernist design. Will Bruder, with whom Rick Joy worked for three years, says of his work that it is "of the ages and of our time, reinterpreting simple elements with materials that are responsive to their place."

Die **TYLER RESIDENCE** liegt in der Sonora-Wüste mit Blick auf die Tumacacori-, Santa-Rita- und San-Cayetano-Berge und setzt sich aus zwei Gebäudeteilen zusammen. Das Haupthaus mit Schlaf-, Wohn- und Essbereich sowie zwei Arbeitsräumen hat 240 m^2, das Gästehaus mit zwei Zimmern, einem Atelier und einer Garage ist 150 m^2 groß. Um das circa 20 km nördlich der Grenze zu Mexiko gelegene Gebäude mit dem 1,5 ha großen Grundstück in eine harmonische Beziehung zur Landschaft zu setzen, entschloss sich der Architekt zu einem Flachbau. Für die Fassadenverkleidung wählte Joy einen natürlich verwitterten Stahl und ordnete die Fensteröffnungen des Hauses so an, dass vorher festgelegte Ausblicke optimal zur Geltung kommen. In diesem Gestaltungsaspekt ließen sich sowohl Auftraggeber wie auch Architekt von Wohnhäusern inspirieren, die Jørn Utzon auf Mallorca entworfen hatte. Das modernistische Design wird in den Innenräumen von schwarz geschliffenen Betonböden, hellem Ahornholz, sandgestrahltem Glas, rostfreiem und mattgrauem Stahl ergänzt. Will Bruder, mit dem Rick Joy drei Jahre lang zusammengearbeitet hat, sagt über diese Arbeit, sie sei in ihrer Neuinterpretation schlichter Elemente mit Materialien, die zu ihrer Umgebung in Bezug stehen, ebenso zeitlos wie aktuell.

Implantée dans le désert de Sonora et donnant sur les montagnes de Tumacacori, Santa Rita et San Cayetano, la **TYLER RESIDENCE** est divisée en une structure principale de 240 m^2 contenant la chambre principale, le séjour, les zones de cuisine et de repas, deux bureaux et une maison d'amis de 150 m^2 à deux chambres, atelier et garage. L'architecte a choisi de donner à l'ensemble habillé d'un acier naturellement vieilli un profil bas adapté au terrain de 1,5 hectare situé à 20 km environ de la frontière mexicaine. Il a disposé les ouvertures de façon à cadrer des vues déterminées. À cet égard, le client et son architecte se sont inspirés des maisons dessinées par Jørn Utzon pour Majorque. Sols en béton noir poli, boiseries d'érable clair, verres sablés, acier inoxydable et acier gris mat sont utilisés à l'intérieur dans un esprit moderniste. Will Bruder, avec lequel Rick Joy a travaillé pendant trois ans, a pu dire de cette maison qu'il s'agissait « [d'une maison] de notre âge, de notre temps, réinterprétant des éléments simples par des matériaux qui répondent au lieu ».

A shed-like covering used to shade the kitchen opens toward the south-west where the swimming pool has a spectacular view of the mountains. Above, cast concrete planters in the inner courtyard.

Ein hallenartiger Vorbau beschattet die Küche und öffnet sich nach Süd-westen, wo man vom Swimmingpool aus eine fantastische Aussicht auf die Berge hat (rechts). Die Pflanztöpfe im Innenhof sind aus Gussbeton (oben).

Un toit en sheds abrite la cuisine et s'ouvre vers le sud-ouest et la piscine qui dispose d'une vue spec-taculaire sur les montagnes. En haut, les jardinières en béton armé de la cour intérieure.

ANISH KAPOOR

Anish Kapoor Studio
230 Farmer's Road
London SE5 0TW
UK

Tel: +44 20 7735 5485
Fax: +44 20 7793 9234
E-mail: anish@kapoorstudio.f9.co.uk

Tate Modern Installation ▶

ANISH KAPOOR was born in Mumbai, India, in 1954 and has lived and worked in London since the early 1970s. Not an architect, but a sculptor, he studied at the Hornsey College of Art (1973–77) and the Chelsea School of Art (1977–78), and had his first solo exhibition in 1980. His early work centered on lightweight materials and bright colors. Subsequent to moving into a ground-floor studio space in the late 1980s, he began to experiment with stone sculpture, but in almost all cases he deals with the ambiguities of perception. As he says, "I don't want to make sculpture about form … I wish to make sculpture about belief, or about passion, about experience that is outside of material concern." His work has been exhibited all over the world and is held in many major international collections. He represented Britain at the 44th Biennale in Venice in 1990 and won the Turner Prize in 1991. His work "Marsyas," exhibited in the Turbine Hall of the Tate Modern in London in 2002, was designed in collaboration with Cecil Balmond. He completed "Cloud Gate," a large-scale stainless-steel work for Chicago's Millennium Park, in 2004, and "Sky Mirror" in New York in 2006.

ANISH KAPOOR kam 1954 in Mumbai zur Welt und lebt und arbeitet seit Anfang der 1970er-Jahre in London. Der nicht als Architekt, sondern als Bildhauer am Hornsey College of Art (1973–77) und der Chelsea School of Art (1977–78) ausgebildete Kapoor hatte 1980 seine erste Einzelausstellung. Seine frühen Werke beschäftigten sich mit leichten Materialien und leuchtenden Farben. Nachdem er Ende der 1980er-Jahre sein Studio in eine Erdgeschosswohnung verlegt hatte, begann er mit Steinskulpturen zu experimentieren. In fast allen Fällen beschäftigt er sich dabei mit den Mehrdeutigkeiten der Wahrnehmung. Er sagt: „Meine Skulpturen sollen sich nicht mit Form auseinandersetzen … Ich möchte Skulpturen über Glauben machen oder über Leidenschaft, über Erfahrung, die über materielle Dinge hinausgeht." Seine Arbeiten wurden in der ganzen Welt ausgestellt und sind Bestandteil zahlreicher bedeutender, internationaler Sammlungen. Er vertrat 1990 Großbritannien auf der 44. Biennale in Venedig und gewann 1991 den Turner-Preis. Seine 2002 in der Turbinenhalle der Tate Modern in London ausgestellte Großskulptur „Marsyas" entstand in Zusammenarbeit mit Cecil Balmond. 2002 schuf er für den Millennium Park in Chicago „Cloud Gate", eine großformatige Skulptur aus rostfreiem Stahl, und 2006 für New York den „Sky Mirror".

ANISH KAPOOR, né à Mumbai en Inde, en 1954, vit et travaille à Londres depuis le début des années 1970. Sculpteur et non pas architecte, il a étudié au Hornsey College of Art & Design (1973–77), à l'École d'art de Chelsea (1977–78), et a tenu sa première exposition personnelle en 1980. Ses premières œuvres étaient centrées sur les matériaux légers et les couleurs vives. Après s'être installé dans un vaste atelier à la fin des années 1980, il commence à s'intéresser à la sculpture sur pierre tout en poursuivant ses recherches sur les ambiguïtés de la perception : « Je ne veux pas faire de sculptures sur la forme… je souhaite faire des sculptures sur la foi, la passion, l'expérience hors de nos préoccupations matérielles. » Son œuvre a été exposée dans le monde entier et figure dans de nombreuses grandes collections internationales. Il a représenté la Grande-Bretagne à la 44e Biennale de Venise en 1990 et remporté le Turner Prize en 1991. Son œuvre « Marsyas », présentée au Turbine Hall de la Tate Modern à Londres en 2002, a été conçue en collaboration avec Cecil Balmond. Il a réalisé « Cloud Gate », œuvre en acier inoxydable de grandes dimensions pour le Millennium Park de Chicago en 2004, et « Sky Mirror » à New York en 2006.

MARSYAS

Turbine Hall, Tate Modern, London, UK, October 9, 2002–April 6, 2003

Client: Tate Modern/Unilever. Size: 155 x 23 x 35 m. Costs: not specified.

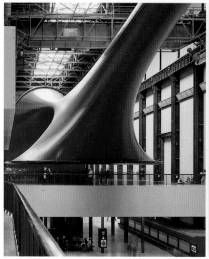  

After Louise Bourgeois and Juan Muñoz, Anish Kapoor was the third artist to participate in The Unilever Series of commissions for the Turbine Hall at Tate Modern. He was, though, the first to make use of the entire length of Tate Modern's enormous Turbine Hall, which measures 155 meters long, 23 meters wide and 35 meters high. **MARSYAS** was comprised of three steel rings joined by a single span of PVC membrane. The geometry generated by these three rigid steel structures determined the sculpture's overall form, a shift from vertical to horizontal and back to vertical again. As Kapoor stated, "the Turbine Hall at Tate Modern is an enormously difficult space, the great problem is that it demands verticality. This is contrary to every notion about sculpture that I've ever engendered in my work. So I felt that the only way to deal with the vertical is to deal with the full horizontal." The title of the work refers to Marsyas, a satyr in Greek mythology, who was flayed alive by Apollo. Unsurprisingly, Anish Kapoor described the impression he intended with the choice of dark red PVC as being "rather like flayed skin." Because of its large dimensions and positioning, it was impossible to view the entire sculpture from any one vantage point, but the artist succeeded not only in altering the architectural space itself, but in creating a new, almost anti-geometric volume suspended in the void of the Turbine Hall.

Anish Kapoor war nach Louise Bourgeois und Juan Muñoz der dritte Künstler, der an der von Unilever organisierten Serie von Auftragsarbeiten für die Turbinenhalle der Tate Modern teilnahm. Er war jedoch der erste, der mit seiner Arbeit den gesamten Raum der riesigen Halle in Anspruch nahm. Die Installation mit dem Titel **MARSYAS** bestand aus drei Stahlringen, die durch eine durchgehende Haut aus PVC-Folie miteinander verbunden waren. Die Geometrie, die durch die drei feststehenden Stahlringe entstand, bestimmte die Gesamtform der Skulptur, die durch eine Verlagerung vom Vertikalen ins Horizontale und wieder zurück gekennzeichnet war. Dazu Anish Kapoor: „Die Turbinenhalle in der Tate Modern ist ein ungeheuer schwieriger Raum, wobei das größte Problem darin besteht, dass sie Vertikalität verlangt. Und das steht im Widerspruch zu allen Vorstellungen von Skulptur, die ich jemals in meinen Arbeiten zum Ausdruck gebracht habe." Der Titel des Werks bezieht sich auf Marsyas, einen Satyr aus der griechischen Mythologie, der von Apollo bei lebendigem Leib gehäutet wurde. Wenig überraschend sagt Anish Kapoor über die Wirkung, die er mit der Wahl der dunkelroten PVC-Folie erzielen wollte, dass sie einer abgezogenen Haut ähneln sollte. Obwohl die Skulptur wegen ihrer riesigen Dimensionen und ihrer Anordnung im Raum von keinem einzigen Punkt aus zur Gänze überschaubar war, ist es dem Künstler dennoch gelungen, nicht nur den Raum selbst zu verändern, sondern einen neuen, beinahe antigeometrischen Baukörper durch die Leere der Turbinenhalle schweben zu lassen.

Après Louise Bourgeois et Juan Muñoz, Anish Kapoor a été le troisième artiste à bénéficier d'une commande Unilever pour le Turbine Hall de la Tate Modern. Cependant, il a été le premier à utiliser intégralement cet énorme volume. **MARSYAS** était constitué de trois anneaux d'acier entre lesquels était tendue une membrane de PVC. La géométrie issue des rapports de ces éléments rigides déterminait la forme d'ensemble de la sculpture, qui passait de la verticale à l'horizontale pour revenir à la verticale. Comme Kapoor l'explique : « Le Turbine Hall est un espace extrêmement difficile, le grand problème étant qu'il demande une verticalité, ce qui était contraire à toute notion de sculpture rencontrée dans mes travaux jusqu'à présent. » Le titre de l'œuvre renvoie à Marsyas, satyre de la mythologie grecque, qui fut écorché vif par Apollon. Kapoor décrit l'impression recherchée par le choix de PVC rouge sombre comme un effet de « peau d'écorché ». Du fait de ses grandes dimensions et du positionnement de l'œuvre, il était impossible de la voir en totalité d'un seul point de vue. L'artiste a réussi non seulement à modifier le volume architectural, mais à créer un volume presque anti-géométrique suspendu dans le vide de ce hall gigantesque.

Filling the vast space of the Tate Modern Turbine Hall has been a challenge that artists have risen to with varying success. Anish Kapoor managed to reconfigure the space in the image of his own new geometry.

Den riesigen Raum der Turbinenhalle in der Tate Modern haben die beauftragten Künstler mit unterschiedlichem Erfolg ausgefüllt. Anish Kapoor gestaltete den Raum nach dem Bild seiner eigenen, neuen Geometrie um.

Occuper l'énorme espace du hall de la turbine de la Tate Modern est un défi que quelques artistes ont relevé avec un succès varié. Anish Kapoor a réussi à reconfigurer l'espace par une géométrie originale.

REI KAWAKUBO

Comme des Garçons Co., Ltd.
5-11-5 Minamiaoyama
Minato-ku
Tokyo, 107-0062
Japan

Tel: +81 3 3407 2480
Web: www.comme-des-garcons.com

REI KAWAKUBO created the Comme des Garçons label in 1969 and established Comme des Garçons Co. Ltd. in Tokyo in 1973. She opened her Paris boutique in 1982, and one in New York one year later. Although she is best known as a fashion designer, she has long had an interest in furniture and architecture. Rei Kawakubo introduced the Comme des Garçons furniture line in 1983. In 1997, she received an honorary doctorate from the Royal College of Art, London. The Flagship Store in Aoyama, Tokyo, which she redesigned in 1999 with the assistance of Takao Kawasaki (interior design), Future Systems (architect/façade), Christian Astuguevieille (art director/interior), and Sophie Smallhorn (artist/interior), was opened in 1989. Since 2004, Rei Kawakubo has sold her clothes in so-called guerilla stores, which are set up in abandoned shops for only a couple of months at a time before moving on to other locations. In 2007, there were guerilla stores in Athens, Cracow, The Hague, among other cities.

REI KAWAKUBO schuf 1969 das Modelabel Comme des Garçons und gründete 1973 die Firma Comme des Garçons Co. Ltd. in Tokio. 1982 eröffnete sie ihre Boutique in Paris und ein Jahr später eine in New York. Obwohl sie vor allem als Modedesignerin bekannt ist, hat sie seit Langem ein großes Interesse an Inneneinrichtung und Architektur. 1983 brachte sie ihre erste Kollektion von Comme-des-Garçons-Möbeln heraus, 1997 wurde ihr vom Royal College of Art in London der Titel eines Ehrendoktors verliehen. Rei Kawakubo hat ihren 1989 eröffneten Flagship-Store in Aoyama in Tokio 1999 in Zusammenarbeit mit Takao Kawasaki (Inneneinrichtung), Future Systems (Fassade), Christian Astuguevieille (Art Director/Interieur) und Sophie Smallhorn (Künstlerin/Interieur) neu gestaltet. Seit 2004 verkauft Rei Kawakubo ihre Mode in sogenannten Guerilla Stores, die jeweils nur für ein paar Monate in alten Ladenlokalen bleiben, bevor sie sich einen neuen Standort suchen. 2007 gab es Guerilla Stores u. a. in Athen, Krakau und Den Haag.

REI KAWAKUBO a créé la marque Comme des Garçons en 1969 et fondé Comme des Garçons Co. Ltd. à Tokyo en 1973. Elle a ouvert sa boutique parisienne en 1982, puis celle de New York en 1983. Bien qu'elle soit surtout connue comme styliste de mode, elle s'intéresse depuis longtemps au design de mobilier et à l'architecture. Elle a lancé une ligne de meubles Comme des Garçons en 1983. Le Flagship Store à Aoyama, Tokyo, qu'elle a rénové en collaboration avec Takao Kawasaki (architecte d'intérieur) en 1999, Future Systems (architecture, façade), Christian Astuguevieille (directeur artistique, aménagements intérieurs) et Sophie Smallhorn (artiste, aménagements intérieurs) avait été ouvert en 1989. Elle est docteur honoraire du Royal College of Arts de Londres (1997). Depuis 2004, Rei Kawakubo écoule sa mode dans des Guerilla Stores, magasins qui ne restent que quelques mois dans des locaux vacants avant d'aller s'installer ailleurs. En 2007, il y a eu des Guerilla Stores à Athènes, La Haye et Cracovie.

COMME DES GARÇONS FLAGSHIP STORE

Tokyo, Japan, 1999

Planning: 1998. Construction: 1999 (one month).
Client: Comme des Garçons. Floor area: 698 m².

Set on Aoyama Street as are several other exclusive fashion boutiques, the **COMME DES GARÇONS FLAGSHIP STORE** was built under the direction of Rei Kawakubo by Takao Kawasaki (interior design), Future Systems (architect/façade), Christian Astuguevieille (art director/interior), and Sophie Smallhorn (artist/interior). The undulating glass façade, overlaid with blue circular dots, allows passersby to look in, but not enough to really capture the interior of the space. The large enameled forms of the interior partitions, designed by Kawakubo, divide the space, at the same time making it appear rather complex. Visitors discover clothes or shoes, displayed in small quantities, as they stroll through and around Kawakubo's units. Here architecture and fashion converge, and the design further contributes to setting out the intention Comme des Garçons wishes to project – an image that goes beyond clothing.

Der in der Aoyama-Straße neben mehreren anderen exklusiven Modeboutiquen gelegene Tokioter **COMME DES GARÇONS FLAGSHIP STORE** wurde unter der Leitung von Rei Kawakubo von Takao Kawasaki (Innenarchitekt), Future Systems (Architekt/Fassade), Christian Astuguevieille (Art Director/Interieur) und Sophie Smallhorn (Künstlerin/Interieur) ausgeführt. Die wellenförmige, mit blauen, kreisrunden Tupfen bedeckte Glasfront erlaubt den Vorübergehenden hineinzusehen, ohne dass sie jedoch das Innere konkret erkennen könnten. Die voluminösen Formen der von Kawakubo entworfenen emaillierten Trennwände gliedern den Raum einerseits und lassen ihn gleichzeitig sehr komplex erscheinen. Während man in und zwischen diesen Einheiten umhergeht, entdeckt man die sparsam dekorierten Kleidungsstücke und Schuhe. Hier ergänzen sich Architektur und Mode, und das Design trägt zusätzlich zu dem Image bei, das Comme des Garçons vermitteln möchte: ein Image, das über den Verkauf von Bekleidung hinausgeht.

Situé rue Aoyama, comme de nombreuses boutiques de mode de luxe, le **COMME DES GARÇONS FLAGSHIP STORE** a été aménagé sous la direction de Rei Kawakubo par Takao Kawasaki (architecture intérieure), Future Systems (architecte/façade), Christian Astuguevieille (directeur artistique/aménagements intérieurs) et Sophie Smallhorn (artiste/aménagements intérieurs). La façade en verre ondulé, plaquée de disques bleus, permet aux passants de voir l'intérieur, sans qu'il puisse en capter le volume. Les grands cocons émaillés, dessinés par Kawakubo, divisent l'espace tout en lui conférant une plus grande complexité. Les visiteurs découvrent les vêtements ou les chaussures présentés en très petit nombre, en se promenant autour d'eux. Cette convergence de la mode et de l'architecture contribue à l'image de Comme des Garçons qui va bien au-delà de l'univers vestimentaire.

The undulating glass façade of Comme des Garçons's Aoyama Flagship Store was designed by the architects Future Systems, transforming a relatively innocuous modern space into a remarkable boutique.

Die wellenförmige Glasfront des Tokioter Hauptgeschäfts von Comme des Garçons wurde vom Architekturbüro Future Systems entworfen, das damit ein konventionelles Ladenlokal in eine auffallende Boutique verwandelte.

La façade ondulée en verre du Flagship Store de Comme des Garçons d'Aoyama a été conçue par Future Systems. Elle fait d'un volume moderne relativement anodin un lieu remarquable.

Rei Kawakubo designed the interior
volumes of the shop with the assistance of architect Takao Kawasaki.
Their unusual shapes give an almost
labyrinthine aspect to the space.

Die Innenräume wurden von Rei Kawakubo in Zusammenarbeit mit dem
Architekten Takao Kawasaki ausgeführt. Die ungewöhnlichen Formen
geben dem Raum fast labyrinthischen
Charakter.

Rei Kawakubo a conçu les volumes
intérieurs de son magasin avec
l'assistance de l'architecte Takao
Kawasaki. Leur forme inhabituelle
donne l'impression d'être dans un
labyrinthe.

Art director Christian Astuguevieille
and artist Sophie Smallhorn collaborated with Rei Kawakubo on the
artistic elements of the interior.

Art Director Christian Astuguevieille
und die Künstlerin Sophie Smallhorn
schufen gemeinsam mit Rei Kawakubo die Kunstwerke im Verkaufsraum.

Le directeur artistique Christian
Astuguevieille et l'artiste Sophie
Smallhorn ont collaboré avec Rei
Kawakubo pour créer le décor
intérieur du magasin.

COMME DES GARÇONS STORE

New York, New York, USA, 1999

Planning: 1998. Construction: 1999 (3 months).
Client: Comme des Garçons. Floor area: 465 m².

The striking aluminum monocoque
structure, designed by Future Systems, sits just inside the unmarked
entrance to the New York store in the
Chelsea gallery district of Manhattan.

Die auffallende, von Future Systems
entworfene Tunnelkonstruktion aus
Aluminium wurde in einen Eingang
integriert, der keinerlei Hinweis auf
die Boutique im Gebäude gibt.

L'étonnante structure monocoque
en aluminium conçue par Future
Systems annonce l'entrée sans
enseigne du magasin new-yorkais
de Rei Kawakubo à Chelsea, le
quartier des galeries de Manhattan.

Set in the midst of the gallery district in Chelsea in Manhattan, the **COMME DE GARÇONS STORE** is located in the former car repair shop Heavenly Body Works, whose sign has been retained over the door. The original brick façade was also kept intact. The only clear signal that there is an unusual space is the entrance to a seamless aluminum monocoque tunnel leading into the store, designed by Future Systems and built in a Cornwall shipyard, with a large, free-form glass door. Inside, the large space is divided using the same system of enameled partitions (or "pods" as she calls them) used by Rei Kawakubo in her Tokyo Flagship Store. Both store interiors have a maze-like quality, allowing visitors to discover the clothing or objects for sale in an unexpected or surprising way. Just as she broke traditional merchandizing rules by deciding, from the very outset, that this boutique should have no windows, Kawakubo breaks new ground as to how her clothes should be presented within the space.

Der inmitten des Manhattaner Kunstviertels Chelsea gelegene New Yorker **COMME DE GARÇONS STORE** ist in den Räumen der ehemaligen Autowerkstatt Heavenly Body Works untergebracht, deren Schild über der Eingangstür belassen wurde. Ebenfalls beibehalten wurde die ursprüngliche Backsteinfassade. Einzige Anzeichen für die Existenz eines architektonisch ungewöhnlichen Raums hinter dieser Fassade sind der Eingang zu einem Tunnel in selbsttragender Schalenbauweise, der von Future Systems entworfen und in einer Schiffswerft im englischen Cornwall gefertigt wurde, sowie eine große, frei geformte Glastür, die in das Ladeninnere führt. Der großzügig angelegte Verkaufsraum ist durch die gleichen emaillierten Trennwände (oder „Kokons", wie die Designerin sie nennt) unterteilt, die Rei Kawakubo für die Gestaltung ihres Flagship-Stores in Tokio eingesetzt hat. Die Ladeninterieurs ermöglichen den Kunden durch ihre labyrinthartige Anlage, die Verkaufsobjekte auf neue und ungewöhnliche Weise zu entdecken. Ebenso wie sie herkömmliche Vermarktungsregeln brach, als sie von Anfang an beschloss, dass diese Boutique keine Fenster haben sollte, ist Kawakubo wegweisend in der Art, wie sie ihre Modeartikel innerhalb des Verkaufsraums präsentiert.

Situé au milieu du quartier des galeries de Chelsea, à Manhattan, le **MAGASIN COMME DES GARÇONS** abritait naguère un atelier de carrosserie, Heavenly Body Works, dont l'enseigne a été conservée tout comme la façade d'origine en brique. Le seul signal évident annonçant l'originalité du lieu est l'entrée, un tunnel monocoque en aluminium, dessiné par Future Systems et fabriqué par un chantier naval de Cornouailles. Il est fermé par une grande porte vitrée de forme libre. À l'intérieur, le vaste espace est divisé par le même système de cloisonnements émaillées ou « cocons » que Rei Kawakubo a utilisé dans son magasin de Tokyo. Les deux boutiques donnent l'impression d'un parcours labyrinthique, qui permet aux visiteurs de découvrir les vêtements ou les objets en vente comme par surprise. De même qu'elle rompt avec les règles traditionnelles de la commercialisation en éliminant toute vitrine, Kawakubo expérimente ainsi de nouvelles façons de présenter ses vêtements dans l'espace.

The same dark curving volumes used in Tokyo grace the interior of the New York Comme des Garçons store, giving a continuity of spirit to two very different spaces.

Das Interieur des New Yorker Comme des Garçons Store ist mit den gleichen dunklen, geschwungenen Trennwänden ausgestattet, wie sie für das Tokioter Hauptgeschäft verwendet wurden. Dies verleiht den beiden sonst sehr unterschiedlichen Räumen einen einheitlichen Stil.

Les mêmes volumes sombres et incurvés utilisés à Tokyo décorent la boutique de New York, en signe de continuité d'esprit entre des espaces très différents.

Alternating light and dark volumes, Rei Kawakubo sets out a relatively limited number of her designs for shoppers to see. Although her approach may not follow strict commercial logic, it does set her apart from other fashion designers.

Im Wechsel zwischen hellen und dunklen Elementen präsentiert Rei Kawakubo eine begrenzte Auswahl an Kleidungsstücken. Indem sie sich einer streng kommerziellen Logik verweigert, hebt sie sich von anderen Modedesignern ab.

En alternant des volumes sombres et clairs, Rei Kawakubo ne met en valeur qu'un nombre limité de ses créations de vêtements. Sa démarche éloignée des règles commerciales strictes la distingue de celle des autres stylistes de mode.

WARO KISHI

Waro Kishi + K. Associates/Architects
Kishi Lab.
Department of Architecture and Engineering, Kyoto University
Katsura, Nishikyo-ku, Kyoto 615-8540
Japan

E-mail: mail@k-associates.com
Web: www.k-associates.com

House in Kurakuen II ▶

Born in Yokohama in 1950, **WARO KISHI** graduated from the Department of Electronics at Kyoto University in 1973, and from the Department of Architecture of the same institution two years later. He completed his postgraduate studies in Kyoto in 1978, and worked in the office of Masayuki Kurokawa in Tokyo from 1978 to 1981. He created Waro Kishi + K. Associates/Architects in Kyoto in 1993. His completed works include: the Autolab automobile showroom, Kyoto (1989); the Kyoto-Kagaku Research Institute, Kizu-cho, Kyoto (1990); the Yunokabashi Bridge, Ashikita-cho, Kumamoto (1991); Sonobe SD Office, Sonobe-cho, Funai-gun, Kyoto (1993); as well as numerous private houses. In 1997 the Memorial Hall, Ube, Yamaguchi (1997) and a house in Higashi-nada, Kobe (1997) were built, a house in Suzaku, Nara, followed (1997–98). Waro Kishi also designed the House in Fukaya, Saitama (2000), and House in Kurakuen II, Nishinomiya, Hyogo (2001).

WARO KISHI, geboren 1950 in Yokohama, studierte bis 1973 Elektrotechnik und bis 1975 Architektur an der Universität Kioto. 1978 schloss er sein Graduiertenstudium an der Universität Kioto ab und arbeitete danach bis 1981 im Büro von Masayuki Kurokawa in Tokio. 1993 gründete Kishi seine eigene Firma, Waro Kishi + K. Associates/Architects in Kioto. Zu Waro Kishis in Japan realisierten Entwürfen zählen der Automobilsalon Autolab in Kioto (1989), das Forschungsinstitut Kioto-Kagaku in Kizu-cho, Kioto (1990), die Yunokabashi-Brücke in Ashikita-cho, Kumamato (1991), das Bürogebäude Sonobe SD in Sonobe-cho, Funai-gun, Kioto (1993) sowie zahlreiche Wohnhäuser. 1997 wurden die Memorial Hall in Ube, Yamaguchi und ein Wohnhaus in Higashi-nada, Kobe gebaut, es folgte ein Wohnhaus in Suzaku, Nara (1997–1998). Weitere Arbeiten sind ein Haus in Fukaya, Saitama (2000), und das Haus in Kurakuen II, Nishinomiya, Hyogo (2001).

Né à Yokohama en 1950, **WARO KISHI** est diplômé du Département d'électronique de l'Université de Kyoto en 1973 et du Département d'architecture de la même institution en 1975. Il poursuit des études de spécialisation à Kyoto de 1978 à 1981, puis fonde Waro Kishi + K. Associates/Architects à Kyoto en 1993. Au Japon, il a réalisé, entre autres, le hall d'exposition automobile Autolab (Kyoto, 1989) ; l'Institut de Recherches Kyoto-Kagaku (Kizu-cho, Kyoto, 1990) ; le pont Yunokabashi (Ashikita-cho, Kumamoto, 1991) ; les bureaux de Sonobe SD (Sonobe-cho, Funai-gun, Kyoto, 1993) et de nombreuses résidences privées. En 1997 furent construits le Mémorial (Ube, Yamaguchi), une maison à Higashi-nada (Kobe) et une résidence à Suzaku (Nara, Japon, 1997–98). Parmi ses autres chantiers : une maison à Fukaya (Saitama, 2000) et la maison à Kurakuen II (Nishinomiya, Hyogo, 2001).

HOUSE IN KURAKUEN II

Nishinomiya, Hyogo, Japan, 2000–01

Client: Sogo Jisho Co. Ltd. Site area: 618 m². Building area: 242 m².
Floor area: 268 m². Structure: steel frame.

This 268 m² house (floor area) was designed in 1996–97 and built beginning in March 2000. It is a two-story steel frame and reinforced concrete house set on a 618 m² site. It is located in a sloping residential area facing the sea. There is a view from the house of the suburbs of Osaka and the bay. Of this exceptional site, Waro Kishi says, "I created two blocks of floating steel reinforced structure. On the left is the private room zone, while on the right are the public living and dining room areas, and both are joined by a sloping ramp. The roof of the topmost floor on the left side individual room block is made to appear as thin as possible," he concludes. The architect chose to frame the view with smaller openings in the living and dining area, while offering a wider, horizontal vista from the private spaces. The metal cladding and dramatic volumes of this house, together with its exceptional site, make it one of Waro Kishi's most exceptional buildings.

Das Wohnhaus mit einer Nutzfläche von 268 m² wurde 1996–97 geplant und ab März 2000 gebaut. Der zweistöckige Bau aus Stahlrahmen und Stahlbeton wurde auf einem 618 m² großen Grundstück errichtet, das in einer zum Meer hin abfallenden Wohngegend liegt. Vom Haus aus überblickt man die Vororte von Osaka und die Bucht. Waro Kishi über seinen außergewöhnlichen Entwurf: „Ich konstruierte zwei Blöcke mit Stahlarmierung. Im linken liegen die Privaträume, während sich im rechten die öffentlichen Bereiche mit Wohn- und Esszimmer befinden. Beide Gebäudeteile sind durch eine Schrägrampe miteinander verbunden. Das Dach auf dem obersten Geschoss des linken Blocks ist so gestaltet, dass es so dünn wie möglich erscheint." Während der Architekt den Ausblick im Wohn- und Essbereich durch kleinere Fensteröffnungen begrenzte, gewährte er in den Privaträumen einen weiten Rundblick. Die Metallverkleidung, die interessante Gestaltung der beiden Baukörper und die herausragende Lage machen das Haus zu einem von Waro Kishis außergewöhnlichsten Bauwerken.

Le chantier de cette maison de 268 m² sur deux niveaux conçue en 1996–97 a débuté en mars 2000. Élevée sur un terrain incliné de 618 m² face à la mer, elle est en béton armé sur ossature en acier. Elle donne d'un côté sur la banlieue d'Osaka et la baie. Waro Kishi décrit ainsi son projet : « J'ai créé deux blocs de structure flottante en acier renforcé. À gauche, se trouve la zone privative, et à droite celle du séjour et des repas, reliées par une rampe en pente. Le toit du niveau supérieur au-dessus de la chambre de gauche est réalisé de manière à paraître aussi mince que possible. » L'architecte a cadré la vue par de petites ouvertures dans les zones de séjour et des repas, mais offre une vision élargie et horizontale dans les espaces plus privés. Le bardage en métal et les spectaculaires volumes de cette maison, ainsi que son site exceptionnel, en font une des réalisations les plus remarquables de Waro Kishi.

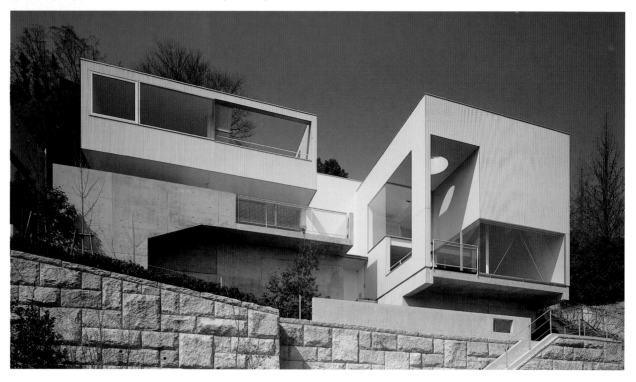

This house is divided into two blocks with a floating steel reinforced structure. On the right in this image (above and right page) the living-dining zone, and on the left the bedroom area.

Das Haus ist in zwei Blöcke aufgeteilt, die aus einer Schwebekonstruktion mit Stahlarmierung bestehen. Wohn- und Essbereich (oben und rechte Seite) sowie Schlafzimmer (oben links).

La maison est divisée en deux blocs à l'intérieur d'une ossature flottante renforcée en acier ; à droite dans cette même image (en haut et page de droite) la zone séjour-repas, et à gauche, la chambre.

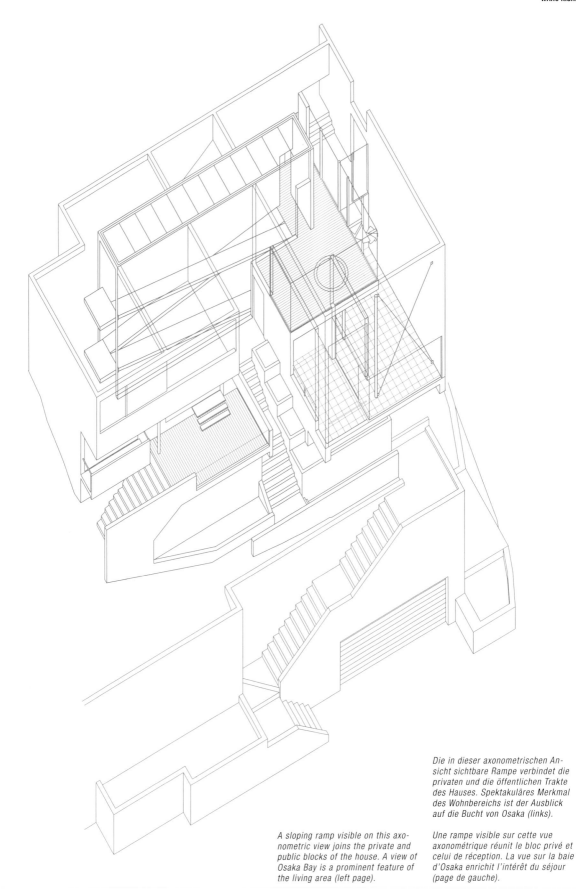

Die in dieser axonometrischen Ansicht sichtbare Rampe verbindet die privaten und die öffentlichen Trakte des Hauses. Spektakuläres Merkmal des Wohnbereichs ist der Ausblick auf die Bucht von Osaka (links).

A sloping ramp visible on this axonometric view joins the private and public blocks of the house. A view of Osaka Bay is a prominent feature of the living area (left page).

Une rampe visible sur cette vue axonométrique réunit le bloc privé et celui de réception. La vue sur la baie d'Osaka enrichit l'intérêt du séjour (page de gauche).

The architect's use of opacity and transparency, or heaviness versus lightness is illustrated in these images. Above, the ramp connecting the public and private zones.

Kishi wechselt opake und transparente Elemente ab und setzt Kontraste aus Schwere und Leichtigkeit. Die Rampe verbindet öffentliche und private Bereiche (oben).

L'alternance d'opacité et de transparence, ou de poids et de légèreté, se manifeste avec évidence. En haut, la rampe qui connecte les zones privées et de réception de la maison.

MARCIO KOGAN

Marcio Kogan
Alameda Tiête, 505
01417-020 São Paulo, São Paulo
Brazil

Tel: +55 11 3081 3522
E-mail: info@studiomk27.com.br
Web: www.marciokogan.com.br

BR House ▶

Born in 1952, **MARCIO KOGAN** graduated in 1976 from the School of Architecture at Mackenzie University in São Paulo. He received an IAB (Brazilian Architects Institute) Award for UMA Stores (1999 and 2002), Coser Studio (2002), Gama Issa House (2002) and Quinta House (2004). He also received the Record House Award for Du Plessis House (2004) and BR House (2005). In 2002, he completed the Museum of Microbiology in São Paulo and in 2003 he made a submission for the World Trade Center Site Memorial. He worked with Isay Weinfeld on the Fasano Hotel in São Paulo. He also participated with Weinfeld in the 25th São Paulo Biennale (2002) with the project for a hypothetical city named Happyland. Kogan is known for his use of boxlike forms, together with wooden shutters, trellises and exposed stone. Amongst Kogan's residential projects are the Cury House (São Paulo, 2006); the E-Home, a "super-technological" house (Santander, Spain); Warbler House (Los Angeles); a villa in Milan; an "extreme house" on an island in Paraty, Rio de Janeiro; as well as two other houses in Brasília.

Der 1952 geborene **MARCIO KOGAN** schloss 1976 an der Architekturfakultät der Universidade Mackenzie in São Paulo sein Studium ab. Er erhielt mehrfach Auszeichnungen des IAB (Instituto do Arquitetos do Brasil): für seine UMA Stores (1999 und 2002), das Coser Studio (2002), das Gama Issa House (2002) und das Quinta House (2004). Ebenfalls erhielt er den Record House Award für das Du Plessis House (2004) und das BR House (2005). 2002 stellte er das Museum für Mikrobiologie in São Paulo fertig und reichte 2003 einen Beitrag für die Gedenkstätte am ehemaligen World Trade Center ein. Mit Isay Weinfeld arbeitete er am Hotel Fasano in São Paulo. Ebenfalls mit Weinfeld beteiligte er sich mit dem Projekt für eine fiktive Stadt namens Happyland an der 25. Biennale in São Paulo (2002). Kogan ist bekannt für die Verwendung kastenförmiger Elemente zusammen mit hölzernen Jalousien und Gittern sowie Sichtstein. Unter Kogans aktuellen Wohnprojekten befinden sich das Haus Cury (São Paulo, 2006), das E-Home, ein „Supertechnologiehaus" (Santander, Spanien), Warbler House (Los Angeles), eine Villa in Mailand, ein „Extremhaus" auf einer Insel in Paraty, Rio de Janeiro, sowie zwei weitere Häuser in Brasília.

Né en 1952, **MARCIO KOGAN**, diplômé en 1976 de l'École d'architecture de l'Universidade Mackenzie à São Paulo, reçoit en 1999 et 2002 un prix de l'IAB (Instituto do Arquitetos do Brazil) pour ses magasins UMA, le Studio Coser (2002), la maison Gama Issa (2002), la maison Quinta (2004), et le prix Record House pour la maison Du Plessis (2004) et la maison BR (2005). En 2002, il a achevé le Musée de microbiologie de São Paulo et, en 2003, a participé au concours pour le mémorial du World Trade Center. Il a collaboré avec Isay Weinfeld sur l'hotel Fasano ainsi qu'à la 25e Biennale de São Paulo sur un projet de ville utopique, Happyland (2002). Il est connu pour ses formes en boîtes, ses voûtes en bois, ses treillis et son utilisation de la pierre apparente. Parmi ses projets résidentiels figurent la maison Cury à São Paulo (2006) ; la E-Home, une maison « supertechnologique » à Santander, Espagne ; la maison Warbler à Los Angeles ; une villa à Milan ; une « maison extrême » sur une île à Paraty, Rio de Janeiro, et deux autres maisons à Brasília.

BR HOUSE

Araras, Rio de Janeiro, Brazil, 2002–04

Floor area: 739 m². Client: not disclosed.
Costs: $ 1 million.

Located on a 6820 m² site, the rectangular **BR HOUSE** has a floor area of 739 m². The architect describes the residence himself in clear terms: "The two-story house is made of concrete, metal, wood, aluminum and glass and is totally integrated with the forest landscape of this mountainous region of Rio de Janeiro (Petrópolis). The first floor has four suites, guest bathroom, kitchen and living/dining rooms. The ground floor has a heated pool, dry sauna with a large fixed glass wall so that one can contemplate the landscape. The house represents the idea of two monolithic concrete blades containing the boxes of the first floor, raised on stilts and stone box. The wood-covered façade consists of a light filter (vertical wooden strips) which, on the terraces of the suites, open completely. At nightfall, this 'skin' looks as though it is totally lit, surrounded by the beautiful mountainous forest." The idea of lifting structures up on pilotis is fairly common in Brazil. What is not at all obvious in this house, is that Marcio Kogan was called into the project after another architect had been dismissed by the clients and Kogan had to deal with an existing steel frame. Seemingly making this apparent handicap into an advantage, the essentially geometric rigor of the architectural solutions blends seamlessly with a sensual and very Brazilian presence of nature.

Das rechteckige, 739 m² große **BR HOUSE** befindet sich auf einem Grundstück mit einer Fläche von 6820 m². Der Architekt beschreibt das Wohnhaus so: „Das zweigeschossige Haus besteht aus Beton, Metall, Holz, Aluminium und Glas und ist vollständig in die Waldlandschaft der bergigen Region Petrópolis von Rio de Janeiro integriert. Im ersten Obergeschoss gibt es vier Suiten, ein Gästebadezimmer, eine Küche sowie Ess- und Wohnräume. Auf der Erdgeschossebene liegen ein beheiztes Schwimmbad und eine Trockensauna mit einer großen festverglasten Glaswand, so dass die Landschaft gegenwärtig ist. Bestimmt wird das Haus von der Idee zweier monolithischer Platten aus Beton (die Decken), die die ‚Kisten' des ersten Obergeschosses aufnehmen. Sie wurden mithilfe der Stützen und einer ‚Steinkiste' angehoben. Die holzverkleidete Fassade wirkt als Lichtfilter und besteht aus vertikalen Holzlamellen. Sie lässt sich im Bereich der Terrassen der Schlafräume komplett öffnen. Nachts scheint diese Hülle – umgeben von dem wunderbaren Bergwald – komplett zu leuchten." Die Idee, Gebäude auf Stützen zu stellen, ist in Brasilien nicht ungewöhnlich. Man bemerkt es gar nicht, aber Marcio Kogan wurde beauftragt, nachdem sich die Bauherren von einem anderen Architekten getrennt hatten. Kogan musste daher die schon fertige Stahlkonstruktion in seinen Entwurf integrieren. Dieses scheinbare Handicap wendete er zum Guten: Die im Grundsatz geometrische Strenge der Lösung fügt sich ohne Schwierigkeiten in die sinnliche und sehr brasilianische Präsenz der Natur ein.

Située sur un terrain de 6820 m², la **MAISON BR** rectangulaire dispose de 739 m² de surface utile. L'architecte la décrit ainsi lui-même : « Cette maison sur deux niveaux est en béton, métal, bois, aluminium et verre, et totalement intégrée au paysage forestier de cette région montagneuse de l'État de Rio de Janeiro (Petrópolis). L'étage réunit quatre suites, des salles de bains pour invités, une cuisine et le séjour/salle à manger. Le rez-de-chaussée est occupé par une piscine chauffée, un sauna sec à grande paroi fixe en verre d'où l'on peut contempler le paysage. La maison est construite sur l'idée de deux lames de béton monolithes contenant les boîtes de l'étage soutenues par des pilotis et une boîte en pierre. La façade en bois se présente sous forme d'un écran léger (baguettes de bois verticales) qui s'ouvre entièrement sur les terrasses des suites. La nuit, cette ‹ peau › semble totalement lumineuse, entourée par la magnifique forêt de cette zone montagneuse. » L'idée d'élever les maisons sur pilotis est assez courante au Brésil, ce qui ne l'est pas, en revanche, c'est que Kogan a été appelé sur ce projet après qu'un de ses confrères ait été écarté, et qu'il a dû composer avec une structure en acier existante. Transformant ce handicap en avantage, la rigueur essentiellement géométrique des solutions architecturales retenues les fait se fondre dans une nature très présente, sensuelle, très typiquement brésilienne.

Lifting his house up on pilotis like many modern Brazilian buildings, Kogan also contrasts a rough stone base with smoother or more sophisticated surfaces in wood, glass, steel or concrete.

Wie viele andere moderne Häuser in Brasilien steht das BR House auf Stützen. Der grobe Steinsockel kontrastiert mit glatteren und edleren Oberflächen aus Holz, Glas, Stahl und Beton.

En élevant la maison sur des pilotis, Kogan a également fait contraster la base en pierre brute avec des surfaces plus douces et plus sophistiquées en verre, bois, acier ou béton.

An elevation shows the strictly rectangular shape of the house, with its essential living space lifted up off the ground.

Die Ansicht zeigt die streng rechtwinklige Form des Hauses. Der Wohnraum liegt im ersten Obergeschoss.

Élévation montrant la forme strictement rectangulaire de la maison, dont la partie séjour est surélevée par rapport au sol.

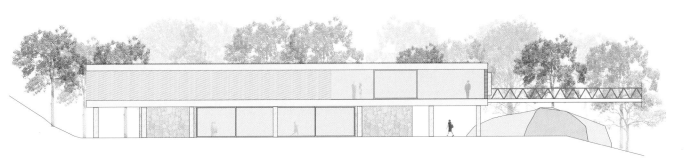

Trees come up through the wooden surface of a terrace, emphasizing the proximity of nature, which is in any case visible through the large glazed surfaces of the house.

Bäume wachsen durch den Holzfußboden der Terrasse und betonen die Nähe zur Natur. Diese ist ohnehin aufgrund der großen Verglasungen des Hauses sehr präsent.

Des arbres poussent à travers la terrasse en bois. Ils renforcent la proximité de la nature, visible à travers les vastes pans de verre de la maison.

Floor-to-ceiling windows bring the surrounding natural setting almost into the living room, while ample but strictly aligned furniture also contrasts with the profusion of greenery seen outside.

Geschosshohe Fenster bringen die natürliche Umgebung fast in den Wohnraum hinein. Großzügige, streng ausgerichtete Möbel bilden dabei einen Gegensatz zum verschwenderischen Grün der Natur.

Des ouvertures sol-plafond font quasiment entrer l'environnement naturel dans la maison, tandis que le mobilier, de proportions généreuses mais strictement aligné, contraste avec la profusion végétale que l'on aperçoit à l'extérieur.

A site plan shows the car park and approach bridge, leading to the outdoor terrace and into the rectangular volume of the house. Rough stones and water define lower level spaces, while the living room (right) remains smoothly horizontal.

Der Lageplan zeigt die überdachten Stellplätze und die Zugangsbrücke, die auf die Außenterrasse führt, von wo aus das Haus betreten wird. Grobes Felsgestein und Wasser definieren die Räume der unteren Ebene. Rechts: Der Wohnraum ist elegant horizontal gegliedert.

Le plan du site montre le parking et la passerelle qui mène à la terrasse et à l'intérieur du rectangle de la maison. Un mur de pierres brutes et un bassin délimitent les espaces du niveau inférieur, tandis que le séjour (à droite) affiche une horizontalité douce et reposante.

REM KOOLHAAS/OMA

Office for Metropolitan Architecture
Heer Bokelweg 149
3032 AD Rotterdam
The Netherlands

Tel: +31 10 243 82 00
Fax: +31 10 243 82 02
E-mail: office@oma.com
Web: www.oma.nl

REM KOOLHAAS created the Office for Metropolitan Architecture (**OMA**) in 1975 together with Elia and Zoe Zenghelis and Madelon Vriesendorp. Born in Rotterdam in 1944, Koolhaas tried his hand as a journalist for the *Haagse Post* and as a screenwriter before studying at the Architectural Association in London. He became well known after the 1978 publication of his book *Delirious New York*. OMA is led today by four partners: Rem Koolhaas, Ole Scheeren, Ellen van Loon, and Joshua Prince-Ramus. Their built work includes a group of apartments at Nexus World, Fukuoka (1991), and the Villa dall'Ava, Saint-Cloud (1985–91). Koolhaas was named head architect of the Euralille project in Lille in 1988, and has worked on a design for the new Jussieu University Library in Paris. His 1400 page book *S,M,L,XL* (Monacelli Press, 1995) has more than fulfilled his promise as an influential writer. He won the 2000 Pritzker Prize and the 2003 Praemium Imperiale Award for architecture. More recent work of OMA includes Maison à Bordeaux, France (1998); the campus center at the Illinois Institute of Technology (1998); the new Dutch Embassy in Berlin (2000–04); as well as the Guggenheim Las Vegas (2000–01); Prada boutiques in New York and Los Angeles; and the 1850-seat Porto Concert Hall (2005). OMA participated in the Samsung Museum of Art (Leeum, 2004) in Seoul with Mario Botta and Jean Nouvel. Recent work includes the design of OMA's largest project ever: the 575 000 m² Headquarters and Cultural Center for China Central Television (CCTV, 2012) in Beijing. OMA has also drawn up the master plan for the New City Center for Almere.

Zusammen mit Elia und Zoe Zenghelis sowie Madelon Vriesendorp gründete **REM KOOLHAAS** 1975 das Office for Metropolitan Architecture (**OMA**). Der 1944 in Den Haag geborene Koolhaas arbeitete als Journalist für die *Haagse Post* und als Drehbuchautor, bevor er an der Architectural Association in London studierte. Er wurde mit seinem 1978 erschienenen Buch *Delirious New York* weithin bekannt. OMA wird heute von vier Partnern geführt: Rem Koolhaas, Ole Scheeren, Ellen van Loon und Joshua Prince-Ramus. Zu ihren Bauten gehören u. a. die Villa dall'Ava im französischen Saint-Cloud (1985–91) und Wohnungen in Nexus World im japanischen Fukuoka (1991). 1988 wurde Koolhaas die Leitung des Euralille-Projekts in Lille übertragen; außerdem erarbeitete er einen Entwurf für die neue Bibliothek der Universität Jussieu in Paris. Mit seinem 1400 Seiten starken Buch *S,M,L,XL* (Monacelli Press, 1995) hat er seinen Status als einflussreicher Theoretiker und Autor bestätigt. Im Jahr 2000 erhielt Koolhaas den Pritzker-Preis und 2003 den Architekturpreis Praemium Imperiale. Gebäude von OMA sind u. a. ein Wohnhaus in Bordeaux (1998), das Campus-Zentrum des Illinois Institute of Technology (1998), die niederländische Botschaft in Berlin (2000–04), das Guggenheim Museum in Las Vegas (2000–01), Boutiquen für Prada in New York und Los Angeles und ein Konzertsaal in Porto mit 1850 Plätzen (2005). Mit Mario Botta und Jean Nouvel hat Koolhaas das Samsung Museum für Kunst (Leeum, 2004) in Seoul realisiert. Zu den jüngsten Projekten gehört der bislang größte Auftrag für OMA: das rund 600 000 m² umfassende Verwaltungs- und Kulturgebäude für China Central Television (CCTV, 2012) in Peking. OMA hat auch den Masterplan für das neue Stadtzentrum von Almere in den Niederlanden entworfen.

REM KOOLHAAS est né à Rotterdam en 1944. Avant d'étudier à l'Architectural Association de Londres, il s'essaye au journalisme pour le *Haagse Post* et à l'écriture de scénarii. Il fonde l'Office for Metropolitan Architecture (**OMA**) à Londres en 1975 et devient célèbre grâce à la publication, en 1978, de son ouvrage *Delirious New York*. OMA est dirigé par quatre partenaires, Rem Koolhaas, Ole Scheeren, Ellen van Loon et Joshua Prince-Ramus. Parmi leurs réalisations : un ensemble d'appartements à Nexus World, Fukuoka, Japon (1991) ; la villa dall'Ava, Saint-Cloud, France (1985–91). Koolhaas est nommé architecte en chef du projet Euralille à Lille en 1988 et propose un projet de bibliothèque pour la Faculté de Jussieu à Paris. Son livre de 1400 pages, *S,M,L,XL* (Monacelli Press, 1995), confirme son influence et son impact de théoricien. Il a remporté le prix Pritzker en 2000 et le Praemium Imperiale en 2003. Parmi ses réalisations : une maison à Bordeaux (1998), le campus de l'Illinois Institute of Technology (1998), la nouvelle ambassade des Pays-Bas à Berlin (2000–04), le Guggenheim Las Vegas (2000–01), des boutiques Prada à New York et Los Angeles et tout récemment, la Casa da Musica, salle de concert de 1850 places, à Porto, Portugal (2005). Son agence a réalisé le Samsung Museum of Art (Leeum, 2004) à Seoul en coopération avec Mario Botta et Jean Nouvel. Parmi ses récents travaux, citons son plus important projet à ce jour : le siège et le centre culturel (575 000 m²) de la Télévision nationale chinoise (CCTV, 2012) à Pékin. OMA a également effectué le plan directeur pour le nouveau centre-ville d'Almere (Pays-Bas).

GUGGENHEIM LAS VEGAS

Las Vegas, Nevada, USA, 1999–2001

Costs: $ 30 million (estimate).
Area: 710 m² (Guggenheim Hermitage), 5900 m² (Guggenheim Las Vegas).

This extravagant project was a "folly" of Thomas Krens, the former Director of the Guggenheim. Naturally, after the success of the Guggenheim Bilbao, designed by Frank O. Gehry, public tolerance of the innovations of Mr. Krens had reached a high before the attacks of September 11, 2001. The climate of hesitation that ensued made the gamble of the **GUGGENHEIM LAS VEGAS** somewhat less of an obvious success. Ever conscious of the "star quality" of the architects he employs, Krens called on the very fashionable Rem Koolhaas to insert not one but two museum spaces into the heart of a Las Vegas casino, The Venetian. The hotel is nothing less than an imitation of Venice, complete with Saint Mark's tower and the Rialto Bridge. Taking on the image of commercial and gambling excess incarnated by The Venetian, Koolhaas designed the Guggenheim Hermitage with Corten steel walls and the larger Guggenheim Las Vegas in a less restrictive mode to receive large exhibitions like "The Art of the Motorcycle," with its decor designed by Frank O. Gehry. Krens was one of the few very visible museum figures to bet in a big way on the drawing power of "star" architects. Be it Gehry, Koolhaas, Jean Nouvel, or Zaha Hadid, the architectural profession has benefited from the interest of Thomas Krens in architecture.

Das extravagante Projekt war ein „verrückte Einfall" von Thomas Krens, dem ehemaligen Direktor des Guggenheim Museums. Nach dem Erfolg von Frank O. Gehrys Guggenheim Museum in Bilbao hatte die öffentliche Akzeptanz für Thomas Krens' Innovationen ihren Höhepunkt erreicht. Die Terroranschläge des 11. September 2001 und die darauf folgende Verunsicherung ließen das Wagnis, das mit dem **GUGGENHEIM LAS VEGAS** eingegangen worden war, allerdings etwas weniger erfolgreich ausfallen. Wie stets auf die „Star-Qualität" der von ihm beschäftigten Architekten bedacht, beauftragte Krens den sehr in Mode gekommenen Rem Koolhaas, gleich zwei Museen in das Hotelcasino The Venetian zu integrieren. Das Gebäude, das tatsächlich Elemente der Lagunenstadt inklusive Markusplatz und Rialto-Brücke imitiert, ließ Koolhaas das Image von Kommerz und Glücksspiel aufnehmen. So wählte er für das Guggenheim Hermitage Museum eine Innenraumgestaltung aus Stahlwänden. Das größere Museum Guggenheim Las Vegas, das für umfangreiche Ausstellungen wie die von Gehry eingerichtete „The Art of the Motorcycle" gedacht ist, entwarf er dagegen in einem weniger restriktiven Stil. Krens war einer der wenigen namhaften Museumsverantwortlichen, der in hohem Maß auf die Anziehungskraft berühmter Architekten setzte. Ob nun Gehry, Koolhaas, Jean Nouvel oder Zaha Hadid die Ausführenden waren, der Berufsstand der Architekten hat ganz allgemein von Thomas Krens' Interesse an der Baukunst enorm profitiert.

Ce projet extravagant était une « folie » de Thomas Krens, l'ancien directeur du Guggenheim. Le succès remporté par Krens avec le Guggenheim Bilbao lui avait attiré la faveur enthousiaste du public avant les événements du 11 septembre 2001. Le climat actuel fait du projet d'un **GUGGENHEIM LAS VEGAS** un pari plus difficile. Toujours très conscient de la « qualité de star » des architectes qu'il emploie, Krens a fait appel à Rem Koolhaas, tellement à la mode, pour insérer non pas un mais deux musées dans un casino de Vegas, The Venetian. Cet hôtel est tout simplement une reconstitution de Venise, campanile de Saint-Marc et Rialto compris. Relevant le défi des excès commerciaux incarnés par le Venitian, Koolhaas a conçu un Guggenheim Hermitage à murs en acier Corten et un Guggenheim Las Vegas, plus vaste, de style plus ouvert, pour accueillir de grandes expositions comme « L'art de la moto » et sa mise en scène signée Frank O. Gehry. Thomas Krens a été l'un des rares responsables de musée connu à tabler à ce point sur le pouvoir d'attraction des « architectes stars ». Que ce soit Gehry, Koolhaas, Nouvel ou Zaha Hadid, toute la profession architecturale a bénéficié de son intérêt pour l'architecture.

Above, the Guggenheim Las Vegas is located within the Venetian Resort-Hotel-Casino with its fake Doge's Palace and grand entrance (above). To the right, the installation, by Frank O. Gehry, of the inaugural "The Art of the Motorcycle" exhibition.

Das Guggenheim Las Vegas befindet sich im Hotelcasino The Venetian, das mit einer Imitation des Dogenpalastes und einem imposanten Eingang aufwartet (oben). Die von Frank O. Gehry für die Eröffnungsausstellung „The Art of Motorcycle" entworfene Architektur (rechts).

En haut, le Guggenheim Las Vegas est situé à l'intérieur du Venitian Resort-Hotel-Casino doté d'un faux palais des Doges et d'une entrée palatiale. À droite, l'installation de l'exposition inaugurale « L'Art de la moto » signée Frank O. Gehry.

Left and above, within the Guggenheim Hermitage, with its unexpected
exhibition walls made of Corten steel,
the inaugural exhibition of modern
masterpieces by such artists as
Delaunay or Kandinsky.

Links und oben, die Innenräume der
Guggenheim Hermitage mit ihren
ungewöhnlichen Stahlwänden; die
Eröffnungsausstellung mit Meister-
werken von Künstlern wie Delaunay
und Kandinsky.

À gauche et en haut, l'intérieur du
Guggenheim Hermitage aux curieux
murs d'exposition en acier Corten ;
l'exposition d'inauguration avec des
chefs-d'œuvre d'artistes comme
Delaunay ou Kandinsky.

The Guggenheim Las Vegas space
again photographed at the time of the
Frank O. Gehry "Motorcycle" exhibition in late 2001. The dynamic inter-
play of the shed-like space designed
by Koolhaas and Gehry's undulating
metal surfaces made the presentation
of the show a work of art in itself.

Der Ausstellungsraum im Guggenheim
Las Vegas, aufgenommen während
der „Motorcycle"-Ausstellung Ende
2001. Das dynamische Zusammen-
spiel von Koolhaas' hallenähnlichem
Raum und Gehrys geschwungenen
Metallbändern machte aus der
Präsentation ein Kunstwerk für sich.

L'espace du Guggenheim Las Vegas
photographié lors de l'exposition
« Moto » de Frank O. Gehry, fin 2001.
Le jeu dynamique de l'espace en
forme de shed conçu par Koolhaas
et les plans métalliques ondulés de
Gehry faisaient de cette mise en
scène une œuvre d'art en soi.

PRADA BOUTIQUE
New York, New York, USA, 1999–2001

Client: Prada. Costs: $ 40 million. Amphitheater capacity: 200 seats.

Koolhaas has made the two levels of the Prada shop (street level and basement) into a continuous whole, so that part of the descent slope is an amphitheater.

Koolhaas verband Erdgeschoss und Untergeschoss der Prada Boutique zu einer Einheit, indem er einen Teil der Schräge als eine Art Amphitheater gestaltete.

Koolhaas a transformé les deux niveaux de la boutique Prada (rez-de-chaussée + sous-sol) en un continuum, et profité de la pente pour créer une sorte d'amphithéâtre.

The co-author (with his students from the GSD) of the magnum opus of 2002, *The Harvard Design School Guide to Shopping*, Rem Koolhaas has willingly allowed an ambiguity to arise about his own attitude to commercially inspired architecture. Seeking at once to enter the surprisingly vital retail sector with projects such as the **PRADA BOUTIQUE** in New York, and to question the proliferation of what he calls "junk space," the Dutch architect appears to want to "have his cake and eat it too." Be that as it may, Prada, located on the corner of Broadway and Prince Street in the Soho area of Manhattan, is a highly visible work. Located in the former space of the Guggenheim Soho (originally designed by Arata Isozaki), the shop runs on two levels. As he often has, Koolhaas employs industrial materials such as the metal grating "cages" that serve to present the chic wares. Cleverly turning a sweeping curve leading from the ground floor to the lower level into a ready-made theater and/or shoe sales space, Koolhaas proves his mastery of volumes and materials. At the juncture between retail sales and architecture, between commerce and art, between fashion and serious design, Koolhaas defines a unique place for himself as an arbiter of taste. With the museum boom waning, it may be that fashion boutiques will be the new place for "star" architects to express their talents.

2002 erschien Rem Koolhaas' zusammen mit seinen Studenten von der Harvard Graduate School of Design (GSD) verfasstes Opus *The Harvard Design School Guide to Shopping*. Koolhaas hat es zugelassen, dass über seine Haltung gegenüber kommerzieller Architektur eine gewisse Ambiguität entstand. Während er bestrebt ist, den überraschend vitalen Einzelhandelssektor mit Projekten wie der neuen **PRADA BOUTIQUE** in New York für sich zu erobern, kritisiert er gleichzeitig die zunehmende Verbreitung dessen, was er „Junk-Bauten" nennt. Aber trotz dieser scheinbaren Widersprüchlichkeit ist die an der Ecke von Broadway und Prince Street im New Yorker Stadtteil Soho gelegene Prada-Niederlassung eine herausragende Arbeit. Das Geschäft, in dessen ursprünglich von Arata Isozaki entworfenen Räumen vorher das Guggenheim Soho untergebracht war, ist auf zwei Ebenen angelegt. Wie schon so oft hat Koolhaas auch hier industrielle Materialen verwendet, zum Beispiel die „Käfige" aus Metallgitter, in denen die edlen Modeartikel präsentiert werden. Raffiniert führt Koolhaas eine schwungvolle Bogenlinie vom Erdgeschoss zum Untergeschoss und verwandelt sie in eine halbkreisförmig ansteigende Bühne für Konfektionsbekleidung und/oder Schuhe. So beweist er sein Können im Umgang mit Baukörper und Material. An der Grenze zwischen Geschäft und Architektur, zwischen Kommerz und Kunst, zwischen Mode und ernsthaftem Design nimmt Koolhaas eine einzigartige Position als Schiedsrichter in Fragen des Geschmacks ein. Mit dem Abflauen des Museumsbooms kann es durchaus sein, dass Modeboutiquen eine neue Möglichkeit für „Stararchitekten" werden, ihr Talent zum Ausdruck zu bringen.

Auteur, avec ses étudiants, d'un opus *The Harvard Design School Guide to Shopping*, paru en 2002, Rem Koolhaas a volontairement laissé une certaine ambiguïté se développer sur son attitude envers l'architecture d'inspiration commerciale. Cherchant à la fois à pénétrer le secteur de la vente de détail – d'une vitalité étonnante – à travers des projets comme la **BOUTIQUE PRADA** et à mettre en cause la prolifération de ce qu'il appelle les « junk space », espaces-poubelles, l'architecte néerlandais semble courir deux lièvres à la fois. Prada, à l'angle de Broadway et de Prince Street dans le quartier de Soho à Manhattan, n'en est pas moins une réalisation très remarquable. Installé dans l'ancien Guggenheim Soho (conçu à l'origine par Arata Isozaki), le magasin s'étend sur deux niveaux. Comme souvent, Koolhaas emploie des matériaux industriels dont des « cages » en treillis métallique qui servent à présenter les vêtements tellement chics. Transformant avec intelligence la rampe incurvée qui mène du rez-de-chaussée au sous-sol en une sorte de théâtre ready-made ou d'espace de vente pour les chaussures, il prouve sa maîtrise des volumes et des matériaux. À la jonction entre espace de vente et architecture, entre commerce et art, mode et design sérieux, Koolhaas se crée au passage un espace personnel d'arbitre du goût. La vague de construction de musées étant terminée, il se peut que les boutiques de mode soient le nouvel espace d'expression qu'attendent les « stars » de l'architecture.

The Prada designs are often placed in contrast with elements of the architecture such as the track-mounted steel cages where clothes can be displayed.

Die Modedesigns von Prada kontrastieren mit architektonischen Elementen wie den auf Schienen montierten Stahlkäfigen, die Kleidungsstücke präsentieren.

Les modèles de Prada sont placés en contraste avec des éléments d'architecture comme les cages d'acier de présentation des vêtements, accrochées à des rails suspendus.

SEATTLE CENTRAL LIBRARY

Seattle, Washington, USA, 2004

Floor area: 30 000 m². Client: Seattle Central Library. Costs: $ 165.5 million (including Temporary Central Library).

The **CENTRAL LIBRARY**, located on Fourth Avenue in Seattle, is drawing more than 8000 visitors a day, or twice as many as the old building. OMA worked with the Seattle firm LMN Architects on this project, which was the third Central Library built on the same site. The total cost of the 30 000 m² structure, including 10 million dollars for the Temporary Central Library, was 165.5 million dollars. It has a capacity for 1.45 million books. The structure is covered with nearly 10 000 pieces of glass, of which half are triple-layered with an expanded metal mesh sandwiched between the two outer layers in order to protect the interior against heat and glare. A reason for the use of this much glass was the architects' desire to make the building "transparent and open," qualities not always associated with libraries. Passersby can see activity on every floor of the building. The unusual shape of the building is partially related to efforts to control the type and quantity of light reaching interior spaces. A particularly striking overhang covers the entry on the Fourth Avenue side of the library. A system of "floating platforms" and a diagonal grid designed to protect against earthquakes or wind damage are amongst other structural innovations in the design. Within the library, a unique "Books Spiral" penetrates four levels of the stacks and contains the nonfiction collection, allowing for increased capacity and easier expansion of the number of books in the future. The 275-seat Microsoft Auditorium, located on Level 1, is considered by the Library to be its "centerpiece." Level 2 is a staff floor, and Level 3 includes the base of the building's atrium, book return and check out facilities, or the "Norcliffe Foundation Living Room," a reading area with a ceiling height of fifteen meters. Four meeting rooms are located on Level 4, and a large space called the "Mixing Chamber" compared by the architects to a "trading floor for information" is used to "go for help with general questions or in-depth research." The "Books Spiral" reaches from Level 6 to Level 9, while a reading room with a capacity for 400 persons is located on Level 10. The top floor is occupied by administrative offices and a staff lunch room.

8000 Besucher kommen täglich in die **ZENTRALBIBLIOTHEK** an der Fourth Avenue in Seattle, doppelt so viele wie in die alte. An dem Projekt – es ist bereits die dritte Zentralbibliothek auf dem Grundstück – waren neben OMA auch LMN Architects aus Seattle beteiligt. Die Gesamtkosten des 30 000 m² großen Gebäudes belaufen sich auf umgerechnet 139 Millionen Euro. Darin enthalten sind etwa 8,5 Millionen Euro für eine temporäre Bibliothek. 1,45 Millionen Bücher haben hier ihren Platz. Der Bau ist mit fast 10 000 Glaspaneelen eingedeckt. Die Hälfte dieser Paneele hat einen dreilagigen Aufbau: Zwischen zwei Glasscheiben ist ein Metallnetz angeordnet, um den Innenraum vor zu viel Hitze und vor Spiegelungen zu schützen. Ein Grund für die Verwendung von so viel Glas ist der Wunsch des Architekten, das Gebäude „transparent und offen" zu gestalten – Qualitäten, die man nicht unbedingt mit einer Bibliothek in Verbindung bringt. Passanten können sehen, dass auf jeder Ebene des Hauses Aktivitäten stattfinden. Die ungewöhnliche Form des Gebäudes hängt z. T. mit Überlegungen zusammen, wie die Tageslichtart und -menge in den Räumen kontrolliert werden können. Der Eingang an der Fourth Avenue wird von einer besonders eindrucksvollen Auskragung überdeckt. Ein System von „schwebenden Ebenen" und ein diagonaler Gitterrost, der die seismischen Kräfte sowie die Windlasten aufnimmt, gehören zu den konstruktiven Neuerungen des Gebäudes. Im Inneren der Bibliothek durchdringt eine „Bücherspirale", die alle Sachbücher enthält, die vier aufeinandergestapelten Büchergeschosse. Die Spiralform erlaubt es, die Nutzerkapazitäten und die Zahl der Bücher in Zukunft zu erhöhen. Das „Microsoft-Auditorium" mit 275 Plätzen auf der Ebene eins wird von den Bibliotheksmitarbeitern als Herz des Baus betrachtet. Auf der Ebene zwei liegen die Räume für die Angestellten. Das Atrium des Gebäudes beginnt auf Ebene drei, außerdem befinden sich hier u. a. die Buchrückgabe und der „Norcliffe Foundation Living Room", eine Lesezone mit einer Deckenhöhe von 15 m. Ebene vier nimmt vier Konferenzräume und einen großen Raum, die sogenannte „Mixing Chamber", auf. Dieser Raum wird von den Architekten mit einem Börsenparkett für Informationen verglichen. Er wird benutzt, wenn man „in grundsätzlichen Fragen Hilfe sucht oder Grundsatzforschung betreibt". Die Bücherspirale reicht von Ebene sechs bis Ebene neun, auf der Ebene zehn befindet sich ein Lesesaal für 400 Personen. Die Büros der Verwaltung und eine Kantine für die Mitarbeiter sind auf der obersten Ebene angeordnet.

Située sur Fourth Avenue, la **BIBLIOTHÈQUE CENTRALE** de Seattle, dont la capacité est de 1,45 million d'ouvrages, attire déjà plus de 8000 visiteurs par jour, soit deux fois la fréquentation de la précédente. OMA a collaboré sur ce projet – la troisième bibliothèque édifiée sur le même site – avec l'agence de Seattle LMN Architects. Le budget total de ce bâtiment de 30 000 m² s'est élevé à 139 millions d'euros dont 8,5 millions pour la Bibliothèque centrale temporaire, le temps du chantier. L'ensemble est habillé de près de 10 000 panneaux de verre dont la moitié de triple épaisseur : entre les deux vitrages externes est inséré un tissu de métal étiré qui protège l'intérieur de la lumière excessive et de la chaleur. La raison de cette utilisation massive du verre était le souhait de l'architecte de rendre le bâtiment « transparent et ouvert », qualités qui ne vont pas forcément de pair avec les bibliothèques. Les passants peuvent ainsi voir toutes les activités qui s'y déroulent, à chaque niveau. La forme originale du bâtiment est due en partie à la volonté de contrôler le type et la quantité de lumière susceptible d'atteindre l'intérieur. Un porte-à-faux spectaculaire protège l'entrée sur Fourth Avenue. Un système de « plates-formes flottantes » et une structure en diagonale, conçus pour résister aux tremblements de terre ou aux tornades, font partie des autres innovations structurelles du projet. Une « Spirale des livres » accueillant les ouvrages documentaires court sur quatre niveaux de rayonnages, permettant aussi d'augmenter la capacité de stockage dans le futur. Au niveau 1, l'auditorium Microsoft de 250 places est considéré comme le point central de la bibliothèque. Au niveau 2 se trouvent les bureaux du personnel et au niveau 3 la base de l'atrium, le bureau de prêt des ouvrages et la Norcliffe Foundation Living Room, une zone de lecture bénéficiant d'une hauteur sous plafond de 15 mètres. Quatre salles de réunion sont situées au niveau 4, ainsi qu'un vaste espace appelé « Chambre de mixage » comparé par les architectes à « une salle de marché de l'information, pour aider à répondre aux questions d'ordre général et aux recherches approfondies ». La « Spirale des livres » s'élève du niveau 6 au niveau 9 tandis qu'une salle de lecture de 400 places occupe le niveau 10. Le dernier niveau est occupé par des bureaux et par le restaurant du personnel.

The dynamic angles of the library set it aside from its urban neighbors. It looks almost as though it might be capable of moving away from the site under its own power.

Durch ihre dynamischen Winkel unterscheidet sich die Zentralbibliothek von ihren innerstädtischen Nachbarn. Fast meint man, sie könne sich aus eigener Kraft von dem Grundstück entfernen.

Les pans inclinés dynamiques de la Bibliothèque la détachent visuellement de son voisinage urbain. On pourrait presque la croire capable de se déplacer d'elle-même.

Despite the unexpected angles of the building, each facet is calculated on the basis of function and sunlight considerations.

Die Winkel im Gebäude mögen zufällig erscheinen, tatsächlich wurde aber jede Facette auf der Basis von Funktion und Belichtung berechnet.

Les étonnantes facettes des façades ont été calculées en fonction de critères fonctionnels pour un éclairage naturel.

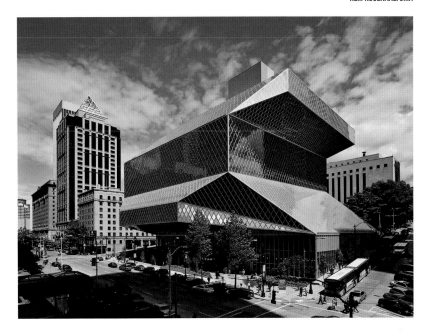

The angled glass façades of the library allow for generous and active interior spaces, where one level proceeds to the next without the usual strict division of floors.

Die geneigten Glasfassaden ermöglichen großzügige und aktiv zu nutzende Innenräume. Ohne die übliche Trennung der Geschosse geht eine Ebene in die nächste über.

Les parois de verre inclinées de la Bibliothèque laissent place à des salles spacieuses et fonctionnelles, où l'on passe d'un niveau à l'autre sans séparation traditionnelle.

Interior features and the vast overhead array of metal and light create an impression of a city within the city, where certain spaces are defined by their function but also, clearly, by their architecture.

Besondere räumliche Elemente und die riesigen Überkopfverglasungen aus Metall und Licht vermitteln den Eindruck einer Stadt in der Stadt. Spezielle Zonen werden durch ihre Funktion definiert – natürlich aber auch durch die Architektur.

L'aménagement intérieur, les immenses volumes de métal et la lumière créent une impression de ville dans la ville. Certains espaces sont définis par leur fonction autant que par leur architecture.

Although many more traditional libraries have had vast reading rooms, the Seattle Library has a profusion of unexpected spaces, where floor levels shift and develop before the visitor's eyes.

Große Lesesäle gab und gibt es auch in vielen älteren Bibliotheken. Die Zentralbibliothek in Seattle wartet jedoch mit einer Fülle von überraschenden Räumen auf, in denen sich die Ebenen neigen und sich dem Besucher sukzessiv erschließen.

Si beaucoup de bibliothèques plus traditionnelles possèdent de vastes salles de lecture, celle de Seattle offre une profusion d'espaces inattendus dans lesquels les niveaux s'entrecroisent et se déploient devant le visiteur.

In contrast with the many vast open spaces, the library also offers more intimate areas near the bookshelves (right). Stairways are not hidden like fire escapes, but participate in the invitation to explore the building (below).

Im Gegensatz zu den vielen riesigen offenen Räumen gibt es in der Zentralbibliothek im Bereich der Buchregale auch intimere Bereiche (rechts). Die Treppen werden nicht wie Sicherheitstreppenhäuser versteckt, sondern sind Teil der Einladung, das Gebäude zu erkunden (unten).

Outre ses vastes espaces ouverts, la bibliothèque met à disposition des aires plus intimes à proximité des rayonnages de livres (à droite). Les escaliers ne sont pas dissimulés comme des issues de secours, mais sont au contraire une invitation à visiter le bâtiment (en bas).

Rem Koolhaas has been quoted as saying that the Seattle Library is his "masterpiece." Though it can be expected that the Dutchman and his firm (OMA) will build many more significant buildings, the library is a symphonic orchestration that allays function and form in new ways, no small accomplishment where the handling of books is concerned.

Rem Koolhaas hat die Bibliothek in Seattle als sein Meisterstück bezeichnet. Man kann von dem Niederländer erwarten, dass er noch viele weitere bedeutende Gebäude realisiert – die Bibliothek wird als „sinfonische Orchestrierung", die Form und Funktion auf neue Weise miteinander in Einklang bringt, Bestand haben. Keine geringe Leistung, wenn es um den Umgang mit Büchern geht.

Rem Koolhaas aurait dit que cette bibliothèque était son « chef-d'œuvre ». On peut espérer que le Néerlandais et son équipe d'OMA réaliseront d'autres projets encore plus significatifs, mais cette bibliothèque est une orchestration symphonique qui réunit de manière novatrice la forme et la fonction, ce qui n'est pas une mince réussite dans le domaine de la conservation des livres.

KENGO KUMA

Kengo Kuma & Associates
2-24-8 Minamiaoyama
Minato-ku
Tokyo 107-0062
Japan

Tel: +81 3 3401 7721
Fax: +81 3 3401 7778
E-mail: kuma@ba2.so-net.ne.jp
Web: www.kkaa.co.jp

Great Bamboo Wall ►

Born in 1954 in Kanagawa, **KENGO KUMA** graduated in 1979 from the University of Tokyo, with a master's degree in architecture. In 1985–86, he received an Asian Cultural Council Fellowship Grant and was a visiting scholar at Columbia University. In 1987, he established the Spatial Design Studio and, in 1991, he created Kengo Kuma & Associates. His work includes: the Gunma Toyota Car Show Room, Maebashi (1989); the Maiton Resort Complex, Phuket, Thailand; Rustic, office building, Tokyo; Doric, office building, Tokyo; M2, headquarters for Mazda New Design Team, Tokyo (all in 1991); the Kinjo Golf Club, club house, Okayama (1992); the Atami Guest House, guesthouse for Bandai Corp, Atami (1992–95); the Karuizawa Resort Hotel, Karuizawa (1993); the Tomioka Lakewood Golf Club House, Tomioka (1993–96); the Kiro-san Observatory, Ehime (1994); the Japanese Pavilion for the Venice Biennale, Italy (1995) and the Toyoma Noh-Theater, Miyagi (1995–96). He has also completed the Stone Museum in Nasu, Tochigi, and the Museum of Ando Hiroshige in Batou, Nasu-gun, Tochigi. More recently, he finished the Great (Bamboo) Wall guesthouse, Beijing (2002); One Omotesando, Tokyo (2003); the boutique and office for Moet Hennessy Louis Vuitton (LVMH) in Osaka (2004); the Fukusaki Hanging Garden (2005); and the Nagasaki Prefecture Art Museum (2005).

KENGO KUMA, geboren 1954 in Kanagawa, Japan, schloss 1979 sein Studium an der Universität Tokio mit dem Master in Architektur ab. Von 1985 bis 1986 arbeitete er mit einem Stipendium des Asian Cultural Council als Gastwissenschaftler an der Columbia University in New York. 1987 gründete Kuma das Spatial Design Studio und 1991 das Büro Kengo Kuma & Associates in Tokio. Zu seinen Bauten gehören der Gunma Toyota Car Showroom in Maebashi (1989), die Ferienanlage Maiton auf Phuket in Thailand, die Bürogebäude Rustic und Doric sowie M2, der Hauptsitz für die Designabteilung von Mazda, alle 1991 in Tokio ausgeführt; ferner das Clubhaus des Kinjo Golf Club in Okayama (1992), das Gästehaus für die Firma Bandai Corporation in Atami (1992–95), eine Hotelanlage in Karuizawa (1993), das Clubhaus des Lakewood Golf Club in Tomioka (1993–96), das Observatorium Kiro-san in Ehime (1994), der japanische Pavillon auf der Biennale in Venedig (1995) und das Noh-Theater in Toyama, Miyagi (1995–96). Er baute weiterhin das Steinmuseum in Nasu, Tochigi, sowie ein Museum für die Werke von Ando Hiroshige in Batou, Nasu-gun, Tochigi. Danach beendet er die Arbeit an dem Hotel Große (Bambus-) Mauer in Peking (2002), an One Omotesando in Tokio (2003), Boutique und Büro für Moet Hennessy Louis Vuitton (LVHM) in Osaka (2004), den Hängenden Gärten in Fukusaki (2005) und am Kunstmuseum der Präfektur Nagasaki (2005).

Né en 1954 à Kanagawa, Japon, **KENGO KUMA** est Master en architecture de l'Université de Tokyo (1979). En 1985–86, il bénéficie d'une bourse de l'Asian Cultural Council et est chercheur invité à la Columbia University. En 1987, il crée le Spatial Design Studio, et en 1991 Kengo Kuma & Associates. Parmi ses réalisations : le Car Show Room Toyota de Gunma (Maebashi, 1989) ; le Maiton Resort Complex (Phuket, Thaïlande, 1991) ; le Rustic Office Building (Tokyo, 1991) ; l'immeuble de bureaux Doric (Tokyo, 1991) ; le siège du département de design de Mazda (Tokyo, 1991) ; le Kinjo Golf Club, Club House (Okayama, 1992) ; l'Observatoire Kiro-san (Ehime, Japon, 1994) ; l'Atami Guest House pour Bandaï Corp (Atami, 1992–95) ; le Karuizawa Resort Hotel (Karuizawa, 1993) ; le Club House du Tomioka Lakewood Golf (Tomioka, 1993–96) ; le Théâtre Nô Toyoma (Miyagi, 1995–96). En outre, il réalisa le Musée de la pierre (Nasu, Tochigi) et le Musée Ando Hiroshige (Batou, Nasu-gun, Tochigi). Puis il termina les travaux concernant l'Hôtel de la Grande Muraille (de bambou) à Pékin (2002), One Omotesando à Tokyo (2003), les boutique et bureaux pour Moet Hennessy Louis Vuitton (LVHM) à Osaka (2004), les jardins suspendus à Fukusaki (2005) et le Musée d'art de la préfecture de Nagasaki (2005).

GREAT BAMBOO WALL

Badaling, China, 2000–02

Client: SOHO China Ltd. Floor area: 528 m². Costs: not specified.

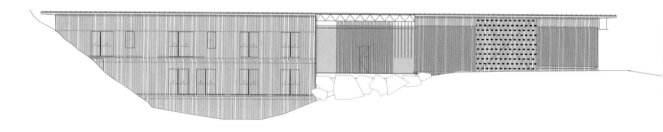

In October 2002, the SOHO (Small Office, Home Office) China group inaugurated the first 11 of 59 planned guesthouses located near the Great Wall of China. Created by the young couple Pan Shiyi and his wife Zhang Xin, SOHO China has called on a number of well-known architects for this project, including Shigeru Ban. Their intention is to make a weekend community mainly for wealthy Chinese clients, and aside from the first 11 villas they have created a 4000 m² club with pools, restaurants, cinemas and art galleries. The cost of the houses ranges from 500 000 to one million euros and they are between 330 and 700 m² in size. Each house has its own style, or rather that of its architect, though the complex does not give the impression of being a kind of architectural "zoo." The structure designed by Kengo Kuma, called the **GREAT BAMBOO WALL**, is set on a 1930 m² site and has a total floor area of 528 m². Intended as a small hotel unit, it is a reinforced concrete one-story structure (and basement) with a partly steel frame. The partial basement takes advantage of a natural dip in the site under part of the structure. An extensive use of glass and bamboo walls with fairly large openings between each pole and bamboo cladding on pillars gives an impression of lightness and a relationship to the traditional architecture of Asia. Kuma attains a simplicity and a modernity that have more to do with the most recent trends in architecture than with the ancient past, however. As he says about bamboo, "skin and outer surface are different. Concrete has an outer surface, but not skin. On top of that, I don't find concrete to be particularly attractive. That's because without skin, the soul within never appears. Bamboo has particularly beautiful skin. And, bamboo has a soul residing within. In Japan there is a famous children's tale about how 'Princess Kakuyahime,' the Moon Goddess, was born inside a stalk of bamboo. People believed the story that she was born inside a stalk of bamboo because bamboo has a peculiar type of skin and possesses a soul." After this structure, Kuma has undertaken the realization of seven houses in the same project area.

Im Oktober 2002 eröffnete die Firmengruppe SOHO (Small Office, Home Office) China in einem Gebiet nahe der Chinesischen Mauer die ersten elf von insgesamt 59 geplanten Gästehäusern. Das von Pan Shiyi und seiner Frau Zhang Xin gegründete Unternehmen SOHO China beauftragte eine Reihe bekannter Architekten mit der Planung, darunter auch Shigeru Ban. Die Zielgruppe sind Wochenendgäste, hauptsächlich wohlhabende Chinesen, für die neben den Villen ein 4000 m² großes Clubareal mit Schwimmbädern, Restaurants und Kunstgalerien angelegt wurde. Die zwischen 330 und 700 m² großen Häuser kosten 500 000 bis eine Million Euro. Zwar hat jedes von ihnen seinen eigenen Stil oder besser gesagt den seines Architekten, trotzdem macht die Anlage nicht den Eindruck, als sei hier eine Art „Architektur-Zoo" entstanden. Das von Kengo Kuma entworfene **GREAT-BAMBOO-WALL-GEBÄUDE** steht auf einem 1930 m² großen Grundstück und hat eine Nutzfläche von 528 m². Es ist als kleines Hotel gedacht und besteht aus einem eingeschossigen Bauteil aus Stahlbeton mit einem Stahlrahmenteilstück. Der zusätzliche Untergeschossraum ergab sich durch Ausnutzung einer natürlichen Senke, die sich unter einem Teil des Gebäudes befindet. Das Haus selbst vermittelt durch die großzügige Ausstattung mit Glas und Bambus den Eindruck von Leichtigkeit und Nähe zur traditionellen Architektur Asiens. Kuma überzeugt hier jedoch mit einer Schlichtheit und Modernität, die mehr mit den neuesten Architektur-trends als mit der Vergangenheit zu tun haben. Zum Thema Bambus erläutert er: „Es gibt einen Unterschied zwischen Haut und Außenfläche. Beton hat eine Außenfläche, aber keine Haut. Außerdem finde ich Beton nicht besonders attraktiv. Und zwar deshalb, weil ohne Haut die Seele nicht zum Vorschein kommt. Bambus dagegen hat eine besonders schöne Haut. Und Bambus besitzt eine Seele. In Japan gibt es ein berühmtes Kindermärchen, in dem erzählt wird, wie Prinzessin Kakuyahime, die Mondgöttin, aus einem Bambusrohr geboren wurde. Die Menschen glaubten diese Geschichte, eben weil Bambus so eine charakteristische Haut hat und eine Seele besitzt." Nach der Fertigstellung dieses Gebäudes übernahm Kuma die Planung von weiteren sieben Häusern für dasselbe Projekt.

En octobre 2002, le SOHO (Small Office, Home Office) China group a inauguré les onze premières maisons d'hôtes sur les 59 qu'il compte édifier près de la Grande muraille de Chine. Créé par Pan Shiyi et son épouse Zhang Xin, SOHO China a fait appel pour ce projet à un certain nombre d'architectes connus, dont Shigeru Ban. Leur programme est de réaliser des résidences de week-end, principalement destinées à de riches clients chinois. En dehors des onze villas, ils ont déjà créé un club de 4000 m² comprenant des piscines, des restaurants, des cinémas et une galeries d'art. Le coût des maisons s'élève de 500 000 à 1 million d'euros pour des surfaces de 330 à 700 m². Chacune possède son style propre, ou plutôt celui de son architecte, mais l'ensemble ne donne pas pour autant l'impression de zoo architectural. Le projet de Kengo Kuma, appelé **LA GRANDE MURAILLE DE BAMBOU**, est érigé sur un terrain de 1930 m² pour 528 m² utiles. Ce petit ensemble hôtelier est une construction en béton armé d'un seul niveau (+ sous-sol) et ossature partiellement en acier. Le sous-sol profite d'un creux naturel du sol. Le recours extensif au verre et aux murs de bambou avec d'assez grandes ouvertures entre chaque pilier de bambou et des espacements marqués entre les lattes du même bois donne une impression de légèreté et rappelle l'architecture traditionnelle de l'Asie. Kuma atteint une simplicité et une modernité néanmoins plus en rapport avec les tendances récentes de l'architecture qu'avec un passé lointain. Il explique à propos du bambou : « Peau et surface extérieure sont différentes. Le béton possède une surface, pas une peau. De plus, je ne trouve pas le béton particulièrement séduisant. Quand il n'y a pas de peau, l'âme est absente. Le bambou possède précisément une peau magnifique. Et il a une âme en lui. Un célèbre conte japonais pour enfants parle de la Princesse Kakuyahime, déesse de la lune, née dans une tige de bambou. Les gens croient qu'elle est née dans une tige de bambou parce que celle-ci possède une peau particulière et une âme. » Après ce projet, Kuma a entrepris la construction de sept résidences dans la même région.

The Great Bamboo Wall building fits naturally into its site, as can be seen in the elevation on the left and in the photos.

Das Great-Bamboo-Wall-Gebäude fügt sich harmonisch in seine Umgebung ein, wie im Querschnitt links und in den Fotos zu sehen ist.

La maison d'hôtes s'intègre naturellement dans son site, comme le montrent l'élévation à gauche et les photos.

A light, open structure permits views to the hilly setting and a basin brings an unexpected freshness into the building itself. Though far less durable than the stones of the Great Wall, bamboo is of course a very popular Asian building material.

Eine helle, offene Raumaufteilung ermöglicht Ausblicke auf die umliegende Berglandschaft und bringt eine überraschende Frische in das Gebäude. Wenn auch weit weniger dauerhaft als die Steine der Chinesischen Mauer, ist Bambus in Asien ein sehr beliebtes Baumaterial.

La structure légère et ouverte favorise les vues sur le cadre montagneux environnant, tandis qu'un bassin apporte une fraîcheur inattendue dans le bâtiment lui-même. Moins résistant que les pierres de la Grande muraille, le bambou n'en reste pas moins un matériau de construction très populaire en Asie.

The simplicity and directness of the design might reveal the architect's effort to mediate the divide that exists between the architecture of his own country and that of China.

Mit der Einfachheit und Geradlinigkeit des Designs stellte der Architekt eine Verbindung zwischen der Architektur seines eigenen Landes und der von China her.

La simplicité et la franchise de conception révèlent cependant un effort pour trouver une voie entre l'architecture de son propre pays et celle de la Chine.

DANIEL LIBESKIND

Studio Daniel Libeskind
2 Rector Street
New York, New York 10006
USA

Tel: +1 212 497 9100
Fax: +1 212 285 2130
E-mail: info@daniel-libeskind.com
Web: www.daniel-libeskind.com

Jewish Museum ▶

Born in Poland in 1946 and now a US citizen, **DANIEL LIBESKIND** studied music in Poland, Israel and New York before taking up architecture at the Cooper Union in New York. He has taught at Harvard, Yale, Hanover, Graz, Hamburg, and UCLA. His work includes the Jewish Museum in Berlin (1989–99), and numerous projects such as his 1997 plan for an extension to the Victoria and Albert Museum in London, and his prize-winning scheme for the Musicon Bremen (1995). Like Zaha Hadid, he has had a considerable influence through his theory and his projects, rather than through his limited built work. The Felix Nussbaum Museum in Osnabrück, Germany, is in fact one of his first completed works. His work includes the Imperial War Museum, Manchester (2001), the Contemporary Jewish Museum, San Francisco, California (2008) and the extension for the Denver Art Museum (2006). In 2003, the Studio Daniel Libeskind won the competition for the master plan for the Memory Foundations, the rebuilding of Ground Zero in New York (2003–14).

DANIEL LIBESKIND, geboren 1946 in Polen, ist amerikanischer Staatsbürger. Zunächst studierte er Musik in Polen, Israel und New York, anschließend Architektur an der Cooper Union in New York. Er hat in Harvard, Yale, Hannover, Graz, Hamburg und an der UCLA gelehrt. Seine wichtigsten Projekte sind das Jüdische Museum in Berlin (1989–99), ein Entwurf zur Erweiterung des Victoria & Albert Museum in London (1997) und der preisgekrönte Wettbewerbsentwurf für das Musicon Bremen, ein Veranstaltungszentrum (1995). Wie Zaha Hadid hat er mehr Einfluss ausgeübt durch seine Theorien und Entwürfe als durch seine wenigen ausgeführten Bauten, deren erstes das Felix-Nußbaum-Haus in Osnabrück war. Er baute auch das Imperial War Museum in Manchester (2001) und das Contemporary Jewish Museum in San Francisco (2008) sowie die Erweiterung des Denver Art Museum (2006). 2003 gewann das Studio Daniel Libeskind den Wettbewerb für den Masterplan für die Memory Foundations, die Wiederbebauung von Ground Zero in New York (2003–14).

Né en Pologne en 1946, et aujourd'hui citoyen américain, **DANIEL LIBESKIND** étudie la musique en Pologne, en Israël et à New York avant de s'orienter vers l'architecture à Cooper Union, New York. Il a enseigné à Harvard, Yale, Hanovre, Graz et UCLA. Il est l'auteur, entre autres, du Musée juif de Berlin (1989-99) et de nombreux projets comme l'extension du Victoria & Albert Museum à Londres et le centre de spectacles Musicon de Brême, primé en 1995. Comme Zaha Hadid, Libeskind a exercé une influence considérable à travers ses théories et ses écrits plus qu'à travers ses réalisations en nombre limité. Le Felix Nussbaum Museum d'Osnabrück, Allemagne, est en fait l'une de ses premières œuvres achevées. Il a construit également l'Imperial War Museum à Manchester (2001), le Musée juif de San-Francisco (2008) ainsi que l'extension du Musée d'art de Denver (2006). En 2003, l'agence Daniel Libeskind remporte le concours pour le plan des Memory Foundations, la reconstruction de Ground Zero à New-York (2003–14).

JEWISH MUSEUM

Berlin, Germany, 1989–99

Competition: 1989. Start of planning: 1989. Construction: 1991–99. Floor area: 12 500 m².
Exhibition space: 9500 m². Costs: c. € 36.9 million.

Given Libeskind's ideas about the concept of absence in this architecture, meaning that of the absence of the Jews who were murdered, the fact that it opened empty seems appropriate.

Die Tatsache, dass das Museum ohne Exponate eröffnet wurde, unterstreicht Libeskinds Idee von der „Abwesenheit", womit er die Abwesenheit der ermordeten Juden meint.

Que le musée soit vide illustre aussi le concept d'absence de son architecture exprimant la disparition des Juifs assassinés.

The **JEWISH MUSEUM** has had a long and complicated history. The project was launched in 1988 as an addition to the Berlin Museum, originally intended to contain a "Jewish Department," as well as theater, fashion and toy displays. Daniel Libeskind's project won first prize in a competition held in 1989. The fall of the Berlin Wall and the decision to return the capital to the now unified city affected plans. A decision to include "the entire history of the relationship between German Jews and non-Jews from Roman times to the present," in the words of the museum's director W. Michael Blumenthal, has left the structure at least temporarily without any exhibition or other contents. A fractured Star of David, or a fragment of the SS symbol? Such are the suggested sources of the plans of this structure, which is unlike any other contemporary museum. Many sections of the building will in any case remain intentionally empty, symbolizing the void left by the absence of Jews who died as a result of the Holocaust.

Das **JÜDISCHE MUSEUM** hat eine lange Vorgeschichte. Das Projekt wurde 1988 als Erweiterung des Berlin-Museums ins Leben gerufen und war ursprünglich für die Aufnahme einer „Jüdischen Abteilung" sowie von Theater-, Mode- und Spielzeugexponaten gedacht. Libeskinds Entwurf erhielt im Wettbewerb von 1989 den ersten Preis. Der Fall der Mauer und der Beschluss, das wiedervereinigte Berlin zur Bundeshauptstadt zu erklären, hatten eine Änderung der Pläne zur Folge. Die Entscheidung, „die gesamte Geschichte der Beziehungen zwischen deutschen Juden und Nichtjuden von der Zeit der Römer bis zur Gegenwart" darzustellen, wie der Museumsdirektor W. Michael Blumenthal es formulierte, hat dazu geführt, dass das Museum zumindest vorerst ohne Exponate geblieben ist. Die Form eines gebrochenen Davidsterns (oder der SS-Runen) sind als Quellen für den Grundriss des Baus vorstellbar, der sich von allen anderen zeitgenössischen Museen deutlich abhebt. Viele Teile des Hauses werden bewusst leer bleiben, um die Leere zu symbolisieren, die durch den Verlust der im Holocaust ermordeten Juden entstand.

L'histoire du **MUSÉE JUIF** est complexe. Le projet a été lancé en 1988 en extension du Berlin Museum, qui prévoyait de s'équiper d'un « département juif », d'un théâtre et d'expositions de mode et de jouets. Le projet de Libeskind a remporté le premier prix lors d'un concours organisé en 1989. La chute du mur de Berlin et la décision de réinstaller la capitale de l'Allemagne dans la ville réunifiée affecta le projet. La décision d'inclure « la totalité de l'histoire de la relation entre les Juifs allemands et les non-Juifs de l'époque romaine à aujourd'hui », selon les mots du directeur du musée, W. Michael Blumenthal, a eu pour conséquence que le bâtiment se trouve pour l'instant sans expositions ni collections. Une étoile de David fracturée – ou un fragment du symbole SS – a pu inspirer les plans de ce bâtiment très différent de tous les musées récemment construits. Plusieurs de ses parties resteront volontairement vides pour symboliser le sentiment d'absence laissé par la disparition des Juifs victimes de l'Holocauste.

A zigzagging pattern of openings evokes the idea of rupture, destruction and absence.

Die im Zickzacksystem angelegten Öffnungen rufen die Vorstellung von Brüchen, Zerstörung und Abwesenheit hervor.

Un motif de découpes en zigzag évoque l'idée de rupture, de destruction et d'absence.

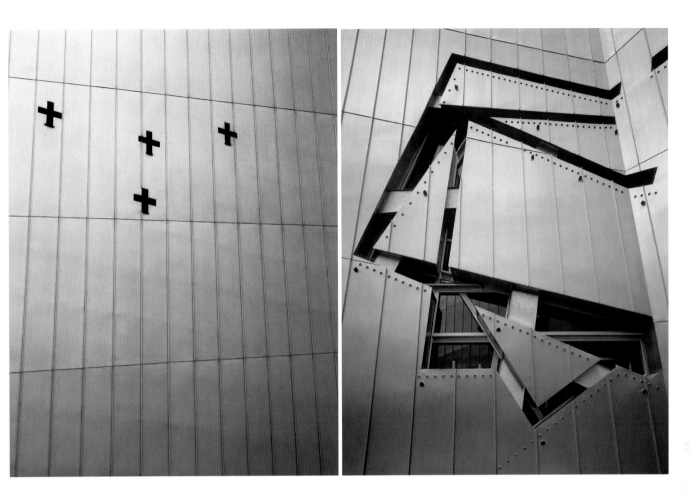

Just as some contemporary art seeks out the uncomfortable, so the Jewish Museum proposes no easy solutions. Where much contemporary architecture seeks simplicity and ease, this design is intentionally difficult.

Das Jüdische Museum erschließt sich dem Besucher nicht ohne Weiteres. Im Gegensatz zu vielen anderen Bauten ist das Museum bewusst kompliziert gestaltet.

De même que certaines œuvres d'art contemporain cherchent à mettre le spectateur mal à l'aise, le Musée juif ne propose pas d'interprétation évidente. Alors que la plupart des œuvres architecturales contemporaines recherchent la simplicité, la conception du musée joue la difficulté.

MAYA LIN

Maya Lin Studio
112 Prince Street
New York, New York 10012
USA

Tel: +1 212 941 6463
Fax: +1 212 941 6464
E-mail: studio@mlinstudio.com
Web: www.mayalin.com

Norton Apartment ▶

MAYA LIN, born in 1959, attended Yale College and the Yale School of Architecture, receiving her M.Arch. in 1986. She created her office, Maya Lin Studio, in New York the same year. By that time she had already created what remains her most famous work, the Memorial Wall of the Vietnam Veterans in Washington D. C. (1981). Other sculptural work includes her Civil Rights Memorial in Montgomery, Alabama (1989); and "Groundswell," at the Wexner Center of the Arts, Columbus, Ohio (1993). She completed the design for the Museum of African Art in New York (with David Hotson, 1993); the Weber Residence, Williamstown, Massachusetts (1994); and the Asia/Pacific/American Studies Department, New York University, New York (1997). Other projects are the Greyston Bakery, Greyston Foundation, Yonkers, New York (2003); the Langston Hughes Library, Childrens' Defense Fund, Clinton, Tennessee (1999, with Martella Associates, Architects); and the Riggio-Lynch Chapel, Children's Defense Fund (2004), published here, as well as her architectural and artistic project "Confluence" in Washington State (2002–05) and the Arts Plaza for the University of California, Irvine (2004–05).

MAYA LIN, geboren 1959, studierte am Yale College und an der Yale School of Architecture, wo sie 1986 ihren Master of Architecture erwarb. Im selben Jahr gründete sie ihr eigenes Büro Maya Lin Studio. Zu diesem Zeitpunkt hatte sie schon ihr bis heute bekanntestes Werk, die Memorial Wall of the Vietnam Veterans in Washington D. C. geschaffen (1981). Andere bildhauerische Arbeiten sind u. a. das Civil Rights Memorial in Montgomery, Alabama (1989), und „Groundswell" für das Wexner Center of Arts in Columbus, Ohio (1993). Realisierte Bauten sind das Museum of African Art in New York (mit David Hotson, 1993), die Weber Residence in Williamstown, Massachusetts (1994), und das Asia/Pacific/American Studies Department der New York University in New York (1997). Weitere Projekte sind die Greyston Bäckerei der Greyston Foundation in Yonkers, New York (2003), sowie die Langston-Hughes-Bibliothek (mit Martella Associates, Architects, 1999) und die Riggio-Lynch-Kapelle, beide für den Childrens' Defense Fund in Clinton, Tennessee (2004), außerdem das Kunst- und Architekturprojekt „Confluence" im US-Bundesstaat Washington (2002–05) und die Arts Plaza für die University of California, Irvine (2004–05).

MAYA LIN, née en 1959, a fait ses études au Yale College et à la Yale School of Architecture, Master of Architecture (1986). Elle ouvre son agence, Maya Lin Studio, à New York la même année, mais a déjà créé ce qui reste à ce jour son œuvre la plus célèbre, le Mémorial des vétérans de la guerre du Vietnam sur le National Mall de Washington (1981). Elle a réalisé d'autres œuvres de nature sculpturale, comme le Mémorial des droits civiques à Montgomery, Alabama (1989) et « Groundswell » pour le Wexner Center for the Arts, Columbus, Ohio (1993). Par ailleurs, elle a réalisé le Museum for African Art, New York (avec David Hotson, 1993) ; la Weber Residence, Williamstown, Massachusetts (1994) et le département des études Asie/Pacifique/Amérique de la New York University, New York (1997). Parmi ses autres travaux : la Greyston Bakery, Greyston Foundation, Yonkers, New York (2003) ; la Langston Hughes Library (avec Martella Associates, Architects) et la Riggio-Lynch Chapel publiée ici, pour le Children's Defense Fund, Clinton, Tennessee (1999 et 2004). Citons enfin le projet d'architecture et d'art « Confluence » (2002–05) à Washington et la Arts Plaza à l'University of California, Irvine (2004–05).

LANGSTON HUGHES LIBRARY

Knoxville, Tennessee, USA, 1997–99

Planning: 1997–98. Completion: 3/99. Clients: Len and Louise Reggio, donors; Children's Defense Fund, sponsors; Marian Wright Edelman, director of CDF. Total floor area: 186 m².

Designed as a library of African-American culture, the unusual **LANGSTON HUGHES LIBRARY** is based on a 100-year-old cantilevered Tennessee barn that the architect literally took apart and set up on two supporting cribs. The library space, measuring about 153 m², is the single upper-level room, whose interior surfaces are clad in maple paneling, beige carpeting and brown recycled particleboard. Located on a farm owned by the Children's Defense Fund, the library's interior has little relation to the rough-hewn timber of the barn – a feature for which the architect has been criticized. Lin compares the design to a "diamond in the rough." "When you cut into it," she says, "it reveals a more-polished inner self." Despite its relatively closed appearance, the library receives good natural light through "cuts made throughout the stacks, reading areas and the entry stair hall."

Die ungewöhnliche, für die Bibliothek der afroamerikanischen Kultur konzipierte **LANGSTON HUGHES LIBRARY** entstand aus der Umnutzung einer 100 Jahre alten, freitragenden „Tennessee-Scheune", die von der Architektin buchstäblich auseinandergenommen und auf eine Balkenkonstruktion gesetzt wurde. Der gut 153 m² große Bibliothekssaal nimmt das gesamte Obergeschoss ein, dessen Inneres mit Ahorntäfelung, beigen Teppichböden und recycelten braunen Spanplatten ausgestattet ist. Obwohl der Bau auf einem im Besitz des Children's Defense Fund befindlichen Farmgelände steht, hat das Interieur der Bibliothek wenig mit der ursprünglichen, grob gearbeiteten Holzauskleidung der Scheune zu tun – ein Aspekt, für den die Architektin kritisiert wurde. Lin vergleicht ihren Entwurf mit einem „Rohdiamanten" und fügt hinzu: „Erst wenn man ihn aufschneidet, kommt sein glattes Inneres zum Vorschein." Trotz ihrer relativ geschlossenen Form erhält die Bibliothek viel natürliches Licht durch Schlitze, die überall zwischen den Regalen, im Lesebereich und im Eingangstreppenhaus angebracht wurden.

Destinée à devenir la Bibliothèque de la culture afro-américaine, la **LANGSTON HUGHES LIBRARY** est implantée dans une propriété agricole du Children's Defense Fund. Ce curieux projet resulte de la reconversion d'une grange à encorbellement séculaire du Tennessee, démontée et remontée sur deux systèmes de pilotis. La bibliothèque, d'environ 153 m², occupe la totalité de la pièce unique de l'étage, dont les murs sont habillés de lambris d'érable, de médium brun, et les sols recouverts de moquette beige. L'intérieur de la bibliothèque n'a que peu de rapport avec l'aspect extérieur de la grange, ce qui a valu certaines critiques à l'architecte. M. Lin compare le projet à « un diamant brut ». « Lorsque vous le taillez, il révèle un intérieur plus lisse. » En dépit de son aspect assez fermé, la bibliothèque reçoit un éclairage naturel de qualité par « des découpes pratiquées entre les rayonnages, dans les zones de lecture et l'escalier d'entrée ».

One very surprising aspect of this project is that the interior and the exterior of the original, elevated wood structure have very little to do with each other. Indeed the sophistication of the interior does contradict the rural surroundings.

Die wohl durchdachte und elegante Innenausstattung des auf eine Holzkonstruktion gesetzten Baus steht in deutlichem Widerspruch zu seinem Äußeren und der ländlichen Umgebung.

Un des aspects les plus surprenants de ce projet est l'absence presque totale de rapports entre le bâtiment d'origine, en bois, et son aménagement. Son intérieur raffiné est même en contradiction avec le cadre naturel.

The rough-hewn exterior of the original barn building gives way to a sophisticated interior that houses the Langston Hughes Library.

Über die Unterbauten, die in ihrer Gestaltung an die grob gearbeitete Außenfassade der ehemaligen Scheune angepasst sind, gelangt man in den sachlich-kühlen Innen-raum der Langston Hughes Library.

On accède à la belle salle de lecture de la Langston Hughes Library par la partie inférieure de cette ancienne grange de construction rustique.

LTL LEWIS.TSURUMAKI.LEWIS

LTL Architects
227 West 29th Street
New York, New York 10001
USA

Tel: +1 212 505 5955, Fax: +1 212 505 1648
E-mail: office@LTLwork.net, Web: www.LTLarchitects.com

Paul Lewis received his M.Arch. from Princeton University in 1992, and studied previously at Wesleyan University (BA, 1988). He is a principal and founding partner of **LEWIS.TSURUMAKI.LEWIS**, created in 1993. He was an associate at Diller + Scofidio, New York (1993–97). Marc Tsurumaki received his M.Arch. degree from Princeton in 1991, after attending college at the University of Virginia. He worked as a project architect in the office of Joel Sanders in New York (1991–97) prior to creating Lewis.Tsurumaki.Lewis. David J. Lewis completed his architectural studies at Princeton in 1995 after attending Cornell and Carlton College. He was the Publications Director, Cornell University, College of Architecture, Art, and Planning (1997–98). He worked at Peter Guggenheimer, Architects, PPC, New York as an assistant (1995–96) and in the office of Daniel Libeskind in Berlin (1993) before creating LTL. The firm's projects include: Bornhuetter Hall, Wooster, Ohio (2004); Tides Restaurant, New York (2005); Figge Residence, Wooster, Ohio (2004); Xing Restaurant, New York (2005); and the Ini Ani Coffee Shop, New York (2004). Later projects are: renovation and expansion of Arthouse at the Jones Center, Austin, Texas (2010); Vegas 888, Nevada (unbuilt); Dash Dogs Restaurant, New York (2005); Alexakos Gymnasium, Southampton, New York (2006); renovation of Brown University's Biomedical Center, Providence, Rhode Island (2005); Glenmore Gardens, East New York, New York (2006); Allentown House, Allentown, Pennsylvania (2006); and the Burns Townhouse, Philadelphia, Pennsylvania (2006).

Paul Lewis studierte erst an der Wesleyan University (B. A. 1988), dann machte er 1992 an der Princeton University seinen Master of Architecture. Er ist Gründungspartner und Geschäftsführer des 1993 eröffneten Büros **LEWIS.TSURUMAKI.LEWIS**. Bei Diller + Scofidio in New York war er von 1993 bis 1997 assoziierter Partner. Marc Tsurumaki studierte an der University of Virginia und an der Princeton University (Master of Architecture 1991). Bevor er Lewis.Tsurumaki.Lewis gründete, war er von 1991 bis 1997 Projektarchitekt bei Joel Sanders in New York. David J. Lewis schloss sein Architekturstudium 1995 in Princeton ab, davor studierte er in Cornell und am Carlton College. Von 1997 bis 1998 war er Publications Director am College of Architecture, Art and Planning der Cornell University. Vor der Gründung von LTL arbeitete David Lewis als Assistent bei Peter Guggenheimer, Architects, PPC, in New York und 1993 bei Daniel Libeskind in Berlin. Projekte des Büros sind u. a. die Bornhuetter Hall in Wooster, Ohio (2004), das Tides Restaurant in New York (2005), die Figge Residence in Wooster, Ohio (2004), das Xing Restaurant in New York (2005) und der Ini Ani Coffee Shop in New York (2004). Zu ihren weiteren Projekten gehören die Sanierung und Erweiterung des Arthouse im Jones Center (ein Museum für zeitgenössische Kunst) in Austin, Texas (2010), Vegas 888, ein Wohnhochhaus in Las Vegas (nicht realisiert), das Dash Dogs Restaurant in New York (2005), die Alexakos-Sporthalle in Southampton, New York (2006), ferner die Sanierung des Biomedizinischen Zentrums der Brown University in Providence, Rhode Island (2005), Glenmore Gardens in East New York, New York (2006), das Allentown House in Allentown, Pennsylvania (2006), und das Burns Townhouse in Philadelphia, Pennsylvania (2006).

Après avoir étudié à la Wesleyan University (Bachelor of Arts, 1988), Paul Lewis a reçu son Master of Architecture de Princeton University en 1992. Il est le cofondateur et directeur de **LEWIS.TSURUMAKI.LEWIS** (LTL), agence créée en 1993. Il a été associé de Diller + Scofidio, New York (1993–97). Marc Tsurumaki est Master of Architecture M. Arch. de Princeton (1991) après des études à l'Université de Virginie. Il a travaillé comme architecte de projet chez Joel Sander à New York (1991–97) avant de créer LTL. David J. Lewis, après Cornell et Carlton College, a achevé ses études d'architecture à Princeton en 1995. Il a été directeur des publications au College of Architecture, Art and Planning de Cornell University (1997–98), a travaillé comme assistant chez Peter Guggenheimer, Architects, PPC, New York (1995–96) et dans l'agence de Daniel Libeskind à Berlin (1993), avant de créer LTL. Parmi les réalisations de l'agence : Bornhuetter Hall, Wooster, Ohio (2004) ; Tides Restaurant Restaurant à New York (2005) ; Ini Ani Coffee Shop à New York (2004). Citons également : la rénovation et l'extension de l'Arthouse au Jones Center, Austin, Texas (2010) ; Vegas 888, Nevada (non réalisé) ; le Dash Dogs Restaurant à New York (2005) ; l'Alexakos Gymnasium à Southampton, New York (2006) ; la rénovation du Centre biomédical de Brown University, Providence, Rhode Island (2005) ; les logements Glenmore Gardens, East New York (2006) ; Allentown House, Allentown, Pennsylvanie (2006) et l'hôtel de ville Burns, Philadelphie, Pennsylvanie (2006).

FLUFF BAKERY

New York, New York, USA, 2004

Floor area: 72 m². Client: Chow Down Mgt. Inc. Costs: $ 250 000.

Created at 751 Ninth Avenue in New York for a cost of $ 250 000, this 72 m² space has unusual walls and ceilings, created with strips of felt and stained plywood each individually put in place. A ceiling light was "designed as a custom horizontal chandelier, composed of 42 dimmable incandescent lights connected to a series of branching stainless steel metal armatures." As the architects explain, "This design/build project explores a new architectural surface made from an excessive repetition and assembly of common, banal and cheap materials. More akin to a gallery installation, the interior surface and the chandelier were built and installed by the architects." The strip cladding also creates a dynamic effect that sweeps visitors into the space beginning with a floor-to-ceiling glass façade. Despite their rather sophisticated background, the architects demonstrate with the **FLUFF BAKERY** that they are willing to get directly involved in an original, small-scale project.

751 Ninth Avenue lautet die Adresse der Bäckerei Fluff in New York. Die Baukosten für den 72 m² großen Raum betrugen umgerechnet 210 500 Euro. Die ungewöhnliche Wand- und Deckenverkleidung besteht aus dünnen Filzstreifen und gebeiztem Sperrholz, jeder Streifen wurde einzeln montiert. Die Deckenbeleuchtung bildet ein "speziell angefertigter ,horizontaler Kronleuchter'. Er besteht aus 42 dimmbaren Leuchtstoffröhren, die an sich verzweigenden Stahlarmen befestigt sind." Die Architekten erläutern: „Mit dem Entwurf bzw. dem realisierten Raum erforschen wir eine neue architektonische Oberfläche, die aus der exzessiven Wiederholung und der Verwendung von gewöhnlichen, einfachen und billigen Materialien entsteht. Die Oberflächen und der ,Kronleuchter' – Elemente, die eher Installationen in einer Galerie ähneln – wurden von den Architekten selbst hergestellt und montiert." Die streifenartige Wandverkleidung hat auch einen dynamischen Effekt, der den Besucher in den Raum hineinzieht. Eingeleitet wird dieser Effekt durch die raumhoch verglaste Fassade. Ihren eher intellektuellen Anspruch hinter sich lassend beweisen die Architekten mit der **BÄCKEREI FLUFF**, dass sie bereit sind, sich auf ein originelles, kleines Projekt einzulassen.

Aménagé 751 Ninth Avenue à New York pour un budget de 210 000 euros, ce local de 72 m² présente de curieux murs et plafonds revêtus de minces bandes de feutre et de contreplaqué teinté, mises en place une par à une. Au plafond est suspendu un luminaire « conçu comme un lustre horizontal sur mesure composé de 42 tubes fluorescents rhéostatés montés sur une série de branches en acier inoxydable ». Comme l'expliquent les architectes : « De sa conception à sa réalisation, ce projet explore une nouvelle surface architecturale composée d'une répétition et d'un assemblage pléthoriques de matériaux communs et bon marché dans un esprit d'excès. Tenant plus de l'installation d'une galerie d'art, ces surfaces et ce lustre ont été fabriqués et installés par nous. » Le « bardage » de fins bandeaux crée un effet dynamique qui happe les clients dans le volume ouvert sur la rue par une façade en verre du sol au plafond. Malgré leur formation assez sophistiquée, les architectes démontrent avec la **BOULANGERIE FLUFF** qu'ils n'hésitent pas à s'impliquer directement à fond dans un projet original, même de petite échelle.

The architects are given to complex effects created with "ordinary" materials. Here, reflections and lighting combine to make it difficult to determine where inside begins and outside ends.

Mit „gewöhnlichen" Materialien erzielen die Architekten komplexe Effekte. Reflexionen und die Belichtung führen hier dazu, dass nicht ohne Weiteres erkennbar ist, wo innen anfängt und außen aufhört.

Les architectes ont privilégié les effets complexes créés par des matériaux « ordinaires ». Ici, reflets et éclairage naturel se combinent pour rendre indiscernable la limite entre l'intérieur et l'extérieur.

GREG LYNN FORM

Greg Lynn FORM
1817 Lincoln Boulevard, Venice
California 90291, USA

Tel: +1 310 821 2629, Fax: +1 310 821 9729
E-mail: node@glform.com, Web: www.glform.com

GREG LYNN was born in 1964. He received his Bachelor of Philosophy and Bachelor of Environmental Design from Miami University of Ohio (1986) and his Master of Architecture from Princeton University (1988). He worked in the offices of Antoine Predock (1987) and Peter Eisenman (1987–91) before creating his present firm, **FORM**, in 1994. He has worked on the New York Korean Presbyterian Church, Long Island City, New York (1997–99) with Garofalo Architects and Michael McInturf and the Ark of the World Museum and Interpretive Center, Costa Rica (1999), as well as PGLife.com Showroom, Stockholm, Sweden, designed in collaboration with Dynamo Sthlm, Stockholm (2000); "Predator," designed with Fabian Marcaccio at Wexner Center for the Arts, Columbus, Ohio (2001); and a piece for "Expanding the Gap," Rendel + Spitz Gallery, Cologne, Germany (2002). Greg Lynn's other projects include: Transformation of Kleiburg, Bijlmermeer, Amsterdam, The Netherlands, encompassing 500 nits of housing, urban planning and design (2000–05); Uniserve Corporation Headquarters, Los Angeles (designed with House and Robertson Architects, Inc., 2011); and Imaginary Forces New York Offices (designed in collaboration with Open Office Architects). Recent work includes the Biennale Park Pavilion no.3, Saadiyat Island Cultural District, Abu Dhabi (2006–present); 5900 Wilshire Blvd. Restaurant & Trellis Pavilion, Los Angeles (thus far unbuilt); BA8: BMW Design Headquarters Competition, Munich, Germany (2007); and Blob Wall (2006–07), "an innovative redefinition of architecture's most basic building unit, the brick; in lightweight, plastic, colorful, modular elements custom shaped using the latest CNC technology."

GREG LYNN, 1964 geboren, erwarb 1986 den Bachelor of Philosophy und den Bachelor of Environmental Design an der Miami University of Ohio und 1988 den Master in Architektur an der Princeton University. 1987 arbeitete er im Büro von Antoine Predock und von 1987 bis 1991 bei Peter Eisenman, bevor er 1994 seine eigene Firma **FORM** gründete. Zu seinen Projekten gehören die in Zusammenarbeit mit Garofalo Architects und Michael McInturf entstandene New York Korean Presbyterian Church in Long Island City (1997–99) sowie das Ark of the World Museum und Interpretive Center in Costa Rica (1999), außerdem der in Zusammenarbeit mit Dynamo Sthlm (Dynamo Stockholm) gestaltete Showroom für PGLife.com in Stockholm (2000), die mit Fabian Marcaccio gestaltete Ausstellung „Predator" und die Ausstellung „Imaginary Forces" (2001), beide am Wexner Center for the Arts in Columbus, Ohio, sowie Expanding the Gap, ein Designprojekt für Rendel + Spitz in Köln (2002). Weitere Projekte von Greg Lynn sind: „Transformation of Kleiburg" in Bijlmermeer, Amsterdam, ein Projekt, das 500 Wohnungen sowie städtebauliche Planungen umfasst (2000–05), die Uniserve Corporation Headquarters, Los Angeles (zusammen mit House and Robertson Architects, Inc., 2011), sowie die New Yorker Büros von Imaginary Forces (in Zusammenarbeit mit Open Office Architects). In jüngerer Zeit entwarf Lynn den Biennale-Park-Pavillon Nr. 3 sowie den Kulturbereich für Saadiyat Island in Abu Dhabi (seit 2006), 5900 Wilshire Blvd. Restaurant & Trellis Pavilion in Los Angeles (bisher nicht realisiert) und Blob Wall (2006/07), „eine innovative Definition der grundlegendsten Baueinheit der Architektur, des Ziegels, der leicht, aus Kunststoff und farbenfroh als modulares Element mithilfe modernster CNC-Technologie maßgeschneidert hergestellt wird."

GREG LYNN, né en 1964, est Bachelor de philosophie et de design environnemental de l'University of Ohio (1986) et Master of Architecture de la Princeton University (1988). Il travaille dans les agences d'Antoine Predock (1987) et Peter Eisenman (1987–1991) avant de créer **FORM** en 1994. En collaboration avec Garofalo Architects et Michael McInturf il est intervenu sur la New York Korean Presbyterian Church (Long Island City, New York, 1997–99) et sur l'Ark of the World Museum and Interpretive Center (Costa Rica, 1999). Citons également : le showroom de PGLife.com (Stockholm, Suède, 2000), en collaboration avec Dynamo Sthlm (Dynamo Stockholm) ; l'exposition « Predator » avec Fabian Marcaccio et l'exposition « Imaginary Forces » (2001) toutes deux au Wexner Center for the Arts, Columbus, Ohio ; ainsi que Expanding the Gap, un projet pour Rendel + Spitz (Cologne, Allemagne, 2002). Ses autres projets sont : la « Transformation de Kleiburg » (Bijlmermeer, Amsterdam, Pays-Bas, projet de 500 logements, urbanisme et conception, 2000–2005) ; le siège d'Uniserve Corporation, Los Angeles (conçu avec House and Robertson Architects, Inc., 2011) ; les bureaux de Imaginary Forces à New York (avec Open Office Architects). Enfin, Lynn a conçu le pavillon de biennale n° 3 ainsi que l'espace culturel pour Saadiyat Island à Abu Dhabi (depuis 2006) ; 5900 Wilshire Blvd. Restaurant & Trellis Pavillon à Los Angeles (non réalisé jusqu'ici) et Blob Wall (2006/07), « une definition innovante de l'élément de base de l'architecture, la brique, qui, fabriquée à l'aide de la technique moderne CNC à partir de matière synthétique, devient un élément modulaire léger et coloré ».

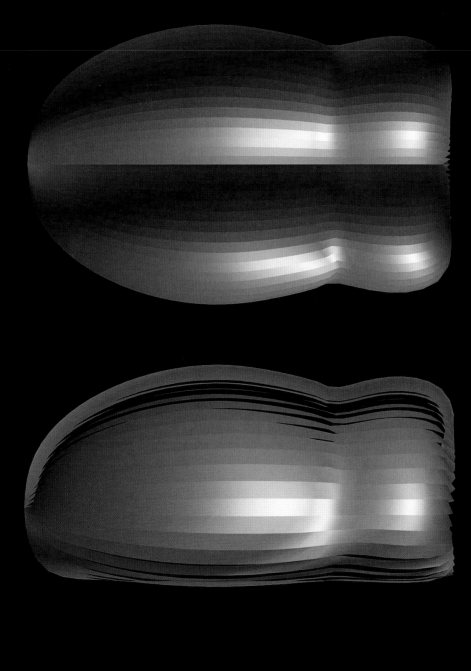
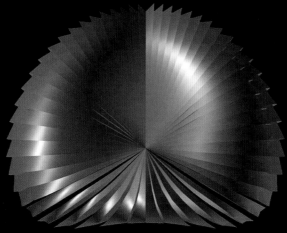

EMBRYOLOGICAL HOUSE

California, USA

*Structure: 2048 panels, 9 steel frames,
and 72 aluminum struts networked together to form a monocoque shell.*

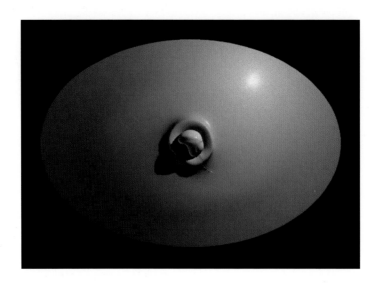

Greg Lynn declares, "The **EMBRYOLOGICAL HOUSE** can be described as a strategy for the invention of domestic space that engages contemporary issues of brand identity and variation, customization and continuity, flexible manufacturing and assembly, and most importantly an unapologetic investment in the contemporary beauty and voluptuous aesthetics of undulating surfaces rendered vividly in iridescent and opalescent colors. The Embryological House employs a rigorous system of geometrical limits that liberate an exfoliation of endless variations." Unlike many architects who work extensively with computer technology, Lynn says, "At this point, I would have to say it is the software making the calls. There is a language of form that comes with the computer, and at first you do what the software does." Lynn has codified the assembly of the Embryological House very strictly: "The domestic envelope of every house is composed of 2048 panels, 9 steel frames, and 72 aluminum struts are networked together to form a monocoque shell, where each component is unique in its shape and size. Using design techniques of flexible manufacturing borrowed from the industrial, automotive, naval and aeronautical design industries, every house in the line is of a unique shape and size while conforming to a fixed number of components and fabrication operations. The form and space of the houses is modified within the predefined limits of the components."

Der Architekt beschreibt das **EMBRYOLOGICAL HOUSE** „als eine Strategie zur Erfindung von Wohnräumen. Eingebunden in diese Strategie sind aktuelle Kernfragen von Markenidentität und Variationsbreite, Kundenspezifizierung und Kontinuität, flexibler Fertigung und Montage sowie vor allem eine offensive Investition in die zeitgemäße Schönheit und sinnliche Ästhetik geschwungener Oberflächen mit der intensiven Ausdruckskraft bunt schillernder Farben. Das Embryological House setzt ein exaktes System begrenzter geometrischer Elemente ein, die eine Entwicklung endloser Variationsmöglichkeiten bieten." Im Gegensatz zu vielen anderen Architekten, die in großem Umfang mit Computertechnologie arbeiten, erklärt Lynn: „An diesem Punkt müsste ich ja eingestehen, dass es die Software ist, auf die es ankommt. Der Computer bringt eine gewisse Formensprache mit sich und da macht man zunächst all das, was die Software vorgibt." Greg Lynn hat die Montage des Embryological House streng kodifiziert: „Die aus 2084 Tafeln, 9 Stahlrahmen und 72 Aluminiumverstrebungen bestehende Hülle der Häuser wird zu einer selbsttragenden Schalenbaukonstruktion zusammengefügt, in der jedes Bauteil seine individuelle Form und Größe hat. Unter Einsatz von Entwurfstechniken flexibler Fertigungssysteme, wie sie in der Automobil-, Schiffbau- und Luftfahrtindustrie verwendet werden, ist jedes Haus dieser Serie einzigartig in seiner Form und Größe. Gleichzeitig entspricht es einer bestimmten Anzahl von Bauteilen und Fertigungsarbeiten. Innerhalb dieser festgesetzten Grenzen werden Form und Aufteilung der Häuser modifiziert."

Pour Greg Lynn : « La **MAISON EMBRYOLOGIQUE** peut se décrire comme la stratégie d'invention d'un espace domestique qui met en jeu les problématiques contemporaines d'image de marque et de variation, de ‹ customisation › et de continuité, de construction et d'assemblage flexibles. Plus important encore, elle illustre un investissement généreux dans la beauté contemporaine et l'esthétique voluptueuse de surfaces ondulées aux couleurs iridescentes et opalescentes. Elle fait appel à un système rigoureux de contraintes géométriques qui libère une exfoliation de variations infinies. » À la différence de nombreux architectes qui utilisent beaucoup l'informatique, Lynn précise : « Je dois dire que c'est le logiciel qui prend le dessus. Il existe un langage formel qui relève de l'ordinateur, et, au départ, vous faites ce que fait le logiciel. » Lynn a codifié très strictement l'assemblage : « L'enveloppe domestique de chaque maison se compose de 2048 panneaux, 9 cardes d'acier et 72 étais d'aluminium qui constituent une coquille monocoque dans laquelle chaque élément est unique, que ce soit par sa taille ou sa forme. À partir de techniques de conception de fabrication flexible empruntées aux industries de l'automobile, de la construction navale et de l'aéronautique, chaque maison est ainsi originale dans sa forme et ses dimensions tout en se conformant à un nombre déterminé de composants et d'opérations de montage. La forme et l'espace de la maison se modifient dans des limites prédéfinies qui sont celles de ses composants. »

"This marks a shift from a Modernist mechanical kit-of-parts design and construction technique to a more vital, evolving, biological model of embryological design and construction." G. Lynn

„Dies markiert eine Wende vom Baukastendesign und einer modernistisch-mechanischen Konstruktionstechnik hin zu einem lebendigeren, sich entwickelnden, biologischen Modell embryologischer Entwurfs- und Konstruktionsart." G. Lynn

« Ce projet marque le passage d'une conception et d'une technique de construction modernistes et mécanique en kit à un modèle biologique, plus vivant, de conception évolutive et de construction embryologique. » G. Lynn

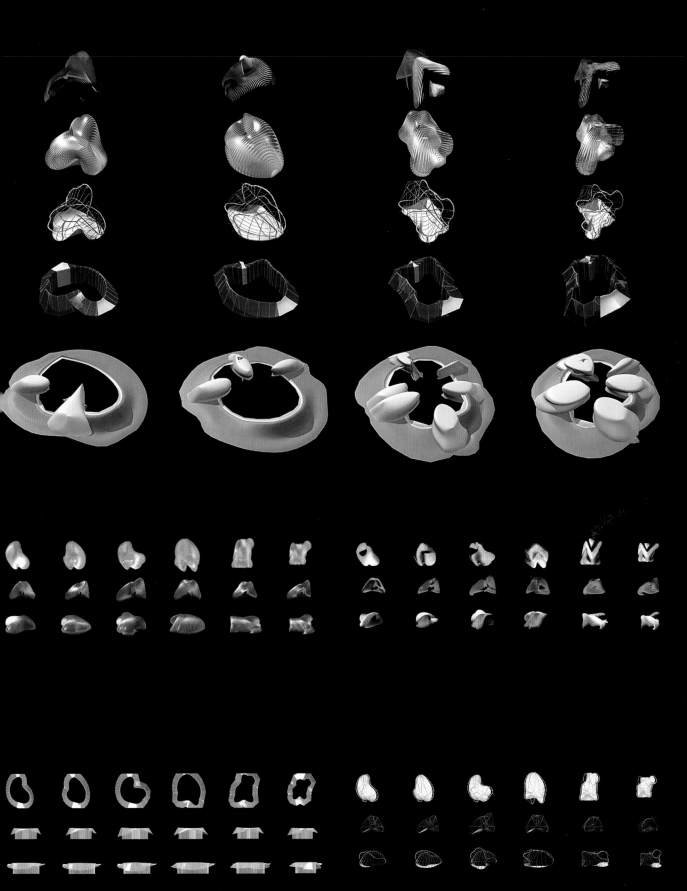

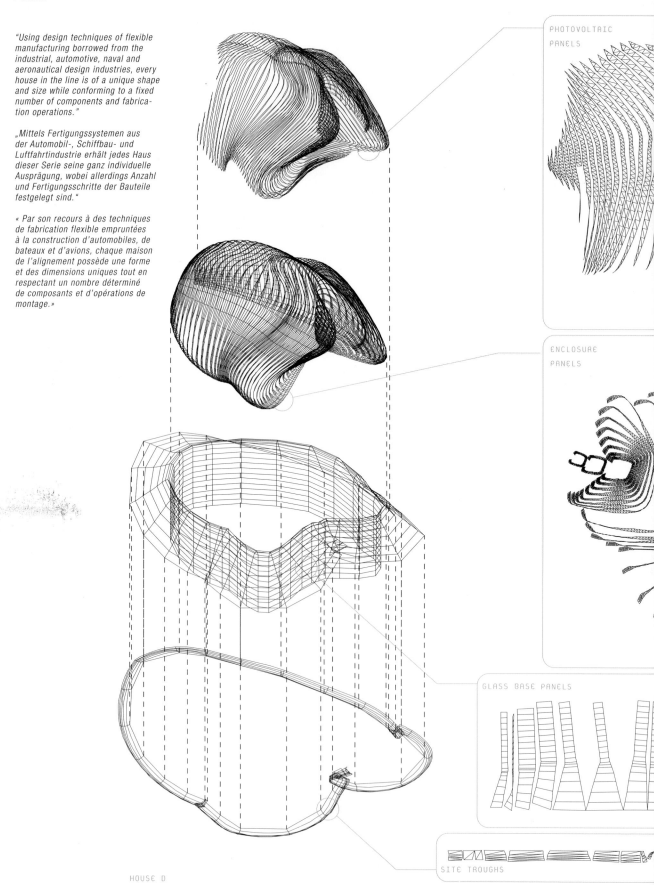

"Using design techniques of flexible manufacturing borrowed from the industrial, automotive, naval and aeronautical design industries, every house in the line is of a unique shape and size while conforming to a fixed number of components and fabrication operations."

„Mittels Fertigungssystemen aus der Automobil-, Schiffbau- und Luftfahrtindustrie erhält jedes Haus dieser Serie seine ganz individuelle Ausprägung, wobei allerdings Anzahl und Fertigungsschritte der Bauteile festgelegt sind."

« Par son recours à des techniques de fabrication flexible empruntées à la construction d'automobiles, de bateaux et d'avions, chaque maison de l'alignement possède une forme et des dimensions uniques tout en respectant un nombre déterminé de composants et d'opérations de montage.»

PHOTOVOLTAIC PANELS

ENCLOSURE PANELS

GLASS BASE PANELS

SITE TROUGHS

HOUSE D

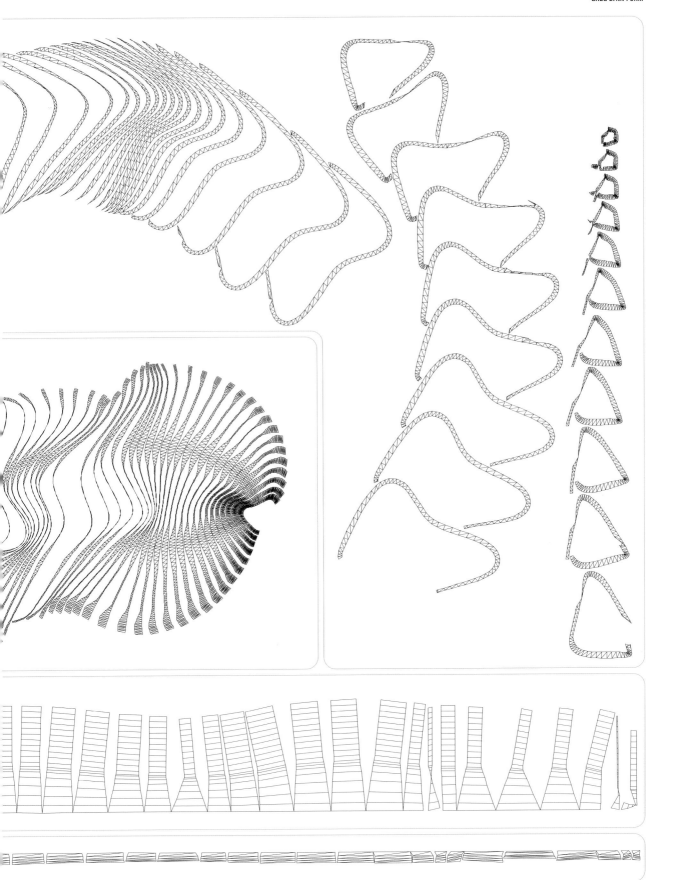

FUMIHIKO MAKI

Maki and Associates
Hillside West Building C
13-4 Hachiyama-cho
Shibuya-ku, Tokyo 150-0035
Japan

Tel: +81 3 3780 3880, Fax: +81 3 3780 3881
E-mail: inquiry@maki-and-associates.co.jp, Web: www.maki-and-associates.co.jp

Born in Tokyo in 1928, **FUMIHIKO MAKI** received his B.Arch. degree from the University of Tokyo in 1952, and M.Arch. degrees from the Cranbrook Academy of Art (1953) and the Harvard Graduate School of Design (1954). He worked for Skidmore, Owings & Merrill in New York (1954–55) and Sert Jackson and Associates in Cambridge, Massachusetts (1955–58) before creating his own firm, Maki and Associates, in Tokyo in 1965. Notable buildings include: the Fujisawa Municipal Gymnasium, Fujisawa, Kanagawa (1984); Spiral, Minato-ku, Tokyo (1985); the National Museum of Modern Art, Sakyo-ku, Kyoto (1986); the Tepia, Minato-ku, Tokyo (1989); the Nippon Convention Center Makuhari Messe, Chiba, Chiba (1989); Tokyo Metropolitan Gymnasium, Shibuya, Tokyo (1990); and the Center for the Arts Yerba Buena Gardens, San Francisco, California (1993). Other projects include the Hillside West buildings (1998), part of his Hillside Terrace project; the Yokohama Bayside Tower, Yokohama, Kanagawa (2003); the TV Asahi Broadcast Center, Minato-ku, Tokyo (2003); the Niigata International Convention Center, Niigata (2003); the MIT Media Laboratory Expansion, Cambridge, Massachusetts (2004); the National Language Research Institute, Tachikawa, Tokyo (2004); the Washington University Visual Arts and Design Center, St Louis, Missouri (2004); and the Nakatsu City Museum, Nakatsu, Oita (2005). A building for the Aga Khan's Ismaili community in Ottawa was completed in 2008. Fumihiko Maki is also working on a tower for the United Nations in New York and a new museum of Islamic Art for the Aga Khan (Toronto).

FUMIHIKO MAKI, geboren 1928 in Tokio, erwarb 1952 den Bachelor in Architektur an der Universität Tokio, den Master in Architektur 1953 an der Cranbrook Academy of Art und 1954 an der Harvard Graduate School of Design. Er arbeitete in den Büros Skidmore Owings & Merrill in New York (1954–55) und Sert Jackson and Associates in Cambridge, Massachusetts (1955–58), bevor er 1965 seine eigene Firma Maki and Associates in Tokio gründete. Zu seinen herausragenden Bauten gehören die städtische Sporthalle in Fujisawa, Kanagawa (1984), das Medienzentrum Spiral, Minato-ku in Tokio (1985), das Nationalmuseum für moderne Kunst in Sakyo-ku, Kioto (1986), das Tepia-Gebäude in Minato-ku, Tokio (1989), die städtische Sporthalle in Shibuya, Tokio (1990), und das Center for the Arts Yerba Buena Gardens in San Francisco (1993). Weitere Projekte sind das Nippon Convention Center Makuhari Messe Phase II in Chiba (1997) und die Hillside-West-Gebäude (1998), Letztere sind Teil seines Hillside-Terrace-Projekts, der Yokohama Bayside Tower in Yokohama, Kanagawa (2003), das TV Asahi Broadcast Center in Minato-ku, Tokio (2003), das International Convention Center in Niigata (2003), die Erweiterung des MIT-Medienlabors in Cambridge, Massachusetts (2004), das Nationale Sprachforschungsinstitut in Tachikawa, Tokio (2004), das Visual Arts and Design Center der Washington University in St. Louis (2004) sowie das städtische Museum in Nakatsu, Oita (2005). Ein Gebäude für die Ismaili-Gemeinde des Aga Khan in Ottawa wurde 2008 fertiggestellt. Fuhimiko Maki arbeitet auch an einem Turm für die Vereinten Nationen in New York und einem neuen Museum für islamische Kunst für den Aga Khan (Toronto).

Né à Tokyo en 1928, **FUMIHIKO MAKI** est Bachelor en architecture de l'Université de Tokyo en 1952, et Master en Architecture de la Cranbrook Aacademy of Art (1953) et de l'Harvard Graduate School of Design (1954). Il travaille pour Skidmore Owings & Merrill à New York (1954–55), et Sert Jackson and Associates à Cambridge, Massachusetts (1955–58), avant de créer sa propre agence, Maki and Associates, à Tokyo (1965). Parmi ses réalisations les plus notables : le gymnase municipal de Fujisawa (Kanagawa, Japon,1984), Spiral (Tokyo, 1985), le Musée national d'art moderne (Kyoto, 1986), Tepia (Tokyo, 1989), le gymnase métropolitain de Tokyo (Shibuya, Tokyo, 1990), le Center for the Arts Yerba Buena Gardens (San Francisco, Californie, 1993). Ses autres projets sont : la Phase II (extension) du Centre de Congrès Nippon de Makuhari (Chiba, 1997) et les immeubles de Hillside West qui font partie de son projet pour Hillside Terrace, la Yokohama Bayside Tower (Kanagawa, 2003), le centre d'émission de TV Asahi (Tokyo, 2003), le centre international de congrès de Niigata (Niigata, Niigata, 2003), l'extension du laboratoire des médias du MIT (Cambridge, MA, USA, 2004), l'Institut national de recherches sur le langage (Tokyo, 2004), le Washington University Visual Arts and Design Center (St. Louis, USA, 2004) et le musée de Nakatsu (Oita, 2005). En 2008, il a achevé un édifice pour la communauté ismaïlienne de l'Aga Khan à Ottawa. Fuhimiko Maki travaille aussi à une tour pour les Nations-Unies à New York et à un nouveau musée d'art islamique pour l'Aga Khan (Toronto).

HILLSIDE WEST

Tokyo, Japan, 1996–98

Planning: 3/96–6/97. Completion: 11/98. Client: Asakura Real Estate.
Floor area: 2958 m². Costs: withheld at owner's request.

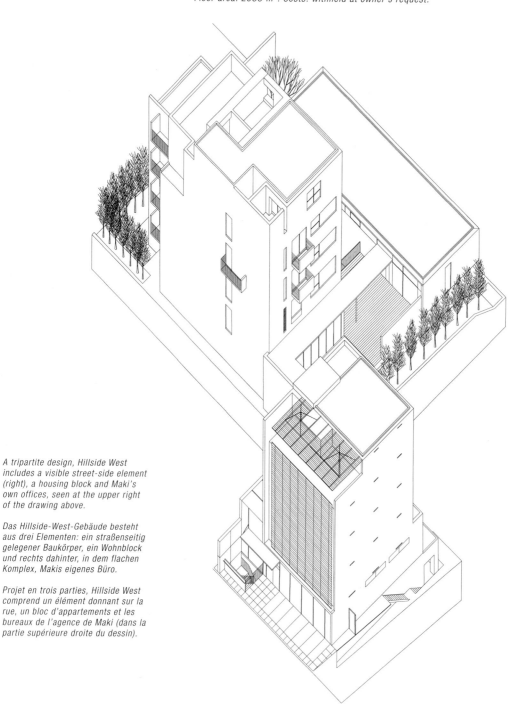

A tripartite design, Hillside West
includes a visible street-side element
(right), a housing block and Maki's
own offices, seen at the upper right
of the drawing above.

Das Hillside-West-Gebäude besteht
aus drei Elementen: ein straßenseitig
gelegener Baukörper, ein Wohnblock
und rechts dahinter, in dem flachen
Komplex, Makis eigenes Büro.

Projet en trois parties, Hillside West
comprend un élément donnant sur la
rue, un bloc d'appartements et les
bureaux de l'agence de Maki (dans la
partie supérieure droite du dessin).

Fumihiko Maki has been building along Old Yamate Street in the Shibuya district of Tokyo since 1967. This building complex, known as Hillside Terrace, is exemplary in its constancy, and contributes to the district's pleasant, urban atmosphere. In 1993, Maki was awarded the Third Prince of Wales Prize in Urban Design for the Hillside Terrace Complex. His most recent addition to the area, **HILLSIDE WEST**, has a total floor area of 2958 m² and is situated down the street from the other buildings on an odd-shaped sloping lot that Maki has transformed into housing, office space (including his own) and an exhibition area. From its most visible façade on Old Yamate Street, shielded with a subtle, perforated aluminum screen, to the interior walkway leading toward his offices, this building is a testimony not only to Maki's talent as an architect, but also to his ability to evoke a civilized understanding of urban life in the midst of Tokyo's sprawling complexity.

Fumihiko Maki arbeitet schon seit 1967 an der Old Yamate Street im Tokioter Shibuya-Distrikt. Der Hillside Terrace genannte Gebäudekomplex, für den Maki 1993 mit dem Third Prince of Wales Prize in Urban Design ausgezeichnet wurde, ist exemplarisch in seiner Konsistenz und trägt zu der urbanen Atmosphäre des Stadtviertels bei. Sein zuletzt hinzugefügter Teil, das Gebäude **HILLSIDE WEST**, hat eine Gesamtnutzfläche von 2958 m². Es wurde ein Stück entfernt von den anderen Gebäuden auf einem unregelmäßig geformten Hanggrundstück errichtet und enthält Wohnungen, Büros (darunter das des Architekten) sowie einen Ausstellungsbereich. Von der mit einem zarten Aluminiumgitter abgeschirmten sichtbaren Front an der Old Yamate Street bis zu dem Gehweg, der zu Makis Büros führt, zeugt dieses Bauwerk nicht nur von Makis Talent als Architekt, sondern ebenso von seiner Fähigkeit, inmitten des ausufernden Stadtgebietes von Tokio den Geist einer kultivierten Urbanität aufleben zu lassen.

Depuis 1967, Fumihiko Maki est responsable d'un long chantier en bordure de la vieille rue Yamate dans le quartier Shibuya de Tokyo. Cet ensemble de bâtiments, appelé Hillside Terrace, est exemplaire par sa continuité et contribue à l'agrément urbain du quartier. En 1993, Maki a obtenu le Third Prince of Wales Prize in Urban Design pour ce projet. **HILLSIDE WEST**, sa plus récente réalisation, a une surface brute de 2958 m². Construite dans la même rue, en contrebas des immeubles déjà achevés, elle se situe sur une parcelle en pente et de forme complexe. Maki a édifié là des logements, des bureaux (dont celui de son agence) et un espace d'exposition. Que ce soit par sa façade sur la rue protégée par un subtil écran d'aluminium perforé, ou ses allées intérieures qui conduisent aux bureaux de l'architecte, cet immeuble témoigne du talent de Maki et de sa capacité de concrétiser une demarche personelle et une certaine idée de l'urbanisme au cœur de l'envahissant désordre de Tokyo.

Right: The passageway, neither fully interior nor fully exterior, leading to Maki's offices.

Rechts: Der überdachte Durchgang zu Makis Büro changiert zwischen Innen- und Außenraum.

Le passage couvert (à droite) qui conduit aux bureaux de Maki n'est ni intérieur ni vraiment extérieur.

MANSILLA+TUÑÓN

Luis M. Mansilla, Emilio Tuñon
Rios Rosas 11, 6°
28003 Madrid
Spain

Tel/Fax: +34 913 99 30 67
Web: www.mansilla-tunon.com

MUSAC Art Center ►

EMILIO TUÑÓN and **LUIS MANSILLA** were both born in Madrid, respectively in 1958 and 1959. Luis Mansilla died in Barcelona in 2012. They created their firm in Madrid in 1992 and received their doctorates from the ETSAM in 1998, where they both later taught as professors in the Architectural Design Department. In 1993, they created a "thinking exchange cooperative" called Circo with Luis Rojo Rojo, which publishes a bulletin of the same name. Their built projects include the Archeological and Fine Arts Museum of Zamora (1996); Indoor Swimming Pool in San Fernando de Henares (1998); Fine Arts Museum of Castellón (2001); Auditorium of León (2002); Regional Library and Archive of Madrid (2003); and the MUSAC Art Center in León (2004). They won competitions for the urban planning of Valbuena in Logroño and a Public Library in Calle de los Artistas in Madrid in 2003. The Town Council of Lalin was built between 2004 and 2011, in 2008 they redesigned and extended the Helga Alvear Foundation in Cáceres. They have been finalists for four Mies van der Rohe Awards (1997, 1999, 2001 and 2003) and eventually won the award in 2007.

EMILIO TUÑÓN, 1958 in Madrid geboren, und **LUIS MANSILLA**, 1959 in Madrid geboren und 2012 in Barcelona verstorben, promovierten 1998 an der ETSAM (Escuela Técnica Superior de Arquitectura) in Madrid. 1992 gründeten sie dort ihr Büro. Luis Mansilla war bis zu seinem Tod Professor im Fachgebiet Architektonischer Entwurf an der ETSAM, wie auch Emilio Tuñón, der nach wie vor an der ETSAM lehrt. 1993 gründeten sie zusammen mit Luis Rojo eine „Gedankenaustausch-Kooperative", Circo genannt, die ein Themenheft mit demselben Namen herausgibt. Zu den realisierten Gebäuden des Büros gehören das Archäologische Museum und Museum für Kunst in Zamora (1996), ein Hallenbad in San Fernando de Henares (1998), das Museum für Bildende Kunst in Castellón (2001) und ein Auditorium in León (2002), ferner die Regionalbibliothek und das Regionalarchiv von Madrid (2003) und das Kunstzentrum MUSAC in León (2004). 2003 haben sie einen städtebaulichen Wettbewerb für Valbuena in Logroño und einen Wettbewerb für eine öffentliche Bücherei in der Calle de los Artistas in Madrid gewonnen. 2004–2011 wurde das Rathaus von Lalín errichtet, 2008 gestalteten sie das Gebäude der Helga-Alvear-Stiftung in Cáceras um und erweiterten es. Sie waren bereits viermal Finalisten für den Mies-van-der-Rohe-Preis (1997, 1999, 2001 und 2003), den sie schließlich 2007 gewannen.

EMILIO TUÑÓN, né à Madrid en 1958, et **LUIS MANSILLA**, né à Madrid en 1959 et décédé à Barcelone en 2012, ont tous deux obtenus leur doctorat à l'Etsam (1998). Ils ont créé leur agence madrilène en 1992. Luis Mansilla a été, jusqu'à sa mort professeur au département de Conception architecturale de l'ETSAM, tout comme Emilio Tuñón, qui y enseigne toujours. En 1993, ils ont créé une « coopérative d'échanges d'idées » appelée « Circo » avec Luis Rojo, qui publie un bulletin du même nom. Parmi leurs réalisations : le Musée d'archéologie et des beaux-arts de Zamora (1996) ; une piscine couverte à San Fernando de Henares (1998) ; le Musée des beaux-arts de Castellon (2001) ; l'Auditorium de León (2002) ; la Bibliothèque régionale et les Archives de Madrid (2003) et le Musac, Musée d'art contemporain de Castille et León (2004). En 2003, ils ont remporté des concours pour l'urbanisme de Valbuena à Logroño et pour une bibliothèque publique, calle de los Artistas à Madrid. De 2004 à 2011, ils ont construit le Conseil municipal de Lalin et en 2008, ils ont réaménagé et agrandi la Fondation Helga Alvear à Cáceres. Ils ont été finalistes de quatre prix Mies van der Rohe (1997, 1999, 2001 et 2003) et ils l'ont remporté en 2007.

MUSAC

Museo de Arte Contemporáneo de Castilla y León, León, Spain, 2002–04

*Floor area: 10 000 m². Client: Gesturcal S. A., Junta de Castilla y León.
Costs: € 24 million.*

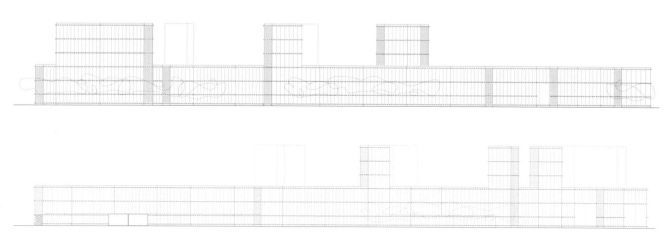

The architects use color like an abstract pattern akin to a work of art executed at architectural scale. With minimal exterior detailing, they allow color to take on a central role in the design.

Die Architekten setzen Farbe als abstraktes Muster ein; dieses wirkt als ein Kunstwerk in einem architektonischen Maßstab. Die äußere Fassade zeigt nur wenige Details und überlässt der Farbe die Hauptrolle.

Les architectes utilisent la couleur comme un motif abstrait, un peu comme dans une œuvre d'art, mais à l'échelle de l'architecture. Avec très peu d'effets extérieurs, ils laissent la couleur prendre la vedette.

Located on the Avenida de los Reyes Leoneses is a 10 000 m² building with white concrete walls and large areas of colored glazing. The architects explain that "**MUSAC** is a new space for culture, regarded as something that visualizes the connections between man and nature. A cluster of chained but independent rooms permit exhibitions of differing sizes and types. Each of the jaggedly shaped rooms constructs a continuous yet spatially differentiated area that opens onto the other rooms and courtyards, providing longitudinal, transversal and diagonal views. Five hundred prefab beams enclose a series of spaces that feature systematic repetition and formal expressiveness. Outside, the public space takes on a concave shape to hold the activities and encounters, embraced by large colored glass in homage to the city as the place for interpersonal relationships." Cheerful and varied in its appearance, MUSAC certainly takes a different esthetic approach than many contemporary art museums, where there is an emphasis on a more discreet Modernism. But the architects have a ready explanation for this difference. "In contrast to other types of museum spaces that focus on the exhibition of frozen historic collections, MUSAC is a living space that opens its doors to the wide-ranging manifestations of contemporary art," they declare.

Das Kunstzentrum **MUSAC** an der Avenida de los Reyes Leoneses in Léon ist ein 10 000 m² großes Gebäude mit weißen Wänden aus Sichtbeton und großen, farbig verglasten Flächen. Die Architekten erläutern: „MUSAC ist ein neuer Ort für Kultur. Kultur wird hier als etwas betrachtet, das die Beziehungen zwischen Mensch und Natur vergegenwärtigt. Eine Gruppe von ineinandergreifenden, aber voneinander unabhängigen Räumen ermöglicht Ausstellungen verschiedener Größe und Art. Jeder der winkligen Räume ist Teil eines Raumkontinuums, gleichzeitig aber räumlich differenziert, und öffnet sich zu anderen Räumen und Innenhöfen, wodurch sich Sichtachsen in Längs-, Quer- und Diagonalrichtung ergeben. 500 vorgefertigte Träger begrenzen das Raumsystem, das von der systematischen Wiederholung und formalen Expressivität bestimmt wird. Der Außenbereich hat eine konkave Form, um den öffentliche Raum für Aktivitäten und Begegnungen zu fassen. Er wird durch große farbige Glasscheiben, eine Hommage an die Stadt als Ort zwischenmenschlicher Beziehungen, gerahmt." Fröhlich und differenziert gestaltet, folgt MUSAC sicherlich einem anderen ästhetischen Ansatz als viele moderne Kunstmuseen, die einem diskreteren Modernismus verpflichtet sind. Für diesen Unterschied haben die Architekten eine Erklärung parat: „Im Gegensatz zu anderen Museumsräumen, die der Ausstellung von ‚gefrorenen' historischen Sammlungen dienen, ist MUSAC ein lebendiger Ort, der seine Türen den sehr unterschiedlichen Äußerungen der neuen Kunst öffnet."

Situé Avenida de los Reyes Leoneses, le bâtiment de ce musée, qui conjugue murs de béton blanc et vastes pans de verre de couleur, totalise 10 000 m². Les architectes expliquent que « le **MUSAC** est un nouvel espace pour la culture, un lieu qui doit mettre en lumière les connexions entre l'homme et la nature. L'assemblage de salles reliées entre elles mais indépendantes permet des expositions de toute nature. Chaque élément découpé de ce ‹ puzzle › détermine un espace continu mais spatialement différencié, qui ouvre sur d'autres salles et des cours tout en ménageant des perspectives longitudinales, transversales et diagonales. Cinq cents poutres préfabriquées enferment une série d'espaces qui jouent de la répétition systématique et de l'expressivité formelle. À l'extérieur, l'espace public s'incurve pour accueillir les activités et les rencontres. Il est couvert de verre de couleurs en hommage à la ville, lieu par excellence des relations humaines. » D'aspect joyeux et très diversifié, le MUSAC a adopté une approche esthétique différente de celle de beaucoup de musées d'art contemporain, où l'on préfère un modernisme plus discret. Mais les architectes ont une explication toute prête à cette différence : « Par contraste avec d'autres types de musées qui se consacrent à l'exposition de collections historiques figées, le MUSAC est un espace vivant qui ouvre ses portes aux multiples manifestations de l'art contemporain. »

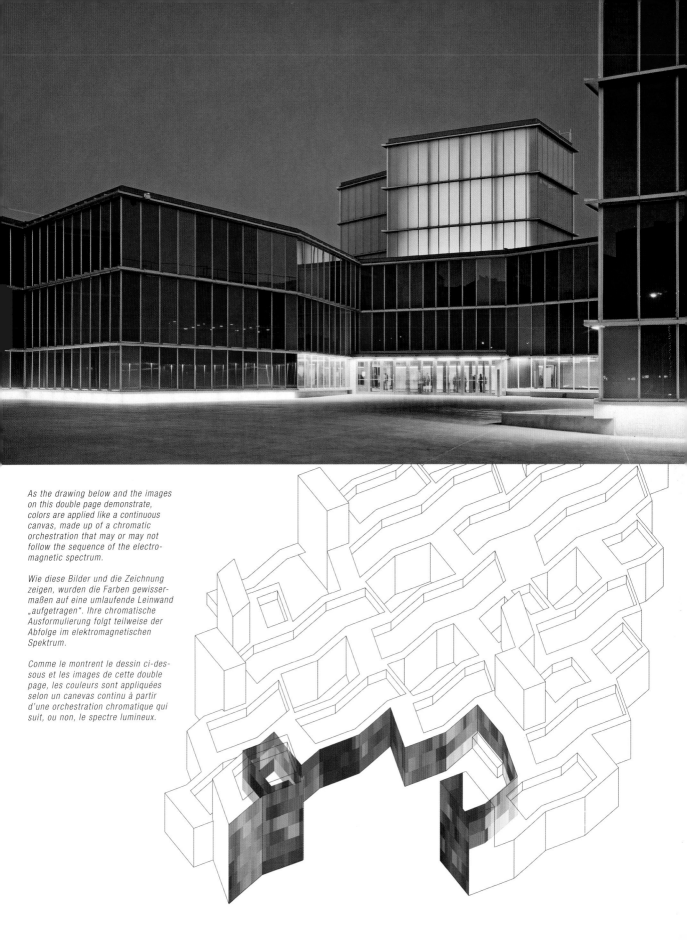

As the drawing below and the images on this double page demonstrate, colors are applied like a continuous canvas, made up of a chromatic orchestration that may or may not follow the sequence of the electromagnetic spectrum.

Wie diese Bilder und die Zeichnung zeigen, wurden die Farben gewissermaßen auf eine umlaufende Leinwand „aufgetragen". Ihre chromatische Ausformulierung folgt teilweise der Abfolge im elektromagnetischen Spektrum.

Comme le montrent le dessin ci-dessous et les images de cette double page, les couleurs sont appliquées selon un canevas continu à partir d'une orchestration chromatique qui suit, ou non, le spectre lumineux.

Interior spaces are generous and sometimes darker than might be expected given the explosion of colors seen on the exterior.

Les généreux volumes intérieurs sont parfois plus sombres que l'on pourrait s'y attendre après l'explosion de couleurs de l'extérieur.

Die Innenräume sind weiträumig und mitunter dunkler als man in Anbetracht der Farbexplosion außen erwarten könnte.

While color is the defining element
of the exterior, it gives way inside to
a limited palette which permits the
exhibition areas to offer a neutral
backdrop to the works to be shown.

Während nach außen die Farbe
das definierende Element ist, wird
im Inneren eine eingeschränkte
Farbpalette verwendet, um einen
neutralen Hintergrund für die Kunst
zu schaffen.

Si la couleur est l'élément clé pour
l'extérieur, elle laisse place, à l'intérieur, à une palette limitée qui permet
aux aires d'exposition d'offrir un environnement neutre aux œuvres d'art.

The plan above shows overlapping zones that house the various museum functions. Within, the symphony of outside colors is left aside, and more solid, concrete surfaces make their appearance.

Der Grundriss zeigt ineinanderübergehende Zonen, in denen die verschiedenen Funktionen des Museums angeordnet sind. Innen wird die Farbigkeit zugunsten massiver Betonoberflächen aufgegeben.

Le plan ci-dessus montre la superposition des zones qui accueillent les différentes fonctions du musée. À l'intérieur, la symphonie de couleurs est écartée au profit de plans de béton brut.

- ENTRANCE
- MAIN LOBBY
- EXHIBITION ROOM 1
- EXHIBITION ROOM 2
- EXHIBITION ROOM 3
- EXHIBITION ROOM 4
- EXHIBITION ROOM 5
- EXHIBITION PATIO

- MULTI-USE ROOM
- RESTAURANT
- SHOP
- TOILETS
- LIBRARY
- EDUCATIONAL WORKSHOP
- OFFICE
- STAFF

- PATIO
- RESTORATION WORKSHOP
- STORAGE
- LOADING AREA
- CONTROL AREA
- TECHNICAL AREA
- VEHICLE ENTRANCE

LOAD AND STORAGE

EXHIBITION

PUBLIC COURTYARD

RECEPTION

INVESTIGATION AND EDUCATION

SERVICES

MARMOL RADZINER

Marmol Radziner
12210 Nebraska Avenue
Los Angeles, California 90025
USA

Tel: +1 310 826 6222
Fax: +1 310 826 6226
E-mail: info@marmol-radziner.com
Web: www.marmol-radziner.com

Restored Kaufmann House ▶

LEONARDO MARMOL, the Managing Principal of Marmol Radziner received his B.Arch. degree from Cal Poly San Luis Obispo in 1987. He has worked as the head of consulting teams on projects for the Los Angeles Unified School District and the LA Department of Airports. Aside from the restoration of the Kaufmann House, he oversaw the restoration of the Raymond Loewy House by Albert Frey, also located in Palm Springs. **RONALD RADZINER** received his M.Arch. degree from the University of Colorado in 1986. He is the Design Principal of the firm, created in 1989. The San Francisco Offices of TBWA/Chiat/Day were completed in 2002 and the Accelerated School in South Central Los Angeles opened in 2005. The firm's work on the Kaufmann House in Palm Springs, California, earned them two American Institute of Architects (AIA) California Council awards for historic preservation, a National AIA Honor Award, and an Honor Award from the California Preservation Foundation. In 2006, Marmol Radziner introduced prefabricated houses onto the market, which have received awards from the AIA and the Industrial Designers Society of America, among other institutions.

LEONARDO MARMOL, Geschäftsführer von Marmol Radziner, erwarb 1987 seinen Bachelor of Architecture an der Cal Poly San Luis Obispo. Er war als leitender Berater für Bauprojekte der Schul- und der Flughafenverwaltung von Los Angeles tätig und beaufsichtigte die Renovierungsarbeiten am Haus Kaufmann und am Haus Raymond Loewy von Albert Frey, beide in Palm Springs. **RONALD RADZINER** machte 1986 seinen Master of Architecture an der University of Colorado und ist heute Planungschef der 1989 gegründeten Firma. Die Niederlassung von TBWA/Chiat/Day in San Francisco war 2002 abgeschlossen, und die Accelerated School in South Central Los Angeles wurde 2005 bezogen. Für ihre Arbeit am Haus Kaufmann in Palm Springs, Kalifornien, erhielten sie zwei Preise für die Erhaltung historisch wertvoller Bauwerke des AIA California Council: den National AIA Honor Award und den Ehrenpreis der California Preservation Foundation. 2006 gingen Marmol Radziner mit Fertighäusern auf den Markt, die u. a. vom American Institute of Architects und der Industrial Designers Society of America prämiert wurden.

LEONARDO MARMOL, directeur de l'agence Marmol Radziner est Bachelor of Architecture de Cal Poly San Luis Obispo (1987). Il a été responsable d'équipes de consultants pour des projets du Los Angeles Unified School District et pour le département des aéroports de Los Angeles. Hormis la restauration de Kaufmann House, il a supervisé la restauration par Albert Frey de la maison de Raymond Loewy, également à Palm Springs. **RONALD RADZINER**, Master of Architecture de l'Université du Colorado (1986), dirige l'agence créée en 1989. Les bureaux de San Francisco de l'agence de publicité TBWA/Chiat/Day ont été achevés en 2002 et l'Accelerated School de South Central Los Angeles accueillit ses élèves dès 2005. Leur intervention sur la Kaufmann House à Palm Springs, Californie, leur a valu deux prix du Conseil de Californie de l'AIA pour la préservation de monuments historiques, un prix d'honneur national de l'AIA et un prix d'honneur de la California Preservation Foundation. En 2006, Marmol Radziner lancèrent sur le marché leurs maisons préfabriquées auxquelles l'American Institute of Architects et l'Industrial Designers Society of America, entre autres, décernèrent des distinctions.

KAUFMANN HOUSE RESTORATION

Palm Springs, California, USA, 1994–98

Planning: 1993–94. Construction: 1994–98. Client: Brent and Beth Harris.
Floor area: 474 m² before restoration, 297 m² after restoration.

Originally designed in 1946 by the architect Richard Neutra, the **KAUFMANN HOUSE** was built for the same client who commissioned Frank Lloyd Wright to design Falling Water. Because successive owners since its original construction had significantly modified the house, the owners decided to return it to its original state. Originally 297 m² in size, the house had been expanded to almost 474 m². The architects removed the later additions, basing the restoration on Julius Shulman's famous photographs of the house, taken in 1947. The architects decided to return the garden to the indigenous desert landscape that existed in Neutra's time. A discreet heating, ventilation and air-conditioning system was added, as was a new pool house, named the Harris Pool House.

Das 1946 von dem Architekten Richard Neutra entworfene **KAUFMANN HOUSE** wurde ursprünglich für denselben Bauherrn gebaut, der Frank Lloyd Wright mit dem Bau von Falling Water beauftragt hatte. Da das Haus von den nachfolgenden Eigentümern stark verändert worden war, beschlossen die Eigentümer, es in seinen Originalzustand zurückzuversetzen. Ursprünglich 297 m² groß, war das Gebäude auf fast 474 m² erweitert worden. Bei ihrer Restauration entfernten die Architekten diese späteren Anbauten, wobei sie sich an Julius Shulmans berühmten Fotografien des Hauses von 1947 orientierten. Außerdem entschieden sie sich, den Garten in jene Wüstenlandschaft zurückzuverwandeln, die das Haus zu Neutras Zeiten umgeben hatte. Neu hinzugefügt wurden eine unauffällige Heizungs-, Belüftungs- und Klimaanlage sowie ein neues Schwimmbad, Harris Pool House genannt.

Œuvre de Richard Neutra (1946), la **KAUFMANN HOUSE** avait été édifiée pour le même client éclairé qui avait commandé Falling Water à Frank Lloyd Wright. Depuis sa construction, les propriétaires successifs avaient fortement modifié la maison. Ils ont décidé de revenir à son état premier, même si la surface d'origine de 297 m² a gagné 177 m². Les architectes ont supprimé certaines extensions tardives en s'appuyant sur des photos prises en 1947 par Julius Shulman. De plus, ils ont entrepris de rendre au jardin l'aspect désertique qu'il avait du temps de Neutra. Un système discret de chauffage, de ventilation et de conditionnement de l'air a été ajouté, ainsi qu'un nouveau pavillon de piscine, appelé la Harris Pool House.

As Julius Shulman's well-known 1947 photograph (below) of the house shows, the restoration (right) of the Kaufmann House has been faithful to the spirit of Neutra.

Wie Julius Shulmans bekannte Fotografie des Hauses von 1947 (unten) zeigt, haben die Architekten bei ihrer Restauration (rechts) den Geist von Richard Neutras Werk bewahrt.

Comme le montre la célèbre photographie de Julius Shulman (ci-dessous) prise en 1947, la restauration de la Kaufmann House (à droite) a été fidèle a l'esprit de Neutra.

The clear, powerful lines of Neutra's design permit an ample degree of openness toward the exterior landscapes.

Neutras Entwurf mit seinen klaren, kraftvollen Linien schafft ein hohes Maß an Offenheit gegenüber der umgebenden Landschaft.

Les lignes simples et fortes imaginées par Neutra permettent une ample ouverture de la maison sur le paysage.

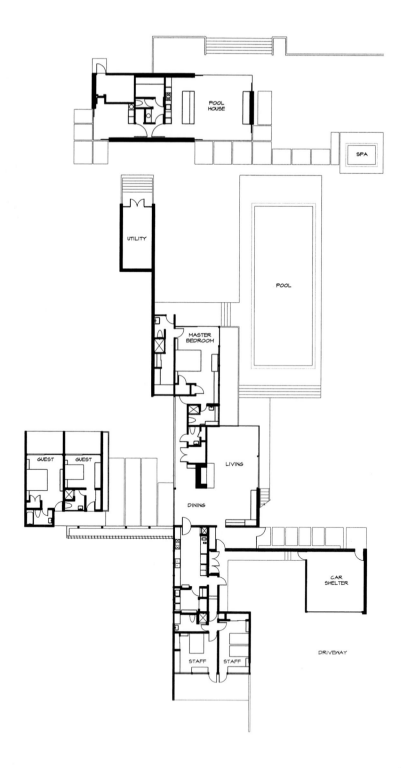

POOL
HOUSE

SPA

UTILITY

POOL

MASTER
BEDROOM

GUEST GUEST

LIVING

DINING

CAR
SHELTER

STAFF STAFF

DRIVEWAY

0'   10'   20'

The minimalist simplicity of the
Kaufmann House honors Neutra's
clairvoyance and the quality of the
restoration carried out by Marmol
Radziner.

Minimalistische Schlichtheit zeichnet
sowohl Neutras wegweisende Gestaltung des Kaufmann House als auch
die sehr gelungene Renovierung von
Marmol Radziner aus.

La qualité de la restauration conduite
par Marmol Radziner est un hommage
à la simplicité minimaliste de la Kaufmann House et à la vision d'avant-
garde de Neutra.

RICHARD MEIER

Richard Meier & Partners Architects LLP
475 Tenth Avenue
New York, New York 10018
USA

Tel: +1 212 967 6060
Fax: +1 212 967 3207
E-mail: mail@richardmeier.com
Web: www.richardmeier.com

RICHARD MEIER was born in Newark, New Jersey, in 1934. He received his architectural training at Cornell University, and worked in the office of Marcel Breuer (1961–63) before establishing his own practice in 1963. In 1984, he became the youngest winner of the Pritzker Prize, and he received the 1989 RIBA Gold Medal. His notable buildings include The Atheneum, New Harmony, Indiana (1975–79); the Museum of Decorative Arts Frankfurt (1979–85); the High Museum of Art, Atlanta, Georgia (1980–83); the Canal Plus Headquarters Paris (1988–92); the City Hall and Library, The Hague (1986–1995); the Barcelona Museum of Contemporary Art, Barcelona (1987–95); and the Getty Center, Los Angeles, California (1984–97). Recent work includes the U.S. Courthouse and Federal Building, Phoenix, Arizona (1994–2000); the Jubilee Church, Rome (1996–2003); the Crystal Cathedral International Center for Possibility Thinking, Garden Grove, California (1998–2003); the Yale University History of Art and Arts Library, New Haven, Connecticut (2001–04); and the 66 restaurant in New York. Other projects include the Beach House, a 12-story glass-enclosed condominium located on Collins Avenue in Miami (2004–07); the ECM City Tower, Pankrac City, Prague, Czech Republic (2004–07); 165 Charles Street (2003–06), a 16-story residential building located in Manhattan near the architect's Perry Street apartments (1999–2002); the Arp Museum, Rolandseck, Germany (1978–2007); and the Ara Pacis Museum, Rome (1995–2006).

RICHARD MEIER, geboren 1934 in Newark, New Jersey, studierte Architektur an der Cornell University und arbeitete bei Marcel Breuer (1961–63), bevor er 1963 sein eigenes Büro eröffnete. Er wurde 1984 als jüngster Preisträger mit dem Pritzker-Preis und 1989 mit der RIBA-Goldmedaille ausgezeichnet. Zu seinen bedeutendsten Bauten gehören das Athenäum in New Harmony, Indiana (1975–79), das Museum für Kunsthandwerk in Frankfurt am Main (1979–85), das High Museum of Art, Atlanta (1980–83), die Hauptverwaltung von Canal Plus in Paris (1988–92), Rathaus und Bibliothek in Den Haag (1986–95), das Museum für Zeitgenössische Kunst in Barcelona (1988–95) und das Getty Center in Los Angeles (1984–97). Um die Jahrtausendwende entstanden das U. S. Courthouse and Federal Building in Phoenix, Arizona (1995–2000), die Kirche Dio Padre Misericordioso in Rom (1996–2003), die Crystal Cathedral International Center for Possibility Thinking in Garden Grove, Kalifornien (1998–2003), die Yale University History of Art and Arts Library in New Haven, Connecticut (2001–04), und das 66 Restaurant in New York. Weitere Projekte sind das Beach House, ein zwölfgeschossiges verglastes Mehrfamilienhaus auf der Colins Avenue in Miami (2004–07), der ECM City Tower in Prag (2004–07), 165 Charles Street (2003–06), ein 16-stöckiges Wohngebäude in Manhattan nahe den ebenfalls von Meier entworfenen Perry-Street-Apartments (1999–2002), das Arp-Museum in Rolandseck (1978–2007) und das Museum Ara Pacis in Rom (1995–2006).

Né à Newark (New Jersey), en 1934, **RICHARD MEIER** étudie à la Cornell University et travaille dans l'agence de Marcel Breuer (1961–63) avant de se mettre à son compte en 1963. Il est le plus jeune lauréat du Prix Pritzker en 1984 et remporte la Royal Gold Medal en 1988. Principales réalisations : The Atheneum, New Harmony (Indiana, 1975–79), le musée des Arts Décoratifs de Francfort-sur-le-Main (1979–1985), le High Museum of Art (Atlanta, Géorgie, 1980–83), le siège de Canal+ (Paris, 1988–92), l'hôtel de ville et la bibliothèque de La Haye (1986–95), le musée d'Art Contemporain de Barcelone (1987–95), le Getty Center (Los Angeles, Californie, 1984–97). Ses travaux au tournant du siècle comprennent le tribunal fédéral et un immeuble de l'administration fédérale à Phoenix (Arizona, 1994–2000), l'Église du Jubilée (Rome, 1996–2003), la Crystal Cathedral International Center for Possibility Thinking, (Garden Grove, Californie, 1998–2003), la bibliothèque de l'histoire de l'art et des arts de la Yale University Connecticut (2001–04) et le restaurant 66 à New York. Ses autres projets sont Beach House, immeuble de verre de 12 étages situés sur la Collins Avenue (Miami, 2004–07), la ECM City Tower, Pankrac City, (Prague, République tchèque, 2004–07), le 165 Charles Street (2003–06), un immeuble résidentiel de 16 étages situé à Manhattan près des appartements Perry Street de l'architecte (1999–2002), le musée Arp (Rolandseck, Allemagne,1978–2007) et le musée Ara Pacis Museum (Rome, 1995–2006).

NEUGEBAUER HOUSE

Naples, Florida, USA, 1995–98

Planning: 1995–96. Construction: 1996–98.
Client: Klaus and Ursula Neugebauer. Floor area: 697 m².

Richard Meier's **NEUGEBAUER HOUSE** is one of his finest. Located on Doubloon Bay, the house has an unusual V-shaped roof. Meier explains that local building regulations required a slanted roof, but did not indicate the direction of the slant. Using 3 cm thick glass for heat insulation, he devised a complex system of brise-soleils. The house's horizontal, shed-like design represents a change in the architect's design options, which are usually more complex, articulated geometric forms, as is the case in another waterfront home, the Ackerberg House in California, but he certainly retains his preference for a white, light-filled architecture.

Richard Meiers **NEUGEBAUER HOUSE** ist eines seiner besten. Es ist an der Bucht von Doubloon gelegen und hat ein ungewöhnliches, V-förmiges Dach. Meier erklärt dazu, dass in den örtlichen Bauvorschriften ein schräges Dach vorgeschrieben, aber nicht die Richtung der Schräge angegeben war. Unter Verwendung einer Wärmedämmung aus 3 cm dickem Glas entwarf er ein komplexes System aus „Brisesoleils" (Sonnenschutz an der Außenseite der Fenster). Die lang gestreckte, schuppenartige Form des Hauses ist eine Erweiterung der Gestaltungsmöglichkeiten des Architekten, der bislang meist mit komplex gegliederten geometrischen Formen gearbeitet hat. Dies war auch bei einem anderen Strandhaus, dem Ackerberg House in Kalifornien, der Fall. Seine Vorliebe für eine weiße, lichterfüllte Architektur behielt Meier jedoch auch in der Gestaltung dieses Hauses bei.

En bordure de la baie de Doubloon, la **MAISON NEUGEBAUER** de Richard Meier, est l'une de ses créations les plus raffinées. Elle se caractérise par un étonnant toit en V. Meier explique que la réglementation locale exigeait un toit en pente, sans en indiquer l'orientation. Il a mis au point un système complexe de brise-soleil en verre de 3 cm d'épaisseur qui isole de la chaleur. L'horizontalité et la simplicité du plan représentent un changement pour l'architecte qui, jusqu'alors, mettait plutôt en œuvre des formes géométriques complexes, comme pour Ackerberg House, une villa construite au bord de l'océan, en Californie. Il conserve néanmoins son goût pour une architecture lumineuse et un blanc immaculé.

Richard Meier quite simply turned the slanted roof required by local zoning restrictions upside down, to allow the house to open out onto the water in a spectacular way.

Durch das „auf den Kopf stellen" des von den örtlichen Bauvorschriften geforderten Satteldachs öffnet sich das Haus auf ganz ungewöhnliche Weise zum Meer.

Richard Meier a tout simplement inversé le toit à deux pentes exigé par la réglementation d'urbanisme locale, permettant ainsi à la maison de s'ouvrir sur l'océan.

In typical fashion, Richard Meier uses the white luminosity of his spaces to their best advantage, particularly in this near tropical climate.

In charakteristischer Weise setzt Richard Meier in seiner Innenraum-gestaltung Licht und weiße Farbe ein, was die Räume, besonders in dieser fast tropischen Umgebung, optimal zur Geltung bringt.

L'une des caractéristiques de Richard Meier est de savoir tirer le meilleur parti de la lumineuse blan-cheur d'espaces situés à proximité des tropiques.

JUBILEE CHURCH

(Dio Padre Misericordioso), Tor Tre Teste, Rome, Italy, 1996–2003

Client: Vicariato of Rome. Floor area: 830 m² (church), 1450 m² (community center), 10 000 m² (site). Costs: not specified.

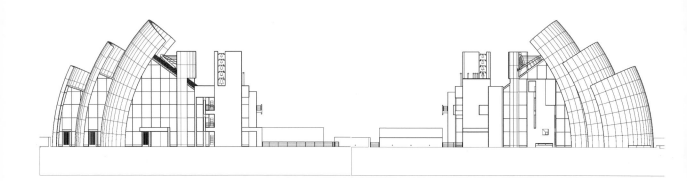

A succession of shells, like sails billowing in the wind, marks this church, set up on its platform in Rome to mark the Jubilee year.

Eine Abfolge von Schalensegmenten, die wie Segel wirken, kennzeichnet die Kirche, die zum katholischen Jubiläumsjahr in Rom errichtet wurde.

Une succession de coques, telles des voiles gonflés par le vent, signalent cette église, édifiée à Rome pour marquer l'année du Jubilée.

Sitting on its glistening plaza, the Jubilee Church at sunset takes on an even more ship-like appearance. Meier has often used nautical metaphors in his work, but in this context the successive sails are surprising.

Die auf einem schimmernden Platz ruhende Jubiläumskirche sieht bei Sonnenuntergang sogar noch schiffsähnlicher aus. Meier hat zwar bereits in früheren Arbeiten nautische Metaphern eingesetzt, aber in diesem Kontext sind die segelartigen Formen neu und ungewöhnlich.

Posée sur une plazza de travertin poli, l'église du Jubilée fait encore plus penser à un bateau au coucher du soleil. Si Meier a souvent utilisé des métaphores nautiques dans son œuvre, l'utilisation de cette succession de voiles n'en est pas moins surprenante.

Commissioned by the Vicariato of Rome, this church is set on a triangular site on the boundary of a public park surrounded by 10-story apartment buildings in a community of approximately 30 000 residents. The project features the use of concrete, stucco, travertine and glass and three dramatic shells or arcs that evoke billowing white sails. Unprecedented in Meier's work, the concrete arcs are graduated in height from 17 to 27 meters. The invited competition to design the structure included Tadao Ando, Günter Behnisch, Santiago Calatrava, Peter Eisenman, and Frank Gehry, as well as Meier, who won in the spring of 1996. Construction began in 1998, and although the architect has designed the Hartford Seminary in Connecticut (1981) and the International Center for Possibility Thinking at the Crystal Cathedral in Southern California (2003), this was his first church. As always, Richard Meier places an emphasis on light. "Light is the protagonist of our understanding and reading of space. Light is the means by which we are able to experience what we call sacred. Light is at the origins of this building," he says. Commenting on the fact that he may be the first Jewish architect asked to design a Catholic church, Meier says, "I feel extremely proud that I was the one chosen to design this church. It is very clear that the Catholic Church chose my design based on its merits, not because of a need to make a statement in regard to their relationship to Jews throughout history. Three of the architects in the competition were Jewish. They were chosen to compete because they were among the top architects of our time." His sources of inspiration, he says, were "the churches in which the presence of the sacred could be felt: Alvar Aalto's churches in Finland, Lloyd Wright's Wayfarers Chapel in the United States along with the Chapel at Ronchamp and La Tourette by Le Corbusier." The **JUBILEE CHURCH** was inaugurated on October 26, 2003 to mark the 25th anniversary of the Pontificate of John Paul II.

Die Jubiläumskirche gehört zu einer Gemeinde mit circa 30 000 Einwohnern. Sie steht auf einem dreiseitigen Grundstück am Rand eines öffentlichen Parks und ist von zehnstöckigen Wohnblocks umgeben. Ein besonderes Gestaltungsmerkmal des mit Beton, Gipsputz, Travertin und Glas ausgestatteten Bauwerks sind drei dramatisch geformte Bögen, die an Segel denken lassen, die sich im Wind blähen. Diese in Meiers Werk noch nie da gewesenen Betonformen sind der Höhe nach von 17 bis 27 m gestaffelt. Neben Meier wurden auch Tadao Ando, Günter Behnisch, Santiago Calatrava, Peter Eisenman und Frank O. Gehry zu dem Wettbewerb für die Gestaltung dieses Projekts eingeladen, den Meier im Frühjahr 1996 für sich entschied. Mit den Bauarbeiten wurde 1998 begonnen, und obwohl der Architekt zuvor das Hartford Priesterseminar in Connecticut (1981) und das International Center for Possibility Thinking der Crystal Cathedral in Südkalifornien (2003) geplant hatte, ist dies sein erster Sakralbau. Wie immer hebt Richard Meier in seinem Entwurf speziell das Licht hervor: „Licht ist der Protagonist unseres Verständnisses und unserer Auffassung von Raum. Das Licht ist das Medium, durch welches wir das erleben können, was wir heilig nennen. Licht liegt am Ursprung dieses Gebäudes." Als Antwort auf die Tatsache, dass er vermutlich der erste jüdische Architekt ist, der mit der Gestaltung einer katholischen Kirche betraut wurde, sagt Meier: „Ich bin ungeheuer stolz darauf, dass ich ausgewählt wurde, um diese Kirche zu entwerfen. Dabei ist ganz klar, dass die katholische Kirche meinen Entwurf aufgrund seiner Vorzüge wählte, und nicht weil es ihr darum ging, eine Aussage über ihr Verhältnis zu Juden zu machen. Drei der Architekten, die am Wettbewerb teilgenommen haben, sind jüdisch. Und sie wurden zu dem Wettbewerb eingeladen, weil sie zu den besten Architekten unserer Zeit gehören." Seine Quelle der Inspiration, erläutert Meier, waren „Kirchen, in denen man die Präsenz des Heiligen fühlen kann: Alvar Aaltos Kirchen in Finnland, Lloyd Wrights Wayfarers-Kapelle in den Vereinigten Staaten und die Wallfahrtskirche zu Ronchamp sowie das Kloster La Tourette von Le Corbusier." Die **JUBILÄUMSKIRCHE** wurde zur Feier des 25-jährigen Pontifikats von Johannes Paul II. am 26. Oktober 2003 eingeweiht.

L'église est implantée sur un terrain triangulaire en bordure d'un parc public entouré d'immeubles de logements de 10 étages dans un ensemble qui compte environ 30 000 résidents. Le projet qui fait appel au béton, au stuc, au travertin et au verre se caractérise par trois coques ou arcs spectaculaires qui évoquent des voiles blanches et gonflées. Motif sans précédent dans l'œuvre de Meier, ces arcs de béton s'étagent de 17 à 27 mètres. Le concours sur invitation comprenait Tadao Ando, Günther Behnisch, Santiago Calatrava, Peter Eisenman et Frank Gehry ainsi que Meier qui le remporta en 1996. C'était son premier projet d'église même s'il a déjà conçu le Séminaire de Hartford (Connecticut, 1981), l'International Center for Possibility Thinking de la Crystal Cathedral (Californie du Sud, 2003). Le chantier débuta en 1998. Comme toujours, Meier a mis l'accent sur la lumière : « La lumière est le protagoniste qui nous fait comprendre et lire l'espace. La lumière est le moyen par lequel nous sommes en mesure de faire l'expérience de ce que nous appelons le sacré. La lumière est à l'origine de ce projet. » Commentant le fait qu'il est peut-être le premier architecte juif à concevoir une église, il ajoute : « Je me sens extrêmement fier d'avoir été choisi… il est clair que l'Église catholique a retenu mon projet pour ses mérites, et non pas pour marquer une position par rapport à sa relation avec les Juifs au cours de l'histoire. Trois des architectes invités étaient juifs. Ils avaient été sélectionnés parce qu'ils faisaient partie des tout premiers architectes de notre temps. » Ses sources d'inspiration ont été « des églises dans lesquelles ont peut sentir la présence du sacré : celles de Alvar Aalto en Finlande, la Wayfarers Chapel de Lloyd Wright aux États-Unis, la chapelle de Ronchamp et le couvent de la Tourette par Le Corbusier ». **L'ÉGLISE DU JUBILÉE** a été inaugurée le 26 octobre 2003, pour marquer le 25ème anniversaire du pontificat de Jean-Paul II.

 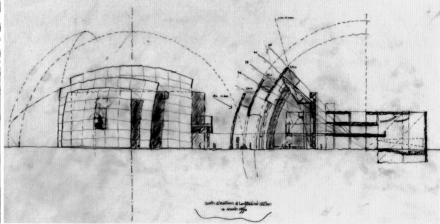

As always attentive to the effects of light in his architecture, Richard Meier has created a light-filled church with a markedly asymmetrical interior design.

Wie immer sorgfältig auf die Wirkung des Lichts in seiner Architektur bedacht, hat Richard Meier eine lichterfüllte Kirche mit einem ausgesprochen asymmetrischen Innenraum entworfen.

Toujours attentif aux effets de la lumière dans son architecture, Meier a créé une église extrêmement lumineuse sur un plan intérieur fortement asymétrique.

MEYER EN VAN SCHOOTEN

Meyer en Van Schooten Architecten BV
Pilotenstraat 35
1059 CH Amsterdam
The Netherlands

Tel: +31 20 5319 800
Fax: +31 20 5319 801
E-mail: office@mvsa.nl
Web: www.meyer-vanschooten.nl

ROBERTO MEYER was born in 1959 in Bogotá, Colombia, while **JEROEN VAN SCHOOTEN** was born in Nieuwer Amstel in 1960. They were both educated at the HTS Architecture, Utrecht, and the Academies of Architecture in Amsterdam and Arnhem. They created their firm, Meyer en Van Schooten Architecten BV, in Amsterdam in 1984. Their work includes housing in Enschede, Apeldoorn, Amsterdam, Rotterdam, Zaandam, and Arnhem. They have also built a number of bridges in IJburg, Amsterdam (1998). Their recent work includes: 60 apartments, Geuzenbaan, Amsterdam; Blok 3, Central Library, 30 apartments, offices, shops, Almere; 150 apartments + parking, Verolme terrain, Alblasserdam; 52 apartments in block 11 and 78 apartments in block 14b Gershwin, south axis, Amsterdam; and 160-apartment Veranda complex in Rotterdam. Their ING Group Headquarters, Amsterdam (1998–2002) won several awards, including the 2002 Netherlands Steel Prize (Nationale Staalprijs 2002) and the Aluminum Architecture Award 2003 (Nederlandse Aluminium Award Architectuur 2003). Rotterdam Central Station (designed together with Benthem Crouwel Architekten and West 8) has been under construction since 2008 and is scheduled to be completed in 2013.

ROBERTO MEYER wurde 1959 in Bogotá in Kolumbien und **JEROEN VAN SCHOOTEN** 1960 im niederländischen Nieuwer Amstel geboren. Beide besuchten die HTS für Architektur in Utrecht und die Architekturakademien in Amsterdam und Arnheim. Zusammen gründeten sie 1984 ihre Firma Meyer en Van Schooten Architecten BV in Amsterdam. Zu ihren Arbeiten gehören Wohnbauten in Enschede, Apeldoorn, Amsterdam, Rotterdam, Zaandam und Arnheim. Außerdem planten sie eine Reihe von Brücken in IJburg in Amsterdam (1998). Zu ihren jüngsten Projekten zählen: 60 Wohnungen in Geuzenbaan in Amsterdam, eine Anlage aus Bücherei, 30 Wohnungen, Büros und Geschäften in Almere-Stad, 150 Wohnungen mit Parkplatz auf dem Verolme-Gelände in Alblasserdam, 52 Wohnungen in Block 11 und 78 Wohnungen in Block 14b der Gershwin-Südachse in Amsterdam sowie die Anlage Veranda mit 160 Wohnungen in Rotterdam. Ihre hier vorgestellte Zentralverwaltung der ING-Gruppe in Amsterdam erhielt zahlreiche Auszeichnungen wie 2002 den Nationale Staalprijs (Niederländischer Stahlpreis) und 2003 den Nederlandse Aluminium Award Architectuur (Niederländischer Aluminiumpreis Architektur). Seit 2008 bauen sie an dem neuen Rotterdamer Hauptbahnhof (zusammen mit Benthem Crouwle Architekten und West 8), der bis 2013 fertiggestellt werden soll.

ROBERTO MEYER est né en 1959 à Bogotá (Colombie) et **JEROEN VAN SCHOOTEN** à Nieuwer Amstel (Pays-Bas) en 1960. Tous deux ont fait leurs études à l'HTS d'architecture d'Utrecht et aux Académies d'architecture d'Amsterdam et d'Arnhem. Ils ont créé leur agence Meyer en Van Schooten Architecten BV à Amsterdam en 1984. Leurs réalisations comprennent des logements à Enschede, Apeldoorn, Amsterdam, Rotterdam, Zaandam et Arnhem. Ils ont également construit plusieurs ponts (IJburg, Amsterdam, 1998). Parmi leurs travaux : 60 appartements (Geuzenbaan, Amsterdam) ; Bibliothèque centrale/30 appartements/bureaux/commerces (Almere-Stad) ; 150 appartements et parkings (Verolme Terrain, Alblasserdam) ; 52 appartements (bloc 11) et 78 appartements (bloc 14) de l'axe méridional Gershwin, Amsterdam, ainsi que le complexe Veranda avec 160 appartements à Rotterdam. L'immeuble ING, publié ici, a remporté plusieurs prix dont le Nationale Staalprijs 2002 (Prix néerlandais de l'acier) et le Prix néerlandais de l'aluminium 2003. Depuis 2008, ils se chargent de la construction de la nouvelle gare centrale de Rotterdam (en collaboration avec Benthem Crouwle Architekten et West 8), qui devrait être achevée en 2013.

ING GROUP HEADQUARTERS

Amsterdam, The Netherlands, 1998–2002

Client: ING Group N.V. Building area: 3500 m², office floor area: 7500 m². Costs: not specified.

Built on a long, narrow site near Amsterdam's ring road, the **ING HEADQUARTERS** lies between the Zuidas area of high-rise buildings and a green zone called De Nieuwe Meer. The architects intentionally kept the structure low on the "green" side and made it rise in the direction of the city. In order to allow motorists a view toward the green zone and at the same time to give the offices a view over the highway, the building is set up on pilotis ranging in height from 9 to 12.5 meters. A great deal of attention was paid to the energy efficiency of the structure, for example with a double-skin façade that facilitates natural ventilation while providing a sound barrier against traffic noise. A pumping system makes use of an aquifer located 120 meters under the building to provide cold/warm thermal storage. Successive stories within the building "intermingle and offer glimpses from one to another." Atriums, loggias and gardens vary the interior space as well. As the architects have written, "the new headquarters symbolizes the banking and insurance conglomerate as a dynamic, fast-moving international network. Transparency, innovation, eco-friendliness and openness were the main starting points for the design." Another interesting element in the design process is the request of the client that the building last between 50 and 100 years. Set up on V-shaped stilts, the structure looks as though it might just move on before that.

Die **ING-ZENTRALE** wurde auf einem lang gestreckten, schmalen Grundstück errichtet, das nahe der Amsterdamer Ringautobahn zwischen der Hochhausgegend Zuidas und dem Naherholungsgebiet De Nieuwe Meer liegt. Bewusst hielten die Architekten das Gebäude zur „grünen Seite" hin niedrig und ließen es zur Stadtseite hin ansteigen. Um den Autofahrern nicht den Blick ins Grüne zu verstellen und den Büros gleichzeitig einen Ausblick über die Schnellstraße hinweg zu gewähren, wurde das Gebäude auf 9 bis 12,5 m hohe Stützpfeiler gesetzt. Große Sorgfalt wurde auch auf ein effizientes Energiesystem verwendet, beispielsweise mit einer doppelwandigen Fassade, die für natürliche Belüftung sorgt und einen Schutz gegen den Verkehrslärm bietet. Außerdem wird durch eine Pumpanlage eine 120 m unterhalb des Gebäudes liegende, Wasser führende Schicht als Thermospeicher genutzt. Im Inneren sind die Stockwerke nicht klar abgegrenzt, sondern gehen ineinander über, so dass sich immer wieder Durchblicke von einem Geschoss zum anderen öffnen. Auch Atrien, Loggien und Wintergärten bringen Abwechslung in den Innenraum. Die Architekten über ihr Projekt: „Mit der neuen Zentrale stellt sich der Bank- und Versicherungskonzern als ein dynamisches, internationales Netzwerk dar. Dabei waren die Aspekte Transparenz, Innovation, Umweltfreundlichkeit und Offenheit für uns entwurfsbestimmend." Wichtig war zudem die Anforderung des Auftraggebers, das Gebäude solle eine Lebensdauer von 50 bis 100 Jahren haben. Mit seinen V-förmigen Stelzen sieht es jedoch aus, als könnte es schon vor dieser Zeit einfach weiterziehen.

Édifié sur un long terrain étroit en bordure de l'autoroute périphérique d'Amsterdam, le **SIÈGE D'ING** est situé entre le quartier de tours de Zuidas et une zone verte, De Nieuwe Meer. Sur le côté « vert », les architectes ont volontairement maintenu une faible hauteur qui s'accroît rapidement vers le côté ville. Pour permettre aux automobilistes de conserver une vision de la zone verte et offrir aux bureaux une vue qui passe par-dessus l'autoroute, l'immeuble est posé sur des pilotis dont la hauteur varie de 9 à 12,5 m. Une grande attention a été portée à l'autonomie énergétique du bâtiment, par exemple grâce à une façade à double-peau qui permet une ventilation naturelle et protège du bruit de la circulation. Un système de pompage utilise la nappe phréatique à 120 m de profondeur pour le stockage thermique. Les différents étages « s'imbriquent et offrent des vues l'un sur l'autre ». Atriums, loggias et jardins diversifient l'intérieur de l'espace. Comme le précisent les architectes : « La nouvelle approche internationale, de transparence, d'innovation, de sensibilité écologique et d'ouverture a constitué le principal point de départ du projet. » Un autre élément intéressant, à la demande du client, est que l'immeuble dure de 50 à 100 ans. Posé sur ses pilotis en V, on a l'impression qu'il pourrait bien avoir envie de se transporter ailleurs avant cette date.

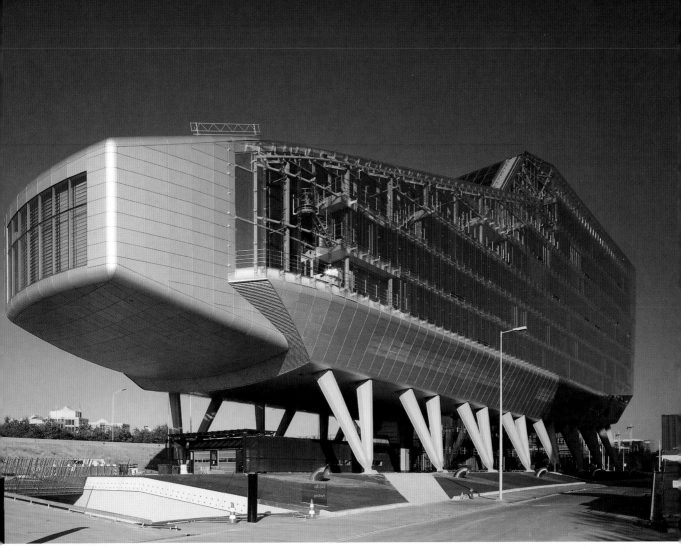

Like an apparition out of a Star Wars movie, the ING Headquarters building looks almost as though it is ready to move forward on its legs.

Die an ein Wesen aus Star Wars erinnernde ING-Zentrale sieht fast so aus, als könne sie sich auf ihren Stelzen vorwärtsbewegen.

Comme sorti d'un film de la série Star Wars, le siège d'ING donne l'impression d'être prêt à déambuler sur ses grandes jambes inclinées.

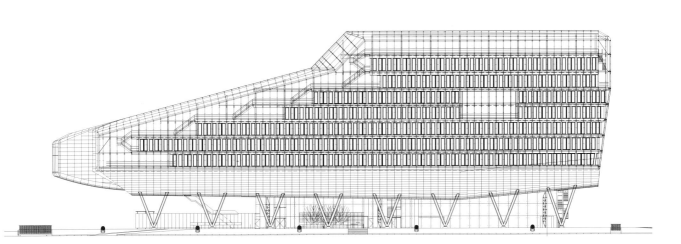

Massive as seen from almost any angle, the weight of the structure seems all the more imposing since it is lifted off the ground.

Das Gewicht des von fast jedem Blickwinkel massiv aussehenden Gebäudes wirkt umso eindrucksvoller, wenn man bedenkt, dass es auf Stützpfeilern ruht.

Massif sous presque tous ses angles, l'immeuble semble d'un poids d'autant plus imposant qu'il est surélevé par rapport au sol.

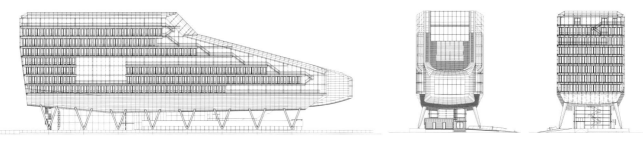

Though the image above gives the impression that the structure spreads wider as it rises, sections show that this is not the case.

Obwohl das Bild oben den Eindruck erweckt, dass das Gebäude nach oben breiter wird, beweist der Querschnitt das Gegenteil.

Contrairement à l'impression donnée par l'image ci-dessus, la structure n'est pas évasée vers le haut comme le montrent ces coupes.

Ground-level images give an impression of lightness since the weight of the structure is carried on the external tilted "legs."

Die Bilder vom Innenraum im Erdgeschoss vermitteln einen Eindruck von Leichtigkeit, während das Gewicht des Gebäudes von den schräg gestellten „Beinen" getragen wird.

Les photos prises au niveau du sol donnent une impression de légèreté du fait de la surélévation sur pilotis.

The glazed airiness of the ground floor is repeated in this space, where a zigzagging stairway goes up the glass façade.

Die luftige Atmosphäre im Erdgeschoss wiederholt sich in diesem Raum, wo eine Treppe im Zickzack die Glasfassade entlang nach oben führt.

La transparence aérienne du rez-de-chaussée se retrouve à l'intérieur du volume, marqué par un escalier en zigzag qui semble escalader la façade de verre.

Though the density of the metallic structure gives a technical or mechanical appearance to the whole, the space is filled with light.

Obwohl die dichte Metallkonstruktion dem Ganzen eine technische Note verleiht, ist der Innenraum von Licht erfüllt.

Si la densité de la présence du métal donne un aspect technique ou mécanique, les volumes sont très lumineux.

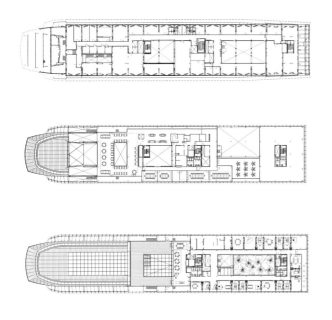

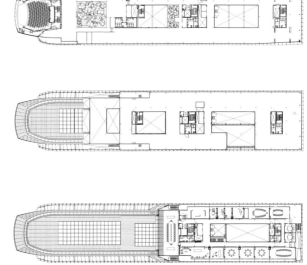

Floor plans show the fundamental regularity of the design and the effect of the progressively increasing area of the glazed roof. Above, a boardroom in the upper level.

Die Grundrisse zeigen die Regelmäßigkeit der Gestaltung und die mit jedem Stockwerk größer werdende Fläche der Dachverglasung. Oben: ein Sitzungsraum im Obergeschoss.

Les plans des niveaux montrent le parti pris de régularité de la conception et l'effet du toit de verre dont la taille croît peu à peu. Ci-dessus, une salle du conseil au niveau supérieur.

JOSÉ RAFAEL MONEO

José Rafael Moneo
Cinca 5
28002 Madrid
Spain

Tel: +34 91 564 2257
Fax: +34 91 563 5217

JOSÉ RAFAEL MONEO was born in Tudela, Navarra, in 1937. He graduated from the Escuela Técnica Superior de Arquitectura in Madrid (ETSAM) in 1961. The following year, he went to work with Jørn Utzon in Denmark. Rafael Moneo has taught extensively at the ETSA in Madrid and Barcelona. He was chairman of the Department of Architecture at the Graduate School of Design at Harvard from 1985 to 1990. He won the 1995 Pritzker Prize, and the 2003 RIBA Gold Medal. His work includes: the National Museum of Roman Art, Mérida (1980–86); the San Pablo Airport Terminal in Seville (1989–91) built for Expo '92; Kursaal Auditorium and Congress Center, San Sebastián, Guipuzcoa (1990–99); the Atocha railway station in Madrid (1992); the interior architecture of the Thyssen-Bornemisza Collection in Madrid (1992); the Miró Foundation in Palma de Mallorca (1993); the Davis Museum at Wellesley College, Wellesley, Massachusetts (1993); Potsdamer Platz Hotel and Office Building, Berlin, Germany (1993–98); Murcia Town Hall, Murcia (1995–99); the Cathedral of Our Lady of the Angels, Los Angeles, California (2000–02); an enlargement of the Prado Museum, Madrid (2000–07). He is also working on the Souks in Beirut; the Laboratory for Interface and Engineering at Harvard; the Student Center for the Rhode Island School of Design, Providence, Rhode Island; and the Northwest Science Building at Columbia University in New York. Other work in Spain includes apartments in Carrer Tres Creus, Sabadell (with José Antonio Martínez Lapeña and Elías Torres, 2000–05); and an extension for the Bank of Spain, Madrid (2001–06).

JOSÉ RAFAEL MONEO, 1937 in Tudela in Spanien geboren, schloss 1961 sein Studium an der Escuela Técnica Superior de Arquitectura (ETSA) in Madrid ab. Im darauffolgenden Jahr ging er nach Dänemark, um dort bei Jørn Utzon zu arbeiten. Rafael Moneo hat an der ETSA in Madrid und in Barcelona gelehrt. Von 1985 bis 1990 war er Leiter des Department of Architecture der Graduate School of Design in Harvard. 1995 erhielt er den Pritzker-Preis, 2003 die RIBA-Goldmedaille. Zu Moneos Bauten gehören das Nationalmuseum für Römische Kunst im spanischen Mérida (1980–86), der für die Expo '92 gebaute Flughafen San Pablo in Sevilla (1989–91), das Kursaal-Auditorium und Kongresszentrum in San Sebastián (1990–99), der Bahnhof Atocha in Madrid (1992), die Innengestaltung der Thyssen-Bornemisza-Sammlung in Madrid (1992), die Miró-Stiftung in Palma de Mallorca (1993), das Davis Art Museum am Wellesley College in Wellesley, Massachusetts (1993), ein Hotel und ein Bürogebäude am Potsdamer Platz in Berlin (1993–98), das Rathaus von Murcia (1995–99), die Kathedrale Our Lady of the Angels in Los Angeles (2000–02) und eine Erweiterung des Prado in Madrid (2000–07). Des Weiteren arbeitet er an den Souks von Beirut, am Laboratorium Interface and Engineering in Harvard, am Studentenzentrum für die Rhode Island School of Design in Providence und am Northwest Science Building der Columbia-Universität in New York. Weitere Arbeiten in Spanien sind die Apartments in Carrer Tres Creus, Sabadell (mit José Antonio Martínez Lapeña und Elías Torres, 2000–05), und ein Erweiterungsbau für die Bank von Spanien in Madrid (2001–06).

JOSÉ RAFAEL MONEO naît à Tuleda, Espagne, en 1937. Il est diplômé de l'Escuela Técnica de Arquitectura de Madrid en 1961. En 1962, il part au Danemark pour travailler avec Jørn Utzon. Il enseigne aux ETSA de Madrid et de Barcelone. Président du département d'architecture de la Graduate School of Design de Harvard de 1985 à 1990. Il obtient le Prix Pritzker en 1995 et la Médaille d'or de RIBA en 2003. Parmi ses réalisations : le Musée national d'art romain (Merida, Espagne, 1980–86), le terminal de l'aéroport de San Pablo (Séville, 1989–91) édifié pour l'Expo '92, l'auditorium Kursaal et le centre culturel de San Sebastián (1990–99), la gare d'Atocha (Madrid, 1992), l'architecture intérieure de la collection Thyssen-Bornemisza à Madrid, la Fondation Miró (Palma de Mallorca, 1993), le Davis Art Museum du Wellesley College (Wellesley, Massachusetts, 1993), un hôtel et un immeuble de bureaux, Potsdamer Platz (Berlin, 1993–98), l'Hôtel de Ville de Murcia (1995–99), la cathédrale Our Lady of the Angels à Los Angeles (2000–02) et l'extension du Prado à Madrid (2000–07). De plus, il travaille aux souks de Beyrouth, au laboratoire Interface and Engineering à Harvard, à la Cité universitaire pour la Rhode Island School of Design à Providence et au Northwest Science Building de la Columbia University à New York. Parmi ses autres réalisations en Espagne comptent les studios de Carrer Tres Creus, Sabadell (en collaboration avec José Antonio Martínez Lapena et Elías Torres, 2000–05) et l'extension de la Banque d'Espagne à Madrid (2001–06).

MURCIA TOWN HALL ANNEX

Murcia, Spain, 1991–98

Planning: 1991–95. Construction: 1995–98. Client: Municipal Government of Murcia.
Floor area: 3000 m². Costs: c. € 3 million.

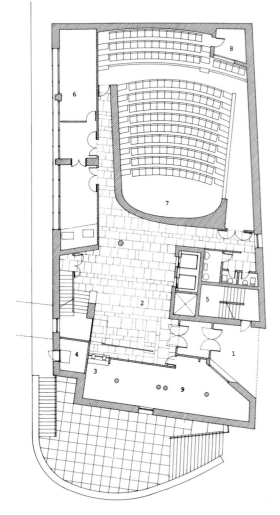
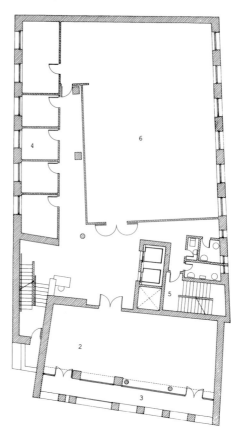

Ground floor	Erdgeschoss	Rez-de-chaussée
1 - Entrance hall	1 - Eingangshalle	1 - Entrée
2 - Vestibule/Information	2 - Vorhalle/Information	2 - Accueil, information
3 - Cashier	3 - Kasse	3 - Caisse
4 - Garbage room	4 - Abstellraum	4 - Local pour les poubelles
5 - Emergency stair	5 - Feuertreppe	5 - Escalier de secours
6 - Office	6 - Büro	6 - Bureau
7 - Lecture hall	7 - Vorlesungssaal	7 - Salle de lecture
8 - Projection room	8 - Projektionsraum	8 - Salle de projections
9 - General office	9 - Verwaltung	9 - Administration centrale

First floor	1. Obergeschoss	Premier étage
1 - Vestibule/Information	1 - Vorhalle/Information	1 - Accueil, information
2 - Reception room	2 - Empfang	2 - Accueil
3 - Gallery	3 - Galerie	3 - Galerie
4 - Office	4 - Büro	4 - Bureau
5 - Emergency stair	5 - Feuertreppe	5 - Escalier de secours
6 - General offices	6 - Verwaltung	6 - Administration centrale

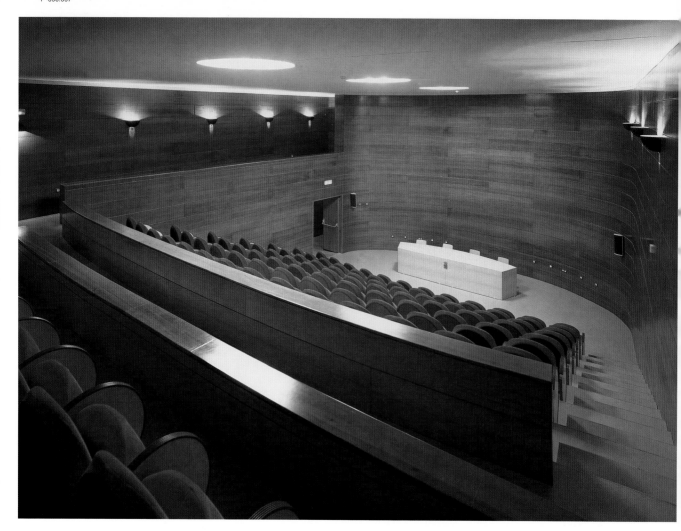

Situated on Plaza Cardenal Belluga, near the cathedral and the Cardinal's Palace, the **MURCIA TOWN HALL ANNEX** presented Rafael Moneo with the difficult task of designing a building that neither challenged the architectural power of the older structures nor timidly denied contemporary municipal power. The reinforced concrete town hall is clad in local sandstone and brick. The interior finishes are plaster and wood paneling, with stone and wood floors. The building specifications required space for the municipal offices, a tourist and information center, a lecture hall, a reception room and a cafeteria. As Rafael Moneo says, "The façade/retable is organized like a musical score, numerically accepting the horizontal levels of the floor slabs. It resists symmetries, and offers, as the key element, the balcony of the gallery that rests on exactly the same horizontal plane as the central balcony of the piano nobile of the Palace, both at the same height."

Der 3000 m² umfassende, an der Plaza del Cardenal Belluga nahe der Kathedrale und dem Kardinalspalast gelegene **MURCIA-RATHAUS-ANNEX** stellte Rafael Moneo vor die schwierige Aufgabe, ein Gebäude zu entwerfen, das weder die architektonische Kraft der alten Bauwerke schmälert, noch schüchtern die Vitalität der modernen Provinzhauptstadt leugnet. Das neue Rathaus ist aus Stahlbeton erbaut und mit örtlichem Sandstein verkleidet. Die Innenraumausstattung besteht aus Gipsputz und Holztäfelung sowie Stein- und Holzfußböden. Der Bauplan verlangte Büros für die Stadtverwaltung, ein Fremdenverkehrsamt, einen Hörsaal, einen Empfangsraum und ein Café. Rafael Moneo erläutert seinen Entwurf: „Die vorgelegte Fassade ist wie eine Partitur angelegt, wobei sich die Anzahl der Geschosse zahlenmäßig an der Fassade widerspiegelt. Entgegen jeder Symmetrie gestaltet, bietet sie als beherrschendes Bauelement den Balkon der Galerie, der auf derselben horizontalen Ebene ruht wie der zentrale Balkon im Hauptgeschoss (piano nobile) des Kardinalspalasts."

Situé Plaza del Cardenal Belluga près de la cathédrale et du palais du Cardinal, l'**ANNEXE DE L'HÔTEL DE VILLE DE MURCIE** de 3000 m² représentait pour l'architecte un défi délicat : comment respecter la forte présence des bâtiments anciens sans nuire, par timidité, à l'autorité que représente la municipalité moderne. Construit en béton armé, l'hôtel de ville est paré de grès local. Les murs intérieurs sont en plâtre ou en lambris, les sols en bois ou pierre. Le programme comprenait des bureaux administratifs, un centre d'information pour les touristes, une salle de conférence, un salon de réception et une cafétéria. Comme Rafael Moneo le précise : « La façade-retable est organisée à la manière d'une partition musicale, et laisse s'affirmer la présence horizontale des dalles de niveau. Contrairement aux principes de symétrie, l'élément majeur, le balcon de la galerie, est aligné sur le même plan que le balcon central (piano nobile) du palais. »

Rafael Moneo has met the challenge of integrating a decidedly modern structure into a tight, traditional urban environment. A view from the inside of a balcony shows the proximity to the older buildings of the city.

José Rafael Moneo ist es gelungen, ein sehr modernes Gebäude in eine dicht bebaute, traditionelle Umgebung zu integrieren. Oben: Der Ausblick vom Balkon macht die Nähe der alten Bauwerke deutlich.

Rafael Moneo relève ici le défi d'intégrer une construction résolument moderne dans un tissu urbain traditionnel et serré. Une vue de l'intérieur d'un balcon montre la proximité des bâtiments anciens.

KURSAAL AUDITORIUM AND CULTURAL CENTER

San Sebastián, Guipuzcoa, Spain, 1990–99

*Planning: 3/1990–11/1993. Construction: 6/1995–8/1999.
Total floor area: 60 440 m². Usable floor area: 49 908 m².
Client: Centro Kursaal – Kursaal Elkargunea, S. A. Costs: c. € 54.1 million.*

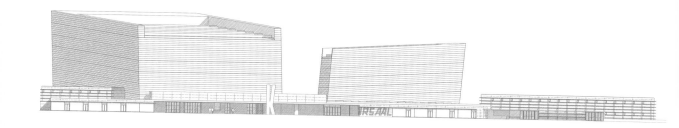

One major objective of Rafael Moneo's design for this complex was to integrate, as intact as possible, much of the natural setting of the mouth of the Urumea River by placing the **KURSAAL AUDITORIUM AND CULTURAL CENTER** like "two gigantic rocks stranded at the river mouth that are part of the landscape, not the city." The "rock" containing the 1806-seat auditorium is a 65 x 46 x 22 m prismatic volume, inclined toward the sea. The other 43 x 32 x 20 m independent prism, which is also inclined, is a chamber music hall. The unusual wall surfaces, made up of a metal structure with flat glass on the interior and curved glass on the exterior, permit adequate resistance to high winds. This system provides a certain transparency during the day, and permits a glowing, overall lighting effect at night. Other facilities are located in the base of the complex. Set near the water, the Center is at once an abstract composition and, at the same time, a discreet homage to its geographic and urban setting. With its purity of line and dynamic inclinations, the Kursaal Auditorium would appear to be one of Rafael Moneo's most successful recent buildings.

Eines der Hauptziele von Rafael Moneos Entwurf bestand darin, die natürliche Umgebung an der Mündung des Urumea Flusses so weit wie möglich in die Gestaltung der Anlage zu integrieren. Die Formen des **KURSAAL-AUDITORIUM UND KULTURZENTRUMS** erinnern an „zwei gigantische, ans Flussufer angeschwemmte Felsbrocken, die mehr Teil der Landschaft als der Stadt sind". Der das Auditorium mit 1806 Sitzen enthaltende „Fels" ist ein zum Meer hin abfallender, prismenförmiger Baukörper mit den Maßen 65 x 46 x 22 m. Der andere, 43 x 32 x 20 m große, ebenfalls prismenförmige Bauteil mit schrägen Wänden beherbergt eine Konzerthalle. Im Fundament der Anlage sind die Serviceeinrichtungen untergebracht. Die Oberflächen der Wände, die eine angemessene Windfestigkeit bieten sollen, sind ungewöhnlich: Die Innenwände sind mit einem Metallgefüge und Tafelglas verkleidet, die Außenfassaden bestehen aus gewölbtem Glas. Darüber hinaus wird durch diese Konstruktion tagsüber eine gewisse Transparenz erreicht, nachts leuchtet der Baukörper weithin sichtbar. Der gesamte Komplex ist eine abstrakte Komposition und eine diskrete Huldigung an die geografische und urbane Umgebung zugleich. Mit seinen klaren Linien und dynamischen Schrägen lässt sich das Kursaal-Auditorium als eines von Rafael Moneos erfolgreichsten Bauwerken bezeichnen.

L'un des principaux objectifs du projet de Rafael Moneo était, si possible, d'intégrer l'**AUDITORIUM DU KURSAAL ET LE CENTRE CULTUREL**, dans le cadre naturel de l'embouchure de l'Urumea en disposant les bâtiments à la manière de « deux gigantesques rochers échoués sur les berges du fleuve et faisant partie du paysage, et non de la ville ». Le « rocher » qui contient l'auditorium de 1806 places est un parallélépipède de 65 x 46 x 22 m, incliné vers la mer. Le second de 43 x 32 x 20 m, également un parallélépipède indépendant et incliné, sert de salle de musique de chambre. Les curieuses parois extérieures sont constituées d'une structure métallique recouverte de verre plat à l'intérieur et bombé à l'extérieur pour renforcer la résistance aux vents. Ce principe permet une certaine transparence de jour et crée un effet lumineux en nocturne. D'autres installations sont implantées à la base du complexe. Au bord de l'océan, le Centre est à la fois une composition abstraite et un hommage discret à son cadre géographique et urbain. Par sa pureté de lignes et sa dynamique due à son inclinaison, ce Kursaal est l'une des récentes réalisations de Rafael Moneo les plus réussies.

Above right: As seen in its urban context the Kursaal Auditorium and Cultural Center affirms a geometric presence whose angling gives a certain dynamism to forms that might have threatened to be too static otherwise.

Oben rechts: Im städtebaulichen Kontext fällt das Kursaal-Auditorium und Kulturzentrum deutlich durch seine geometrische Anlage auf. Unten rechts: Die schräg gestellten Fassaden verleihen den sonst sehr statisch wirkenden Gebäudeformen eine gewisse Dynamik.

Ci-dessus à droite : Dans son contexte urbain, l'Auditorium et centre culturel affirme la forte présence de leur géométrie. L'inclinaison donne un certain dynamisme à des formes qui auraient pu être statiques.

Right: Rafael Moneo shows a surprising capacity to renew his architectural vocabulary according to the circumstances, though he does tend to favor rather closed structures, preferring to modulate internal lighting conditions in a more intimate way.

Rechts: Moneo besitzt die ungewöhnliche Fähigkeit, seine Formensprache den jeweiligen Umständen entsprechend zu erneuern. Grundsätzlich tendiert er zu eher geschlossenen Baukörpern und einer intimen Gestaltung der Lichtverhältnisse im Inneren.

À droite : Rafael Moneo fait preuve d'une étonnante capacité à renouveler son vocabulaire architectural selon les circonstances, même s'il préfère toujours les structures assez fermées dont il peut moduler l'éclairage intérieur de façon plus intime.

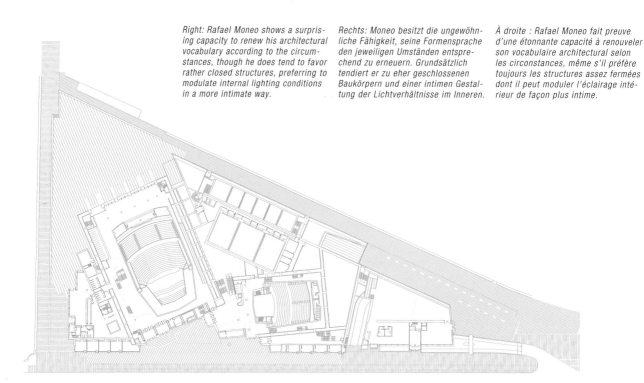

Stairways and façades present an intricate arrangement of opaque and translucent surfaces. The articulation of the stairways gives an impression that solid slabs of stone or metal are hovering in space.

Treppenaufgänge und Fassaden bilden ein ausgeklügeltes System lichtundurchlässiger und durchscheinender Oberflächen. Die Anordnung der Treppen erweckt den Eindruck, als schwebten die massiven Körper aus Stein- und Metallplatten im Raum.

Les escaliers et les façades s'imbriquent de façon à produire une étonnante composition de surfaces opaques et transparentes. L'articulation des escaliers donne l'impression que les dalles de pierre ou de métal sont en suspension dans l'espace.

MORPHOSIS

Morphosis
3440 Wesley Street
Culver City, California 90232
USA

Tel: +1 424 258 6200
E-mail: studio@morphosis.net
Web: www.morphosis.net

MORPHOSIS principal Thom Mayne, born in Connecticut in 1944, received his B.Arch. degree in 1968 from USC, and his M.Arch. degree from Harvard in 1978. He created Morphosis in 1972 with Jim Stafford. Thom Mayne has taught at UCLA, Harvard, Yale, and SCI-Arc, of which he was a founding faculty member. Some of the main buildings by Morphosis are, in California, the Lawrence House (Hermosa Beach, 1981); Kate Mantilini Restaurant (Beverly Hills, 1986); Cedar's Sinai Comprehensive Cancer Care Center (Beverly Hills, 1987); Crawford Residence (Montecito, 1987–92); Yuzen Vintage Car Museum (project, West Hollywood, 1992); Blades Residence (Santa Barbara, 1992–97); International Elementary School (Long Beach, 1997–99); Diamond Ranch High School (Pomona, 1996–2000); as well as in Austria the Hypo Alpe-Adria Center (Klagenfurt, 1996–2002). More recent work includes the Caltrans District 7 Headquarters (Los Angeles, 2001–04); Science Center School (Los Angeles, 2004); San Francisco Federal Building; the University of Cincinnati Student Recreation Center (Cincinnati, Ohio, 1999–2005); NOAA Satellite Operation Facility in Suitland (Maryland, 2001–05); Wayne L. Morse U. S. Courthouse (Eugene, Oregon, 1999–2006); New Academic Building for the Cooper Union for the Advancement of Science and Art (New York, 2004–08); proposal for the 2012 Olympics in New York City made prior to the selection of London; and Phare Tower (Paris, unbuilt). Thom Mayne was the winner of the 2005 Pritzker Prize.

Der Leiter von **MORPHOSIS**, Thom Mayne, wurde 1944 in Connecticut geboren, erwarb 1968 den Grad eines B.Arch. an der University of Southern California (USC) und 1978 den eines M.Arch. in Harvard. 1972 gründete er Morphosis mit Jim Stafford. Tom Mayne lehrte an der UCLA, in Harvard, Yale und am SCI-Arc, zu dessen Gründungsmitgliedern er gehörte. Zu den wichtigsten Bauten von Morphosis zählen in Kalifornien: Lawrence House (Hermosa Beach, 1981), Kate Mantilini Restaurant (Beverly Hills, 1986), Cedar's-Sinai-Krebsklinik (Beverly Hills, 1987), Wohnhaus Crawford (Montecito, 1987–92), Yuzen-Vintage-Automuseum (Projekt, West Hollywood, 1992), Wohnhaus Blades (Santa Barbara, 1992–97), Internationale Grundschule (Long Beach, 1997–99), Diamond Ranch High School (Pomona, 1996–2000) und in Österreich das Hypo Alpe-Adria Center (Klagenfurt, 1996–2002). In jüngerer Zeit entstanden die Caltrans-District-7-Zentrale (Los Angeles, 2001–04), die Science Center School (Los Angeles, 2004), das San Francisco Federal Building, das Studentenzentrum an der University of Cincinnati (Cincinnati, Ohio, 1999–2005), die Satellitenbetriebseinrichtung der NOAA in Suitland (Maryland, 2001–05), das Wayne L. Morse U. S. Courthouse (Eugene, Oregon, 1999–2006), das New Academic Building der Cooper Union zur Förderung von Wissenschaft und Kunst (New York, 2004–08) sowie ein Entwurf für die Olympischen Spiele 2012 in New York City (vor der Wahl Londons als Austragungsort entstanden). Ein weiteres Projekt, der Phare Tower in Paris (2006–), wurde nicht realisiert. Thom Mayne erhielt 2005 den Pritzker-Preis.

Le directeur de **MORPHOSIS**, Thom Mayne, né dans le Connecticut en 1944, est B. Arch de USC (1968) et M. Arch. d'Harvard (1978). Il crée Morphosis en 1972 avec Jim Stafford. Thom Mayne a enseigné à UCLA, Harvard, Yale, et SCI-Arc dont il est un des fondateurs. Parmi les principales réalisations de Morphosis, en Californie : Lawrence House, Hermosa Beach (1981) ; Kate Mantilini Restaurant, Beverly Hills (1986) ; le Cedar's Sinai Comprehensive Cancer Care Center, Beverly Hills, (1987) ; la Crawford Residence, Montecito (1987–92) ; le Yuzen Vintage Car Museum (projet, West Hollywood, 1992) ; la Blades Residence, Santa Barbara (1992–97) ; l'International Elementary School de Long Beach (1997–99) ; la Diamond Ranch High School, Pomona (1996–2000), et, en Autriche, le Hypo-Alpe Adria Center à Klagenfurt (1996–2002). Plus récemment, il a réalisé le siège de Caltrans District 7, Los Angeles (2001–04) ; the Science Center School Los Angeles (2004) ; l'immeuble fédéral de San Francisco ; le centre de loisirs de l'Université de Cincinnati, Ohio (1999–2005) ; le centre opérationnel satellitaire NOAA à Suitland, Maryland (2001–05) ; le tribunal fédéral Wayne L. Morse, Eugene, Oregon (1999–2006) ; le nouvel immeuble du Cooper Union for the Advancement of Science and Art, New York (2004–08), et une proposition pour les Jeux Olympiques 2012 à New York, avant la sélection de Londres. Le projet de la Tour Phare, Paris La Défense, n'a pas été réalisé. Thom Mayne a reçu le Pritzker Prize en 2005.

CALTRANS DISTRICT 7 HEADQUARTERS

Los Angeles, California, USA, 2002–04

Floor area: 69 677 m². Client: California Department of Transportation.
Costs: $ 170 million.

This large office building was erected for a cost of 170 million dollars. Located on South Main Street opposite City Hall close to Frank Gehry's Walt Disney Concert Hall and Arata Isozaki's MoCA, it is the **HEADQUARTERS FOR THE CALIFORNIA DEPARTMENT OF TRANSPORTATION (CALTRANS) DISTRICT 7**, and serves 1850 Caltrans employees and 500 employees of the Los Angeles Department of Transportation. Awarded to Morphosis after a competition held in 2001, it is the first building to be commissioned under the State of California's Design Excellence Program. The building is L-shaped in plan, composed of two main volumes. The larger one is 13 stories high, 43 meters wide and 110 meters long, running from north to south. The secondary block is four stories high. The main exterior materials are an exposed galvanized steel structure, and coated perforated aluminum panels. The design features an outdoor lobby and plaza, and a public art installation by Keith Sonnier. A super-graphic sign four stories high features the building's street address, "100." The architects have also been attentive to environmental concerns. As they explain, "The building's south glass façade is entirely screened with sunshade panels incorporating photovoltaic cells, an original system designed by Morphosis, Clark Construction and a team of special consultants. The cells generate approximately 5% of the building's energy while shielding the façade from direct sunlight during peak summer hours, without obstructing the spectacular views towards the city all the way to the ocean."

Das umgerechnet 141 Millionen Euro teure Bürogebäude ist die **ZENTRALE DER VERKEHRSBEHÖRDE VON KALIFORNIEN (CALTRANS)**. 1850 Mitarbeiter von Caltrans und 500 Mitarbeiter der Verkehrsbehörde von Los Angeles arbeiten hier. Das Gebäude liegt an der South Main Street gegenüber dem Rathaus der Stadt, nicht weit entfernt von Frank Gehrys Walt Disney Concert Hall und Arata Isozakis MoCA. Morphosis wurde nach einem Wettbewerb 2001 mit dem Projekt betraut; das Gebäude ist das erste, das innerhalb des „Programms für herausragende Architektur des Bundesstaates Kalifornien" ausgeführt wurde. Das L-förmige Gebäude besteht aus zwei Hauptbaukörpern. Der größere Flügel in Nord-Süd-Richtung hat 13 Geschosse, ist 43 m tief und 110 m lang. Der zweite Flügel ist viergeschossig. Die Außenfassaden sind durch eine sichtbare verzinkte Stahlkonstruktion und beschichtete, perforierte Aluminiumpaneele charakterisiert. Der öffentliche Raum umfasst eine Lobby und eine Plaza, außerdem eine Installation des Künstlers Keith Sonnier; die Hausnummer 100 wurde als vier Geschosse hohe „Supergrafik" gestaltet. Auch auf ökologische Aspekte legten die Architekten Wert. Sie erklären: „Die gesamte Südfassade ist von Sonnenschutzpaneelen mit Fotovoltaikzellen bedeckt. Das neuartige System wurde von Morphosis, Clark Construction und einem Team aus Spezialisten entwickelt. Die Zellen generieren ungefähr fünf Prozent des Energiebedarfs des Gebäudes und schützen die Fassade in der Mittagszeit im Sommer vor direkter Sonneneinstrahlung, ohne die spektakuläre Sicht in Richtung Stadt und bis zum Pazifik zu behindern."

Ce grand immeuble de bureaux a été construit pour un budget de 141 millions d'euros. Situé South Main Street, face à l'hôtel de ville et proche du Walt Disney Concert Hall de Frank Gehry et du MoCA d'Arata Isozaki, il est le **SIÈGE DU DÉPARTEMENT DES TRANSPORTS DE CALIFORNIE (CALTRANS), DISTRICT 7**, et accueille 1850 employés de ce département et 500 de celui des transports de Los Angeles. Contrat remporté par Morphosis après un concours organisé en 2001, c'est le premier immeuble commandé dans le cadre du programme d'excellence de l'État de Californie. L'immeuble en L se compose de deux volumes principaux. Le plus grand, orienté nord-sud, mesure 110 m de long, 43 m de large et compte 13 niveaux. Le second en comporte quatre seulement. Les principaux matériaux des façades sont l'acier galvanisé pour la structure, et l'aluminium perforé enduit pour les panneaux de l'habillage. L'ensemble comprend également une plaza, un accueil extérieur et une installation artistique de l'artiste Keith Sonnier. Un signe graphique de quatre niveaux de haut rappelle le numéro de l'adresse de l'immeuble : « 100 ». Les architectes ont également été sensibles aux préoccupations environnementales. Comme ils l'expliquent : « La façade sud de l'immeuble, en verre, est entièrement doublée par des panneaux de protection solaire à cellules photovoltaïques, système original conçu par Morphosis, Clark Construction et une équipe de consultants. Ces cellules génèrent environ 5 % de l'énergie consommée par l'immeuble et protègent la façade des rayons solaires directs lors des heures d'ensoleillement maximum, sans obstruer la vue spectaculaire sur la ville jusqu'à l'océan. »

As the program undoubtedly required,
the Caltrans building appears to be
quite simply massive in its urban
context.

*Das umfangreiche Raumprogramm
führt dazu, dass das Caltrans-Gebäude in seiner städtischen Umgebung
sehr massiv wirkt.*

*Comme le programme l'exigeait sans
doute, l'immeuble Caltrans s'inscrit
assez massivement dans son contexte
urbain.*

With its jutting elements and band-like openings, the building gives a sense of dynamism that is not evident when it is viewed from a greater distance.

Mit seinen Auskragungen und horizontalen Öffnungen in der Fassade wirkt das Gebäude aus der Nähe dynamischer als aus größerer Entfernung betrachtet.

Avec ses éléments en saillie et ses ouvertures en bandeaux, l'immeuble crée une certaine dynamique, même si elle devient moins évidente dès que l'on s'en éloigne.

As has been the case in much of Thom Mayne's work, the Caltrans building takes on a very definitely sculptural aspect through many of its design details.

Wie viele andere Projekte von Thom Mayne wird das Caltrans-Gebäude von einem dezidiert skulpturalen Ansatz geprägt, der sich in zahlreichen Entwurfsdetails zeigt.

Comme la plupart des réalisations de Thom Mayne, le Caltrans prend une allure vraiment sculpturale par le biais de multiples détails de sa conception.

ERIC OWEN MOSS

Eric Owen Moss Architects
8557 Higuera Street
Culver City, California 90232
USA

Tel: +1 310 839 1199
Fax: +1 310 839 7922
E-mail: mail@ericowenmoss.com
Web: www.ericowenmoss.com

The Umbrella ▶

Born in Los Angeles, California, in 1943, **ERIC OWEN MOSS** received his Bachelor of Arts degree from UCLA in 1965, and his M.Arch. from UC Berkeley in 1968. He also received a M.Arch. degree from Harvard in 1972. He opened his own firm, located in Culver City, California, in 1973. He has been a professor of design at the Southern California Institute of Architecture (SCI-Arc) since 1974, and has been director of the school since 2003. His built work includes the Central Housing Office, University of California, Irvine, California (1986–89); the Lindblade Tower, Culver City (1987–89); the Paramount Laundry, Culver City (1987–89); the Gary Group, Culver City (1988–90); The Box, Culver City (1990–94); the I. R.S. Building, Culver City (1993–94); and the Samitaur Complex, Culver City (1994–96). Recent built work includes the Stealth; the Umbrella; and the Beehive, all in Culver City, California. Other projects include Queens Museum of Art, Queens, New York (2001–03); a proposal for the Mariinsky Cultural Center, St. Petersburg (2001–03); New Holland, St. Petersburg (2001–03); the Jose Vasconcelos Library of Mexico, Mexico City (2003–04); the Conjunctive Points Theater Complex; the Gateway Art Tower; and a parking garage and offices (the Pterodactyl, 2007), located in Culver City.

ERIC OWEN MOSS, geboren 1943 in Los Angeles, erwarb 1965 den Bachelor of Arts an der University of California, Los Angeles (UCLA) und 1968 den Master of Architecture an der University of California, Berkeley, dem er 1972 einen weiteren Master of Architecture in Harvard hinzufügte. Ein Jahr später gründete er in Culver City in Kalifornien sein eigenes Büro. Seit 1974 hat er eine Professur für Entwurf am Southern California Institute of Architecture (SCI-Arc) inne, dessen Direktor er seit 2003 ist. Zu seinen ausgeführten Bauten zählen das Central Housing Office an der University of California in Irvine (1986–89), in Culver City der Lindblade Tower (1987–89), die Paramount Laundry (1987–89), Gary Group (1988–90), The Box (1990–94), das Gebäude der Steuerbehörde (1993–94) sowie der Samitaur-Komplex (1994–96). Ebenfalls in Culver City entstanden The Stealth, The Umbrella und The Beehive. Weitere Projekte sind das Kunstmuseum im New Yorker Stadtteil Queens (2001–03), ein Entwurf für das Mariinsky-Kulturzentrum in St. Petersburg (2001–03), Neuholland in St. Petersburg (2001–03), die mexikanische Jose-Vasconcelos-Bibliothek in Mexiko-Stadt (2003/04) sowie in Culver City der Conjunctive-Points-Theaterkomplex, der Gateway Art Tower und der Pterodactyl mit Parkhaus und Büros (2007).

Né en 1943 à Los Angeles, **ERIC OWEN MOSS** est diplômé en architecture de University of California, Los Angeles (Bachelor of Arts, 1965) et titulaire de deux masters : University of California, Berkeley (1968) et Harvard (1972). Il crée sa propre agence à Culver City en 1973 et enseigne la conception architecturale au Southern California Institute of Architecture (SCI-Arc) depuis 1974. Parmi ses réalisations aux États-Unis : Central Housing Office, University of California at Irvine (Irvine, 1986–89), à Culver City : Lindblade Tower (1987–89), Paramount Laundry (1987–89), Gary Group (1988–90), The Box (1990–94), le bâtiment du service des impôts (1993–94) et le complexe Samitaur (1994–96). C'est aussi à Culver City que se trouvent The Sealth, The Umbrella et The Beehive. Citons également : le Musée d'art dans le quartier de Queens, New York (2001–03), un projet pour le Centre culturel Mariinsky à Saint-Pétersbourg (2001–03), New Holland à Saint-Pétersbourg (2001–03), la Bibliothèque Jose-Vasconcelos à Mexico (2003–04), ainsi que le complexe théâtral Conjunctive Points, la Gateway Art Tower et le Pterodactyl (avec parking à étages et bureaux, 2007) à Culver City.

THE UMBRELLA

Culver City, California, USA, 1998–99

*Completion: 12/1999. Client: Samitaur Constructs.
Floor area: 1468 m².*

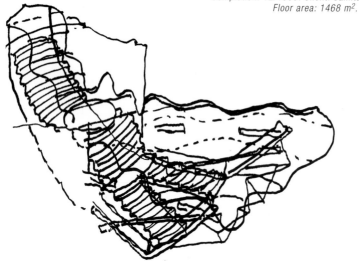
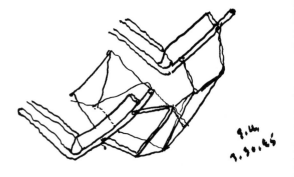

As he has done in other buildings in Culver City, Eric Owen Moss here adds a spectacular sculptural element to the outside of the corner of this structure.

Wie schon bei seinen anderen Bauprojekten in Culver City fügte Moss auch der Fassade dieses Gebäudes ein spektakulär gestaltetes plastisches Element hinzu.

Comme il l'a fait précédemment pour d'autres projets à Culver City, Eric Owen Moss greffe un élément sculptural spectaculaire à l'angle extérieur d'un bâtiment.

Part of the architect's ongoing effort to renovate industrial buildings in Culver City, sponsored by a promoter who owns the Hayden Tract in this district in Los Angeles, **THE UMBRELLA** is a 1468 m^2 project undertaken at a cost of $ 1 185 000. It consists of two contiguous warehouses built in the 1940s and renovated to provide 20 private office spaces, two conference areas and large open workspaces. According to Moss, the name "Umbrella" derives from "an experimental piece of construction." "It is a conceptual bowl," says the architect, "an arena the slope of which is determined by the curving top chord of two inverted wood trusses salvaged from the demolition of an adjacent project and inserted here." Like most of his Culver City projects, this renovation does not fundamentally alter the exterior forms of the existing structures but rather adds a sculptural element whose origin is linked to the spaces. It is this added piece that gives an unusual identity to the completed building.

Als Teil der laufenden Renovierungsarbeiten des Architekten an den Industriebauten in Culver City und gesponsert von einem Veranstalter, dem der Hayden Tract in diesem Distrikt von Los Angeles gehört, ist **THE UMBRELLA** (der Regenschirm) ein 1468 m^2 umfassendes Projekt, das für 1 850 000 $ realisiert wurde. Es besteht aus zwei aneinandergrenzenden Lagerhäusern aus den 1940er-Jahren, die nun zur Unterbringung von 20 Privatbüros, zwei Konferenzsälen und einigen großflächigen, offenen Arbeitsräumen umgebaut wurden. Laut Moss bezieht sich der Name „Umbrella" auf ein experimentelles Bauteil, das der Architekt so beschreibt: „Es beruht auf der Grundidee einer Schüssel und stellt eine Arena dar. Deren Schräge wird von der oberen gekrümmten Spannweite zweier nach innen gekehrter Balken vorgegeben, die beim Abriss eines benachbarten Gebäudes geborgen und hier eingesetzt wurden." Wie bei den meisten seiner Bauprojekte in Culver City verändert Moss bei dieser Renovierung die äußeren Formen der bestehenden Gebäude nicht grundlegend, sondern fügt lediglich ein plastisch gestaltetes Element hinzu, das sich auf die ursprünglichen Gebäude bezieht. Auch bei The Umbrella ist es dieses zusätzliche Element, das dem fertigen Gebäude seine Individualität verleiht.

Dans le cadre d'un programme permanent de rénovation de bâtiments industriels à Culver City financé par le promoteur propriétaire du Hayden Tract, **THE UMBRELLA** (le parapluie) est un projet de $ 1 885 000 pour une surface de 1468 m^2. Il se compose de deux entrepôts contigus édifiés dans les années 1940 puis transformés par Moss en 20 bureaux indépendants, deux salles de conférence et de vastes plateaux ouverts. Selon l'architecte, le nom de « Umbrella » désigne « une construction expérimentale. Un ‹ bol › conceptuel, une arène, dont la pente est déterminée par la courbe supérieure de deux fermes de bois récupérées dans la démolition d'un projet voisin… » Comme pour la plupart de ses réalisations à Culver City, cette rénovation ne modifie pas fondamentalement les formes extérieures des constructions existantes, mais leur ajoute un élément sculptural lié à la nature de chaque espace. C'est cet ajout qui confère à chaque bâtiment son identité originale.

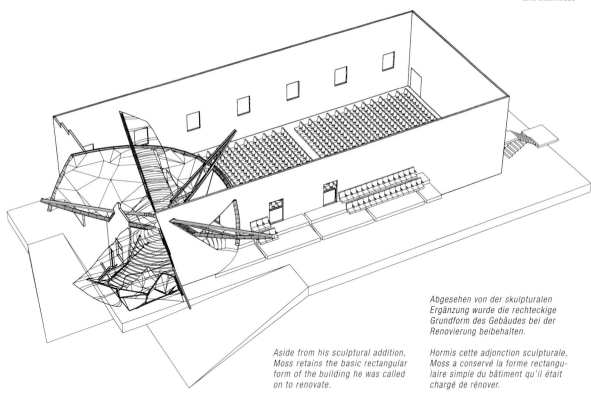

Aside from his sculptural addition, Moss retains the basic rectangular form of the building he was called on to renovate.

Abgesehen von der skulpturalen Ergänzung wurde die rechteckige Grundform des Gebäudes bei der Renovierung beibehalten.

Hormis cette adjonction sculpturale, Moss a conservé la forme rectangulaire simple du bâtiment qu'il était chargé de rénover.

Inside the building, Moss uses his sense of materials and complex spaces to enliven the visitor's experience. Thus a run-down warehouse is transformed into a up-to-date office.

Im Inneren steigert Moss das Raumgefühl mit dem ihm eigenen Gespür für Materialien und komplexe Räume und verwandelt ein baufälliges Lagerhaus in ein modernes Büro.

Moss use de son sens des matériaux et des espaces complexes pour créer un univers stimulant. Un entrepôt abandonné se transforme en bureaux d'avant-garde.

GLENN MURCUTT

Glenn Murcutt & Associates P/L
Sydney, Australia

Private Residence ►

GLENN MURCUTT was born in London in 1936 of Australian parents. He received his Diploma of Architecture from the Sydney Technical College (UNSW) in 1961 and joined Ancher Mortlock Murray & Woolley Architects, Sydney from 1964 to 1969 before he established his own practice in 1969. He has taught at numerous universities, among them the University of Pennsylvania, Philadelphia, (1990/91/95); University of Technology, Sydney (1990/92/95); University of Arizona, Tucson, (1991); University of Technology, Helsinki, Finland (1994); University of Hawaii, Honolulu (1996); University of Texas at Austin (1997); University of Virginia, Charlottesville (1997); School of Architecture, Aarhus, Denmark (1999); in 2001 he held the William Henry Bishop Chair at Yale University. He was honored with national and international awards such as the Alvar Aalto medal (1992), Royal Australian Institute of Architects Gold Medal (1992), and the Thomas Jefferson Medal for Architecture (2001). He has traveled extensively in Europe and the United States. His built work in Australia includes numerous private houses, such as the Magney House (Bingi Point, New South Wales, 1982–84), the Meagher House (Bowral, New South Wales, 1988–92), or the Marika-Alderton House (Yirrkala, Northern Territory, 1991–94), a private residence (Mount Wilson, New South Wales, 1989–94), the Museum of Local History and the Tourism Office (Kempsey, New South Wales, 1979–82, 1986–88), a restaurant (Berowra Waters, Sydney, 1977–78, 1982–83), and The Arthur and Yvonne Boyd Education Centre, Riversdale, West Cambewarra, New South Wales, Australia (1995–98).

GLENN MURCUTT wurde 1936 als Sohn australischer Eltern in London geboren. Sein Studium am Sydney Technical College der University of New South Wales schloss er 1961 mit dem Diplom ab. Von 1964 bis 1969 arbeitete er für Ancher Mortlock Murray & Woolley Architects, Sydney. 1969 gründete er sein eigenes Büro. Er lehrte an zahlreichen Universitäten, u.a. an der University of Pennsylvania, Philadelphia, (1990/91/95), University of Technology, Sydney (1990/92/95), University of Arizona, Tucson (1991), University of Technology, Helsinki, Finnland (1994), University of Hawaii, Honolulu (1996), University of Texas at Austin (1997), University of Virginia, Charlottesville (1997), School of Architecture, Aarhus, Dänemark (1999), und hatte 2001 den William-Henry-Bishop-Lehrstuhl an der Yale University inne. Er unternahm ausgedehnte Reisen nach Europa und in die Vereinigten Staaten. Er wurde u.a. mit folgenden nationalen und internationalen Preisen ausgezeichnet: Alvar Aalto Medal (1992), Royal Australian Institute of Architects Gold Medal (1992) und der Thomas Jefferson Medal for Architecture (2001). Sein Werk umfasst zahlreiche Privathäuser: Haus Magney in Bingi Point, NSW (1982–84), Haus Meagher in Bowral, NSW (1988–92), und Haus Marika-Alderton in Yirrkala, Northern Territory (1991–94). Außerdem entwarf er das lokalgeschichtliche Museum und Fremdenverkehrsamt in Kempsey, NSW (1979–82, 1986–88), das Restaurant Berowra Waters in Sydney (1977–78, 1982–83) und das Arthur and Yvonne Boyd Education Centre, Riversdale, West Cambewarra, NSW, Australien.

GLENN MURCUTT naît à Londres en 1936 de parents australiens. Il étudie au Sydney Technical College de l'Université de Galles du Sud, dont il obtient le diplôme d'architecte en 1961. De 1964 à 1969, il travaille pour Ancher Mortlock Murray & Wooley architectes à Sydney et crée sa propre agence en 1969. Il a enseigné dans de nombreuses universités parmi lesquelles : University of Pennsylvania, Philadelphia, (1990/91/95), University of Technology, Sydney (1990/92/95), University of Arizona, Tucson, (1991), University of Technology, Helsinki, Finlande (1994), University of Hawaii, Honolulu, (1996), University of Texas at Austin (1997), University of Virginia, Charlottesville, (1997), School of Architecture, Aarhus, Danemark (1999), et a été professeur à l'Université de Yale en 2001. Il a beaucoup voyagé en Europe et aux États-Unis. Il a obtenu des prix nationaux et internationaux dont l'Alvar Aalto Medal (1992), la Royal Australian Institute of Architects Gold Medal (1992), et le Thomas Jefferson Medal for Architecture (2001). Parmi ses réalisations en Australie : de nombreuses maisons privées dont la Magney House (Bingi Point, NSW, 1982–84), la Meagher House (Bowral, NSW, 1988–92), ou la Marika-Alderton House (Yirrkala, Northern Territory, 1991–94), ainsi que le musée d'histoire locale et l'office du tourisme de Kempsey, NSW, (1979–82, 1986–88), le restaurant Berowra Waters à Sydney (1977–78, 1982–83) et le centre d'éducation, Riversdale, West Cambewarra, NSW, Australie.

PRIVATE RESIDENCE

Mount Wilson, New South Wales, Australia, 1989–94

Client: withheld. Costs: AU$ 2300/m².

Situated in the Blue Mountains, 150 km northwest of Sydney, this **RESIDENCE** is set on a 3-hectare site at an altitude of 1000 m. The spartan design for a retired couple includes a house and an atelier, which is separated by an elevated wooden walkway and a basin. This presence of wood is exceptional in a house that is made of aluminum, painted steel, glass, and polished concrete for the floors. Characterized by an evident horizontality, the house is strictly aligned except for the atelier, which is set at a slight angle to the rest of the composition because of a rock outcropping. The house faces toward the east and northeast, and the bedrooms are lodged toward the rear under the lower point of the sloping roof. The inclined roof and rectilinear layout bring to mind Murcutt's Meagher House (Bowral, New South Wales, 1988–92). Despite its apparently extreme austerity and simplicity, the house took more than five years to design and build.

Das in den Blue Mountains 150 km nordwestlich von Sydney gelegene **HAUS** steht auf einem 3 ha großen Grundstück in 1000 m Höhe. Der spartanische Entwurf umfasst ein Wohnhaus und ein Atelier, die durch einen erhöhten hölzernen Steg verbunden sind, sowie ein Wasserbecken. Die Verwendung von Holz bei einem Haus aus Aluminium, gestrichenem Stahl, Glas und geschliffenen Betonböden wirkt außergewöhnlich. Das lang gestreckte Gebäude ist streng rechtwinklig ausgerichtet, mit Ausnahme des Ateliers, das einem Felsen ausweicht und im leichten Winkel zum Rest der Anlage steht. Das Gebäude ist nach Osten und Nordosten orientiert; die Schlafräume liegen im rückwärtigen Bereich unter der tiefer gezogenen Seite des Schrägdachs. Dies und der rechtwinklige Grundriss erinnern an Murcutts Haus Meagher (Bowral, NSW, 1988–92). Trotz seiner extremen Strenge und Schlichtheit betrugen Planungs- und Bauzeit mehr als fünf Jahre.

Située dans les Blue Montains, à 150 km au nord-ouest de Sydney, cette **RÉSIDENCE** se dresse sur un terrain de 3 hectares à 1000 m d'altitude. Ce projet spartiate conçu pour un couple de retraités comprend une maison et un atelier séparés par une allée de bois surélevée et un bassin. La présence du bois est étonnante dans cette maison toute d'aluminium, acier laqué, verre et sols de béton poli. Résolument horizontal, le plan de la maison est entièrement aligné, à l'exception de l'atelier implanté légèrement en biais pour éviter un affleurement de rocher. La façade regarde vers l'est et le nord-est et les chambres sont installées à l'arrière, sous la partie la plus basse du toit. L'inclinaison de celui-ci et le plan rectiligne font penser à la Meagher House, également de Murcutt (Bowral, Nouvelle-Galles du Sud, 1988–92). Malgré cette apparente austère simplicité, il a fallu plus de cinq ans pour concevoir et construire la maison.

Mixing the idea of an ephemeral shed with a bright, clear architecture, Murcutt creates this modern refuge.

Murcutt verbindet hier die Vorstellung von einem einfachen Schuppen mit einer hellen, klaren Architektur.

Refuge moderne, imaginé par Murcutt à partir de principes de simplicité et de luminosité.

Set into the woods and responding to them, the house nonetheless carves out a domain of its own.

Trotz seiner Einbindung in die Natur bewahrt das Haus durch seine strengen Formen seine Eigenständigkeit.

Au milieu des bois et en harmonie avec eux, la maison n'en a pas moins su se créer son territoire.

TAKEHIKO NAGAKURA

Takehiko Nagakura
Associate Professor of Design and Computation
Department of Architecture
Massachusetts Institute of Technology
77 Massachusetts Avenue, 10-472M
Cambridge, Massachusetts 02139
USA

Tel: +1 617 253 0781
E-mail: takehiko@mit.edu

TAKEHIKO NAGAKURA is an architect from Tokyo. He received undergraduate education in architectural design under Professor Fumihiko Maki at the University of Tokyo and was a Ishizaka Memorial Foundation Scholar (1985-87) while he studied in the M.Arch. program at the Harvard University Graduate School of Design (GSD). He has served as Associate Professor of Design and Computation at the Department of Architecture of the Massachusetts Institute of Technology (MIT) since 1999. After graduation from GSD, Nagakura established a design practice in Japan, where he is a registered architect and engaged in building projects in Tokyo and Okinawa. His project for the Gushikawa Orchid Center in Okinawa was selected for the SD Review Award in 1998. Nagakura, together with research scientist Kent Larson, initiated Team Unbuilt, which developed computer graphics visualizations of significant unbuilt projects of early Modernism.

All following images were originally developed at the Massachusetts Institute of Technology by Team Unbuilt, sponsored by the Takenaka Corporation of Japan under supervision of Takehiko Nagakura and Kent Larson.

TAKEHIKO NAGAKURA wurde in Tokio geboren. Er studierte Architektur bei Professor Fumihiko Maki an der Universität Tokio und von 1985 bis 1987 als Stipendiat der Ishizaka Memorial Foundation an der Harvard University's Graduate School of Design (GSD), wo er den Master of Architecture erwarb. Seit 1999 ist er als Professor für Entwurf und Computersimulation im Fachbereich Architektur des Massachusetts Institute of Technology (MIT) tätig. Nach seinem Abschluss an der GSD eröffnete Nagakura ein Planungsbüro in Japan, wo er mehrere Bauprojekte in Tokio und Okinawa ausführte. Sein Entwurf für das Gushikawa Orchid Center in Okinawa wurde 1998 mit dem SD Review Award ausgezeichnet. Zusammen mit dem Forscher Kent Larson initiierte Nagakura das Team Unbuilt, das Computergrafiken zur Veranschaulichung bedeutender, aber unrealisiert gebliebener Architekturentwürfe der frühen Moderne entwickelte.

Die folgenden Bilder wurden mit finanzieller Unterstützung der Takenaka Corporation of Japan unter Leitung von Takehiko Nagakura und Kent Larson vom Team Unbuilt am Massachusetts Institute of Technology (MIT) entwickelt.

TAKEHIKO NAGAKURA est un architect basé à Tokyo. Il étudie la conception architecturale auprès du Professeur Fumihiko Maki à l'Université de Tokyo, et obtient une bourse de la Fondation mémoriale Ishikaza (1985-87) pour son Master of Architecture de la Graduate School of Design de l'Université de Harvard. Depuis 1999, il est professeur de conception et d'informatique au département d'architecture du Massachusetts Institute of Technology (MIT). Actif au Japon, il travaille sur des projets à Tokyo et Okinawa. Son projet pour le centre de l'orchidée Gushikawa à Okinawa a été sélectionné pour le SD Review Award (1998). En compagnie du chercheur Kent Larson, il a créé le Team Unbuilt qui se propose de visualiser par des moyens informatiques d'importants projets modernistes jamais réalisés.

Toutes les images publiées ici ont été développées au Massachusetts Institute of Technology par Team Unbuilt, financé par la Takenaka Corporation of Japan et supervisé par Takehiko Nagakura et de Kent Larson.

MONUMENT TO THE THIRD INTERNATIONAL

Petrograd, Soviet Union, 1919/98

Computer Graphics Visualization Project. Producer/Director: Takehiko Nagakura.
Computer graphics: Andrzej Zarzycki, Takehiko Nagakura, Dan Brick, Mark Sich.
Production period: 1997–98. Film length: 3 min. 10 sec.
Funding support: Takenaka Corporation.

Vladimir Tatlin's Constructivist project for a **MONUMENT TO THE THIRD INTERNATIONAL** was a machine in which the various sections would rotate within an exposed steel armature. Because of Stalin's dislike of modern architecture, the tower was never completed. Its foundation was later used for an outdoor swimming pool. "Tatlin was a sculptor," says Nagakura, "and his project was a wildly shaped 400 m tower in the middle of the great classic city of St. Petersburg (then Petrograd). The computer graphics (by Takehiko Nagakura, Andrzej Zarzycki, Dan Brick, and Mark Sich) attempt to show the visual effect that this jarring addition would have today, with its double-spiral form, rusting-iron materiality and enormous out-scaled size, none of which had any precedents in the context of the old Russian city."

Wladimir Tatlins konstruktivistischer Entwurf für das **MONUMENT DER DRITTEN INTERNATIONALE** war eine Maschine, deren verschiedene Teile innerhalb einer freiliegenden Stahlkonstruktion rotieren sollten. Wegen Stalins Abneigung gegen moderne Architektur wurde dieser Turm jedoch nie realisiert. Sein Fundament wurde später für ein Freibad genutzt. „Tatlin war Bildhauer", erklärt Nagakura, „und sein Projekt war ein kühn geformter 400 m hoher Turm, der mitten im klassizistischen Zentrum von Petrograd, dem heutigen St. Petersburg, stehen sollte. Die Computergrafiken (von Takehiko Nagakura, Andrzej Zarzycki, Dan Brick und Mark Sich) versuchen deutlich zu machen, welche optische Wirkung dieses Bauwerk heute haben würde: Mit seiner Gestalt in Form einer Doppelspirale, der Massivität des rostigen Stahls und seiner enormen Größe verkörpert es Eigenschaften, für die es in dieser alten russischen Stadt keinerlei Vorläufer gab."

Le projet constructiviste de **MONUMENT À LA IIIᵉ INTERNATIONALE** proposé par Vladimir Tatline était en fait une machine dont les diverses sections devaient tourner à l'intérieur d'une armature d'acier. Staline n'appréciant pas l'architecture moderne, la tour ne fut jamais achevée. Par la suite, ses fondations servirent à la construction d'une piscine en plein air. « Tatline était un sculpteur », explique Nagakura, « et son projet était celui d'une incroyable tour au milieu de cette grande cité néoclassique qu'est Saint-Pétersbourg. Le traitement en image de synthèse (par Takehiko Nagakura, Andrzej Zarzycki, Dan Brick et Mark Sich) tente de montrer l'effet visuel que cette provocante incursion exercerait aujourd'hui, avec sa double spirale, son aspect de fer rouillé et ses gigantesques dimensions, sans précédent dans le contexte de l'ancienne capitale impériale. »

Takehiko Nagakura and his Team Unbuilt group at MIT chose to give their
computer perspectives of Tatlin's
Monument to the Third International
the look and feeling of an aging
structure, as though the monument
had actually been built in 1919.

Nagakura und seine Gruppe am MIT,
Team Unbuilt, gaben ihren Computer-
ansichten von Tatlins Monument der
Dritten Internationale das Aussehen
und die Aura eines gealterten Bauwerks, um den Eindruck zu erzeugen,
es sei tatsächlich 1919 erbaut
worden.

Takehiko Nagakura et son équipe
Team Unbuilt du MIT ont choisi de
traiter en image de synthèse le
Monument à la troisième Internationale de Tatline, en vieillissant
artificiellement la construction,
comme si elle avait été réalisée.

PALACE OF THE SOVIETS

Moscow, Soviet Union, 1931/98

Computer Graphics Visualization Project. Producer/Director: Takehiko Nagakura.
Computer graphics: Shinsuke Baba. Production period: 1997–98. Film length: 5 min. 20 sec.
Funding support: Takenaka Corporation.
(Unrealized project by Le Corbusier, graphic interpretation by responsibility of the author.)

During a trip to Moscow, Le Corbusier came into contact with the Constructivists. As Takehiko Nagakura says, "In 1931, Le Corbusier participated in and lost the competition for the **PALACE OF THE SOVIETS**. Corbusier's entry comprised two symmetric structures: a roof suspended by a giant arch, and another folded roof, along the riverside of Moscow. Corbusier's exterior model for this project has been well published in the architectural media, but its interior space had existed only in the mind of the architect. The computer graphics (by Shinsuke Baba) attempt here to put viewers at the foot of the giant arch and to let the visitor proceed inside of this widely acknowledged modern masterpiece for the first time."

Während einer Reise nach Moskau kam Le Corbusier mit den russischen Konstruktivisten in Kontakt. Takehiko Nagakura meint: „1931 nahm Le Corbusier am Wettbewerb für den **PALAST DER SOWJETS** teil, den er jedoch verlor. Sein Beitrag bestand aus zwei symmetrischen Strukturen: einem Dach, das an einem riesigen Bogen aufgehängt, und einem weiteren Faltdach, das zum Flussufer ausgerichtet war. Le Corbusiers Modell vom Äußeren des Baus wurde in zahlreichen Architekturzeitschriften veröffentlicht, während die Innenraumgestaltung bislang nur in der Vorstellung des Architekten existierte. Die Computergrafiken (von Shinsuke Baba) führen nun den Besucher zum ersten Mal vom Fuß des riesigen Bogens in das Innere dieses berühmten Meisterwerks der Moderne."

Lors d'un voyage à Moscou, Le Corbusier entra en contact avec les constructivistes russes. Comme le fait remarquer Takehiko Nagakura : « En 1931, Le Corbusier avait participé au concours pour le **PALAIS DES SOVIETS** qu'il avait perdu. Son projet comprenait deux constructions symétriques : un toit suspendu à une arche géante et un toit replié le long de la Moscova. La maquette de l'extérieur de ce projet a été amplement publiée dans la presse architecturale, mais l'intérieur n'existait que dans l'esprit de Le Corbusier. Les images de synthèse (de Shinsuke Baba) placent le visiteur au pied de l'arche géante et, pour la première fois, le font pénétrer à l'intérieur de ce chef-d'œuvre reconnu de l'architecture moderne. »

Using their knowledge of the original architectural plans and software capable of modeling light patterns, Nagakura and Team Unbuilt virtually resurrected this essentially unknown masterpiece.

In Kenntnis der Originalentwürfe und einer Software, die selbst die Wirkung des Lichteinfalls veranschaulichen kann, erweckten Nagakura und sein Team Unbuilt dieses fast unbekannte Meisterwerk zu virtuellem Leben.

À partir de leur connaissance des plans d'origine et de leur maîtrise du traitement de la lumière par ordinateur, Nagakura et Team Unbuilt ont littéralement donné vie à ce chef-d'œuvre en grande partie inconnu.

NEUTELINGS RIEDIJK

Neutelings Riedijk Architecten bv
P. O. Box 527
3000 AM Rotterdam
The Netherlands

Tel: +31 10 404 6677
E-mail: info@neutelings-riedijk.com
Web: www.neutelings-riedijk.com

WILLEM JAN NEUTELINGS was born in 1959 in Bergen op Zoom. He studied at the Technical University in Delft (1977–81), before working for OMA with Rem Koolhaas (1981–86). He has taught at the Academy of Architecture in Rotterdam and at the Berlage Institute in Amsterdam (1990–99). **MICHIEL RIEDIJK** was born in Geldrop, The Netherlands, in 1964. He attended the Technical University in Delft (1983–89), before working with J. D. Bekkering in Amsterdam (1989–91). He has also taught at the Technical Univeristy in Delft and Eindhoven, and at the Academies of Architecture in Amsterdam, Rotterdam and Maastricht since 1990. Their built work, mainly in The Netherlands, includes the Prinsenhoek Residential Complex (Sittard, 1992–95); Tilburg Housing (1993–96); Hollainhof Social Housing (Ghent, Belgium, 1993–98); Borneo Sporenburg Housing (Amsterdam, 1994–97); Lakeshore Housing (Huizen, 1994–2003); and building for Veenman Printers (Ede, 1995–97). One of their most widely published projects is the Minnaert Building (Utrecht, 1994–98). They have also built fire stations in Breda (1996–98) and Maastricht (1996–99). In 2004, they won the competition for the Kolizej Centre in Ljubljana, Slovenia, which is to include a 1400-seat concert hall, 25 000 square meters of office space, 100 apartments, a shopping arcade, and a parking lot. They completed the Shipping and Transport College in Rotterdam in 2005, and the Netherlands Institute for Sound and Vision in Hilversum in 2006.

WILLEM JAN NEUTELINGS wurde 1959 in Bergen op Zoom geboren. Er studierte an der Technischen Universität in Delft (1977–81), ehe er von 1981 bis 1986 bei OMA mit Rem Koolhaas arbeitete. Anschließend lehrte er an der Architekturakademie in Rotterdam und am Berlage-Institut in Amsterdam (1990–99). **MICHIEL RIEDIJK** wurde 1964 in Geldorp in den Niederlanden geboren. Er besuchte die Technische Universität in Delft (1983–89), ehe er mit J. D. Bekkering in Amsterdam arbeitete (1989–91). Seit 1990 lehrt er an den Technischen Universitäten Delft und Eindhoven sowie an den Architekturakademien in Amsterdam, Rotterdam und Maastricht. Zu den gemeinsamen Bauten der beiden, fast alle in den Niederlanden, gehören: Wohnanlage Prinsenhoek (Sittard, 1992–95), Wohnbauten Tilburg (1993–96), Sozialwohnungen Hollainhof (Gent, Belgien, 1993–98), Wohnbauten Borneo Sporenburg (Amsterdam, 1994–97), Lakeshore Housing (Huizen, 1994–2003) und das Gebäude für Veenman Printers (Ede, 1995–97). Eines ihrer bekanntesten Projekte ist das Minnaert-Gebäude (Utrecht, 1994–98). Außerdem erbauten sie Feuerwachen in Breda (1996–98) und Maastricht (1996–99). 2004 gewannen sie den Wettbewerb für das Kolizej-Zentrum in Ljubljana, Slowenien, zu dem eine Konzerthalle mit 1400 Plätzen, 25 000 m² Bürofläche, 100 Apartments, eine Ladenpassage und ein Parkgelände gehören sollen. 2005 stellten sie die Hochschule für Schifffahrts- und Transportwesen in Rotterdam fertig und 2006 das Niederländische Institut für Bild und Ton in Hilversum.

WILLEM JAN NEUTELINGS, né en 1959 à Bergen Op Zoom, Pays-Bas, a étudié à l'Université Technique de Delft (1977–81) et travaillé pour l'Office for Metropolitan Architecture de Rem Koolhaas (1981–86). Il a enseigné à l'Académie d'architecture de Rotterdam et au Berlage Institute d'Amsterdam (1990–99). **MICHIEL RIEDIJK**, né à Geldrop, Pays-Bas, en 1964, a étudié à l'Université Technique de Delft (1983–89), avant de travailler avec J. D. Bekkering à Amsterdam (1989–91). Depuis 1990, il enseigne en outre à l'Université Technique de Delft et d'Eindhoven et aux Académies d'architecture d'Amsterdam, Rotterdam et Maastricht. Parmi leurs réalisations, dont la plupart aux Pays-Bas : le Complexe résidentiel de Prinsenhoek, Sittard (1992–95) ; un immeuble d'appartements à Tilburg (1993–96) ; l'immeuble de logements Borneo Sporenburg, Amsterdam (1994–97) ; des logements à Lakeshore, Huizen (1994–2003) ; l'immeuble de Veenman Printers, Ede (1995–97). L'un de leurs projets les plus publiés est l'immeuble Minnaert, Utrecht (1994–98). Ils ont construit des casernes de pompiers à Breda (1996–98) et Maastricht (1996–99). En 2004, ils ont remporté le concours pour le Centre Kolizej à Ljubljana, Slovénie, comprenant une salle de concert de 1400 places, 25 000 m² de bureaux, 100 appartements, un centre commercial et un parking. Ils ont achevé le Collège de la navigation et des transports en 2005 et l'Institut néerlandais de l'audiovisuel à Hilversum en 2006.

MINNAERT BUILDING

Utrecht, The Netherlands, 1994–97

Planning: 1994–96. Construction: 1996–97.
Client: University of Utrecht. Floor area: c. 9000 m².

Located on the campus of Uithof University, the **MINNAERT BUILDING** includes three main components – a restaurant, classrooms and laboratories, and workspace. Characterized by its sienna pigmented undulating skin of sprayed concrete, the building includes a 50 x 10 m pond that collects rainwater and is situated in a main hall. The water is pumped in and out of the building by the roof for cooling purposes. Water falls into the basin during rainy periods, adding the element of sound to a composition that intends to evoke the five senses. Large-scale letters spelling the name Minnaert replace columns on part of the south elevation, making the building immediately recognizable to passersby.

Das **MINNAERT-GEBÄUDE** liegt auf dem Uithof-Campus der Universität Utrecht und besteht aus drei Bauteilen, in denen ein Restaurant, Klassen- und Arbeitsräume sowie Laboratorien untergebracht sind. Das durch seine ockerfarben pigmentierte und gewellte Haut aus gespritztem Beton gekennzeichnete Gebäude besitzt in der Haupthalle einen 50 x 10 m großen Brunnen, in dem Regenwasser aufgefangen wird. Zum Zweck der Kühlung wird das Wasser vom Dach aus in das Gebäude hinein- und wieder herausgepumpt. Wenn es regnet, fällt Wasser in das Becken, was der Komposition, die alle Sinne ansprechen will, das akustische Element hinzufügt. Auf der Südseite ruht der Bau auf Stützen in Form von großformatigen Buchstaben. Diese ergeben den Namen Minnaert, wodurch das Gebäude für Passanten sofort kenntlich gemacht wird.

Situé sur le campus de l'Université Uithof, ce bâtiment se compose de trois parties principales : un restaurant, des salles de cours et des laboratoires. Caractérisé par sa peau externe ondulée en béton projeté de couleur terre de Sienne, il possède un bassin de 50 x 10 m dans le hall principal qui récupère les eaux de pluie ; cet élément sonore enrichit une composition qui évoque les cinq sens. L'eau est pompée ou rejetée sur le toit en fonction de la température. Les énormes lettres qui composent le nom de **MINNAERT** remplacent les colonnes sur la façade sud et rendent le bâtiment facilement identifiable.

As the drawing (below right) shows, the architects share a typical Dutch concern for the environmental efficiency of their building, this in spite of the rather massive appearance of the structure.

Das Minnaert-Gebäude ist nach umweltfreundlichen Gesichtspunkten konzipiert (unten rechts). Diese energiesparende Bauweise, die in den Niederlanden Tradition hat, ist an den eher massiv und geschlossen wirkenden Oberflächen nicht ablesbar.

Le dessin en bas à droite montre que les architectes ont conçu le bâtiment dans un souci de respect de l'environnement traditionnel aux Pays-Bas, préoccupation qui ne transparaît pas dans l'aspect massif de sa structure.

The rather heavy feeling of the interior spaces is somewhat alleviated by the use of some bright colors. The angled ceilings and walls are typical of the architects.

Die eher schweren Innenräume werden durch einige helle Farbtöne aufgelockert. Charakteristisch für den Stil des Büros sind die schrägen Decken und Wände.

Une certaine lourdeur perçue dans les espaces intérieurs est allégée par le recours à des couleurs vives. Les plafonds et les murs inclinés sont typiques du style des architectes.

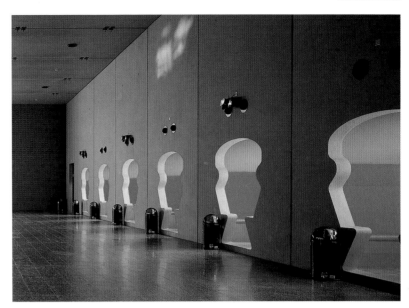

OSCAR NIEMEYER

Fundação Oscar Niemeyer
R. Conde lages, 25
CEP: 22610-210, Rio de Janeiro, RJ
Brazil

Tel/Fax: +55 21 2509 1844
E-mail: arquitetura@oscarniemeyer.com.br
www.niemeyer.org.br

Born in Rio de Janeiro in 1907, **OSCAR NIEMEYER** studied at the Escola Nacional de Belas Artes. He graduated in 1934 and joined a team of Brazilian architects collaborating with Le Corbusier on a new Ministry of Education and Health in Rio de Janeiro. It was Lucio Costa, for whom he worked as an assistant, who introduced Niemeyer to Le Corbusier. Between 1940 and 1954, his work was based in three cities: Rio de Janeiro, São Paulo and Belo Horizonte. In 1956, Niemeyer was appointed architectural adviser to Nova Cap—an organization responsible for implementing Lúcio Costa's plans for Brazil's new capital, Brasília. The following year, he became its chief architect, designing most of the city's important buildings. In 1964, he sought exile in France for political reasons. There, amongst other structures, he designed the building for the French Communist Party, in Paris. With the end of the dictatorship, he returned to Brazil, immediately resuming his professional activities. He was awarded the Gold Medal of the American Institute of Architecture in 1970 and the 1988 Pritzker Prize. Niemeyer continued to work on numerous large projects beyond his 100th birthday, including an Administrative Center for the province of Minas Gerais in Belo Horizonte; an Auditorium completed in 2005 to celebrate the 50th anniversary of his Ibirapuera Park in São Paulo; and a Cultural Center in Goiânia completed in 2007. Oscar Niemeyer died in 2012.

Der 1907 in Rio de Janeiro geborene **OSCAR NIEMEYER** studierte an der Escola Nacional de Belas Artes. Er machte seinen Abschluss 1934 und schloss sich einem Team brasilianischer Architekten an, die mit Le Corbusier beim Bau eines neuen Ministeriums für Erziehung und Gesundheit zusammenarbeiteten. Er war Assistent bei Lúcio Costa, der ihn mit Le Corbusier bekannt machte. Zwischen 1940 und 1954 baute er in drei Städten: Rio de Janeiro, São Paulo und Belo Horizonte. 1956 wurde Niemeyer zum architektonischen Berater von Nova Cap berufen – einer Organisation, die für die Umsetzung von Lucio Costas Plänen für Brasília, die neue Hauptstadt Brasiliens, verantwortlich war. Im folgenden Jahr wurde er leitender Architekt von Nova Cap und entwarf die meisten wichtigen Bauten der Stadt. Aus politischen Gründen ging er 1964 ins Exil nach Frankreich. Dort entwarf er u. a. das Gebäude der Kommunistischen Partei Frankreichs in Paris. Nach dem Ende der Diktatur in Brasilien kehrte er dorthin zurück und nahm seine Arbeit unverzüglich wieder auf. 1970 erhielt er die Goldmedaille des American Institute of Architecture und 1988 den Pritzker-Preis. Auch als über 100-Jähriger arbeitete Niemeyer an zahlreichen Großprojekten, darunter ein Verwaltungszentrum für die Provinz Minas Gerais in Belo Horizonte, ein zur Feier des 50. Jahrestags seines Ibirapuera-Parks in São Paulo 2005 fertiggestelltes Auditorium sowie das 2007 vollendete Kulturzentrum von Goiânia. Oscar Niemeyer verstarb Ende 2012.

Né à Rio de Janeiro en 1907, **OSCAR NIEMEYER** étudie à la Escola Nacional de Belas Artes. Diplômé en 1934, il fait partie de l'équipe d'architectes brésiliens qui collabore avec Le Corbusier sur le projet du nouveau ministère de l'éducation et de la santé à Rio. Lúcio Costa, dont il est l'assistant, l'introduit auprès de Le Corbusier. De 1940 à 1954, il intervient essentiellement dans trois villes : Rio de Janeiro, São Paulo et Belo Horizonte. En 1956, il est nommé conseiller pour l'architecture de Nova Cap, organisme chargé de la mise en œuvre des plans de Costa pour la nouvelle capitale, Brasília. L'année suivante, il en devient l'architecte en chef, dessinant la plupart de ses bâtiments importants. En 1964, il s'exile en France pour des raisons politiques, où il construit entre autres le siège du parti communiste à Paris. À la fin de la dictature, il retourne au Brésil, et reprend immédiatement ses responsabilités professionnelles. Il reçoit la médaille d'or de l'American Institute of Architecture en 1970 et le Pritzker Prize en 1988. Même centenaire Niemeyer n'en continue pas moins à travailler sur de nombreux projets, dont un Centre administratif pour l'État du Minas Gerais à Bel Horizonte ; un auditorium achevé en 2005 pour la célébration du 50ᵉ anniversaire de son parc d'Ibirapuera à São Paulo et le Centre culturel à Goiânia, achevé en 2007. Oscar Niemeyer est décédé fin 2012.

SERPENTINE GALLERY PAVILION 2003

Kensington Gardens, London, UK, 2003

Client: Serpentine Gallery, Kensington Gardens. Floor area: 250 m². Costs: not specified.

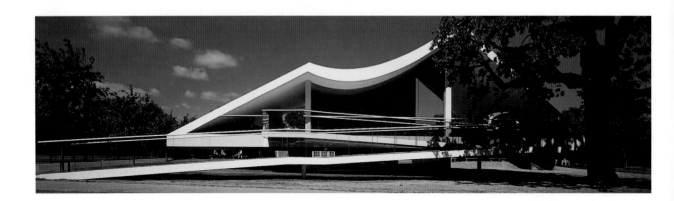

"I am delighted to be designing the **SERPENTINE GALLERY PAVILION**, my first structure in the United Kingdom," wrote Oscar Niemeyer. "My idea was to keep this project different, free and audacious. That is what I prefer. I like to draw, I like to see from the blank sheet of paper a palace, a cathedral, the figure of a woman appearing. But life for me is much more important than architecture." In these times of computer-generated architecture, it is a rare privilege to see the recent work of an architect who worked with Le Corbusier in the mid-1930s. The pavilion he created for the Serpentine Gallery does have very much the spirit of one of his own sketches brought to life. After first refusing to design this small structure, Niemeyer accepted when the director of the Serpentine, Julia Peyton-Jones, went to Rio to meet him. One of his long-time collaborators, the engineer Jose Carlos Sussekind, and Arup in London actually made certain that the pavilion was built. Made of concrete and steel, the structure looks more like a permanent addition to the Kensington Gardens than it is. "My architecture followed the old examples," said Niemeyer when he received the 1988 Pritzker Prize. "The beauty prevailing over the limitations of the constructive logic. My work proceeded, indifferent to the unavoidable criticism set forth by those who take the trouble to examine the minimum details, so very true of what mediocrity is capable of." It appears that in these circumstances, Niemeyer wanted to create nothing else than a resumé of his own work. "I wanted to give a flavor of everything that characterizes my work," he said to *The Financial Times*. "The first thing was to create something floating above the ground. In a small building occupying a small space, using concrete, and few supports and girders, we can give an idea of what my architecture is all about."

„Ich bin hocherfreut, den **SERPENTINE GALLERY PAVILION** zu entwerfen, mein erstes Bauwerk in Großbritannien", schrieb Oscar Niemeyer. „Meine Idee war, dieses Projekt anders wirken zu lassen – frei und verwegen. Das ist es, was ich bevorzuge. Ich zeichne gern, und ich mag es, auf einem weißen Blatt Papier einen Palast, eine Kathedrale, die Gestalt einer näher kommenden Frau entstehen zu sehen. Aber das Leben ist für mich viel wichtiger als die Architektur." In diesen Zeiten computer-generierten Gestaltens ist es ein seltenes Privileg, die neueste Arbeit eines Architekten zu sehen, der schon Mitte der 1930er-Jahre mit Le Corbusier zusammengearbeitet hat. Der von Niemeyer entworfene Pavillon hat in der Tat eine spirituelle Energie – er wirkt, als sei seine Zeichnung zum Leben erwacht. Die aus Beton und Stahl bestehende Konstruktion sieht allerdings dauerhafter aus, als sie wirklich ist. Der Architekt sagte 1988 in seiner Dankesrede zur Verleihung des Pritzker Prize: „Meine Architektur folgte den alten Vorbildern. Das heißt, die Ästhetik hat immer die Begrenzungen der konstruktiven Logik überwunden. Meine Arbeit entwickelte sich unabhängig von der unvermeidlichen Kritik derer, die sich die Mühe machen, jedes kleinste Detail zu untersuchen – was so treffend charakterisiert, wozu Mittelmäßigkeit fähig ist." Es scheint, als habe Niemeyer mit dem Serpentine Gallery Pavilion ein Resümee seiner architektonischen Arbeit präsentieren wollen. In einem Interview mit der *Financial Times* fasste er zusammen: „Ich wollte einen Eindruck von all dem vermitteln, was für mein Werk charakteristisch ist. Dabei ging es mir vornehmlich darum, etwas zu gestalten, das über dem Erdboden schwebt. Indem wir in einem kleinen Gebäude, das wenig Raum einnimmt, Beton, ein paar Stützen und Träger verwenden, können wir eine Vorstellung davon vermitteln, worum es in meiner Architektur geht."

« Je suis ravi de concevoir le **PAVILLON DE LA SERPENTINE GALLERY**, ma première réalisation au Royaume-Uni », a écrit Oscar Niemeyer. « Mon idée a été de trouver une approche différente, libre et audacieuse. C'est ce que je préfère. J'aime dessiner, j'aime voir apparaître sur la feuille blanche un palais, une cathédrale, la figure d'une femme. Mais pour moi la vie est beaucoup plus importante que l'architecture. » En ces temps d'architecture générée par ordinateur, c'est un privilège rare de voir naître une œuvre récente d'un architecte qui a travaillé avec Le Corbusier au milieu des années 1930. Son pavillon pour la Serpentine Gallery fait penser à l'animation de l'un de ses croquis. En béton et en acier, la structure pourrait être une addition permanente aux Kensington Gardens, ce qu'elle n'est pas. « Mon architecture a suivi des exemples anciens », a déclaré Niemeyer en recevant le Pritzker Prize 1988. « La beauté prend le pas sur les limites de la logique de construction. Mon œuvre a progressé, indifférente aux critiques inévitables avancées par ceux qui perdent leur temps à examiner des détails sans importance, bon exemple de ce dont la médiocrité est capable. » Niemeyer souhaitait créer un résumé de son œuvre. « Je voulais donner le goût de tout ce qui caractérise mon œuvre », a-t-il déclaré au *Financial Times*. « La première étape a été de créer quelque chose qui flotte au-dessus du sol. À travers une petite construction qui occupe une petite parcelle, à partir du béton, de quelques poutres et supports, on peut donner une idée de ce qu'est l'architecture. »

Succeeding Toyo Ito in Kensington Gardens as the architect of the Serpentine's temporary summer pavilion Oscar Niemeyer calls on a typically daring use of wide expanses of white concrete.

Der auf Toyo Ito als Architekt des Sommerpavillons der Serpentine Gallery in Kensington Gardens folgende Oscar Niemeyer präsentiert einen typisch wagemutigen Einsatz großer, weißer Betonflächen.

Succédant à Toyo Ito pour construire le pavillon d'été temporaire de la Serpentine dans les Kensington Gardens, Oscar Niemeyer utilise les grands plans de béton blanc qui lui sont familiers.

Using as few supports and girders as possible, the structure offers light, open spaces that appear more tent-like than solid.

Unter Verwendung so weniger Stützen und Träger wie möglich bietet der Bau helle, offene Räume, die ihn mehr wie ein Zelt als ein massives Gebäude wirken lassen.

À partir d'un nombre aussi réduit que possible de poutres et de poteaux, la structure offre des espaces ouverts et lumineux qui font davantage penser à une tente qu'à une construction lourde.

Oscar Niemeyer clearly still mastered the dramatic design that made him famous in Brasília and elsewhere.

Oscar Niemeyer war ein Meister der dramatischen Formgebung, die ihn in Brasília und anderswo berühmt gemacht hat.

Oscar Niemeyer a toujours maîtrisé le style spectaculaire qui l'avait rendu célèbre à Brasília et dans le monde entier.

JEAN NOUVEL

Ateliers Jean Nouvel
10, Cité d'Angoulême
75011 Paris
France

Tel: +33 1 4923 8383, Fax: +33 1 4314 8110
E-mail: info@jeannouvel.fr, Web: www.jeannouvel.fr

Born in 1945 in Fumel, France, **JEAN NOUVEL** studied in Bordeaux and then at the Paris École des Beaux-Arts (1964–72). From 1967 to 1970, he was an assistant of Claude Parent and Paul Virilio. In 1970, he created his first office with François Seigneur. His first widely noticed project was the Institut du Monde Arabe (Paris, 1981–87, with Architecture Studio). Other works include his Nemausus Housing (Nîmes, 1985–87); Lyon Opera House (1986–93); Vinci Conference Center (Tours, 1989–93); Euralille Shopping Center (Lille, 1991–94); Fondation Cartier (Paris, 1991–94); Galeries Lafayette (Berlin, 1992–95). His unbuilt projects include the 400-meter-tall "Tours sans fins," La Défense (Paris, 1989); Grand Stade for the 1998 World Cup (Paris, 1994); Tenaga Nasional Tower (Kuala Lumpur, 1995). In 2003, Jean Nouvel won a competition sponsored by the Aga Khan Trust for Culture for the design of the waterfront Corniche in Doha, Qatar, and was called on to design the new Guggenheim Museum in Rio de Janeiro (unbuilt). His major completed projects since 2000 are the Music and Conference Center (Lucerne, Switzerland, 1998–2000); the Agbar Tower (Barcelona, Spain, 2001–03); social housing at the Cité Manifeste (Mulhouse, Germany, 2004); the extension of the Reina Sofia Museum (Madrid, 1999–2005); the Quai Branly Museum (Paris, 2001–06); an apartment building in SoHo (New York, 2006); and the Guthrie Theater (Minneapolis, Minnesota, 2006). Recent projects also include port facilities in Le Havre (2004) and the city hall in Montpellier (2002–09). Jean Nouvel received the RIBA Gold Medal in 2001.

JEAN NOUVEL, geboren 1945 im französischen Fumel, studierte in Bordeaux und anschließend an der Paris École des Beaux-Arts (1964–72). 1967 bis 1970 war er Assistent von Claude Parent und Paul Virilio. 1970 gründete er zusammen mit François Seigneur sein erstes Architekturbüro. Sein erstes bekanntes Bauwerk war das Institut du Monde Arabe in Paris (1981–87, mit Architecture Studio). Zu seinen weiteren Arbeiten zählen die Wohnanlage Nemausus in Nîmes (1985–87), das Opernhaus in Lyon (1986–93), das Kongresszentrum Vinci in Tours (1989–93), das Einkaufszentrum Euralille in Lille (1991–94), die Fondation Cartier in Paris (1991–95) und die Galeries Lafayette in Berlin (1992–96). Nouvels 400 m hoher „Tour sans fin" in La Défense in Paris (1989), sein Stadion für die Fußball-Weltmeisterschaft von 1998 in Paris (1994) und der Tenaga Nasional Tower in Kuala Lumpur (1995) wurden nicht realisiert. 2003 gewann Jean Nouvel den vom Aga-Khan-Kulturfonds gesponserten Wettbewerb für die Gestaltung des Hafengebiets Corniche in Doha (Katar) und wurde mit der Planung des neuen Guggenheim-Museums in Rio de Janeiro (nicht realisiert) beauftragt. Seine wichtigen, seit 2000 fertiggestellten Projekte sind das Musik- und Kongresszentrum in Luzern (1998–2000), der Agbar Tower in Barcelona (2001–03), Sozialwohnungen in der Cité Manifeste im französischen Mulhouse (2004), die Erweiterung des Museums Reina Sofia in Madrid (1999–2005), das Museum Quai Branly in Paris (2001–06), ein Apartmenthaus in SoHo in New York (2006) sowie das Guthrie-Theater in Minneapolis (2006). Zu seinen jüngeren Arbeiten zählen Hafenanlagen in Le Havre (2004) und das Rathaus von Montpellier (2002–09). Jean Nouvel wurde 2001 mit der RIBA-Goldmedaille ausgezeichnet.

Né en 1945 à Fumel (France), **JEAN NOUVEL** fait ses études à Bordeaux, puis est admis à l'École des Beaux-Arts de Paris (1964–72). De 1967 à 1970, il est l'assistant de Claude Parent et de Paul Virilio. En 1970, il crée une première agence avec François Seigneur. Son premier projet remarqué sur le plan international est l'Institut du Monde Arabe, à Paris (1981–87, avec Architecture Studio). Parmi ses autres réalisations : les immeubles d'appartements Nemausus (Nîmes, 1985–87), l'Opéra de Lyon (1986–93), le palais des congrès Vinci (Tours, 1989–93), le centre commercial Euralille (Lille, 1991–94), la Fondation Cartier (Paris, 1991–94), les galeries Lafayette (Berlin, 1992–95). Parmi ses projets non réalisés : une tour de 400 m « La tour sans fin » (La Défense, Paris, 1989), le Grand Stade de la Coupe du monde de football 1998 (Paris, 1994), la Tour Nasional Tenaga (Kuala Lumpur, Malaisie, 1995). En 2003, il a remporté un concours organisé par l'Aga Khan Trust for Culture pour la nouvelle corniche de Doha au Qatar, et a été choisi pour le nouveau Guggenheim Museum de Rio de Janeiro (non réalisé). Ses principales réalisations depuis 2000 sont : le Centre culturel et de Congrès (Lucerne, Suisse, 1998–2000), la tour Agbar (Barcelone, Espagne, 2001–03), les logements sociaux de la Cité Manifeste (Mulhouse, France, 2004), l'extension du musée Reina Sofia (Madrid, 1999–2005), le musée du Quai Branly (Paris, 2001–06), un immeuble d'appartements à SoHo (New York, 2006), le Guthrie Theater (Minneapolis, Minnesota, 2006), le complexe portuaire au Havre (2004) et la nouvelle mairie de Montpellier (2002–09). Jean Nouvel a remporté la médaille d'or RIBA en 2001.

LUCERNE CULTURE AND CONGRESS CENTER

Lucerne, Switzerland, 1992–2000

Client: Trägerstiftung Kultur- und Kongresszentrum Luzern. Start of planning: 1992.
Construction: 1995–98 (1st phase), 1995–2000 (2nd phase). Floor area: 35 000 m².
Costs: c. SFR 2 million.

Set in a highly visible location in Lucerne, next to the railroad station and at the edge of the lake, this is the most important building by Jean Nouvel since his Fondation Cartier in Paris (1995). Comprising a 1900-seat symphony hall, a 900-seat multi-purpose hall, a 300-seat congress hall, a 2400 m² art museum and three restaurants, the complex has a total usable floor area of 35 000 m². The budget for the building, whose symphony hall opened in 1998, was 200 million Swiss francs. A first proposal by Nouvel made in 1989 that would have modified the existing shores of the lake by building out into the water was rejected by a referendum, and the city asked him to propose a new scheme in 1992. The most stunning feature of the Center is its razor-thin roof, which projects out toward the lake and the tour boat dock. A truly mature work, it is full of surprises, ranging from the use of light to the surprising materials. Another unexpected feature of the building is that Nouvel actually brings water inside, with long, narrow basins separating each unit of the complex.

Weithin sichtbar, neben dem Bahnhof und am Ufer des Vierwaldstätter Sees gelegen, ist das **LUZERNER KULTUR- UND KONGRESSZENTRUM** der bedeutendste Bau Jean Nouvels seit seiner Fondation Cartier in Paris (1995). Der Komplex besteht aus einem Konzertsaal mit 1900, einer Mehrzweckhalle mit 900 und einer Kongresshalle mit 300 Sitzen. Hinzu kommen ein 2400 m² großes Kunstmuseum und drei Restaurants. Das Budget des Gebäudes, dessen großer Konzertsaal 1998 eröffnet wurde, betrug 200 Millionen Schweizer Franken. Ein erster Vorschlag Nouvels von 1989, der eine in den See hineinragende Bebauung vorsah, wurde in einem Referendum verworfen. 1992 forderte die Stadt ihn zu einem neuen Entwurf auf. Das auffälligste Merkmal des Zentrums ist sein papierdünnes Dach, das über den See und die Anlegestelle der Ausflugsboote auskragt. Dieses wahrhaft meisterliche Werk steckt voller Überraschungen – von der Nutzung des Lichts bis zu den ungewöhnlichen Materialien. Eine weitere Eigenheit des Baus besteht darin, dass Nouvel das Wasser – mittels langer, schmaler Becken, welche die einzelnen Trakte voneinandertrennen – in den Innenraum führt.

Occupant une position particulièrement en vue au centre de Lucerne, près de la gare et en bordure du lac, ce Centre est la plus importante réalisation de Jean Nouvel depuis la Fondation Cartier à Paris (1995). Il abrite sur une surface totale de 35 000 m² une salle de concerts symphoniques de 1900 places (inaugurée en 1998), une salle polyvalente de 900 places, une salle de congrès de 300 places, une galerie d'art de 2400 m² et trois restaurants. Le budget de construction s'est élevé à 200 millions de francs suisses. En 1989, une première proposition de l'architecte qui modifiait le profil de la rive du lac en édifiant le bâtiment au-dessus de l'eau, avait été rejetée par référendum. La ville lui demanda un nouveau projet en 1992. L'élément le plus étonnant est le toit en lame de rasoir qui se projette vers le lac et un appontement. Œuvre de grande maturité, ce bâtiment réserve de nombreuses surprises, de la maîtrise de la lumière à celle de matériaux inhabituels, en passant par de longs bassins étroits qui séparent intérieurement chaque partie du bâtiment.

The overhanging roof of course pro-
tects visitors from the weather, but
its razor-sharp form also defines the
visual identity of the complex.

Das auskragende Dach dient als
Wetterschutz, seine rasiermesser-
scharfe Form verleiht dem Komplex
aber auch visuelle Identität.

Le toit en surplomb protège les
visiteurs de la pluie, mais sa forme
de rasoir effilé définit également
l'identité visuelle du Centre.

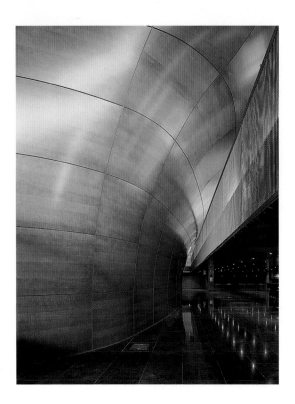

The main concert hall seats 1900
persons. Its form and materials
are naturally related to acoustical
considerations.

Die große Konzerthalle fasst 1900
Personen. Ihre Form und die Wahl der
Materialien sind durch akustische
Anforderungen bedingt.

La salle de concert principale compte
1900 places. Sa forme et ses matériaux sont déterminés par des consi-
dérations acoustiques.

Inside, Jean Nouvel retains his taste for unexpected materials, and creates spaces that are less claustrophobic than those of the Lyon Opera House for example.

Im Innern beweist Nouvel sein Geschick im Umgang mit ungewöhnlichen Materialien und erzeugt Räume, die weniger eng wirken als zum Beispiel in seinem Opernhaus von Lyon.

À l'intérieur, Nouvel manifeste son goût pour les matériaux inattendus et crée des espaces moins claustrophobiques que ceux de l'Opéra de Lyon.

MONOLITH, EXPO.02

Morat, Switzerland, 2000–01

Client: Swiss Expo.02. Dimensions: 34 x 34 x 34 m. Costs: € 36 million (all interventions).

For the Swiss National Exhibition, in principle organized every 25 years, it was decided in 2002 to situate the pavilions in four different cities near Neuchatel. In each case, the buildings had to be temporary and situated whenever possible on the lakes of Neuchatel and Morat. Jean Nouvel was chosen as the main architect involved in the attractive historic city of Morat. He conceived a series of interventions, the most visible of which was a monolithic block of rusting steel sitting off the shore in the lake. Another unexpected structure was an exhibition area occupied by the Fondation Cartier and made of stacks of logs. Actually, with its reference to logging, this structure may have had more to do with Switzerland than some of the other elements of the exhibitions. Using tents, containers and military camouflage, Nouvel occupied Morat with his temporary designs in a manner and style that in some cases approached installation art more than architecture. Unlike the other cities involved in **EXPO.02**, Morat, at Nouvel's instigation, did not create a closed-off area for the pavilions – rather the different elements were dispersed in proximity to the lake, with a simple ticketing system allowing entry to each area in whatever order the visitor preferred. This spreading of the Expo throughout the city was in part due to the relatively dense town configuration but it also permitted a real discovery of the city. For those interested in Nouvel, seeking out and recognizing his interventions became a part of the adventure of visiting the Expo. Nouvel's Expo.02 became part of Morat rather than being an incoherent addition. Although Expo.02 in Morat has not been as widely published as many other recent works by Jean Nouvel, it is amongst his most inventive and surprising efforts. He showed in particular that he was sensitive to changing circumstances, where astonishing new buildings may not be as much in the spirit of the times as an ability to use simple materials and designs to redefine space and serve a specific purpose.

Die Organisatoren der Schweizer Landesausstellung, die in der Regel alle 25 Jahre stattfindet, beschlossen für das Jahr 2002, die Ausstellungspavillons auf vier verschiedene Standorte nahe der Kantonshauptstadt Neuchâtel zu verteilen. Die Bauten sollten temporär sein und, wenn möglich, direkt auf dem Neuenburger oder Murtensee liegen. Jean Nouvel, der als leitender Architekt für die historische Gemeinde Murten ausgewählt worden war, entwarf eine Reihe von Arbeiten, deren hervorstechendste ein monolithischer Block aus rostigem Stahl war, der in einiger Entfernung vom Ufer aus dem Wasser ragte. Ebenfalls sehr ungewöhnlich war eine andere Arbeit, eine Ausstellungsfläche für die Fondation Cartier, die aus übereinandergestapelten Holzstämmen bestand. Mit ihrem Bezug auf die Holzindustrie hatte diese Konstruktion mehr mit der Schweiz zu tun als viele andere Beiträge. Einige von Nouvels Konstruktionen waren mit Bestandteilen wie Zelten, Containern und Tarnnetzen der Installationskunst näher als der Architektur. Im Gegensatz zu anderen Standorten der **EXPO.02** verzichtete Murten – auf Nouvels Betreiben – auf einen abgegrenzten Bereich für die Pavillons. Stattdessen wurden die einzelnen Objekte in Seenähe verteilt. Ein unkompliziertes Kartensystem erlaubte den Besuchern, alle Ausstellungsbereiche in beliebiger Reihenfolge zu besichtigen. Dass sich die Expo so über die ganze Stadt ausbreiten konnte, ergab sich aus Murtens relativ dichtem Stadtgefüge, das den Ausstellungsbesuchern die Gelegenheit bot, die Stadt wirklich zu entdecken. Für die Fans von Nouvel trug das Aufspüren und Identifizieren seiner Arbeiten zu der besonderen Qualität dieser Expo bei. Nouvel ließ seine Expo-Beiträge mehr zu einem Teil der Stadt werden, als sie nur zusammenhanglos hinzuzufügen. Obwohl die Ausstellung nicht so große Beachtung in den Medien fand wie andere seiner Projekte, gehört sie zu seinen einfallsreichsten und überraschendsten Arbeiten. Er bewies hier eine besondere Sensibilität gegenüber sich verändernden Verhältnissen, in denen spektakuläre neue Gebäude möglicherweise weniger zeitgemäß sind als die Fähigkeit, mit einfachen Materialien und Gestaltungsformen einen Raum zu definieren und einem bestimmten Zweck zu dienen.

L'Exposition nationale suisse, qui se tient en principe tous les 25 ans, avait décidé de s'implanter dans la région de Neuchâtel. Les bâtiments devaient être temporaires et situés dans une large mesure sur les lacs de Neuchâtel et de Morat. Jean Nouvel a été choisi pour le projet de la charmante petite cité historique de Morat. Il a conçu une série d'interventions dont la plus visible était un bloc monolithique en acier rouillé posé à quelques encablures de la rive. Une autre création étonnante était l'espace d'exposition occupé par la Fondation Cartier, construite à partir d'empilements de grumes. Par sa référence aux rondins, elle était sans doute plus en rapport avec la Suisse que certains autres éléments des expositions. À l'aide de tentes, de conteneurs et de camouflage militaire, les projets temporaires de Nouvel ont occupé Morat d'une façon et dans un style plus proches de l'installation que de l'architecture. À la différence d'autres villes participant à **EXPO.02**, Morat, à l'instigation de l'architecte, n'avait pas créé de zone fermée mais préféré disperser les divers lieux à proximité du lac, un système de billetterie permettant à chacun de visiter ce qu'il voulait dans l'ordre de ses préférences. Cette dilution de l'Expo, due en partie à la configuration relativement dense de la ville, en permettait cependant une authentique découverte. Pour ceux qui s'intéressent au travail de Nouvel, la recherche et la reconnaissance de ses interventions participaient au plaisir de la visite. Son intervention faisait partie de la ville, plutôt que de se contenter de n'être qu'un simple ajout sans cohérence. Bien que ce travail n'ait pas reçu une couverture médiatique aussi abondante que celle d'autres réalisations récentes de l'architecte, il fait partie de ses réalisations les plus inventives et les plus étonnantes. Il a montré en particulier qu'il était sensible à des circonstances particulières, que créer une construction qui surprenne était peut-être moins dans l'esprit du moment que la capacité à faire appel à des plans et des matériaux simples pour redéfinir l'espace et répondre à un objectif bien défini.

Nouvel's contribution to Expo.02 in Morat was not limited to the rusting metal Monolith. He also conceived a number of the lakeside installations.

Nouvels Beitrag zur Expo.02 beschränkte sich nicht auf den Monolith aus rostigem Metall. Er entwarf auch etliche der um den Murtensee herum installierten Arbeiten.

La contribution de Nouvel à Expo.02 à Morat ne se limitait pas à ce monolithe d'aspect rouillé. Il y a également conçu un certain nombre d'autres installations en bordure du lac.

MARCOS NOVAK

Marcos Novak
510 Venice Way
Venice, California 90291
USA

E-mail: marcos@centrifuge.org
Web: www.centrifuge.org/marcos

AlloBio ▶

Born in Caracas, Venezuela, **MARCOS NOVAK** grew up in Greece and received a Bachelor of Science in architecture, a M.Arch. and a certificate of specialization in computer-aided architecture from Ohio State University (Columbus, Ohio), completing his studies in 1983. He has worked as a research fellow at the Center for Advanced Inquiry in the Interactive Arts at the University of Wales, and as Co-Director of the Transarchitectures Foundation in Paris (with Paul Virilio). He has numerous publications to his credit. His work has been essentially virtual, and he is regarded as the "pioneer of the architecture of virtuality" according to the organizers of the 7th International Architecture Exhibition in Venice, in which he participated (Greek Pavilion). He is known for such projects as his "Sensor Space," "From Immersion to Eversion," "Transmitting Architecture," "Liquid Architectures," and "Metadata Visualization." Marcos Novak has taught at Ohio State University and at the University of Texas Austin, the architecture program at UCLA, the digital media program at UCLA, Art Center College of Art & Design, Pasadena, and is currently a professor at the University of California Santa Barbara.

MARCOS NOVAK wurde in Caracas geboren und wuchs in Griechenland auf. Er hat einen Bachelor of Science in Architecture, einen Master of Architecture und ein Zertifikat für Spezialwissen im Bereich CAD (Architektur) von der Ohio State University in Columbus, Ohio. 1983 schloss er sein Studium ab. Er war Forschungsstipendiat am Center for Advanced Inquiry in the Interactive Arts der University of Wales und stellvertretender Leiter der Transarchitectures Foundation in Paris (mit Paul Virilio). Ferner hat er zahlreiche Beiträge veröffentlicht. Seine Projekte sind hauptsächlich virtuell. Von den Organisatoren der 7. Architekturbiennale in Venedig, an der er mit dem griechischen Pavillon teilnahm, wurde er als „Pionier der virtuellen Architektur" bezeichnet. Er ist bekannt durch Projekte wie das „Sensor Space", „From Immersion to Eversion", „Transmitting Architectures", „Liquid Architectures" und „Metadata Visualization". Marcos Novak hat an der Ohio State University und an der University of Texas, Austin, unterrichtet, und war außerdem beim „Architecture Program" und „Digital Media Program" an der UCLA und am Art Center College of Design in Pasadena tätig. Er ist Professor an der University of California (Santa Barbara).

Né à Caracas, Venezuela, **MARCOS NOVAK** a été élevé en Grèce et a étudié à l'Ohio State University (Columbus, Ohio) où il obtenu son Bachelor of Science in Architecture, son Master of Architecture et un certificat de spécialisation en CAA (conception architecturale assistée par ordinateur, 1983). Il a travaillé comme chercheur au Center for Advanced Inquiry in the Alternative Arts de l'Université du Pays de Galles et a dirigé (avec Paul Virilio) la Fondation Transarchitectures à Paris. Il a beaucoup publié. Ses œuvres sont essentiellement virtuelles et il est considéré comme le « pionnier de l'architecture de la virtualité » selon les organisateurs de la 7ᵉ Biennale d'architecture de Venise à laquelle il a participé (pavillon grec). Il est connu pour des projets comme son « Sensor Space », « From Immersion to Eversion », « Transmitting Architecture », « Liquid Architectures » et « Metadata Visualisation ». Marcos Novak a enseigné à l'Ohio State University (Columbus), à l'University of Texas (Austin), l'Architecture Program de UCLA, le Digital Media Program de UCLA, à l'Art Center College of Art & Design de Pasadena. Il est actuellement professeur à l'Université de Californie Santa Barbara.

V4D_TRANSAURA, ECHINODERM, ALIENWITHIN, ECHINODERM_RP, ALLOBIO

2001

Marcos Novak is the most visible proponent of cyberspace as an autonomous architectural field of inquiry. He actively uses non-Euclidean spatial concepts with the idea of algorithmic unfolding, the mathematical modeling of data-space-navigable computer environments to create unexpected forms. He is at the origin of the idea of "liquid architectures" and "transarchitectures" which he sees as part of a larger movement that he terms "transmodernity." Novak can be considered an artist as much as an architect. His liquid architectures are intended to combine opposites – soft and hard, real and virtual, masculine and feminine to create a third or "alien" condition. Novak worked with Kas Oosterhuis on the trans-ports 2001 project. Novak seeks nothing less than "warpings into alien territory, true transmutations into unpredictable conceptual spaces, phase transitions into completely new states of being."

Marcos Novak ist der bekannteste Verfechter der Idee des Cyberspace als einem autonomen Bereich der Architektur. Er verwendet nichteuklidische Raumkonzepte und verknüpft sie mit der Idee algorithmischer Entfaltung, der mathematischen Modellierung von Daten und steuerbaren Computer-Environments, um neue Formen zu kreieren. Die von ihm ausgehende Vorstellung „fließender Architekturen" oder „Transarchitekturen" sieht er als Teil einer größeren Bewegung, für die er den Begriff „Transmodernität" geprägt hat. Novak kann ebenso sehr als Künstler wie als Architekt angesehen werden, der mit seinen fließenden Bauwerken versucht, Gegensätze miteinander zu verbinden – weich und hart, real und virtuell, maskulin und feminin –, um damit einen jeweils dritten oder „fremden" Zustand zu schaffen. Marcos Novak, der zusammen mit Kas Oosterhuis an dem Projekt trans-ports 2001 gearbeitet hat, beschreibt seine künstlerischen Ziele als „Verzerrungen, die in fremdes Terrain reichen, als echte Transmutationen in unvorhersehbare konzeptionelle Räume und Phasenumwandlungen in vollkommen neue Seinszustände."

Marcos Novak est l'un des représentants les plus célèbres du cyberespace, considéré comme un champ de recherches architecturales. Il met en œuvre des concepts spatiaux non-euclidiens, des déploiements algorithmiques et des modélisations mathématiques d'environnements spatiaux numériques navigables pour créer des formes inattendues. Il est à l'origine de l'idée « d'architectures liquides » et de « transarchitectures » dans laquelle il voit les éléments d'un mouvement plus vaste nommé « transmodernité ». Il est autant artiste qu'architecte. Ses architectures liquides combinent des opposés – mou/dur, réel/virtuel, masculin/féminin – pour créer un troisième état « étranger ». Il a travaillé avec Kas Oosterhuis sur le projet trans-ports 2001. Il ne cherche rien moins que « des gauchissements vers des territoires étrangers, d'authentiques transmutations dans des espaces conceptuels imprévisibles, des phases de transition dans des états entièrement nouveaux ».

V4D_TransAura: higher dimensional geometries are used to create invisible architectures. Shown above is one of these, presented as a sculpture verging on an architectonic scale.
AlloBio: These forms anticipate a radical possibility: that of a literally living architecture, or of an architecture biologically grown of materials that are quasi-alive, while still directly connected to virtual space.

V4D_TransAura: Höherdimensionale Geometrie wird zur Gestaltung unsichtbarer Architekturformen eingesetzt, wie die an architektonische Maßstäbe grenzende Skulptur (oben).
AlloBio: Diese Formen antizipieren die radikale Möglichkeit einer buchstäblich lebendigen Architektur, beziehungsweise einer Architektur, die biologisch aus quasilebendigen und dennoch direkt mit dem virtuellen

Raum verbundenen Materialien entsteht (rechts).

V4D_TransAura : des configurations dimensionnelles plus importantes sont utilisées pour créer des architectures invisibles. En haut, l'une d'elles, présentée comme une sculpture d'une échelle presque architectonique.
AlloBio : ces formes anticipent la possibilité radicale d'une architecture

littéralement vivante, ou d'une architecture d'origine quasi biologique issue de matériaux qui sont à la fois quasi vivants et directement connectés à l'espace virtuel.

AlloBio: Several distinct investigations converge on this project: the overarching question of the theoretical and critical production of the "alien" in our culture; the merging of the technological and the biological; and the continuity between the actual, the virtual, and the invisible.

AlloBio: In diesem Projekt bündeln sich mehrere unterschiedliche Untersuchungsgegenstände: die übergeordnete Frage nach der theoretischen und kritischen Produktion des „Fremden" in unserer Kultur, das Verschmelzen von Technologie und Biologie sowie die Kontinuität zwischen dem Realen, dem Virtuellen und dem Unsichtbaren.

AlloBio : ce projet est l'aboutissement de la convergence de plusieurs recherches distinctes : l'interrogation omniprésente de la production théorique et critique de « l'étranger » dans notre culture ; la fusion du technologique et du biologique ; la continuité entre le réel, le virtuel et l'invisible.

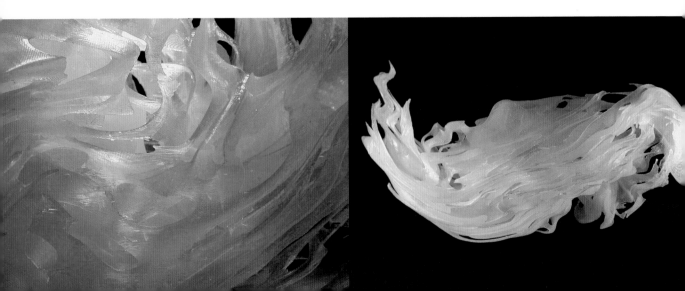

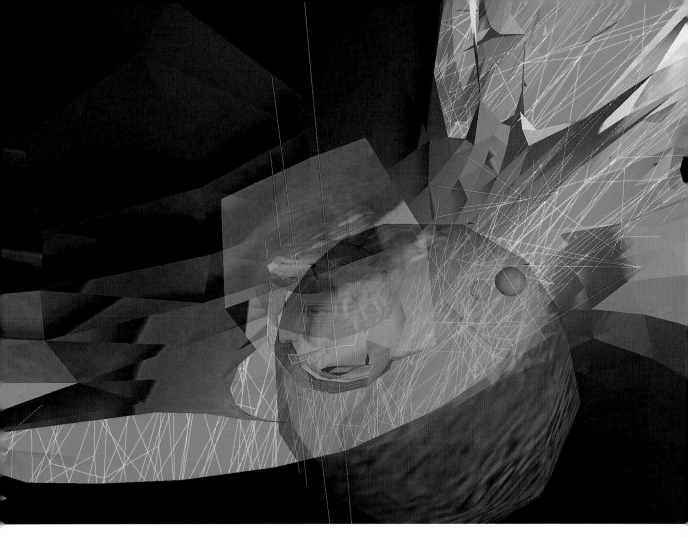

AlloBio: Viewers and participants in the Allotopes of Venice, Florence, and Erice were asked to express their affective state through interactions with sensor-implemented invisible sculptures. These affective data streams were then used to alter and deform the simplified versions of the Echinoderm.

AlloBio: Betrachter und Teilnehmer der Allotope in Venedig, Florenz und Erice wurden gebeten, ihre Gefühle in der Interaktion mit den sensorgeführten unsichtbaren Skulpturen auszudrücken. Diese affektiven Datenströme wurden anschließend dazu verwendet, die vereinfachten Versionen des Echinoderms zu verändern und zu verformen.

AlloBio : les spectateurs et participants des Allotopes montés à Venise, Florence et Erice étaient conviés à exprimer leur état affectif à travers des interactions avec des sculptures invisibles bardées de capteurs. Ces flux de données affectives servaient ensuite à modifier et déformer les versions simplifiées de l'Echinoderm.

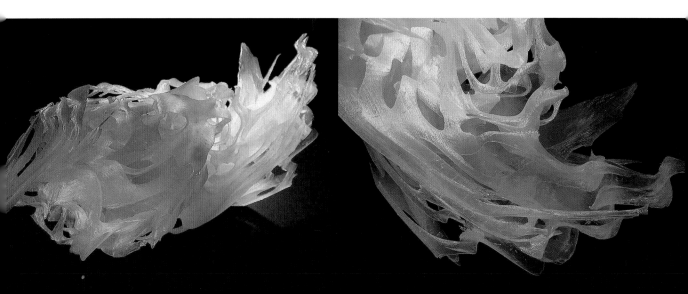

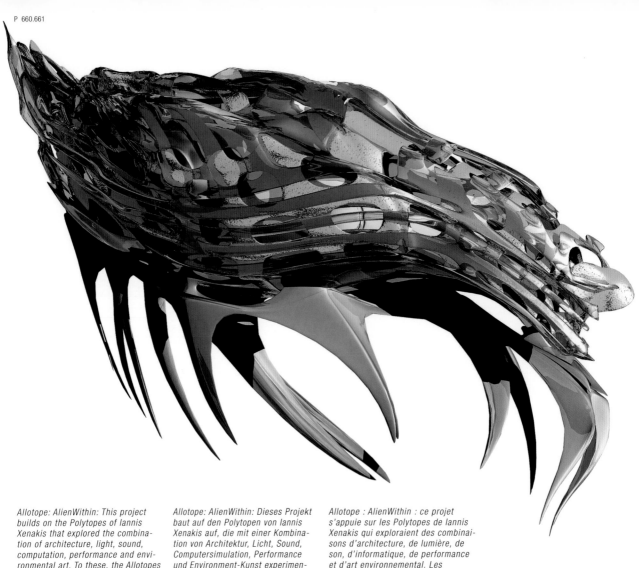

Allotope: AlienWithin: This project builds on the Polytopes of Iannis Xenakis that explored the combination of architecture, light, sound, computation, performance and environmental art. To these, the Allotopes add generativity, transactivity, and virtuality. Shown above are images of navigations through the virtual environments created for this project.

Allotope: AlienWithin: Dieses Projekt baut auf den Polytopen von Iannis Xenakis auf, die mit einer Kombination von Architektur, Licht, Sound, Computersimulation, Performance und Environment-Kunst experimentierten. Die Allotope erweitern diese Elemente um die der Generativität, Transaktivität und Virtualität. Bildliche Darstellung der Navigationen durch die für dieses Projekt erzeugten virtuellen Environments (oben).

Allotope : AlienWithin : ce projet s'appuie sur les Polytopes de Iannis Xenakis qui exploraient des combinaisons d'architecture, de lumière, de son, d'informatique, de performance et d'art environnemental. Les Allotopes y ajoutent reproductivité, transactivité, et virtualité. En haut, images de navigation à travers les environnements virtuels créés pour ce projet.

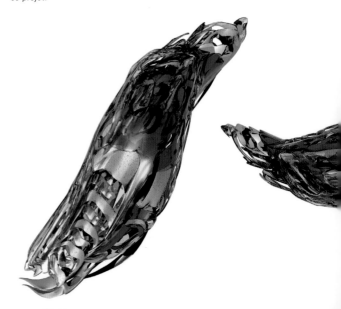

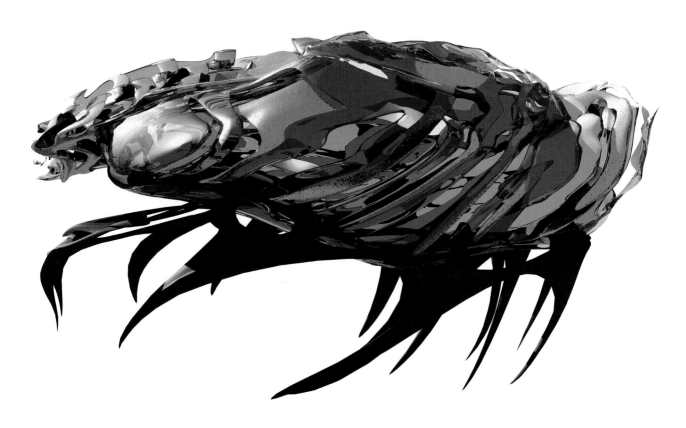

Echinoderm_RP: Using stereolithography, these were realized as solid objects. In conversations with the artists and scientists of Symbiotica, three possibilities arose: that the forms be replaced with living bone tissue; that these forms be covered with living skin; or both. This led to the idea of a genuinely living architecture, subject of the AlloBio, shown on the previous pages.

Echinoderm_RP: Mittels Stereolithografie wurden räumliche Objekte realisiert. In Gesprächen mit den Künstlern und Wissenschaftlern von Symbiotica ergaben sich drei Möglichkeiten: die Formen durch lebendes Knochengewebe zu ersetzen, sie mit lebender Haut zu bedecken oder beides zusammen. Das führte zur Idee einer genuin lebendigen Architektur, Thema des auf den vorigen Seiten abgebildeten AlloBio-Projekts.

Echinoderm_RP : ces formes ont été réalisées en objets réels, par le procédé de stéréophotographie. Au cours des conversations avec les artistes et les chercheurs de Symbiotica, trois possibilités sont apparues : que les formes soient remplacées par des tissus osseux vivants ; qu'elles soient recouvertes de peau vivante ; ou les deux. Ceci a conduit à l'idée d'une architecture authentiquement vivante, sujet de AlloBio, montré dans les pages précédentes.

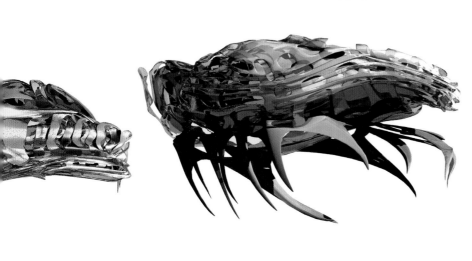

NOX

NOX/Lars Spuybroek
Conradstraat 38
3013 AD Rotterdam
The Netherlands

Tel/Fax: +31 10 477 2853
www.nox-art-architecture.com

LARS SPUYBROEK is the principal of **NOX**. Since the early 1990s, he has been involved in research on the relationship between architecture and media, often more specifically between architecture and computing. He was the editor-publisher of one of the first magazines on the subject (*NOX*, and later also *Forum*), has made videos ("Soft City") and interactive electronic artworks ("Soft Site," "edit Spline," "deep Surface"). More recently, he has focused on architecture (H2Oexpo, Blow Out, V2_lab, wetGRID, D-Tower, Son-O-House, Maison Folie). His work has won several prizes and was shown at the Venice Biennale in 2000 and 2002. In 2003, NOX participated in the important international exhibitions "Zoomorphic" at the Victoria and Albert in London and "Non Standard Architecture" at the Centre Pompidou in Paris. NOX created the interactive tower for the Dutch city of Doetinchem (D-Tower); "a house where sounds live" (Son-O-House); and a complex of cultural buildings in Lille, France (Maison Folie), as well as working on competitions for the European Central Bank in Frankfurt and the New Centre Pompidou in Metz, France (competition won by Shigeru Ban). Lars Spuybroek has lectured widely and has taught at various universities. He is currently a professor at the School of Architecture of the Georgia Institute of Technology in Atlanta, USA. His book, *Machining Architecture,* was published in 2004 (Thames & Hudson).

LARS SPUYBROEK, der Leiter von **NOX**, beschäftigt sich seit Anfang der 1990er-Jahre mit dem Verhältnis zwischen Architektur und Medien, insbesondere zwischen Architektur und Computerwesen. Er war Herausgeber und Verleger einer der ersten Zeitschriften zu diesem Thema, *NOX* (später auch *Forum*), und hat Videos ("Soft City") wie auch interaktive elektronische Kunstwerke ("Soft Site", "edit Spline", "deep Surface") produziert. In jüngerer Zeit hat er sich mehr auf die Architektur konzentriert, mit Projekten wie H2Oexpo, Blow Out, V2_lab, wetGRID, D-Tower, Son-O-House und Maison Folie. Er wurde mit mehreren Preisen ausgezeichnet und war in den Jahren 2000 und 2002 auf der Biennale in Venedig vertreten. 2003 nahm NOX an den bedeutenden internationalen Ausstellungen "Zoomorphic" im Victoria & Albert Museum in London und "Non Standard Architectures" im Pariser Centre Pompidou teil. Weitere Projekte von NOX sind der interaktive Turm D-Tower für die niederländische Stadt Doetinchem, das Son-O-House, "ein Haus, in dem Geräusche leben", das Kulturzentrum Maison Folie im französischen Lille sowie die Wettbewerbsbeiträge für die Europäische Zentralbank in Frankfurt und das Neue Centre Pompidou in Metz (Wettbewerbssieger: Shigeru Ban). Lars Spuybroek hat zahlreiche Vorlesungen und Vorträge gehalten und an verschiedenen Universitäten gelehrt. Zurzeit ist er Professor an der School of Architecture des Georgia Institute of Technology in Atlanta, USA. 2004 erschien sein Buch *Machining Architecture* bei Thames & Hudson.

LARS SPUYBROEK, qui dirige **NOX**, s'intéresse depuis le début des années 1990 aux relations entre l'architecture et les médias, et plus spécifiquement l'architecture et l'informatique. Il a été rédacteur-en-chef de l'un des premiers magazines consacrés à ce sujet (*NOX*, puis plus tard *FORUM*) et a réalisé des vidéos (« Soft City ») et des œuvres artistiques interactives (« SoftSite », « edit Spline », « deep Surface »). Plus tard il s'est davantage impliqué dans l'architecture (H2Oexpo, BlowOut, V2_lab, wetGRID, D-Tower, Son-O-House, Maison Folie). Son travail a remporté plusieurs distinctions et a été présenté aux Biennales de Venise de 2000 et 2002. En 2003, NOX a participé à l'importante exposition « Zoomorphic » au Victoria & Albert Museum à Londres, et à « Architectures non standard » au Centre Pompidou à Paris. Autres réalisations de NOX : une tour interactive pour la ville néerlandaise de Doetinchem (D-Tower), « une maison du son » (Son-O-House) et un complexe d'installations culturelles à Lille, en France (Maison Folie). L'agence a participé à des concours pour la Banque centrale européenne et le Nouveau Centre Pompidou à Metz, en France (remporté par Shigeru Ban). Lars Spuybroek a donné de nombreuses conférences, tenu de nombreux cours, enseigné dans plusieurs universités. Actuellement, il est professeur à la School of Architecture du Georgia Institute of Technology à Atlanta, États-Unis. Il a rédigé un livre *Machining Architecture*, publié par Thames & Hudson en 2004.

SON-O-HOUSE

Son en Breugel, The Netherlands, 2000–03

Client: Enterprise Group. Floor area: 300 m². Costs: € 410 000.

These images demonstrate that the apparently complex design of the Son-O-House evolves from the idea of the assembly of simple strips of paper.

Diese Bilder demonstrieren, dass sich die komplexe Gestaltung des Son-O-House aus der Idee einfacher, miteinander verflochtener Papierstreifen entwickelt hat.

Ces images montrent la conception apparemment complexe de la Son-O-House qui évolue à partir de l'idée d'un assemblage de simples bandes de papier.

As NOX prinicipal Lars Spuybroek explains, "the **SON-O-HOUSE** is one of our typical 'art' projects which allows us to proceed more carefully and slowly (over a period of three to four years) while generating a lot of knowledge that we apply to larger and speedier projects. Son-O-House is what we call 'a house where sounds live,' not being a 'real' house, but a structure that refers to living and the bodily movements that accompany habit and habitation. In the Son-O-House a sound work is continuously generating new sound patterns activated by sensors picking up actual movements of visitors." More specifically, the structure is derived from a set of movements of bodies, limbs and hands (on three scales) that are inscribed on paper bands as cuts. These paper bands are then stapled together, creating an arabesque of complex intertwining lines that is then made into a three-dimensional "porous structure." An analog computing model is then "digitized and remodeled on the basis of combing and curling rules which results in the very complex model of interlacing vaults which sometimes lean on each other or sometimes cut into each other." Spuybroek goes on to explain that "in this house-that-is-not-a-house we position eight sensors at strategic spots to indirectly influence the music. This system of sounds, composed and programmed by sound artist Edwin van der Heide, is based on moiré effects of interference of closely related frequencies. As a visitor one does not influence the sound directly, which is so often the case with interactive art. One influences the landscape itself that generates the sounds. The score is an evolutionary memoryscape that develops with the traced behavior of the actual bodies in the space."

Lars Spuybroek erklärt: „Das **SON-O-HOUSE** ist eins von unseren typischen ‚Kunst'-Projekten … Es ist kein ‚reales' Haus, sondern eine Konstruktion, die sich an den Lebensäußerungen und Bewegungen der Menschen orientiert, die sich darin bewegen oder wohnen. Im Son-O-House erzeugt eine Soundanlage ständig neue Geräuschmuster, die von den durch Sensoren übertragenen Bewegungen der Bewohner ausgelöst werden." Anders gesagt: Die Form entstand aus einer Serie von Bewegungen von Körpern, Gliedmaßen und Händen, die als Schnitte auf Papierstreifen fixiert wurden. Diese Papierstreifen wurden zusammengeheftet, woraus eine Arabeske aus komplexen, miteinander verflochtenen Linien entstand. Diese wurde dann zu einem dreidimensionalen „durchlässigen Gebilde" geformt. Anschließend wurde ein analoges Computermodell „nach demselben Prinzip wie Haare geflochten werden, digitalisiert und umgeformt, was zu unserem komplexen Modell verschlungener Gewölbe führt, die sich aneinander anlehnen oder überschneiden". Spuybroek abschließend: „In diesem Haus-das-kein-Haus-ist haben wir an strategischen Punkten acht Sensoren installiert, um die Musik indirekt zu beeinflussen. Dieses Soundsystem, das von Edwin van der Heide komponiert und programmiert wurde, basiert auf dem Moiré-Effekt, der durch die Überlagerung eng beieinander liegender Frequenzen entsteht. Anders als bei vielen anderen interaktiven Kunstprojekten kann man hier als Besucher die Musik nicht direkt beeinflussen. Man beeinflusst vielmehr die Umgebung selbst, die den Sound hervorbringt. Dabei stellt die Partitur eine evolutionäre Erinnerungslandschaft dar, die sich mit dem aufgezeichneten Verhalten realer Körper im Raum entfaltet."

Comme l'explique Lars Spuybroek : « La **SON-O-HOUSE** est l'un de ces projets ‹ artistiques › typiques qui nous permettent d'avancer plus soigneusement et plus lentement (sur trois ou quatre ans) tout en générant une masse de connaissances dont bénéficieront des projets plus importants et plus pressés … Ce n'est pas une ‹ vraie › maison, mais une structure qui se réfère à la vie et aux mouvements corporels qui accompagnent les habitudes et le fait d'habiter. Dans cette maison une centrale sonore génère en continu de nouveaux motifs sonores activés par des capteurs qui enregistrent les mouvements réels des visiteurs. » Plus précisément, cette structure est issue de l'ensemble des mouvements des corps, des membres et des mains (sur trois échelles) qui s'inscrivent sur des bandes de papiers. Celles-ci sont ensuite agrafées ensemble, pour créer une arabesque de lignes entrelacées complexes qui se transforme en « structure poreuse » en trois dimensions. Un modèle de calcul analogique est ensuite « numérisé et remodelé sur la base de lignes qui donnent un modèle très complexe de voûtes entrelacées qui tantôt s'inclinent l'une ou l'autre, tantôt s'entrecoupent ». Spuybroek explique également que « dans cette maison-qui-n'est-pas-une-maison, nous positionnons huit capteurs à des endroits stratégiques qui influencent indirectement la musique. Ce système de sons, composés et programmés par l'artiste sonore Edwin van der Heide, repose sur des effets de moirages d'interférences de fréquences proches. Le visiteur n'influence pas directement le son, ce qui est si souvent le cas dans l'art interactif, mais influence le paysage lui-même qui génère les sons. Le résultat est un paysage mémorisé évolutif qui se développe concurremment au traçage du comportement des corps dans l'espace. »

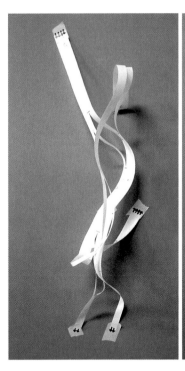
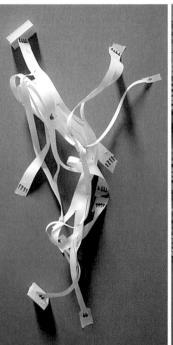

P 666.667

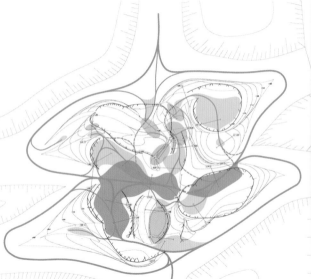

The more finished computer images
of the house show its curious shapes
that might approach biological forms.

*Die Computerdarstellungen des
Hauses zeigen die Nähe der merkwür-
digen Formen zu Naturgebilden.*

*Une image de synthèse montre des
formes curieuses qui ne sont pas très
éloignées de formes biologiques.*

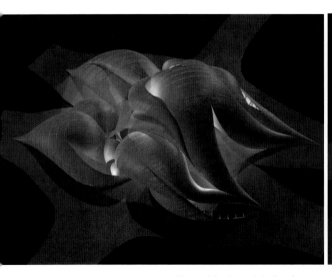

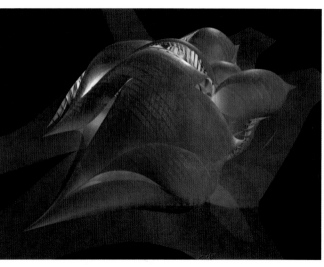

These night views of the Son-O-House give the impression of a living entity, glowing and possibly even moving as its sounds are influenced by visitors' movements.

Die nächtlichen Ansichten des Hauses lassen an ein lebendiges, im Dunkeln leuchtendes Wesen denken, das sich im Rhythmus seiner Besucher bewegt.

Ces vues de nuit de la maison donnent l'impression d'un organisme vivant, irradiant et même mobile puisque les formes sont influencées par les mouvements des visiteurs.

JOHN PAWSON

John Pawson
Unit B
70–78 York Way
London N1 9AG
UK

Tel: +44 20 7837 2929
Fax: +44 20 7837 4949
E-mail: email@johnpawson.co.uk
Web: www.johnpawson.com

Monastery of Novy Dvûr ▶

Born in Halifax in central England in 1949, **JOHN PAWSON** attended Eton and worked in his own family's textile mill before going to Japan for four years. On his return, he studied at the Architectural Association (AA) in London and set up his own firm in 1981. He has worked on numerous types of project, including the flagship store for Calvin Klein in New York, airport lounges for Cathay Pacific Airlines at the Chek Lap Kok Airport in Hong Kong, and a small apartment for the author Bruce Chatwin. Pawson may be even better known to the general public because of his 1996 book *Minimum*, which focused on such essential subjects as light, structure, ritual, landscape, and volume. Because of this book, but also for his style, Pawson has come to be considered an essential figure in the minimalist style of recent years. Other projects include Tetsuka House (Tokyo, 2003–06); Monastery of Novy Dvûr (Toužim, Czech Republic, 2004); Lansdowne Apartments (London, 2004); Baron House (Skane, Sweden, 2005); Sackler Crossing, Royal Botanic Gardens, Kew (Surrey, UK, 2006); Klein Apartment (New York, 2006); 50 Gramercy Park North (New York, 2007). He also worked on the Hotel Puerta America in Madrid.

Der 1949 in Halifax, England, geborene **JOHN PAWSON** besuchte Eton und arbeitete in der Textilfabrik seiner Familie, ehe er für vier Jahre nach Japan ging. Nach seiner Rückkehr studierte er an der AA in London und eröffnete 1981 sein eigenes Büro. Er war mit vielgestaltigen Projekten befasst, darunter dem Flagship-Store von Calvin Klein in New York, den Flughafenlounges für Cathay Pacific am Flughafen Chek Lap Kok in Hongkong sowie einem kleinen Apartment für den Schriftsteller Bruce Chatwin. Der Allgemeinheit ist Pawson besser bekannt wegen seines 1996 erschienenen Buchs *Minimum*, in dem er sich mit solch grundsätzlichen Themen wie Licht, Struktur, Ritual, Landschaft und Raum beschäftigt. Wegen dieses Buchs, aber auch wegen seines Stils gilt Pawson inzwischen als wesentlicher Vertreter des Minimalismus der letzten Jahre. Weitere Projekte sind Haus Tetsuka (Tokio, 2003–06), Kloster Novy Dvûr (Toužim, Tschechische Republik, 2004), Lansdowne Apartments (London, 2004), Haus Baron (Skane, Schweden, 2005), Sackler Crossing, Royal Botanic Gardens, Kew (Surrey, Großbritannien, 2006), Apartment Klein (New York, 2006), 50 Gramercy Park North (New York, 2007). Darüber hinaus arbeitete er am Hotel Puerta America in Madrid.

Né à Halifax en Angleterre en 1949, **JOHN PAWSON**, après des études à Eton, travaille dans l'usine textile familiale avant de séjourner quatre ans au Japon. À son retour, il étudie à l'Architectural Association de Londres et crée son agence en 1981. Il est intervenu sur de nombreux types de projets dont le Flagship Store de Calvin Klein à New York, les salons de l'aéroport de Chek Lap Kok à Hongkong pour Cathay Pacific ou un petit appartement pour l'écrivain Bruce Chatwin. Il est peut-être surtout connu du grand public à travers le succès de son livre *Minimum* (1996) sur les thèmes de la lumière, de la structure, du rituel, du paysage et du volume. À la suite de ce livre, mais aussi parce que c'est son style, il a été considéré comme une figure essentielle du minimalisme contemporain. Parmi ses réalisations : la maison Tetsuka, Tokyo (2003–06) ; le monastère de Novy Dvûr, Toužim, République Tchèque (2004) ; Lansdowne Apartments, Londres (2004) ; la maison Baron, Skane, Suède (2005) ; la passerelle Sackler, Royal Botanic Gardens, Kew, Surrey, Grande-Bretagne (2006) ; l'appartement Klein, New York (2006) ; 50 Gramercy Park North, New York (2007). Il a également participé aux aménagements de l'Hotel Puerta America à Madrid.

MONASTERY OF NOVY DVÛR

Toužim, Czech Republic, 2004

Floor Area: 70 m x 70 m (4900 m²) Client: Monastery of Saint Lieu Sept-Fons.
Costs: not disclosed.

John Pawson was asked to work on a new monastery by French Cistercian monks in 1999. The site they had selected was a 100-hectare estate located west of Prague, with an eighteenth-century manor house that had been uninhabited for forty years. The monks were familiar with Pawson's book *Minimum* and had seen images of his Calvin Klein store in Manhattan before selecting him. Pawson, who has called the **NOVY DVÛR MONASTERY** "the project of a lifetime," recalls that the "monastic cloister has been likened to an enclosed city, with many sub-programs typically including the functions of church, home, office, school, workshop, guesthouse, hospital and farm." Basing his own 6500 m² scheme on the blueprint drawn up in the twelfth century for the Cistercian Order's buildings by Saint Bernard of Clairvaux, which called for simple, pared-down spaces and a respect for light and correct proportions, Pawson restored the baroque manor house and added three wings of new architecture along the lines of pre-existing structures. Pawson was familiar with the Abbaye du Thoronet, a Cistercian abbey located between Draguignan and Brignoles in southern France, but this was the first time he designed a religious building. He explains, "I didn't have to adapt my style particularly. I'd already read Saint Bernard's rules (the Apologia of 1127, against artistic adornment), so the ideas all made sense to me." The challenge of the project as he explains was to design the monastery so that the very precise movements and rituals of the monks could be carried out without hindrance. "The church," he concludes, "had to make praying easier – to bring calm and pleasure – but also to be stimulating without being distracting."

1999 beauftragten französische Zisterziensermönche John Pawson mit der Planung eines neuen Klosters. Als Standort hatten sich die Mönche ein 100 ha großes Grundstück westlich von Prag ausgesucht, mit einem Herrenhaus aus dem 18. Jahrhundert, das 40 Jahre lang nicht bewohnt worden war. Sie kannten Pawsons Buch *Minimum* und hatten Bilder seines Apartments für Calvin Klein in Manhattan gesehen, bevor sie ihn als Architekten auswählten. Pawson, der das **KLOSTER NOVY DVÛR** „das Projekt seines Lebens" nennt, erwähnt, dass ein „Mönchskloster mit einer in sich abgeschlossenen Stadt verglichen wird, mit vielen ‚Unterprogrammen', die typischerweise Funktionen wie Kirche, Wohnraum, Büro, Schule, Werkstatt, Gästehaus, Krankenhaus und Bauernhof beinhalten." Pawsons 6500 m² umfassender Entwurf basiert auf einer Zeichnung aus dem 12. Jahrhundert, die der heilige Bernhard von Clairvaux für die Gebäude des Zisterzienserordens anfertigte. Er sah einfache Räume mit natürlicher Beleuchtung und stimmigen Proportionen vor. Pawson setzte das barocke Herrenhaus instand und fügte drei moderne Flügel an, die sich exakt dort befinden, wo bereits früher Gebäude standen. Die Abbaye du Thoronet, eine Zisterzienserabtei zwischen Draguignan und Brignoles in Südfrankreich, war Pawson bekannt; aber zum ersten Mal hat er selbst ein Gebäude mit einer religiösen Funktion entworfen. Er erläutert: „Ich musste meinen Stil nicht besonders anpassen. Ich hatte schon vorher die Regeln des heiligen Bernhard gelesen (die Apologie von 1127 gegen künstlerische Verzierung), daher fand ich die Ideen alle sehr einleuchtend." Die Herausforderung des Projekts, so Pawson, bestand darin, das Kloster so zu entwerfen, dass die präzisen Ordensregeln und Rituale der Mönche ohne Behinderungen ausgeführt werden können. „Die Kirche", sagt er abschließend, „sollte das Beten vereinfachen – sie sollte Ruhe und Freude vermitteln –, aber sie sollte auch anregend wirken ohne abzulenken."

C'est en 1999 que des moines cisterciens français ont demandé à John Pawson de les aider à édifier un nouveau **MONASTÈRE** dans un domaine de cent hectares à l'ouest de Prague, sur lequel s'élevait un manoir du XVIIIe siècle, inhabité depuis plus de quarante ans. Les religieux connaissaient bien l'ouvrage *Minimum* et avaient vu des photos du magasin Calvin Klein à Manhattan avant de le sélectionner. Pawson, pour lequel cette commande est « le projet de [sa] vie », rappelle que « le monastère a été comparé à une ville fermée, remplissant les multiples fonctions d'église, de foyer, de bureaux, d'école, d'ateliers, de maison d'hôtes, d'hôpital et de ferme ». Appuyant son projet de 6500 m² sur les recommandations établies au XIIe siècle pour les bâtiments de l'Ordre par saint Bernard de Clairvaux, qui voulait des espaces simples et épurés ainsi que le respect de la lumière et de proportions correctes, Pawson a restauré le manoir baroque et lui a ajouté trois ailes sur les traces d'anciennes constructions. Il connaissait bien l'abbaye du Thoronet, ensemble cistercien situé non loin de Draguignan et Brignoles dans le Midi de la France, mais c'était la première fois qu'il devait concevoir un édifice religieux : « Je n'ai pas eu à adapter particulièrement mon style. J'avais déjà lu la règle de saint Bernard [l'Apologie de la vie monastique de 1127 contre l'ornement artistique], aussi toutes ses idées avaient-elles déjà un sens pour moi. » Le défi était dès lors de concevoir un monastère dans lequel les mouvements et les rituels précis des moines pouvaient se dérouler sans la moindre gêne. « L'église », conclut-il, « devait favoriser la prière – apporter le calme et le plaisir – mais également être stimulante sans pour autant distraire. »

Pawson's careful study of the functions of the monastery ultimately led him to create simple forms that do not contradict those of the existing buildings on the site.

Pawsons genaue Analyse der funktionalen Abläufe im Kloster führte letztlich zu den einfachen Formen, die mit dem Bestehenden harmonieren.

L'étude approfondie des fonctions du monastère a finalement incité Pawson à créer des formes simples qui ne heurtent pas celles des bâtiments préexistants.

Passageways and patterns of light are the most obvious traces of architecture in these images, where all extraneous intervention has been set aside.

Die Wege und die Lichtführung sind die deutlichsten Spuren einer Architektur, die jede unwesentliche Intervention vermeidet.

Des passages et des effets de lumière sont les traces d'architecture les plus évidentes dans ces images dont toute intervention extérieure semble avoir été exclue.

Pawson's work shows that there is nothing that prohibits centuries-old traditions from being served by contemporary architecture.

Pawsons Projekt zeigt, dass auch zeitgenössische Architektur im Dienst jahrhundertealter Tradition stehen kann.

Le projet de Pawson montre que même l'architecture contemporaine peut être au service d'une tradition séculaire.

An occasional liturgical object or
piece of wooden furniture enters
this realm of light and worship.
Pawson has sought and surely found
something of the quintessence of
architecture in Novy Dvûr.

Ein liturgisches Objekt oder ein
einzelnes Möbelstück aus Holz findet
sich in diesem Reich des Lichtes und
der Anbetung. Pawson hat in Novy
Dvûr etwas von der Quintessenz von
Architektur gesucht und sicher auch
gefunden.

De temps à autre, un objet liturgique
ou un meuble en bois fait son
apparition dans ce lieu de lumière
et de prière. À Novy Dvûr, Pawson a
cherché et certainement trouvé
quelque chose qui se rapproche de
la quintessence de l'architecture.

DOMINIQUE PERRAULT

Dominique Perrault Architecture
6, rue Bouvier
75011 Paris
France

Tel: +33 1 4406 0000
Fax: +33 1 4406 0001
E-mail: dpa@d-p-a.fr
Web: www.perraultarchitecte.com

DOMINIQUE PERRAULT was born in 1953 in Clermont-Ferrand. He studied in Paris and received his diploma as an architect from the École des Beaux-Arts in 1978. He received a further degree in urbanism at the École Nationale des Ponts et Chaussées in 1979, as well as a master's degree in history at the EHESS in 1980. He founded his own firm in 1981 in Paris. His first well publicized works were the Engineering School (ESIEE), Marne-la-Vallée (1984–87); the Hôtel industriel Berlier, Paris (1986–90); the Applix factory, Cellier-sur-Loire (1991–99); and the Town Hall / Hybrid Hotel, Innsbruck, Austria (2000–02). His major projects include the French National Library in Paris (1989–95) and the Olympic Velodrome, Swimming and Diving Pool, Berlin (1992–99). Further buildings include the Media Library, Vénissieux (1997–2001); the design of several supermarkets for the M-Preis chain in Austria (1999–2003); the refurbishment of the Piazza Gramsci, Cinisello Balsamo, Milan (1999–2004); and the master plan for the Donau City, Vienna (2002–03). His recent projects include: a redesign of the urban waterfront "Las Teresitas" (2000–06) and the construction of a 5-star hotel (2000–08), both in Tenerife, Canary Islands; the Habitat Sky Tower, Barcelona (2002–07); the Olympic Tennis Center, Madrid (2002–07); the Ewha Women's University, Seoul (2004–07); the Sky Tower, Vienna (2004–08); the redevelopment of the banks of the Manzanares, Madrid (2005–08); and an extension of the Court of Justice of the European Community, Luxembourg (2008).

DOMINIQUE PERRAULT, 1953 in Clermont-Ferrand geboren, erwarb 1978 sein Architekturdiplom an der École des Beaux-Arts in Paris, 1979 ein weiteres Diplom in Stadtplanung an der École Nationale des Ponts et Chaussées in Paris sowie 1980 einen Master in Geschichte an der EHESS. 1981 gründete er in Paris seine eigene Firma. Zu seinen ersten bekannteren Arbeiten gehören die Ingenieurschule (ESIEE) in Marne-la-Vallée (1984–87), das Hôtel industriel Berlier in Paris (1986–90), die Applix-Fabrik in Cellier-sur-Loire (1991–99) und das Rathaus/Hybrid Hotel in Innsbruck (2000–02). Zu seinen größten Projekten zählen die französische Nationalbibliothek in Paris (1989–97), die olympische Rad- und Schwimmsporthalle in Berlin (1992–98) sowie eine groß angelegte Studie zur Stadtentwicklung von Bordeaux (1992–2000). Zu seinen weiteren Projekten zählen die Mediathek in Vénissieux (1997–2001), die Planung mehrerer Filialen der Supermarktkette M-Preis in Österreich (1999–2003), die Modernisierung der Piazza Gramsci in Cinisello Balsamo in Mailand (1999–2004), der Masterplan für die Donau City in Wien (2002–03). Unter den neueren Projekten finden sich die Umgestaltung des Uferbezirks Las Teresitas (2000–06) und die Realisierung eines Fünf-Sterne-Hotels auf Teneriffa (2000–08), der Habitat Sky Tower in Barcelona (2002–07), das olympische Tenniscenter in Madrid (2002–07), die Ewha-Frauenuniversität in Seoul (2004–07), der Skytower in Wien (2004–08), die Umgestaltung des Manzanaresufers in Madrid (2005–08) sowie ein Erweiterungsbau für den Gerichtshof der Europäischen Gemeinschaft in Luxemburg (2008).

DOMINIQUE PERRAULT naît en 1953 à Clermont-Ferrand. Il est diplômé d'architecture de l'École des Beaux-Arts de Paris en 1978, diplômé en urbanisme de l'École Nationale des Ponts et Chaussées, Paris (1979) et obtint une maîtrise d'histoire à l' EHESS (1980). Il crée son agence en 1981 à Paris. Parmi ses premières réalisations les plus connues : l'École d'ingénieurs ESIEE (Marne-la-Vallée, 1984–87), l'hôtel industriel Berlier (Paris, 1986–90), l'usine Applix à Cellier-sur-Loire (1991–99) et l'Hôtel de Ville / Hybrid Hotel à Innsbruck (2000–02). Parmi ses projets majeurs : la Bibliothèque de France (Paris, 1989–1997), le vélodrome et la piscine olympiques (Berlin, 1992–98) et une étude urbanistique de fond sur la ville de Bordeaux (1992–2000). Parmi ses réalisations : la médiathèque de Vénissieux (1997–2001) ; la conception de plusieurs supermarchés pour la chaîne M-Preis en Autriche (1999–2003) ; la modernisation de la Piazza Gramsci, Cinisello Balsamo (Milan, 1999–2004) ; le masterplan pour la Donau City à Vienne (2002–03). Entre autres projets plus récents : le réaménagement du front de mer « Las Teresitas » (2000–06) et la construction d'un hôtel de luxe à Ténériffe (Îles Canaries, 2000–08) ; l'habitat Sky Tower à Barcelone (2002–07) ; le centre olympique de tennis à Madrid (2002–07) ; l'Université pour femmes Ewha à Séoul (2004–07) ; le Skytower à Vienne (2004–08) ; le réaménagement des rives du Manzanares à Madrid (2005–08) ainsi que l'agrandissement de la Cour de justice de la Communauté européenne à Luxembourg (2008).

OLYMPIC SWIMMING POOL

Berlin, Germany, 1992–99

*Completion: 11/99. Client: City of Berlin, Department for Construction and Housing, represented by
Olympia 2000 Sportstättenbau GmbH. Landscape: Landschaft Planen & Bauen, Berlin.
Floor area: 28 490 m². Capacity: 1600 seats.
Costs: € 204.5 million (total including the velodrome).*

Originally intended as an element of Berlin's proposal for the 2000 Olympic Games, the swimming pool is located next to the velodrome conceived by Perrault (in collaboration with Rolf Reichert and Hans Jürgen Schmidt) for the same event. Echoing the low-lying geometric circle traced in the ground for the velodrome, Perrault here uses a strict rectangle, set deeply into a surrounding orchard of 450 apple trees. Trying to avoid the heavy-handed symbolism that characterized the 1936 Olympic Games, Perrault opted for a minimalist discretion, a digging into the earth that is atypical of modernist designs. Although the idea of placing a major part of the structure below ground level initially necessitated higher construction costs, it will ensure the thermal stability of the complex, and reduce the building's energy consumption. The 28 490 m² complex was built at a cost of € 138 million.

Ursprünglich für die Bewerbung Berlins um den Austragungsort der Olympischen Spiele 2000 geplant, befindet sich diese Schwimmsporthalle neben der von Perrault (in Zusammenarbeit mit Rolf Reichert und Hans Jürgen Schmidt) für das gleiche Ereignis entworfenen Radsporthalle. Sowohl das tiefer liegende kreisförmige Velodrom als auch die rechteckig angelegte Schwimmsporthalle sind in einen Obstgarten mit 450 Apfelbäumen eingebettet. Um den plumpen Symbolismus, der die Olympischen Spiele von 1936 kennzeichnete, zu vermeiden, entschied sich der Architekt für eine minimalistische Zurückhaltung, die für zeitgenössische Bauten ungewöhnlich ist. Zwar mag die Idee, einen Großteil des Gebäudes unter die Erde zu verlegen, höhere Baukosten verursacht haben, dadurch wird aber andererseits die Wärmestabilität gewährleistet und so letztendlich der Energieverbrauch reduziert. Der 28 490 m² große Komplex wurde für € 138 Millionen erbaut.

Projetée à l'occasion de la candidature de Berlin aux Jeux Olympiques 2000, cette piscine est située à côté du vélodrome olympique, réalisation de Perrault (en collaboration avec Rolf Reichert et Hans Jürgen Schmidt) s'inscrivant dans le même contexte, le vélodrome olympique. En opposition au cercle surbaissé du vélodrome, il utilise ici un forme strictement rectangulaire entourée d'un verger de 450 pommiers. Pour éviter le lourd symbolisme des Jeux Olympiques de 1936, l'architecte a opté pour une discrétion minimaliste atypique des projets contemporains. Bien que l'idée d'implanter la plus grande partie du bâtiment sous le niveau du sol ait entraîné des coûts de construction plus élevés, elle permet d'assurer une meilleure stabilité thermique et de réduire la consommation énergétique. Cet ensemble de 28 490 m² a coûté € 138 millions.

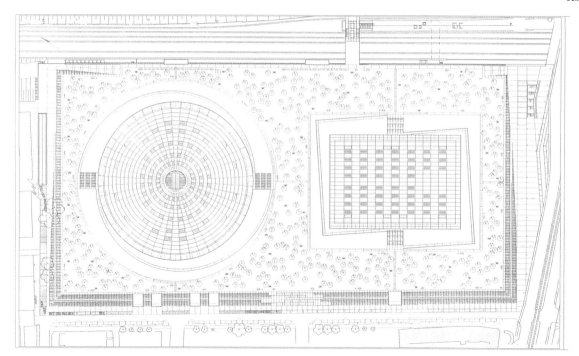

Like the neighboring velodrome, the Olympic Swimming Pool is recessed into the site, making its size and volume much less evident than they might have been.

Die Schwimmhalle wurde ebenso wie die benachbarte Radrennbahn zum Teil unter Bodenniveau angelegt, was den Bauten trotz ihrer Größe die Massivität nimmt.

De même que son voisin, le vélodrome, la piscine olympique est en partie enterrée, ce qui réduit d'autant son volume apparent.

Using the kind of strong minimalist vocabulary with an insistence on hard surfaces that he demonstrated in the Bibliothèque de France in Paris, Dominique Perrault created a strict, efficient swimming facility.

Die kraftvoll-minimalistische Formensprache, die er bei der Bibliothèque de France demonstrierte, bestimmt auch Perraults strenge, funktionalistische Schwimmhalle.

À partir d'un vocabulaire minimaliste vigoureux et du goût pour les surfaces dures telles que celles de la Bibliothèque de France à Paris, Dominique Perrault a créé un centre de natation sobre et fonctionnel.

RENZO PIANO

Renzo Piano Building Workshop
34, rue des Archives
75004 Paris
France

Tel: +33 1 4461 4900, Fax: +33 1 4278 0198
E-mail: france@rpbw.com, Web: www.rpbw.com

RENZO PIANO was born in 1937 in Genoa, Italy. He studied at the University of Florence, and at the Polytechnic Institute, Milan (1964). He formed his own practice (Studio Piano) in 1965, then associated with Richard Rogers (Piano & Rogers, 1971–78). Piano completed the Pompidou Center in Paris in 1977. From 1978 to 1980, he worked with Peter Rice (Piano & Rice Associates). He created the Renzo Piano Building Workshop in 1981 in Genoa and Paris. Piano received the RIBA Gold Medal in 1989. His built work includes: Menil Collection Museum (Houston, Texas, 1981–86); conversion of the Lingotto Factory Complex (Turin, Italy, 1983–2003); Cité Internationale de Lyon (Lyon, France, 1985–96); San Nicola Stadium (Bari, Italy, 1987–90); the 1988–90 extension of the IRCAM (Paris); Kansai International Airport Terminal (Osaka, Japan, 1988–94); Beyeler Foundation Museum (Riehen, Basel, Switzerland, 1991–97); Jean-Marie Tjibaou Cultural Center (New Caledonia, 1991–98); Padre Pio Pilgrimage Church (San Giovanni Rotondo, Foggia, Italy, 1991–2004); Potsdamer Platz reconstruction (Berlin, Germany, 1992–2000); Mercedes-Benz Center (Stuttgart, Germany, 1993–98); Rome Auditorium (Italy, 1994–2002); Parma Auditorium (Italy, 1997–2001); Maison Hermès (Tokyo, Japan, 1998–2001); and renovation and expansion of the Morgan Library (New York, 2000–06). Other projects include: New York Times Tower (New York, 2004–07); Whitney Museum of American Art (New York); High Museum Expansion (Atlanta, Georgia, 1999–2005); The Shard (London Bridge Tower, London, 2000–12); California Academy of Sciences (San Francisco, 2000–08); and the Chicago Art Institute Expansion (Chicago, 1999–2009).

RENZO PIANO wurde 1937 in Genua geboren. Er studierte an der Universität von Florenz und am Polytechnischen Institut in Mailand (1964). 1965 eröffnete er unter dem Namen Studio Piano ein eigenes Büro und schloss sich dann mit Richard Rogers zu Piano & Rogers zusammen (1971–78). 1977 errichteten sie das Centre Pompidou in Paris. Von 1978 bis 1980 arbeitete er mit Peter Rice (Piano & Rice Associates). 1981 eröffnete er in Genua und Paris den Renzo Piano Building Workshop. 1989 erhielt Piano die Goldmedaille der RIBA. Zu seinen realisierten Bauten gehören: Menil Collection Museum (Houston, Texas, 1981–86), Umbau des Fiat-Werks Lingotto (Turin, 1983–2003), Cité Internationale de Lyon (Lyon, 1985–96), Stadion San Nicola (Bari, 1987–90), die Erweiterung des IRCAM (Paris, 1988–90), Kansai International Airport Terminal (Osaka, 1988–94), Museum der Fondation Beyeler (Riehen bei Basel, 1991–97), Kulturzentrum Jean-Marie Tjibaou (Neukaledonien, 1991–98), Pilgerkirche Padre Pio (San Giovanni Rotondo, Foggia, Italien, 1991–2004), Wiederaufbau des Potsdamer Platzes (Berlin, 1992–2000), Mercedes-Benz-Center (Stuttgart, 1993–98), Auditorium in Rom (1994–2002), Auditorium in Parma (1997–2001), Maison Hermès (Tokio, 1998–2001) sowie Renovierung und Ausbau der Morgan Library (New York, 2000–06). Weitere Projekte sind: New York Times Tower (New York, 2004–07), Whitney Museum of American Art (New York), High Museum Expansion (Atlanta, Georgia, 1999–2005), The Shard (London Bridge Tower, London, 2000–12), California Academy of Sciences (San Francisco, 2000–08) und die Erweiterung des Chicago Art Institute Chicago (1999–2009).

RENZO PIANO né en 1937 à Gênes, Italie, étudie à l'Université de Florence et à l'Institut Polytechnique de Milan (1964). Il crée son agence, Studio Piano, en 1965, puis s'associe à Richard Rogers (Piano & Rogers, 1971–78). Ils achèvent le Centre Pompidou à Paris en 1977. De 1978 à 1980, il collabore avec Peter Rice (Piano & Rice Associates). Il fonde le Renzo Piano Building Workshop en 1981 à Gênes et Paris. Il a reçu la médaille d'or du RIBA en 1989. Parmi ses réalisations : le Menil Collection Museum, Houston, Texas (1981–86) ; la conversion de l'usine du Lingotto, Turin, Italie (1983–2003) ; la Cité Internationale de Lyon, France (1985–96) ; le stade San Nicola, Bari, Italie (1987–90) ; l'extension de l'IRCAM, Paris (1988–90) ; le terminal de l'aéroport international du Kansai Airport, Osaka, Japon (1988–94) ; le musée de la Fondation Beyeler, Riehen, Bâle, Suisse (1991–97) ; le Centre culturel Jean-Marie Tjibaou, Nouvelle-Calédonie (1991–98) ; l'église de pèlerinage Padre Pio (San Giovanni Rotondo, Foggia, Italie (1991–2004) ; la reconstruction de la Potsdamer Platz, Berlin (1992–2000) ; le Centre Mercedes-Benz, Stuttgart, (1993–98) ; l'auditorium de Rome (1994–2002) ; l'auditorium de Parme (1997–2001), la Maison Hermès, Tokyo (1998–2001), et la rénovation et l'agrandissement de la Morgan Library (New York, 2000–06). Ses autres projets sont : la New York Times Tower (New York, 2004–07) ; le Whitney Museum of American Art (New York) ; High Museum Expansion (Atlanta, Georgie, 1999–2005) ; The Shard (London Bridge Tower, Londres, 2000–12) ; la California Academy of Sciences (San Francisco, 2000–08) et l'agrandissement du Chicago Art Institute (Chicago, 1999–2009).

JEAN-MARIE TJIBAOU CULTURAL CENTER

Nouméa, New Caledonia, 1992–98

Competition: 1991. Conceptual design: 1992. Construction: 1994–98.
Client: Agency for the Development of Kanak Culture, Marie Claude Tjibaou (President).
Floor area: 7650 m². Costs: c. € 30.5 million.

From the outset, Renzo Piano included the question of the identity of the Kanak people in his concept for a cultural center named after a local proponent of independence from France. Specifically non-European in its concept, this alignment of ten conical wooden "houses" connected by a glass and wood corridor drawn out over some 250 m is surrounded by a garden of carefully chosen local plants. The ten structures are aligned in three groups according to their function: entrance, exhibition space and cafeteria; multimedia and temporary exhibitions; video rooms, and classrooms for courses in local culture. The naturally ventilated "houses" turn their curved backs to the ocean, which is to say against the prevailing winds that can attain a hurricane force of over 240 km/h. There was no question of the architect copying any local architecture – rather he has given a sensitive and unexpected contemporary interpretation to the design of this center, which is located on a small peninsula 10 km northwest of the capital, Nouméa.

Von Anfang an bezog Renzo Piano die Frage nach der Identität der Südseeinsulaner in seinen Entwurf für ein Kulturzentrum ein, das nach einem Kämpfer für die Unabhängigkeit Neukaledoniens von Frankreich benannt ist. Die Folge von zehn kegelförmigen hölzernen „Häusern", die durch einen etwa 250 m langen Korridor aus Glas und Holz miteinander verbunden sind, ist von einem Garten mit sorgfältig ausgewählten einheimischen Pflanzen umgeben. Die zehn Bauten sind entsprechend ihrer Funktion in drei Gruppen aufgeteilt: Eingang, Ausstellungsbereich und Cafeteria; Multimedia und Wechselausstellungen; Video- und Unterrichtsräume für das Studium der einheimischen Kultur. Die natürlich belüfteten „Häuser" wenden ihre gekrümmten Rückseiten dem Meer zu und trotzen dem Wind, der hier eine Geschwindigkeit von mehr als 240 km/h erreichen kann. Piano hat die regionale Architektur mit dieser Anlage auf einer kleinen Halbinsel 10 km nordwestlich der Hauptstadt Nouméa ebenso einfühlsam wie überraschend interpretiert.

Dès le départ, Renzo Piano a intégré dans son projet qui porte le nom d'un leader indépendantiste assassiné, le problème de l'identité du peuple kanak. De concept non-européen, cet alignement de dix « maisons » coniques en bois réunies par un corridor en bois et en verre, se développe sur environ 250 m de long, entouré d'un jardin de plantes locales choisies avec soin. Les deux structures sont disposées en trois groupes selon leur fonction : entrée, espace d'exposition et cafétéria ; expositions temporaires et multi-média ; salles vidéo et salles de cours sur la culture locale. Les « maisons » qui bénéficient d'une ventilation naturelle tournent leurs dos arrondi à l'océan, et donc aux vents dominants qui peuvent atteindre jusqu'à 240 km/h. Plutôt que de copier l'architecture locale, Piano a préféré en donner une interprétation sensible et inattendue. Le Centre se dresse sur une péninsule à 10 km au nord-ouest de la capitale, Nouméa.

Inspired by local architecture, the complex is meant to resemble a village of wooden huts.

Die von der lokalen Architektur inspirierte Anlage ist einem Dorf mit Holzhütten nachempfunden.

Inspiré de l'architecture locale, ce complexe culturel ressemble à un village de huttes modernes.

Despite its surprising wooden shell
construction, the Center makes
use of the most modern technology
available.

Trotz der überraschenden Außenhülle
aus Holz verfügt das Zentrum über
modernste Technologie.

La construction en bois n'empêche
pas le centre de faire appel aux
technologies les plus récentes.

CHRISTIAN DE PORTZAMPARC

Atelier Christian de Portzamparc
1, rue de l'Aude
75014 Paris
France

Tel: +33 1 4064 8000
Fax: +33 1 4327 7479
E-mail: studio@portzamparc.com
www.portzamparc.com

CHRISTIAN DE PORTZAMPARC was born in Casablanca, Morocco, in 1944. He studied at the École des Beaux-Arts, Paris (1962–69), and founded his own firm in 1980. Built projects include his Water Tower, Marne-la-Vallée (1971–74); Hautes Formes public housing, Paris (1975–79); Cité de la Musique, Paris (1985–95); extension for the Bourdelle Museum, Paris (1988–92); Housing, Nexus World, Fukuoka, Japan (1989–92); a housing complex at the ZAC Bercy, Paris (1991–94); and Crédit Lyonnais Tower, Euralille, Lille (1992–95), built over the Lille-Europe railway station in Lille. Other works include a courthouse for Grasse in the south of France (1993–97); the LVMH Tower on 57th Street, New York (1996–99); an addition to the Palais des Congrès, Paris (1996–99); and the Espace Lumière office building, Boulogne-Billancourt (1996–99); the French Embassy, Berlin (1997–2003); the Philharmonic concert hall, Luxembourg (1997–2005); the headquarters of the daily *Le Monde*, Paris (2001–04); and the Champs Libres museum and bookshop, Rennes (2002–06). Other projects include the master plan for the Massena neighborhood, Paris (1995–2010); the Cidade das Artes, Rio de Janeiro (2002–11); and an apartment building on Park Avenue South, New York (2002–09). Christian de Portzamparc was awarded the 1994 Pritzker Prize.

CHRISTIAN DE PORTZAMPARC, geboren 1944 in Casablanca, studierte von 1962 bis 1969 an der École des Beaux-Arts in Paris und gründete 1980 sein eigenes Büro. Zu seinen realisierten Projekten gehören der Wasserturm in Marne-la-Vallée (1971–74), die Wohnanlage Les Hautes Formes in Paris (1975–79), die Cité de la Musique in Paris (1985–95), die Erweiterung des Museums Bourdelle in Paris (1988–92), die Nexus-World-Wohnanlage im japanischen Fukuoka (1989–92), die ZAC-Bercy-Wohnsiedlung in Paris (1991–94) und der über dem Euralille-Bahnhof errichtete Crédit Lyonnais Tower in Lille (1992–95). Weitere Arbeiten sind das Gerichtsgebäude in Grasse in Südfrankreich (1993–97), der LVMH Tower in der 57. Straße in New York (1996–99), das Espace-Lumiére-Bürogebäude in Boulogne-Billancourt (1996–1999). Ab 2000 wurden die französische Botschaft in Berlin (1997–2003), die Philharmonie in Luxemburg (1997–2005), die Zentrale der Tageszeitung *Le Monde* in Paris (2001–04) sowie das Museum und der Buchladen Champs Libres in Rennes (2002–06) fertiggstellt. Weitere Projekte sind die umfassende Neugestaltung des Viertels Massena in Paris (1995–2010), die Cidade das Artes in Rio de Janeiro (2002–2011) und ein Apartmenthaus an der Park Avenue South in New York (2002–2009). 1994 wurde Portzamparc mit dem Pritzker-Preis ausgezeichnet.

Né à Casablanca en 1944, **CHRISTIAN DE PORTZAMPARC** étudie à l'École des Beaux-Arts de Paris (1962–69) et ouvre sa propre agence en 1980. Parmi ses réalisations : un château d'eau (Marne-la-Vallée, 1971–74), l'immeuble de logements économiques Les Hautes Formes (Paris, 1975–79), la Cité de la Musique à Paris (1985–95), l'extension du Musée Bourdelle (Paris, 1988–92), un immeuble d'appartements Nexus World (Fukuoka, Japon, 1989–92), un immeuble d'habitation dans la ZAC de Bercy (Paris, 1991–94) et la tour du Crédit Lyonnais (Euralille, Lille, 1992–95), au-dessus de la gare de Lille-Europe. Entre autres travaux, il convient de citer le Palais de justice de Grasse (1993–97), la tour LVMH 57th Street, à New York (1996–99), l'Espace Lumière, immeuble de bureaux, à Boulogne-Billancourt (1996–99). À partir de l'an 2000, l'ambassade de France à Berlin (1999–2003), la Philarmonie de Luxembourg (1997–2005), le siège du quotidien *Le Monde* à Paris (2001–04) ainsi que le musée et la librairie Champs libres à Rennes (2002–06) ont été achevés. Ses autres projets sont : la restructuration intégrale du quartier Masséna à Paris (1995–2010), la Cidade das Artes à Rio de Janeiro (2002–11), ainsi qu'un immeuble de logements dans la Park Avenue South à New York (2002–09). Il obtient en 1994 le Pritzker Prize.

LVMH TOWER

New York, New York, USA, 1995–99

*Planning: 1995–97. Construction: 1997–99. Client: LVMH Corporation.
Floor area: 8683 m². Costs: withheld.*

By using New York City zoning regulations very efficiently, the architect managed to translate the setbacks in the façade into extra height – used for the three-story "Magic Room" at the top of the structure.

In sehr geschickter Umsetzung der New Yorker Bauvorschriften gelang es dem Architekten, durch das Zurückstufen der Fassade (rechts) zusätzliche Höhe zu gewinnen, die er für die Anlage des dreistöckigen „Magic Room" (oben) als Bekrönung des Gebäudes nutzte.

Par une interprétation habile de la réglementation du zoning new-yorkais, l'architecte a mis à profit des retraits (à droite) pour augmenter la hauteur de la tour et créer sa « Magic Room » (ci-dessus) de trois étages de haut, au sommet de l'édifice.

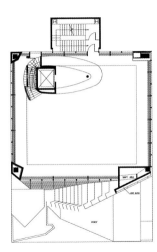

23rd floor

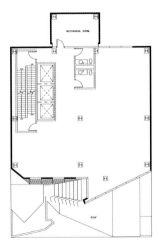

19th floor

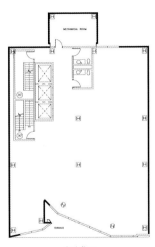

3rd floor

Set near the corner of 57th Street and Madison Avenue, the **LVMH TOWER** represents a shift in the design of tall buildings. Rather than the more common undifferentiated façade generally seen in Manhattan, this 23-story office building represents a complex Saint Gobain glass façade designed to avoid direct reflections of the black IBM Tower just across 57th Street. By carefully studying New York's complex zoning laws after a series of setbacks, the architect managed, through the use of a sophisticated design, to increase the overall height of his building, even edging out the neighboring Chanel Tower. This gave him the possibility of creating the so-called "Magic Room" atop the tower – a spectacular three-story room with views on three sides onto 57th Street, and toward Central Park. Portzamparc's contribution to the tower is in good part limited to this room and the façade, since the design of the offices, and of the boutiques on the ground floor, is the work of other architects. A sophisticated lighting system inserted into a "fault" line running up the façade gives the building a real nighttime identity in the cityscape.

Der nahe der Kreuzung von 57. Straße und Madison Avenue gelegene 23-geschossige **LVMH TOWER** stellt mit seiner komplexen Fassade aus Saint-Gobain-Glas eine Neuerung in der Hochhausarchitektur dar. Die Fassade, die sich deutlich von dem üblichen Erscheinungsbild der Hochhäuser in Manhattan absetzt, ist so strukturiert, dass eine direkte Spiegelung des genau gegenüberliegenden schwarzen IBM-Turms vermieden wird. In Umgehung der komplizierten New Yorker Baugesetze durch den Einsatz eines raffinierten Entwurfs ist es dem Architekten gelungen, die Gesamthöhe seines Bürogebäudes so zu vergrößern, dass es nun sogar den benachbarten Chanel Tower überragt. Dies gab Portzamparc die Möglichkeit, den sogenannten „Magic Room" an die Turmspitze zu setzen – einen spektakulären dreigeschossigen Raum mit freiem, dreiseitigem Ausblick auf die 57. Straße und den Central Park. Portzamparcs Beitrag zur Gestaltung des Hochhauses beschränkt sich im Wesentlichen auf diesen Raum und die Fassade, die Büros und die im Erdgeschoss befindlichen Geschäfte wurden von anderen Architekten entworfen und ausgeführt. Eine kunstvolle Beleuchtung, die in einer an der Fassade verlaufenden „Bruchlinie" eingesetzt wurde, verleiht dem Gebäude auch bei Nacht eine unverkennbare Identität.

Dressée presque à l'angle de la 57th Street et de Madison Avenue, la **TOUR LVMH** marque une évolution dans la conception des immeubles de grande hauteur. Au lieu de ces façades plus ou moins différenciées que l'on voit d'habitude à Manhattan, cette tour de bureaux de 23 étages arbore une complexe façade en verre de Saint-Gobain conçue pour éviter la réflexion directe de l'énorme tour noire d'IBM qui se dresse de l'autre côté de la rue. Après avoir étudié attentivement la réglementation compliquée du zoning de la ville de New York, Portzamparc a réussi, au moyen d'une série d'habiles retraits, à augmenter la hauteur totale de l'immeuble, jusqu'à dépasser sa voisine, la Tour Chanel. Ceci lui a permis de créer, au sommet, la « Magic-Room », une spectaculaire salle de trois étages de haut qui offre des vues sur trois côtés et sur Central Park. La contribution de l'architecte s'est pour une bonne part limitée à la façade et à cette salle, car l'aménagement des bureaux et des boutiques a été confiée à d'autres intervenants. Un système sophistiqué d'éclairage a été inséré dans une « faille » qui court verticalement sur la façade ce qui, la nuit, confère à l'immeuble sa forte identité.

 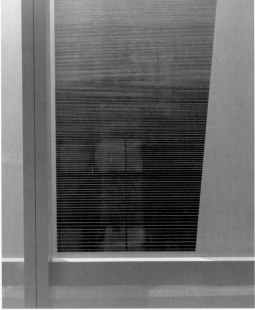

Christian de Portzamparc concentrated his efforts on the façade, and the Magic Room. His responsibility did not extend to interior decoration or to the ground level Christian Dior boutique designed by Peter Marino.

Christian de Portzamparc konzentrierte sich in seiner Gestaltung auf die Fassade und den „Magic Room". Er war weder für die Innenraumausstattung noch für die im Erdgeschoss liegende und von Peter Marino entworfene Christian-Dior-Boutique zuständig.

Christian de Portzamparc a concentré ses efforts sur la façade et la « Magic Room ». Il n'a été chargé ni des aménagements intérieurs ni du magasin Christian Dior du rez-de-chaussée, œuvre de Peter Marino.

RICHARD ROGERS

Rogers Stirk Harbour + Partners
Thames Wharf
Rainville Road
London W6 9HA
UK

Tel: +44 20 7385 1235
Fax: +44 20 7385 8409
E-mail: enquiries@rsh-p.com
Web: www.rsh-p.com

RICHARD ROGERS was born in Florence in 1933. He studied at the Architectural Association (AA) in London, and received his M.Arch. degree from Yale (1954–59). He was the recipient of the 1985 RIBA Gold Medal and the 2000 Praemium Imperiale. He is an Honorary Trustee of the Museum of Modern Art in New York. He founded his present firm Rogers Stirk Harbour + Partners in 1977, just after the completion of the Pompidou Center. "We were young and we wanted to shock them," says Renzo Piano, describing the design of the Georges Pompidou Center (Paris, 1971–77) that he worked on with Rogers. This goal was attained. Piano and Rogers both joined the ranks of the best-known architects in the world, known for a "high-tech" style that Rogers affirmed with very visible structures like the Lloyd's of London Headquarters (1978–86). Rogers subsequently refined his visually complex assemblages in buildings like the Channel 4 Television Headquarters (London, 1990–94), and his Law Courts in Bordeaux (France, 1992–98). Rogers has also participated in large-scale urban schemes like the Lu Jia Zui Masterplan (Shanghai, China, 1992–94). Other projects include the Madrid Barajas Airport (Spain, 1997–2006); Hesperia Hotel and Conference Center (Barcelona, 1999–2006); Maggie's Centre (London, 2001–08); and Terminal 5, Heathrow Airport (London, 1989–2008). Another high-profile project is the National Assembly for Wales building in Cardiff (1998–2005).

RICHARD ROGERS wurde 1933 in Florenz geboren. Er studierte Architektur an der Architectural Association in London und legte die Prüfung zum M.Arch. in Yale (1954–59) ab. 1985 wurde er mit der Goldmedaille der RIBA und im Jahr 2000 mit dem Praemium Imperiale ausgezeichnet. Er ist Treuhänder ehrenhalber des Museum of Modern Art in New York. Sein jetziges Büro Rogers Stirk Harbour + Partners gründete er 1977, unmittelbar nach Fertigstellung des Centre Pompidou. „Wir waren jung und wollten schockieren", sagt Renzo Piano, als er den Entwurf des Centre Georges Pompidou (Paris, 1971–77) beschreibt, das er zusammen mit Richard Rogers baute. Dieses Ziel erreichten sie. Piano und Rogers gehören zu den weltweit bekanntesten Architekten, berühmt für ihren Hightechstil, den Rogers mit sehr prägnanten Bauten wie der Zentrale von Lloyd's of London (1978–86) bestätigte. Rogers verfeinerte in der Folge seine visuell komplexen Projekte bei Bauten wie der Zentrale des Fernsehsenders Channel 4 (London, 1990–94) und seinem Gerichtsgebäude in Bordeaux (1992–98). Darüber hinaus beteiligte sich Richard Rogers an großflächigen Stadtprojekten wie dem Gesamtplan Lu Jia Zui (Shanghai, China, 1992–94). Zu den weiteren Projekten zählen der Flughafen Barajas, Madrid (1997–2006), Hesperia-Hotel mit Konferenzzentrum (Barcelona, 1999–2006), Maggie's Centre (London, 2001–08) und Terminal 5, Flughafen Heathrow (London, 1989–2008). Ein weiteres viel beachtetes Projekt ist das Gebäude der National Assembly for Wales in Cardiff (1998–2005).

Né à Florence, Italie, en 1933, **RICHARD ROGERS** étudie à l'Architectural Association de Londres et passe son M. Arch. à la Yale University School of Architecture (1954–59). Il reçoit la médaille d'or du RIBA en 1985 et le Praemium Imperiale en 2000. Il est administrateur honoraire du Museum of Modern Art de New York. Il fonde son agence actuelle, Rogers Stirk Harbour + Partners, en 1977, juste après l'achèvement du Centre Pompidou. « Nous étions jeunes et nous voulions les choquer », dit Renzo Piano pour décrire ce projet parisien (1971–77) dont il est le co-auteur. Le but fut atteint. Piano et Rogers rejoignirent alors les rangs des architectes les plus célèbres du monde, connus pour ce nouveau style *high-tech* que Rogers poursuivit dans des réalisations très vues comme le siège des Lloyd's, Londres (1978–86) ; le siège de Channel 4, Londres (1990–94) et le Palais de justice de Bordeaux (1992–98). Richard Rogers a également participé à des projets d'urbanisme à grande échelle comme le plan directeur du district de Lu Jia Zui, Shanghai, Chine (1992– 94). Parmi ses autres réalisations : l'aéroport de Barajas à Madrid (1997–2006) ; l'Hesperia Hotel and Conference Center, Barcelone (1999–2006) ; le Maggie's Centre, Londres (2001–08), et le Terminal 5 de l'aéroport d'Heathrow, Londres (1989–2008). Son projet pour l'Assemblée nationale du Pays de Galles à Cardiff (1998–2005) a été très remarqué.

LAW COURTS
Bordeaux, France, 1993–98

Competition: 11/1992. Planning: 1993–94. Construction: 1995–98.
Completion: 2000 (external works). Floor area: 25 000 m².
Costs: £ 27 million.

The Bordeaux **PALAIS DE JUSTICE** is located near the neoclassical heart of this southwestern French city. Intended to be light and open, symbolizing the transparency of the justice system, the building contains seven pod-like wood-clad courtroom structures, aligned behind a 20 x 76 m glass wall. Made with a concrete base and a wood-frame superstructure, the courtroom pods are lined with plywood with an overlay of cedar strips. They are approached by an open and exposed walkway that reveals the full height of the building. Known for his mechanically oriented design, Rogers here appears to make a successful foray into the domain of more organic forms. Directly abutting an ancient wall and surrounded largely by the classical stone buildings of Bordeaux, the Palais de Justice is at once surprising and coherent in this context.

Der **PALAIS DE JUSTICE** liegt nahe dem klassizistischen Zentrum von Bordeaux und ist als helles und offenes Gebäude geplant, um die Transparenz des Justizsystems zu symbolisieren. Der Bau enthält sieben holzverkleidete Gerichtssäle, aufgereiht hinter einer 20 x 76 m großen Glaswand. Die aus einer Betonbasis und einer Holzkonstruktion als Überbau bestehenden Gerichtssäle sind mit Sperrholz und darüberliegenden Zedernholzstreifen verkleidet. Sie sind über einen offenen Steg erschlossen, der die große Höhe des Gebäudes spürbar macht. Rogers, der für seine Hightechentwürfe bekannt ist, macht hier offenbar einen erfolgreichen Abstecher in den Bereich eher organischer Formen. Der direkt an eine alte Mauer angrenzende und überwiegend von klassizistischen Gebäuden umgebene Palais de Justice wirkt in diesem Kontext zugleich überraschend wie auch dazugehörig.

Le **PALAIS DE JUSTICE** de Bordeaux est situé non loin du centre néoclassique de la ville. Voulu ouvert et aérien pour symboliser la transparence du système judiciaire, il contient sept structures de chambres de justice en forme de coques recouvertes de bois, alignées derrière une paroi de verre de 20 x 76 m. Structures en bois montées sur une base de béton, ces coques sont doublées de contreplaqué recouvert de bardeaux de cèdre. On y accède par une passerelle ouverte assez exposée qui permet de prendre conscience de la hauteur du bâtiment. Connu pour son approche technologique, Rogers semble avoir fait ici une incursion réussie dans des formes plus organiques. Appuyé directement contre un ancien rempart et entouré en grande partie d'immeubles classiques de pierre blanche typiques de Bordeaux, ce Palais de Justice est à la fois surprenant et cohérent dans son contexte.

 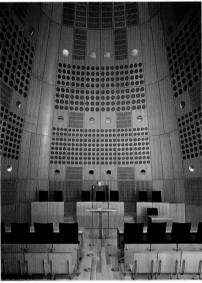 

The internal openness of the building contrasts with the wooden discretion of the actual courtrooms.

Die Transparenz der öffentlich zugänglichen Innenräume steht im Kontrast zur Geschlossenheit der holzverkleideten Gerichtssäle.

L'impression d'ouverture très sensible à l'intérieur du bâtiment contraste avec la neutralité du décor des salles du tribunal.

The wood-clad pods contain the courtroom spaces. A central glass passageway links them.

Die holzverkleideten Gehäuse enthalten die Gerichtssäle, die durch einen zentralen, verglasten Gang miteinander verbunden sind.

Les enceintes recouvertes de bois contiennent les salles du tribunal. Elles sont reliées par une passerelle de verre.

MARC ROLINET

Rolinet et Associés
9, rue Pierre Villey
75007 Paris
France

Tel: +33 1 44 42 01 10
Fax: +33 1 44 42 01 20
E-mail: rolinet@rolinet.fr
Web: www.rolinet.fr

L'Arbresle ▶

Born in Montbéliard, France, in 1956, **MARC ROLINET** earned a master's degree in urbanism from the prestigious Ecole des Ponts et Chaussées in 1980 and created his own architectural office the following year. Rolinet has built a large number of housing projects in Paris, Marseille and Cergy-Pontoise, including the prestigious Gros Caillou complex on the Rue de l'Université in Paris (2001). He also has considerable experience in the area of office buildings, and, more unexpectedly, religious structures. He has completed several projects for the Protestant Deaconesses of Reuilly, as well as churches in Paris, Villeneuve-le-Roi, and Montreuil in the Paris area. Despite the ease with which he works on a large scale, Marc Rolinet has also designed a number of individual homes. In 2002, his studio and residence for the Deaconesses of Reuilly in L'Arbresle in Versailles was also completed, as well as M1L, the headquarters of the French rail-network company Réseau Ferré de France in Paris. Other work includes La Moinerie, a large office building (for Electricité-Gaz de France on a greenfield site in Saint-Malo, 2004), and a residential hospital in Evian with vast glass façades on the shores of Lake Geneva (2006). In 2006 Rolinet also completed two office buildings in central Lisbon, Expobi 2, and opened a second office in Geneva, before building a group of new chalets, Grande Combe, in Grimentz, an Alpine village in the Valais region of Switzerland in 2007.

MARC ROLINET, geboren 1956 im französischen Montbéliard, erwarb 1980 den Master in Stadtplanung an der renommierten École des Ponts et Chaussées und gründete im darauffolgenden Jahr sein eigenes Architekturbüro in Paris. Rolinet hat eine große Zahl von Wohnungsbauprojekten in Paris, Marseille und Cergy-Pontoise realisiert, einschließlich der bekannten Anlage Gros Caillou in der Rue de l'Université in Paris (2001). Er hat auch viel Erfahrung im Bau von Bürogebäuden und – überraschenderweise – von Sakralbauten. So hat er für die protestantische Diakonissen von Reuilly mehrere Projekte realisiert, ebenso wie Kirchen in Paris, Villeneuve-le-Roi und Montreuil bei Paris. Neben seiner souveränen Gestaltung von Großbauten hat er auch eine Reihe von Privathäusern sowie die Hauptverwaltung des französischen Schienennetzbetreibers Réseau Ferré de France in Paris, M1L, entworfen. Weitere Arbeiten sind La Moinerie, ein großes Bürogebäude für Électricité-Gaz de France auf einer Grünfläche in Saint-Malo (2004) und ein Krankenpflegeheim in Évian mit großzügigen Glasfassaden am Ufer des Genfer Sees (2006). 2006 hat Rolinet im Zentrum von Lissabon zwei Bürogebäude, Expobi 2, fertiggestellt. In Grimentz, einem Bergdorf im Wallis in der Schweiz, baute er 2007 eine Reihe von Chalets (Grande Combe). 2006 eröffnete Rolinet ein zweites Büro in Genf.

Né à Montbéliard en 1956, **MARC ROLINET** est diplômé d'urbanisme de la prestigieuse École des Ponts et Chaussées en 1980 et crée son agence l'année suivante. Il a réalisé un grand nombre de logements à Paris, Marseille et Cergy-Pontoise, dont l'ensemble du Gros Caillou, rue de l'Université à Paris (2001). Son expérience dans le domaine du bureau et même des églises est considérable. Il a ainsi réalisé plusieurs projets pour les diaconesses protestantes de Reuilly, ainsi que des églises à Paris, Villeneuve-le-Roi et Montreuil, en région parisienne. En 2002, sa résidence-atelier conçue pour les diaconesses de Reuilly à L'Arbresle, à Versailles, a été terminée ainsi que le siège de la compagnie Réseau Ferré de France à Paris. Entre autres travaux : La Moinerie, grand immeuble de bureaux pour Électricité-Gaz de France sur un terrain viabilisé à Saint-Malo (2004), et une maison de repos aux vastes baies vitrées à Évian, sur les bords du lac Léman (2006). Rolinet a achevé deux immeubles de bureaux au centre de Lisbonne, Expobi 2 (2006). En 2007, il a construit un ensemble de chalets, Grande Combe (Grimentz, canton du Valais, Suisse). En 2006, Rolinet a créé une seconde agence à Genève.

L'ARBRESLE
Versailles, France, 2001–02

Client: Œuvres et Institutions des Diaconesses de Reuilly. Gross floor area: 620 m². Costs: € 7 626 000.

A small activities building set in a park near a Versailles hospital was destroyed by a storm in 1999. Marc Rolinet was called on to replace the structure on a tight budget. For a total cost of 626 000 euros, this 450-square-meter facility was built for an order of Protestant sisters (Communauté des Diaconesses de Reuilly). Aside from the original activities, the new building was to contain rooms for the sisters. The architect divided the project into four zones: on a square base, the activities area; on an oval base a woodworking shop; beneath the residential area, a large storage area, and finally the 37-meter-long living section, set up on pilotis and clad partially in polycarbonate. This cantilevered volume takes advantage of strong metallic supports and a relatively lightweight wood and plastic upper structure. On the whole, this facility has a rather Japanese feeling to it, because of the use of lightweight materials, and because of the four-part angular geometric composition.

Im Jahr 1999 zerstörte ein Sturm ein kleines, zu einem Krankenhaus bei Versailles gehörendes Mehrzweckgebäude. In der Folge beauftragte die protestantische Communauté des Diaconesses de Reuilly Marc Rolinet mit der Planung eines Neubaus. Das knappe Budget hielt er mit Baukosten von insgesamt 626 000 Euro für das fertige 450 m² große Gebäude ein. Zusätzlich zu den ursprünglichen Funktionen sollte das neue Haus auch Wohnräume für die Schwestern enthalten. Der Architekt teilte das Projekt in vier Zonen auf: einen quadratischen Bereich mit Räumen für verschiedene Aktivitäten, einen ovalen Bereich für die Holzwerkstatt, den großen Lagerraum im Untergeschoss und einen Wohnbereich, der mit einer Gesamtlänge von 37 m auf Stützpfeiler aus Metall gesetzt und teilweise mit Polycarbonat verkleidet wurde. Dieser auskragende Baukörper besteht aus einer relativ leichtgewichtigen Konstruktion aus Holz und Kunststoff. Insgesamt wirkt diese Anlage in ihrer Gestaltung ziemlich japanisch, was auf die Verwendung leichter Baumaterialien und die besondere geometrische Komposition der vier Bauteile zurückzuführen ist.

Ce petit bâtiment utilitaire situé dans un parc près d'un hôpital de Versailles avait été détruit au cours d'une tempête en 1999. Marc Rolinet fut appelé par la Communauté des Diaconesses de Reuilly pour le reconstruire, ce qu'il a fait dans le cadre d'un modeste budget de 626 000 euros. En plus de sa fonction d'origine, la nouvelle construction devait également compter des chambres pour les sœurs. Rolinet a divisé le projet en quatre zones, les activités dans une forme carrée, l'atelier de bois dans un ovale, un vaste espace de stockage niché sous la partie résidentielle, qui est un long tube de 37 m posé sur pilotis et partiellement habillé de polycarbonate. Ce volume en porte-à-faux et sa structure relativement légère en bois et plastique repose sur de solides piliers métalliques. La réalisation présente un certain caractère japonais par l'utilisation de matériaux légers et une composition en quatre parties.

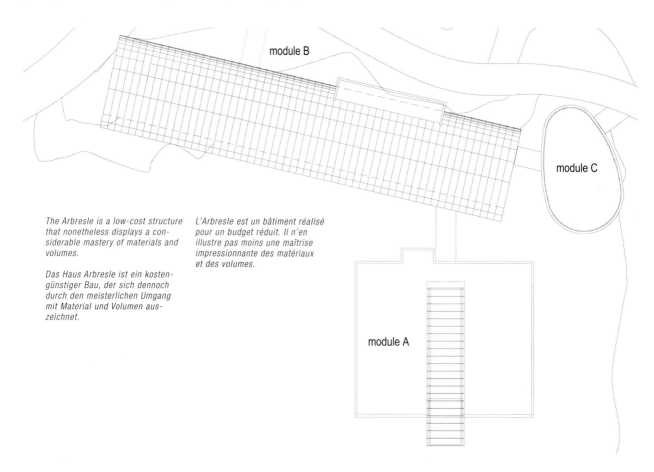

The Arbresle is a low-cost structure that nonetheless displays a considerable mastery of materials and volumes.

Das Haus Arbresle ist ein kostengünstiger Bau, der sich dennoch durch den meisterlichen Umgang mit Material und Volumen auszeichnet.

L'Arbresle est un bâtiment réalisé pour un budget réduit. Il n'en illustre pas moins une maîtrise impressionnante des matériaux et des volumes.

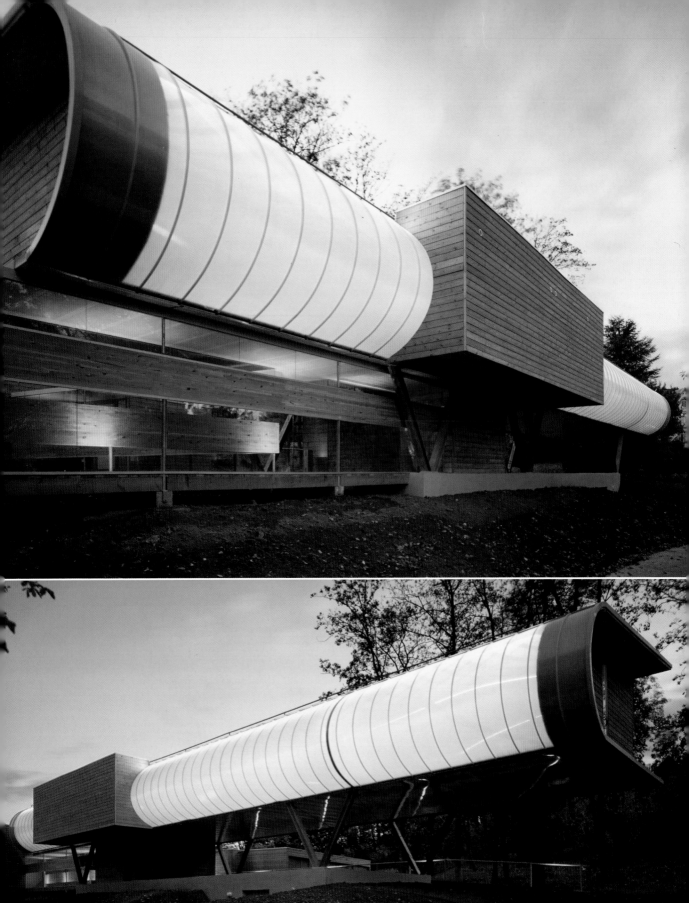

Interior spaces of the residential area include the hallway which is faced on one side with curved polycarbonate. This surface lets a diffused light in during the day and glows from within at night.

Zu den Räumen im Wohntrakt gehört ein Flur, der an einer Seite mit gewölbtem Polycarbonat verkleidet ist. Diese Oberfläche lässt tagsüber ein diffuses Licht ein und leuchtet nachts von innen.

Les espaces intérieurs de la partie résidentielle comprennent un hall qui court le long de la partie incurvée en polycarbonate. Cette surface diffuse une lumière douce pendant la journée et irradie pendant la nuit.

The residential volume is seen above and below, set up on pilotis. To the right, below, the oval workshop space identified as "Module C" on the plans.

Die beiden Fotos oben und unten links zeigen den auf Stützpfeilern ruhenden, auskragenden Wohntrakt. Unten rechts: Der ovale Werkstatt-raum ist auf dem Grundriss mit „Module C" ausgewiesen.

Le volume résidentiel, ci-dessus, et ci-dessous, est posé sur des pilotis. À droite, en bas, l'atelier ovale désigné comme « Module C » sur les plans.

HARRY SEIDLER

Harry Seidler and Associates
Level 5, 2 Glen Street
Milsons Point 2061 Sydney, NSW
Australia

Tel: + 61 2 9922 1388
Fax: + 61 2 9957 2947
E-mail: hsa@seidler.net.au
Web: www.seidler.net.au

Born in Vienna, Austria, **HARRY SEIDLER** studied architecture at the University of Manitoba in Winnipeg (B. Arch., 1944) before winning a scholarship to Harvard, where he participated in the master's class of Walter Gropius (M.Arch., 1946). He also studied design under Josef Albers at Black Mountain College in North Carolina and was the chief assistant of Marcel Breuer in New York from 1946 to 1948. He worked with Oscar Niemeyer in Rio de Janeiro before opening his own practice in Sydney in 1949. He taught at the Harvard Graduate School of Design (1976–77), and at the ETH in Zurich (1993) as well as at the University of Sydney. Winner of the RIBA Gold Medal in 1996, he is the author of the Australian Embassy in Paris (1973–77), the Shell Headquarters in Melbourne, and a social housing complex for 2500 people by the Danube in Vienna. For his Cove Apartments in Sydney, Seidler received the International Skyscraper Award (Internationaler Hochhauspreis) from the City of Frankfurt in 2004. Seidler died in Sydney on March 9, 2006.

Der in Wien geborene **HARRY SEIDLER** schloss 1944 sein Architekturstudium an der University of Manitoba in Winnipeg, Kanada, ab, bevor er ein Stipendium für Harvard erhielt, wo er die Meisterklasse von Walter Gropius besuchte und 1946 seinen Master of Architecture erwarb. Er studierte außerdem Entwurf bei Josef Albers am Black Mountain College in North Carolina und war von 1946 bis 1948 leitender Assistent bei Marcel Breuer in New York. Bevor er 1949 sein eigenes Büro in Sydney gründete, arbeitete er bei Oscar Niemeyer in Rio de Janeiro. Er lehrte an der Harvard Graduate School of Design (1976–77), an der Eidgenössischen Technischen Hochschule (ETH) in Zürich (1993) sowie an der University of Sydney. 1996 erhielt er die RIBA-Goldmedaille. Zu seinen Bauten gehören die australische Botschaft in Paris (1973–77), die Shell-Zentrale in Melbourne und ein Wohnkomplex für 2500 Menschen an der Wiener Donau. Für seine Cove Apartments in Sydney wurde Seidler 2004 mit dem Internationalen Hochhauspreis der Stadt Frankfurt ausgezeichnet. Seidler starb am 9. März 2006 in Sydney.

Né à Vienne, Autriche, **HARRY SEIDLER** étudie l'architecture à l'Université du Manitoba à Winnipeg (B. Arch., 1944) avant de recevoir une bourse pour Harvard où il participe au cours de maîtrise de Walter Gropius (M. Arch., 1946). Il étudie également la conception avec Josef Albers au Black Mountain College de Caroline du Nord et devient premier assistant de Josef Albers à New York de 1946 à 1948. Il travaille auprès d'Oscar Niemeyer à Rio de Janeiro avant d'ouvrir son agence à Sydney en 1949. Il a enseigné à l'Harvard Graduate School of Design (1976–77), et à l'ETH de Zurich (1993) ainsi qu'à l'Université de Sydney. Titulaire de la Médaille d'or du RIBA en 1996, il est l'auteur de l'ambassade d'Australie à Paris (1973–77), du siège social de Shell à Melbourne et d'un ensemble de logements pour 2 500 personnes à Vienne. Pour ses Cove Apartments à Sydney Seidler reçut de la Ville de Francfort l'Internationaler Hochhauspreis. Seidler est décédé à Sydney le 9 mars 2006.

BERMAN HOUSE

Joadja, New South Wales, Australia, 1996–99

Client: Mr. and Mrs. Berman. Site area: 91 hectares. Floor area: 570 m². Costs: $ 1.6 million.

This very clear ground-floor plan
shows the garage at the bottom, and
the irregular swimming pool at the
top. To the right, the rough stone
found on-site borders the swimming
pool and forms a wall above
a fountain.

*Der sehr klar gegliederte Grundriss
des Erdgeschosses ist durch die
Garage am unteren und den unregelmäßig geformten Swimmingpool am
oberen Ende begrenzt. Unbehauene,
vor Ort gefundene Sandsteinblöcke
umranden den Swimmingpool und
einen Springbrunnen (rechts oben).*

*Ce plan au sol très clair montre le
garage, en bas, et la piscine de forme
libre, en haut. À droite, des blocs
de pierre brute trouvés sur le terrain
bordent la piscine et forment un mur
au-dessus d'une fontaine.*

Set on a cliff edge on a one 100-hectare property overlooking a river and a vast wilderness area, the **BERMAN HOUSE** has a suspended living zone and a projecting balcony hung from the roof's steel columns. Using new technologies, the architect has framed the roofs of the living area, bedroom wing and garage with curved steel beams. The floors are made of concrete with Altasite stone paving. Sandstone boulders found on the site form the rough retaining walls that "anchor" the house to its natural setting and surround the irregular-shaped swimming pool. These harsh stone walls contrast dramatically with the sophisticated white curves of the house itself. A lack of municipal water dictates the collection of rainwater from the roofs and the design of the swimming pool to serve as a reservoir in case of bush fires. Inside, stone fireplaces and radiant floor heating are intended to increase energy self-sufficiency. The fireplaces "define specific areas within the most open-planned space."

Das **BERMAN HOUSE** liegt am Rand eines Felsens auf einem 100 ha großen Grundstück mit Blick auf einen Fluss und ein riesiges Wüstengebiet. Zu seinen Besonderheiten gehören der abgehängte Wohnbereich und ein vorspringender, an den Stahlstützen des Daches befestigter Balkon. Unter Einsatz neuer Technologien verwendete der Architekt für die Überdachungen von Wohnbereich, Schlafzimmertrakt und Garage gebogene Stahlrahmenträger. Die Fußböden bestehen aus Beton- und Steinplatten. Im Gelände vorgefundene Sandsteine dienten als Baumaterial für die unbearbeiteten Stützmauern, die das Haus in seiner natürlichen Umgebung „verankern", sowie für die Umgrenzungsmauer des unregelmäßig geformten Swimmingpools. Diese rauen Steinwände bilden einen scharfen Kontrast zu den eleganten weißen Bogenlinien des Hauses selbst. Die fehlende städtische Wasserversorgung machte es notwendig, dass ein Auffangbecken für die Sammlung von Regenwasser installiert wurde und der Swimmingpool auch als Wasservorrat für den Fall eines Buschfeuers dient. Im Inneren des Hauses tragen offene Kamine zur Selbstversorgung mit Energie bei. Die steinernen Kamine dienen zudem zur räumlichen Abgrenzung der einzelnen Wohnbereiche innerhalb des sehr offen angelegten Grundrisses.

Implantée sur l'arrête d'une falaise dans un domaine de 100 ha dominant un fleuve et une vaste étendue sauvage, la **MAISON BERMAN** possède une zone de séjour suspendue et un balcon projeté accroché aux colonnes d'acier du toit. Faisant appel à de nouvelles technologies, l'architecte a structuré les toits de la zone de séjour, l'aile de la chambre et le garage à l'aide de poutres d'acier incurvées. Les sols sont en béton recouvert d'un dallage de pierre d'Altasite. Des rochers de grès trouvés sur place ont été utilisés dans les murs de soutènement qui « ancrent » la maison dans son cadre naturel et entourent la piscine de forme irrégulière. Ces murs de pierre brute contrastent spectaculairement avec les courbes blanches sophistiquées de la maison. L'absence de branchement au réseau d'eau public, explique la récupération d'eau de pluie des toits et le dessin de la piscine qui sert de réservoir en cas de feux naturels. À l'intérieur, les cheminées en pierre et le chauffage central au sol participent à l'autarcie énergétique de la maison ; les cheminées « définissent des zones spécifiques dans l'espace de plan en grande partie ouvert ».

The spectacular wave-like roof lifts above the living space, offering views onto the neighboring countryside. In contrast to the hard surfaces of the house, lighting, a fireplace, and the site itself provide a natural counterpoint.

Das spektakuläre, sich wellenförmig über dem Wohnbereich erhebende Dach mit Ausblicken auf die Umgebung. Im Gegensatz zu den harten Oberflächen des Hauses setzen die Beleuchtung, ein offener Kamin und die Lage selbst einen natürlichen Kontrapunkt.

Le spectaculaire toit en vague se soulève au dessus du séjour, en dégageant des perspectives sur le paysage environnant. L'éclairage, la cheminée et le site lui-même fournissent un contrepoint naturel aux surfaces « dures » de la maison.

A terrace cantilevers out over the abrupt cliff visible on page 709. Like many earlier Modernist houses, the Berman residence sits easily on its rugged site, not visually disturbing the natural rock formations.

Die Terrasse ragt über den auf Seite 709 abgebildeten steil abfallenden Hang hinaus. Wie viele Häuser der frühen Moderne fügt sich das Berman House natürlich in seine zerklüftete Umgebung mit ihren Felsformationen ein.

Une terrasse s'élève en porte-à-faux au-dessus de la falaise abrupte. Comme beaucoup de maisons modernistes antérieures, la résidence des Berman a aisément trouvé sa place dans un site sauvage, sans apparemment déranger le cadre naturel des rochers.

From every vantage point, the house opens out in a spectacular fashion onto the wilderness. The walls and cladding offer varying degrees of roughness, from smooth glass to rough sandstone.

Aus allen Blickwinkeln öffnet sich das Haus auf spektakuläre Weise der Wildnis ringsum. Die Oberflächen der Wände und Verkleidungen reichen von glattem Glas bis zu unbearbeitetem Sandstein.

De tous les côtés, la maison s'ouvre de manière spectaculaire sur la nature. Les murs et l'habillage présentent divers degrés de finition de surface, du verre lisse à la pierre calcaire brute.

ÁLVARO SIZA

Álvaro Siza Arquitecto SA
Rua do Aleixo, 53–2
4150–043 Porto
Portugal

Tel: +351 22 616 72 70
Fax: +351 22 616 72 79
E-mail: geral@sizavieira.pt
Web: www.sizavieira.pt

Church and Parish Center ▶

Born in Matosinhos, Portugal, in 1933, **ÁLVARO SIZA** studied at the University of Porto School of Architecture (1949–55). He created his own practice in 1954, and worked with Fernando Tavora from 1955 to 1958. He received the European Community's Mies van der Rohe Prize in 1988 and the Pritzker Prize in 1992. He built a large number of small-scale projects in Portugal, and worked on the restructuring of the Chiado in Lisbon (Portugal, 1989–); the Meteorology Center in Barcelona (Spain, 1989–92); the Vitra Furniture Factory (Weil am Rhein, Germany, 1991–94); the Porto School of Architecture, Porto University (Portugal, 1986–95); the University of Aveiro Library (Aveiro, Portugal, 1988–95); the Portuguese Pavilion for the 1998 Lisbon World's Fair (with Eduardo Souto de Moura); and the Serralves Foundation (Porto, Portugal, 1996–99). More recent projects include the Adega Mayor Winery (Campo Maior, Portugal, 2005–06); and the Iberê Camargo Foundation (Porto Alegre, Brazil, 2008).

ÁLVARO SIZA, geboren 1933 in Matosinhos, Portugal, studierte von 1949 bis 1955 an der Escola Superior de Belas Artes der Universität Porto. 1954 gründete er sein eigenes Büro und arbeitete von 1955 bis 1958 mit Fernando Tavora zusammen. 1988 wurde er mit dem Mies-van-der-Rohe-Preis der Europäischen Union ausgezeichnet, 1992 erhielt er den Pritzker-Preis. Er hat zahlreiche kleinere Projekte in Portugal realisiert und plante die Neustrukturierung der Altstadt Chiado in Lissabon (1989–92), das meteorologische Zentrum in Barcelona (1989–92), ein Fabrikgebäude für Vitra in Weil am Rhein (1991–94), die Architekturfakultät der Universität Porto (1986–95) sowie eine Universitätsbibliothek in Aveiro, Portugal (1988–95). Er realisierte ebenfalls den portugiesischen Pavillon für die Weltausstellung 1998 in Lissabon (mit Eduardo Souto de Moura) und die Stiftung Serralves in Porto (1996–99). Aktuellere Projekte sind das Weingut Adega Mayor (Campo Maior, Portugal, 2005–06) und die Stiftung Iberê Camargo (Porto Alegre, Brasilien, 2008).

Né à Matosinhos, au Portugal, en 1933, **ÁLVARO SIZA** a fait ses études à l'École d'architecture de l'Université de Porto (1949–55). Il crée son agence en 1954 et travaille avec Fernando Távora de 1955 à 1958. Il a reçu le prix Mies van der Rohe de la Communauté Européenne en 1988 et le prix Pritzker en 1992. Il a réalisé un grand nombre de petits projets au Portugal et est intervenu sur la restructuration du quartier du Chiado à Lisbonne (1989–92) ; le Centre de météorologie, Barcelone, Espagne (1989–92) ; un bâtiment pour l'usine de meubles Vitra, Weil-am-Rhein, Allemagne (1991–94) ; l'École d'architecture de Porto, Université de Porto (1986–95), la bibliothèque de l'Université d'Aveiro, Aveiro (1988–95) ; le pavillon portugais d'Expo 98 à Lisbonne (1998), avec Souto de Moura, ainsi que la Fondation Serralves (Porto, 1996–99). Ses projets plus récents comprennent l'établissement vinicole Adega Mayor, Campo Maior (2005–06) et la fondation Iberê Camargo, Porto Alegre, Brésil (2008).

CHURCH AND PARISH CENTER

Marco de Canavezes, Portugal, 1990–96

Planning: 1990–93. Construction: 1994–96. Client: Comissão Fabriqueira do Marco de Canavezes.
Floor area: 3477 m². Costs: $ 1263/m².

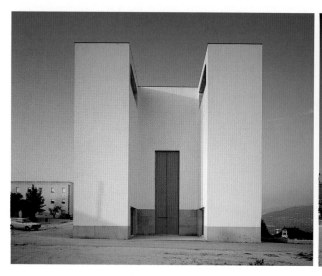 

The powerful simplicity of the church is evident in its unadorned façade and interior. The entrance doors, which will eventually be replaced by bronze ones, are 10 m high.

Die ausdrucksvolle Schlichtheit der Kirche zeigt sich im Innenraum wie auch in der undekorierten Fassade. Die 10 m hohen Eingangstüren aus Holz sollen später eventuell durch Bronzetüren ersetzt werden.

La simplicité et la force de cette église se traduisent dans sa façade et son intérieur presque sans aucun décor. La porte d'entrée qui sera éventuellement remplacée par un modèle en bronze, mesure 10 m de haut.

Designed in close collaboration with the parish priest, Father Nuno Higino, the spare, white church of Santa Maria at Marco de Canavezes is one of Álvaro Siza's purest and most powerful works. The simple, 30 m long nave has 10 m high twin doors that open out onto a square. Within the church, Siza has taken great care in the design of numerous details, ranging from the chairs to the altar and even to the gilt wood cross, which stands to the right of the altar as the priest faces the congregation. Local construction techniques were used to reduce costs, but Siza's touch is visible at every point, particularly in the very successful "light chimneys" that bring two bands of light down behind the altar, suggesting the presence of a cross without actually drawing it out. These light wells also serve the funerary chapel located directly below the altar. Unusual features such as the tile-clad baptistery area sited immediately to the left of the main entrance, and the low strip window that offers the 400 seated parishioners a view of neighboring mountains, ensure that this church is full of surprises, despite its apparent austerity.

Die bescheidene, in enger Zusammenarbeit mit dem Gemeindepriester Nuno Higino geplante Kirche Santa Maria in Marco de Canavezes gehört zu Álvaro Sizas klarsten und kraftvollsten Bauten. Das schlichte, 30 m lange Mittelschiff hat 10 m hohe Doppeltüren, die sich zu einem Vorplatz öffnen. Im Innern der Kirche hat Siza zahlreiche Details, von der Bestuhlung über den Altar bis hin zum vergoldeten Holzkreuz rechts vom Altar, selbst gestaltet. Regionale Bauweisen kamen zum Tragen, um die Kosten zu reduzieren; Sizas Handschrift ist aber überall erkennbar, besonders in den gelungenen „Lichtkaminen", durch die Tageslicht in zwei Streifen hinter den Altar fällt und ein Kreuz andeutet. Diese Lichtschächte beleuchten auch die direkt unter dem Altar gelegene Kapelle. Ungewöhnliche Details, wie die mit Kacheln verkleidete Taufkapelle links vom Haupteingang und das niedrige Fensterband, das von den 400 Sitzplätzen einen Blick auf die nahe gelegenen Berge bietet, beweisen, dass diese Kirche trotz ihrer Nüchternheit voller Überraschungen steckt.

Conçue en collaboration étroite avec le prêtre de la paroisse, le Père Nuno Higino, l'austère église immaculée de Sainte-Marie à Marco de Canavezes est l'une des plus pures et plus puissantes œuvres de Siza. Sa simple nef de 30 m de long se termine sur deux étroites portes de 10 m de haut, qui donnent sur une place. À l'intérieur, Siza a apporté le plus grand soin au dessin de nombreux détails, allant des sièges à l'autel et même à la croix de bois doré qui se dresse à droite de l'autel. Des techniques de construction locales ont permis de réduire les coûts, mais la signature de l'architecte reste omniprésente, en particulier dans les très réussies « cheminées de lumière » qui orientent deux bandeaux lumineux à l'arrière de l'autel pour suggérer la présence d'une croix. Ces puits de lumière éclairent également la chapelle funéraire située juste sous l'autel. Par ses détails inhabituels comme le baptistère en carrelage directement à gauche de l'entrée et la longue baie en bandeau qui offre aux 400 fidèles une vue sur les montagnes avoisinantes, cette église apparemment austère ne manque pas de surprendre.

Using local plaster techniques, Siza
has created subtle undulating wall
surfaces.

The baptismal font, also designed by
Siza, is placed in a tiled area to the
left of the church entrance.

Unter Verwendung lokaler Putztech-
niken hat Siza leicht geschwungene
Wandflächen geschaffen.

Das ebenfalls von Siza entworfene
Taufbecken steht in einer gekachelten
Taufkapelle links vom Eingang.

Grâce à des techniques locales
d'application du plâtre, Siza a créé
des surfaces murales subtilement
ondulées.

Les fonts baptismaux, également
dessinés par Siza, sont situés dans
une pièce carrelée à gauche de
l'entrée de l'église.

PORTUGUESE PAVILION EXPO '98

Lisbon, Portugal, 1996–98

Planning: 1995–96. Construction: 1996–97. Completion: 1998.
Client: Expo '98. Site area: 14 000 m².

The most spectacular architectural element of the Pavilion is the enormous suspended concrete "veil" that covers an outdoor square.

Das spektakulärste Element des Pavillons ist das riesige Beton-„Segel", das einen weitläufigen Freibereich überdeckt.

Le plus spectaculaire élément architectural du Pavillon est un énorme « voile » de béton suspendu qui abrite une place intérieure.

Built on the shores of the Tagus, the **PORTUGUESE PAVILION** occupied an axial site not far from the main entrance to Expo '98. As opposed to many of the surrounding buildings, Siza chose a discreet, horizontal design. His brief included a large outside space for ceremonial functions. He met this requirement with an unusual curved concrete "veil," which is suspended at either end from steel cables. Red and green ceramic cladding is used at the ends of this outdoor space, marking one of Siza's first exterior uses of a traditional Portuguese building material. The main structure, now serving as the seat of the Portuguese Council of Ministers, is designed for maximum flexibility. The large, high-ceilinged rooms on the ground floor were used for the Expo '98 multimedia presentation, in spaces designed by Eduardo Souto de Moura. On the upper level, around a central courtyard, the so-called VIP rooms, including the large table for the Council of Ministers, are entirely designed and decorated by Siza.

Der am Ufer des Tejo gelegene **PORTUGIESISCHE PAVILLON** wurde auf einem symmetrischen Grundstück nahe dem Haupteingang zur Expo '98 errichtet. Siza gab dem Gebäude eine lang gestreckte einfache Form, die im Kontrast zu vielen Bauten der Umgebung steht. Den in der Ausschreibung geforderten Platz für Feste schuf Siza durch ein Betonsegel, eine Art Hängedach aus Beton, das auf beiden Seiten an Stahlseilen aufgehängt ist. Die Wände des Freibereichs sind mit roter und grüner Keramik verkleidet. Siza verwendet dieses traditionelle portugiesische Baumaterial hier erstmals an einem Außenbau. Der Haupttrakt, der jetzt als Sitz des portugiesischen Ministerrats dient, sollte äußerst flexibel sein. Die großen, hohen Räume im Erdgeschoss beherbergten während der Expo '98 eine Multimedia-Präsentation und wurden von Eduardo Souto de Moura gestaltet. Die um einen zentralen Innenhof angeordneten sogenannten VIP-Räume im Obergeschoss wurden einschließlich des großen Tischs für den Ministerrat ebenfalls von Siza entworfen.

Edifié au bord du Tage, ce **PAVILLON OFFICIEL** se trouve sur un site majeur, non loin de l'entrée principale de l'Expo '98. À la différence des nombreux bâtiments environnants, Siza a choisi un parti de discrétion et d'horizontalité. Le programme prévoyait un vaste espace extérieur pour les cérémonies officielles, obligation à laquelle il a répondu par un surprenant « voile » de béton suspendu par des câbles à ses deux extrémités. Des placages de carreaux de céramique rouges et verts – première utilisation extérieure par Siza d'un matériau typiquement portugais – marquent les deux limites de cet espace extérieur. Le bâtiment principal, qui abrite aujourd'hui le siège du Conseil des ministres, a été conçu pour permettre le maximum de souplesse. Au rez-de-chaussée, les vastes salles à haut plafond ont accueilli des expositions multimédias lors de l'Expo '98 dans une mise en espace d'Eduardo Souto de Moura. Au niveau supérieur, autour d'une cour centrale, les salons VIP, dont la grande table du Conseil, ont été entièrement conçus et décorés par Siza.

Openness and a frequent use of asymmetry characterize every façade.

Offenheit und die wiederholt asymmetrische Gliederung charakterisieren die Fassaden.

L'ouverture et l'asymétrie caractérisent chaque façade.

The light concrete veil is solidly anchored in the stone-clad volumes of the main building on one side and a rectangular support structure on the other.

Das leichte Betonsegel ist mit Stahlseilen zwischen das natursteinverkleidete Hauptgebäude und eine orthogonale Stützkonstruktion gespannt.

Le voile de béton est solidement accroché aux volumes parés de pierre du bâtiment principal d'un côté, et à une structure rectangulaire de soutien de l'autre.

Most interior areas of the building were entirely designed by Siza,
including furniture and wall drawings.
One exception to Siza's control is
the large exhibition space designed
by his colleague Eduardo Souto de
Moura.

Auch die Innenbereiche, einschließlich der Möbel und Wandzeichnun-
gen, wurden überwiegend von Siza
gestaltet. Eine Ausnahme bildet der
große Ausstellungsbereich, den sein
Mitarbeiter Eduardo Souto de Moura
ausgestattet hat.

La plupart des intérieurs ont été dessinés par Siza, y compris le mobilier
et les dessins des murs. La seule
exception à l'intervention de Siza est
le vaste espace d'exposition conçu
par son confrère Eduardo Souto de
Moura.

VIEIRA DE CASTRO HOUSE

Famalicão, Portugal, 1984–98

Client: David Vieira de Castro. Floor area: 550 m². Costs: withheld.

More than 14 years in the making, the **VIEIRA DE CASTRO HOUSE** built for a local businessman is on a hilltop site above the modern town of Famalicão, north of Porto. A forest path approaches it, and the visitor first encounters sculptural Corten steel entry gates. Like the rusticated stone walls that define the terraces of the residence, these gates are Siza's work. The visitor is led along a path between the rectangular outdoor swimming pool and an existing rocky outcrop to the discreet main door. Indoors, a gently sloping, slightly curved wooden passage leads down to the living room, with its many views onto the neighboring mountainous countryside. The chimney, the living and dining room furniture, the kitchen fixtures, all are designed by Siza. Committed to a lengthy and complex process, the owners waited patiently for the last pieces of furniture to arrive. Although clearly a house for wealthy clients, a modern discretion bordering on austerity is the rule in this light-filled residence.

Die Entstehung des **HAUSES VIEIRA DE CASTRO**, das für einen ortsansässigen Geschäftsmann entworfen wurde, hat sich über 14 Jahre hingezogen. Es liegt auf einer Anhöhe oberhalb der Stadt Famalicão nördlich von Porto. Das Haus ist über einen Waldweg erreichbar, und der Blick des Besuchers fällt zuerst auf die Tore aus Corten-Stahl, die wie Skulpturen wirken. Sie wurden, ebenso wie das Rustikamauerwerk aus Natursteinen, das die Terrasse des Hauses einfasst, von Siza gestaltet. Innen führt ein sanft abfallender, leicht gekrümmter Holzkorridor hinunter zum Wohnraum mit seinen zahlreichen Ausblicken in die bergige Landschaft. Der Kamin, die Möblierung des Wohn- und Esszimmers und die Kücheneinrichtung wurden ebenfalls von Siza entworfen. Obgleich es sich hier eindeutig um ein Werk für wohlhabende Bauherren handelt, ist das lichterfüllte Haus durch eine moderne, fast an Nüchternheit grenzende Zurückhaltung geprägt.

Il a fallu 14 ans pour mener à bien la construction de la **MAISON VIEIRA DE CASTRO** réalisée pour un chef d'entreprise local, au sommet d'une colline qui surplombe la ville moderne de Famalicão, au nord de Porto. Le visiteur se trouve d'abord face à deux portes sculpturales en acier Corten, œuvres de Siza, de même que les murs de pierre rustiquée qui délimitent les terrasses. Une allée conduit à la porte d'entrée en se glissant entre la piscine rectangulaire et un affleurement de rocher. À l'intérieur, un couloir parqueté en pente douce et légèrement incurvé mène à la salle de séjour. La cheminée, le mobilier du séjour et de la salle à manger, les meubles de cuisine, tous ont été dessinés par Siza. Les propriétaires ont patiemment attendu que les derniers meubles soient livrés pour s'installer. Maison à l'évidence construite pour de riches clients, sa discrétion moderniste et lumineuse frise l'austérité.

 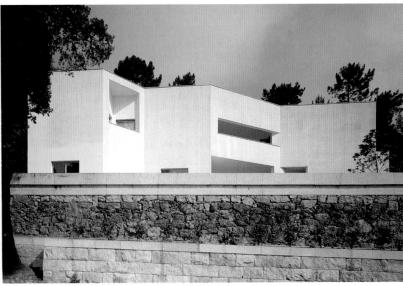

The rock walls and unexpected metal entrance gates were designed by Siza as was the entire interior.

Die Natursteinmauern und die Eingangstore aus Corten-Stahl wurden ebenso wie die gesamte Innenausstattung von Siza gestaltet.

Les murets de pierre et le portail d'entrée en métal ont été dessinés par Siza, comme tous les aménagements intérieurs.

Set into a rocky outcrop overlooking the town of Famalicão, the house is deceptively simple when seen from the exterior.

Das auf einen Felsvorsprung über der Stadt Famalicão gestellte Wohnhaus sieht von außen trügerisch einfach aus.

Implantée sur une excroissance rocheuse qui domine la ville de Famalicão, la maison revêt une apparence simple mais trompeuse vue de l'extérieur.

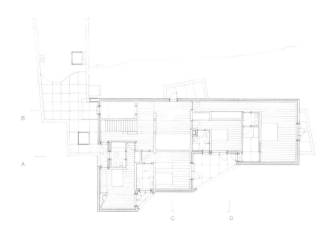

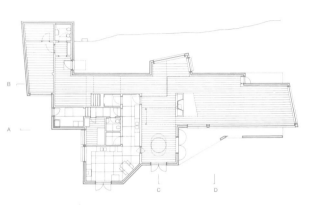

SERRALVES FOUNDATION

Porto, Portugal, 1991–99

Planning: 1991–99. Construction: 1996–99. Client: Serralves Foundation.
Landscape: Global – João Gomes da Silva and Erika Skabar. Floor area: 15 000 m².

The **SERRALVES FOUNDATION,** specializing in contemporary art, was created through a joint venture of the Portuguese government and 50 private investors. Established in the Quinta de Serralves, a large property including the main house built in the 1930s, it is located not far from the center of Porto. Siza's new structure, located in the park of the Foundation, is both substantial in size and ambitious in scope. Using a suspended ceiling system similar to the one he devised for the Galician Center of Contemporary Art, Siza created a number of large, flexible galleries, intended for temporary art shows. Interior courtyards and numerous windows permit the visitor to remain in contact with the attractive park environment (of which Siza designed three hectares).

Die auf zeitgenössische Kunst spezialisierte **STIFTUNG SERRALVES** wurde durch die Zusammenarbeit der portugiesischen Regierung mit 50 Investoren aus der Privatwirtschaft begründet. Ihr in der Quinta de Serralves gelegener Sitz mit dem in den 1930er-Jahren erbauten Haupthaus befindet sich auf einem großen Gelände unweit des Zentrums von Porto. Sizas neues Gebäude, das in dem zur Stiftung gehörenden Park errichtet wurde, ist sowohl von seiner Größe als auch seinem Anspruch her ein groß angelegtes Unternehmen. Der Architekt schuf unter Verwendung einer Hängedeckenkonstruktion, wie er sie in ähnlicher Form bereits für das Galicische Zentrum für Zeitgenössische Kunst entworfen hat, eine Reihe großer, flexibler Galerien, in denen Wechselausstellungen gezeigt werden sollen. Innenhöfe und zahlreiche Fenster erlauben dem Besucher einen ständigen Ausblick auf die reizvolle Parklandschaft (von der Siza 3 ha gestaltet hat).

La **FONDATION SERRALVES** d'art contemporain est née d'un partenariat entre l'État portugais et 50 mécènes privés. Installée dans la Quinta de Serralves, vaste propriété où se trouvait déjà une belle demeure des années 1930, elle est située à proximité du centre de Porto. Le nouveau bâtiment de Siza, édifié dans le parc de la Fondation, est de taille et de propos ambitieux. À partir d'un système de plafonds suspendus ressemblant à celui mis au point pour le Centre d'art contemporain de Galice, Siza a créé plusieurs vastes galeries d'expositions temporaires. Des cours intérieures et de nombreuses ouvertures permettent au visiteur de conserver le contact avec un parc magnifique (dont 3 ha ont été conçus par Siza).

Set at some distance from the old city of Porto, the building of the Serralves Foundation does not give a very open impression from the exterior (above) but its complex forms allow ample light into the appropriate galleries, as well as views out toward the park (right).

Das Gebäude der unweit der Altstadt von Porto gelegenen Stiftung Serralves macht von außen einen eher abweisenden Eindruck (oben). Seine komplexen Formen lassen jedoch viel natürliches Licht in die einzelnen Ausstellungsräume und geben immer wieder Ausblicke auf den Park frei (rechts).

Non loin de la vieille ville de Porto, le bâtiment de la Fondation Serralves semble très peu ouvert sur l'extérieur (ci-dessus), mais ses formes complexes laissent pénétrer une généreuse lumière dans ses galeries, et découvrir des perspectives sur le parc (à droite).

Siza is a master of the subtle manipulation of light and materials, here to the benefit of the art works that are placed in spaces whose architecture and lighting can be modified to accommodate specific types of installation.

Siza ist ein Meister der subtilen Gestaltung mit Licht und Material. Im Vordergrund stehen dabei die Kunstwerke, die in Räumen präsentiert werden, deren Innenausstattung und Lichtdesign je nach Art der Ausstellung verändert werden können.

Siza est un des maîtres de la manipulation subtile de la lumière et des matériaux, ici au bénéfice d'œuvres d'art disposées dans des espaces dont l'architecture et l'éclairage peuvent être modifiés selon les types de présentation.

SNØHETTA

Snøhetta Group
Akershusstranda 21, Skur 39
0150 Oslo
Norway

Tel: +47 24 156 060
Fax: +47 24 156 061
E-mail: contact@snoarc.com
Web: www.snoarc.com

SNØHETTA is a mountain in central Norway. It is a central theme in early Viking sagas and is the mythical home of Valhalla. Henrik Ibsen developed the story of Peer Gynt around Snøhetta, which gave its name to the architectural practice founded in 1987 in Oslo by Craig Dykers, Christoph Kapeller, and Kjetil Trædal Thorsen. Aside from the Alexandria Library published here, Snøhetta also built the Oslo Opera House between 2004 and 2008. Other work of the firm includes the Hamar Town Hall (Hamar, Norway, 2000); the Karmøy Fishing Museum, (Karmøy, Norway, 1999); and the Skistua School (Skistua, Narvik, Norway, 1998). They also took the second prize in the 1997 open international competition for the Kansai-Kan Library in Japan, and built the Lillehammer Art Museum, the centerpiece cultural building for the 1993 Winter Olympics.

SNØHETTA, der Namensgeber für das 1987 in Oslo gegründete Architekturbüro, ist ein Berg in Zentralnorwegen. Er spielt als die mythische Heimstatt von Walhalla eine wichtige Rolle in alten Wikingersagen und auch in Henrik Ibsens Geschichte von Peer Gynt. Craig Dykers, Christoph Kapeller und Kjetil Trædal Thorsen gründeten gemeinsam das Architekturbüro. Neben der hier vorgestellten Bibliothek von Alexandria errichtete Snøhetta von 2004 bis 2008 das Opernhaus in Oslo. Weitere Projekte des Büros sind das Rathaus in Hamar (2000), das Fischereimuseum in Karmøy (1999) und die Skistua-Schule in Skistua, Narvik (1998), alle in Norwegen. 1997 gewann das Büro den zweiten Preis im offenen internationalen Wettbewerb für die Kansai-Kan-Bibliothek in Japan und stellte 1993 mit dem Kunstmuseum in Lillehammer das wichtigste Kulturgebäude für die Winterolympiade fertig.

SNØHETTA, cette montagne du centre de la Norvège qui donne donc son nom à l'agence d'architecture fondée en 1987 à Oslo, figure dans les anciennes sagas des Vikings. Elle y est le siège mythique du Valhalla, et Henrik Ibsen y a situé Peer Gynt. Craig Dykers, Christoph Kapeller et Kjetil Trædal Thorsen ont fondé ensemble l'agence d'architecture. En dehors de la bibliothèque d'Alexandrie présentée ici, Snøhetta a construit de 2004 à 2008 l'Opéra national d'Oslo. Parmi ses autres travaux : l'hôtel de ville de Hamar (Hamar, Norvège, 2000), le musée de la pêche de Karmøy (Karmøy, Norvège, 1999) et l'école de Skistua (Skistua, Narvik, Norvège, 1998). Les architectes ont également remporté le second prix du concours international de 1997 pour la bibliothèque de Kansaï-Kan au Japon et édifié le musée d'art de Lillehammer, à l'occasion des J. O. d'hiver de 1993.

BIBLIOTHECA ALEXANDRINA

Alexandria, Egypt, 1995–2001

Client: Arab Republic of Egypt. Area: 70 000 m². Costs: $ 150 million.

Winners of a 1989 open international competition that drew 524 entries from 52 countries, Snøhetta devised a circular, tilting form for the structure, rising from the ground to reveal rough stone walls heavily carved with inscriptions. Subsequent to the original competition, they were also awarded contracts for the landscape and interior design of this project sponsored by Unesco and the Arab Republic of Egypt. This massive 70 000 m² structure had a budget of $ 150 million. Founded shortly after the creation of the city by Alexander the Great in 331 BC, the **GREAT LIBRARY** was a center of learning in the ancient world. Parts of it burned during the civil war between Caesar and Mark Antony, and the rest was destroyed in the third and fourth centuries after Christ. The intention of Unesco in sponsoring the project was to resurrect a symbol, but also to create a new center in this major Egyptian city. A great reading room, typical of many of the world's major libraries but organized in this case in a cascade of descending terraces, is one of the main interior features. The facility is designed to receive 3500 readers per day.

Der 1989 als Sieger aus einem offenen, internationalen Wettbewerb mit 524 Beiträgen aus 52 Ländern hervorgegangene Entwurf von Snøhetta Architects besteht aus einem kreisförmigen, geneigten Bau. Die vom Erdgeschoss aufsteigenden Wände aus unbearbeitetem Stein sind reich mit gemeißelten Inschriften geschmückt. Im Anschluss an den eigentlichen Wettbewerb erhielten Snøhetta Architects auch die Folgeaufträge für Landschaftsarchitektur und Innenraumgestaltung dieses von der UNESCO und der Arabischen Republik Ägypten unterstützten Projekts. Das massive, 70 000 m² umfassende Gebäude wurde für 150 Millionen US-Dollar realisiert. Die **ALEXANDRINISCHE BIBLIOTHEK**, die einige Jahre nach der Gründung Alexandrias durch Alexander den Großen (331 v. Chr.) erbaut wurde, war in der Antike ein Zentrum der Kunst und Wissenschaft. Während des Krieges zwischen Cäsar und Marcus Antonius fiel sie teilweise den Flammen zum Opfer, Ende des 4. Jahrhunderts n. Chr. wurde sie dann vollständig zerstört. Die UNESCO beabsichtigte mit ihrer finanziellen Unterstützung sowohl die Wiedererrichtung eines symbolischen Bauwerkes als auch die Initiation eines neuen Zentrums des Geisteslebens in dieser ägyptischen Großstadt. Eines der Hauptmerkmale der Innenraumgestaltung ist ein ausgedehnter Lesesaal, der in einer Kaskade abfallender Terrassen angelegt wurde. Der Komplex ist für eine Nutzungskapazität von täglich 3500 Lesern konzipiert.

Vainqueurs en 1989 du concours international qui a attiré 524 participants de 52 pays, l'agence Snøhetta a conçu une structure circulaire inclinée qui se soulève du sol pour découvrir des murs de pierre brute sur lesquels sont gravées des inscriptions. Elle a également été chargée des aménagements paysagers et intérieurs de ce projet financé par l'Unesco et l'Égypte. Cette massive construction de 70 000 m² aura coûté 150 millions de dollars. Fondée peu après la création de la ville par Alexandre le Grand en 331 av. J.-C., la **GRANDE BIBLIOTHÈQUE D'ALEXANDRIE** fut l'un des centres du savoir de l'Antiquité. Une partie brûla lors du conflit entre César et Marc-Antoine, et le reste fut détruit aux IIIe et IVe siècles. L'intention de l'Unesco est de redonner vie à ce symbole, mais également de créer un nouveau pôle de développement pour la grande ville égyptienne. Une vaste salle de lecture, organisée en une cascade de terrasses est l'une des principales caractéristiques intérieures du bâtiment qui devrait recevoir 3500 lecteurs par jour.

The design is a tilted torus with a slanted roof. The footbridge here connects the library to the campus of the University of Alexandria.

Der Entwurf besteht aus einem geneigten Torus mit schräg gestellter Bedachung. Der hier abgebildete Steg (links) verbindet die Bibliothek mit dem Campus der Universität von Alexandria.

Le projet consiste en un tore basculé et un toit incliné. La passerelle connecte la bibliothèque au campus de l'Université d'Alexandrie.

The concrete columns in the main reading room are a variant of the lotus-topped pharaonic designs. Above, a wedge-shaped observation deck is set above the reading room.

Die Betonpfeiler im Hauptlesesaal sind eine Variation der altägyptischen, mit Lotos bekrönten Säulen. Über dem Lesesaal erhebt sich eine keilförmige Aussichtsplattform (oben).

Les colonnes de béton de la salle de lecture principale représentent une variante des colonnes égyptiennes à chapiteau en fleur de lotus. En haut, une terrasse d'observation, au-dessus de la salle de lecture.

JULIE SNOW ARCHITECTS

Julie Snow Architects Inc.
2400 Rand Tower
527 Marquette Avenue
Minneapolis, Minnesota 55402
USA

Tel: +1 612 359 9430
Fax: +1 612 359 9530
E-mail: mail@juliesnowarchitects.com
Web: www.juliesnowarchitects.com

Koehler House ▶

JULIE SNOW created her own firm in 1988 after working since 1974 with the firm of Hammel, Green and Abrahamson. She prides herself on a "certain fascination with the technical aspects of building assembly." Built work includes the Vista Building for Microsoft/Great Plains Software in Fargo, North Dakota (2001); Light Rail Transit Stations for Minneapolis (2004); the New School of Business, University of South Dakota (Vermillion, South Dakota, 2001 competition); and the Koehler House, shown here. Another project is the Jackson Street Roundhouse (St. Paul, Minnesota, 1995–2005). The firm's earlier Origen Center for the Phillips Plastics Corporation (Menomonie, Wisconsin, 1994) won several awards, including an AIA Minnesota Honor Award in 1995.

JULIE SNOW gründete 1988 ihre eigene Firma, nachdem sie seit 1974 im Büro von Hammel, Green and Abrahamson gearbeitet hatte. Laut eigener Aussage faszinieren sie besonders die technischen Aspekte an einem Bauprojekt. Zu ihren Werken zählen das Vista Building für Microsoft/Great Plains Software in Fargo, North Dakota (2001), die Transitbahnhöfe von Light Rail in Minneapolis (2004), die New School of Business der University of South Dakota in Vermillion (Wettbewerb: 2001) sowie die hier vorgestellte Koehler Residence. Ein weiteres Projekt ist das Jackson Street Roundhouse in St. Paul, Minnesota (1995–2005). Für das von ihrer Firma 1994 fertiggestellte Origen Center der Firma Phillips Plastics Corporation in Menomonie, Wisconsin, gewann sie mehrere Preise, so 1995 den AIA Minnesota Honor Award.

JULIE SNOW crée son agence en 1988 après avoir travaillé depuis 1974 chez Hammel, Green and Abrahamson. Elle avoue une « certaine fascination pour les aspects techniques de la construction ». Parmi ses travaux : le Vista Building pour Microsoft/Great Plains Software à Fargo, Dakota du Nord (2001) ; les stations d'un système de transport léger pour Minneapolis (2004) ; la Koehler Residence, présentée dans ces pages. Elle a travaillé aussi au projet de la Jackson Street Roundhouse (St. Paul, Minnesota, 1995–2005). Son Origen Centre pour la Phillips Plastics Corporation (Menomonie, Wisconsin, 1994) a remporté plusieurs prix, y compris un AIA Minnesota Honor Award en 1995.

KOEHLER HOUSE

New Brunswick, Canada, 2000

Client: David and Mary Beth Koehler. Floor area: 150 m².
Structure: wood frame, Douglas fir columns and concrete foundations.

Set on the edge of the Bay of Fundy, this 150 m² house is intended as a family retreat. The Minneapolis residents David and Mary Beth Koehler chose this rugged twenty-hectare site located about 40 kilometers from the Maine border for their open, rectangular, two-level house. Piled like two boxes, one on top of the other, the lower floor is cantilevered over the rock, no more than 30 meters from the average high tide line of the ocean. The owners of the house were apparently inspired by Mies van der Rohe's Farnsworth House, a still-simpler one story structure. The living room, dining room and kitchen are a continuous space on the lower floor, while the master bedroom, porch and sitting room are on the upper level. Poured-in-place concrete foundations with steel pins anchor the house to the rocks while the roof and floors are designed with plywood membranes and wooden trusses – all of this with the intention of protecting the house against the weather conditions that occur frequently in the area.

Das an der Spitze der Bay of Fundy gelegene, 150 m² große Haus ist als Zufluchtsort der in Minneapolis lebenden Familie David und Mary Beth Koehler gedacht. Als Bauplatz für ihr rechteckiges, offen gestaltetes und auf zwei Ebenen angelegtes Haus wählten sie ein 20 ha großes, zerklüftetes Stück Land, circa 40 km von der Grenze zu Maine entfernt. Das Gebäude erweckt den Eindruck von zwei aufeinandergestapelten Kisten, von denen die untere über die Felskante hinausragt, und zwar nur 30 m oberhalb des durchschnittlichen Flutpegels des Atlantiks. Offenbar ließen sich die Bauherren von Mies van der Rohes Farnsworth House inspirieren, einem noch schlichteren einstöckigen Gebäude. Wohnzimmer, Esszimmer und Küche befinden sich in einem offenen Raum im Erdgeschoss, während das Hauptschlafzimmer, eine Veranda und ein kleinerer Wohnraum im Obergeschoss liegen. Durch ein Fundament aus Gussbeton mit Stahlbolzen wird das Haus auf den Felsen verankert, während Dach und Böden aus Sperrholzmembranen und Holzbalken gefertigt sind. All diese bautechnischen Maßnahmen dienen dazu, das Haus gegen die in dieser Region häufig auftretenden Unwetter zu schützen.

Implantée au bord de la baie de Fundy, cette maison de 150 m² est une résidence familiale de loisirs. Ce sont David et Mary Beth Koehler, de Minneapolis, qui ont choisi ce terrain de 20 hectares à 40 km environ de la frontière du Maine pour y créer cette maison ouverte, rectangulaire, de deux niveaux empilés l'un sur l'autre à la manière de boîtes. Le niveau du rez-de-chaussée en porte-à-faux au-dessus du rocher se trouve à 30 m de la ligne des grandes marées. Les propriétaires ont sans doute été sensibles à la Farnsworth House de Mies van der Rohe, également à deux niveaux, mais encore plus épurée. Au rez-de-chaussée, le séjour, la salle à manger et la zone de préparation des repas sont traités en espace continu tandis que la chambre principale, un salon et une véranda occupent le niveau supérieur. Des fondations en béton coulé sur place et broches en acier ancrent la maison au rocher, le toit et les sols sont en poutres de bois et panneaux-membranes de contre-plaqué, le tout calculé pour protéger la maison du mauvais temps fréquent dans cette région.

Although it appears to be very light and transparent, the house is designed to withstand high winds and very cold conditions.

Obgleich es sehr leicht und transparent wirkt, ist das Haus so konstruiert, dass es Stürmen und äußerst kalten Temperaturen standhält.

Bien qu'elle paraisse particulièrement légère et transparente, la maison a été conçue pour résister aux vents et au climat très froid.

The owner comments that the site of this house is much as it must have been when the French explorer Champlain saw the shore for the first time 400 years ago.

Laut Eigentümer sieht die Umgebung des Hauses nicht viel anders aus als vor 400 Jahren, als die Küste von dem Franzosen Samuel de Champlain entdeckt wurde.

Pour les propriétaires, ce site est resté tel qu'il était lorsque l'explorateur Champlain aborda cette côte pour la première fois, il y a 400 ans.

The situation of the house above the ocean gives it something of the feeling of a boat. Furniture selected by the owners is mostly by Le Corbusier or Mies van der Rohe.

Durch seine Lage direkt über dem Ozean hat das Haus etwas von einem Schiff. Die von den Besitzern ausgewählten Möbel sind größtenteils von Le Corbusier oder Mies van der Rohe entworfen.

La situation de la maison au-dessus de l'océan donne parfois le sentiment d'être dans un bateau. Le mobilier choisi par les propriétaires est généralement signé Le Corbusier ou Mies van der Rohe.

WERNER SOBEK

Werner Sobek Engineering & Design
Albstraße 14
70597 Stuttgart
Germany

Tel: +49 711 76750 0
Fax: +49 711 76750 44
E-mail: Stuttgart@wernersobek.com
Web: www.wernersobek.com

House R 128 ►

WERNER SOBEK was born in 1953 in Aalen, Germany. He studied architecture and civil engineering at the University of Stuttgart (1974–80) and did post-graduate research in "Wide-Span Lightweight Structures" at the University of Stuttgart (1980–86). He received his PhD in civil engineering from the same university in 1987. He worked as a structural engineer in the office of Schlaich, Bergermann & Partner (Stuttgart, 1987–91) before creating his own office in 1991. Since 1994 he has been a professor at the University of Stuttgart where he succeeded Frei Otto as Director of the Institute for Lightweight Structures. His projects include: Ecole Nationale d'Art Décoratif (Limoges, France, 1991–94); Dome service hall Deutsche Bank (Hanover, 1992–95); Art and Media Science Center (Karlsruhe, 1992–97); Interbank façade (with Hans Hollein, Lima, Peru, 1996–99); New Bangkok International Airport (Thailand, with Murphy/Jahn, 1995–2004); House R 128 (published here, Stuttgart, 1998–2000), and fair pavilions for Audi and BMW.

WERNER SOBEK, 1953 in Aalen geboren, studierte von 1974 bis 1980 Architektur und Bauwesen an der Universität Stuttgart und führte dort von 1980 bis 1986 Forschungsarbeiten zum Thema „weit gespannte Leichtbauten" durch. 1987 erwarb er an derselben Universität seinen Doktortitel in Bauwesen. Von 1987 bis 1991 arbeitete er als Bauingenieur bei Schlaich, Bergermann & Partner in Stuttgart, bevor er 1991 sein eigenes Büro in Stuttgart gründete. Seit 1994 ist er als Professor an der Universität Stuttgart tätig, wo er als Nachfolger von Frei Otto Direktor des Instituts für Leichtbauten wurde. Zu seinen Projekten zählen: die École nationale d'art décoratif in Limoges (1991–94), die Kuppel in der Schalterhalle der Deutschen Bank in Hannover (1992–95), das ZKM in Karlsruhe (1992–97), der neue internationale Flughafen in Bangkok (mit Murphy/Jahn, 1995–2004), die Fassade der Interbank (mit Hans Hollein) in Lima, Peru (1996–99), das hier vorgestellte Wohnhaus R 128 in Stuttgart (1998–2000) sowie Messepavillons für Audi und BMW.

WERNER SOBEK, né en 1953 à Aalen, en Allemagne, étudie l'architecture et l'ingénierie civile à l'Université de Stuttgart (1974–80) et mène une recherche de post-diplôme sur les structures légères de longue portée également à Stuttgart (1980–86). Il est Ph. D. en ingénierie civile en 1987. Ingénieur structurel à l'agence Schlaich, Bergermann & Partner (Stuttgart, 1987–1991), il fonde la sienne en 1991. Depuis 1994, il est professeur à l'Université de Stuttgart où il a succédé à Frei Otto à la direction de l'Institut des structures légères. Parmi ses projets : École national d'arts décoratifs (Limoges, France, 1991–94) ; dôme du hall de la Deutsche Bank (Hanovre, 1992–95) ; Centre des arts et des médias (Karlsruhe, 1992–97) ; façade d'Interbank (avec Hans Hollein, Lima, Pérou, 1996–99) ; nouvel aéroport international de Bangkok (Thaïlande, avec Murphy/Jahn, 1995–2004) ; résidence privée, R 128, publiée ici (Stuttgart, 1998–2000) et pavillons de salons pour Audi et BMW.

HOUSE R 128

Stuttgart, Germany, 1999–2000

Client: Ursula and Werner Sobek. Total floor area: 250 m². Costs: not specified.

The steep hillside of the 250 m² **HOUSE R 128** made construction difficult. An existing 1923 structure was first demolished, and work such as that on the foundation had to be carried out by hand. A great deal of attention was paid to the ease of construction and finishing. The floors, for example, consist of prefabricated plastic-covered wood panels measuring 3.75 x 2.8 meters that are just placed between the floor beams without using screws. Aluminum ceiling panels are also clipped in place. The electrical or water lines are placed in aluminum ducts in the walls, never under plaster, to facilitate maintenance. The 11.2-meter, four-story building is made of a bolted steel skeleton with twelve columns arranged on a 3.85 x 2.9 meter grid. The façade is made of triple-glazed panels filled with inert gas and measuring 2.8 meters high by 1.36 meters wide on the north and south – 1.42 meters wide on the west and east. A mechanical ventilation system controls airflow and allows heat to be recovered from exhaust air. Air is blown through a heat exchanger situated below the foundation, taking advantage of the more constant temperature of the earth. Solar panels in the roof run the mechanical ventilation system and heat pump. Werner Sobek has announced that he intended to design only three houses in his life, each one requiring ten years of research. This one, made from twelve tons of steel and twenty tons of glass, was erected in an amazing eleven weeks. A second, teardrop-shaped carbon-fiber structure so light it does not need foundations was planned and built between 2001 and 2012.

Die Konstruktion des 250 m² großen **HOUSE R 128** wurde durch seine Lage an einem stark abschüssigen Berghang erschwert. Insgesamt wurde große Sorgfalt auf den glatten Ablauf der Endfertigung verwandt. So bestehen beispielsweise die Böden aus vorgefertigten, 3,75 x 2,80 m großen Holzpaneelen mit Kunststoffüberzug, die ohne Einsatz von Schrauben einfach zwischen die Fußbodenbalken eingesetzt wurden. Auch die Deckenplatten aus Aluminium wurden lediglich mit einer Halterung befestigt. Sowohl elektrische Leitungen wie auch Wasserrohre verlaufen durch Aluminiumröhren in den Wänden, liegen aber nicht unter Gipsputz, was die Instandhaltung erleichtert. Die Konstruktion des 11,20 m hohen, viergeschossigen Hauses besteht aus einem verschraubten Stahlskelett mit zwölf Säulen, die innerhalb eines Grundrasters von 3,85 x 2,9 m angeordnet sind. Die Fassade setzt sich aus dreifach verglasten und mit Schutzgas gefüllten Tafeln zusammen, die an der Nord- und Südseite jeweils 2,80 m hoch und 1,36 m breit sowie an der West- und Ostseite 1,42 m breit sind. Ein mechanisches Belüftungssystem steuert den Luftstrom und ermöglicht eine Wärmerückgewinnung aus Abluft. Die Luft wird durch einen Wärmeaustauscher geblasen, der unter dem Fundament liegt und die konstante Temperatur des Erdbodens nutzt. Das Belüftungssystem und die Wärmepumpe werden durch Solartafeln angetrieben, die im Dach montiert sind. Werner Sobek hat angekündigt, er wolle in seinem ganzen Leben nur drei Häuser entwerfen, da jedes davon zehn Jahre Forschungsarbeit in Anspruch nimmt. Das hier vorgestellte Haus, das aus zwölf Tonnen Stahl und 20 Tonnen Glas gefertigt ist, wurde in der unglaublich kurzen Zeit von nur elf Wochen errichtet. Ein zweiter Entwurf, eine tropfenförmige Konstruktion aus Kunststoff und Karbonträgern, die so leicht ist, dass sie keinerlei Unterbau benötigt, wurde von 2001 bis 2012 geplant und errichtet.

L'escarpement de la pente sur laquelle s'élève la **MAISON R 128** a rendu le chantier difficile. Une grande attention a été portée à la facilité de construction et d'aménagement. Par exemple, les sols consistent en panneaux de bois enduits de plastique de 3,75 x 2,8 m posés entre les solives, sans boulonnage. Les panneaux d'aluminium de la toiture sont simplement clipsés. Les conduites électriques ou d'eau passent par des tuyaux d'aluminium dans les murs, mais jamais sous enduit de plâtre pour faciliter leur maintenance. La maison de 11,2 m de haut et de quatre niveaux fait appel à un squelette d'acier riveté à 12 colonnes disposées selon une trame de 3,85 x 2,9 m. La façade est en panneaux de verre triple épaisseur séparés par une couche de gaz inerte, qui mesurent 2,8 x 1,36 m de haut au nord et au sud, et 2,8 x 1,42 m à l'est et à l'ouest. Un système de ventilation mécanique contrôle l'aération et permet de récupérer la chaleur de l'air usé. L'air est traité par une pompe à chaleur située sous les fondations, pour bénéficier de la température plus constante du sol. Des panneaux solaires en toiture alimentent le système de ventilation mécanique et la pompe à chaleur. Werner Sobek a annoncé sa volonté de ne construire que trois maisons au cours de sa carrière, chacune nécessitant dix années de recherches. Celle-ci, qui a demandé 12 tonnes d'acier et 20 de verre, a été montée très rapidement en 11 semaines. Une seconde construction, en forme de goutte et en fibre de carbone, si légère qu'elle ne nécessite même pas de fondations, a été conçue et édifiée de 2011 à 2012.

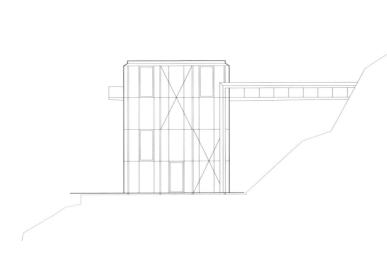

Making an ecologically sensitive house out of glass is already a considerable challenge. Succeeding in making it esthetically attractive and in harmony with its setting is a triumph.

Ein ökologisch sensibles Haus aus Glas zu bauen, ist eine große Herausforderung. Es ästhetisch attraktiv und in Harmonie mit seiner Umgebung zu gestalten, ist ein Triumph.

Réaliser une maison d'esprit écologique est un défi considérable, réussir à la rendre esthétiquement séduisante et en harmonie avec son cadre est une performance rare.

The extreme simplicity of the layout and the entirely glazed walls make the house astonishing to look at from the exterior and allow full views out toward Stuttgart.

Die äußerste Schlichtheit der Anordnung und die zur Gänze verglasten Wände machen das Haus zu einer auffallenden Erscheinung und erlauben einen freien Rundblick.

L'extrême simplicité du plan et les parois entièrement vitrées donnent un aspect étonnant à la maison et permettent une vue panoramique de Stuttgart.

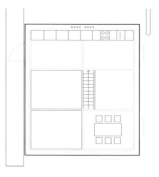

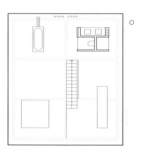

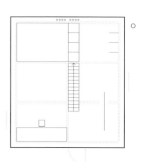

The reduction of this house to its bare minimum does not make it less interesting, quite the contrary. Its highly engineered nature is not at all apparent and that is its success.

Die Reduzierung dieses Gebäudes auf ein absolutes Minimum macht es nicht weniger interessant, ganz im Gegenteil. Dass sein stark ingenieurtechnischer Charakter in keiner Weise spürbar wird, ist ein weiterer Grund für seinen Erfolg.

La réduction de la maison au minimum possible ne la rend pas moins intéressante, bien au contraire. Avoir su faire oublier sa haute technicité est une de ses réussites.

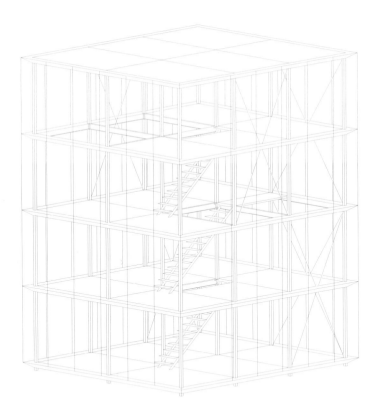

The extreme lightness of the structural elements of the house almost seems to make the floors hover in space with no visible means of support.

Die extreme Leichtigkeit der Konstruktionsteile lassen die Geschossböden fast ohne sichtbare Stützvorrichtungen im Raum schweben.

La légèreté extrême des éléments structurels donne l'impression que les niveaux flottent dans l'espace, sans support visible.

PHILIPPE STARCK

Ubik
1, avenue Paul Doumer
75016 Paris
France

Tel: +33 1 4807 5454
Fax: +33 1 4807 5464
E-mail: info@starcknetwork.com
Web: www.starck.com

PHILIPPE STARCK was born in 1949 and attended the École Nissim de Camondo in Paris. Though he is of course best known as a furniture and object designer, his projects as an architect include the Café Costes (Paris, 1984); Laguiole Knife Factory (Laguiole, France, 1987); Royalton Hotel (New York, 1988); Nani Nani Building (Tokyo, 1989); Asahi Beer Building (Tokyo, 1989); Teatriz Restaurant (Madrid, 1990); Paramount Hotel (New York, 1990); and the Baron Vert Building (Osaka, 1990). He has also designed a number of private houses and apartment blocks, for example Lemoult in Paris (1987); Angle in Antwerp (1991); apartment buildings in Los Angeles (1991); and a private house in Madrid (1991). He was responsible for the interior design of the Saint Martin's Lane and Sanderson Hotels in London, the Delano in Miami, the Mondrian in Los Angeles, the Hudson in New York and the Clift in San Francisco. In 2006, the Japanese restaurant Katsuya opened in Los Angeles. He has also worked on the design of condominium apartments in Toronto (75 Portland Street), and the 24-story JIA boutique hotel in Hong Kong. The 40 000 m² Alhondiga in Bilbao, a "place of discovery, exchange and living," opened in 2010. Starck's other ventures have included his role as Creative Director of Yoo (2001–08), a property development company in which he was associated with the developer John Hitchcox and Jade Jagger.

PHILIPPE STARCK wurde 1949 geboren und besuchte die École Nissim de Camondo in Paris. Obgleich er natürlich mit seinen Möbel- und Objektentwürfen am bekanntesten wurde, umfassen seine architektonischen Projekte das Café Costes (Paris, 1984), die Messerfabrik Forge de Laguiole (Laguiole, Frankreich, 1987), das Royalton Hotel (New York, 1988), das Nani Nani Building (Tokio, 1989), das Asahi Beer Building (Tokio, 1989), das Teatriz Restaurant (Madrid, 1990), das Paramound Hotel (New York, 1990) und das Baron Vert Building (Osaka, 1990). Darüber hinaus entwarf er eine Reihe von Privathäusern und Wohnungsbauten, zum Beispiel Lemoult in Paris (1987), Angle in Antwerpen (1991), Apartmenthäuser in Los Angeles (1991) sowie ein Privathaus in Madrid (1991). Er war verantwortlich für den Innenausbau des Saint Martin's Lane Hotel und Sanderson Hotel in London, des Delano in Miami, des Mondrian in Los Angeles, des Hudson in New York und des Clift in San Francisco. 2006 wurde in Los Angeles das japanische Restaurant Katsuya eröffnet. Außerdem war er am Ausbau einer Eigentumswohnung in Toronto (75 Portland Street) und des 24-geschossigen JIA Boutique Hotel in Hongkong beteiligt. Das 40 000 m² umfassende Alhondiga in Bilbao, ein „Ort für Entdeckung, Austausch und Leben", wurde 2010 eröffnet. Zu Starcks sonstigen Unternehmungen zählt seine Rolle als Creative Director von Yoo (2001–08), einer Wohnungsbaufirma, bei der er Partner des Bauunternehmers John Hitchcox und Jade Jagger war.

PHILIPPE STARCK est né en 1949 et a étudié à l'École Nissim de Camondo à Paris. Bien qu'il soit surtout connu comme designer d'objets et de meubles, il a réalisé un certain nombre de projets d'architecture comme le Café Costes, Paris (1984) ; la manufacture Forge de Laguiole, Laguiole, France (1987) ; le Royalton Hotel, New York (1988) ; l'immeuble Nani Nani, Tokyo (1989) ; l'immeuble Asahi Beer, Tokyo (1989) ; le restaurant Teatriz, Madrid (1990) ; le Paramount Hotel, New York (1990) ; et l'immeuble Baron Vert, Osaka (1990). Il a également conçu un certain nombre de résidences privées et d'immeubles d'appartements, par exemple la maison Lemoult à Paris (1987) ; l'Angle à Anvers (1991) ; un immeuble d'appartements à Los Angeles (1991) et une maison privée à Madrid (1991). Il a été responsable des aménagements intérieurs des hôtels Saint Martin's Lane et Sanderson à Londres, le Delano à Miami, le Mondrian à Los Angeles, l'Hudson à New York et le Clift à San Francisco. En 2006, son restaurant japonais Katsuya a ouvert ses portes à Los Angeles. Il a également travaillé à la conception d'un immeuble d'appartements en copropriété à Toronto (75 Portland Street) et le boutique hôtel de 24 niveaux JIA à Hong Kong. L'Alhondiga de 40 000 m², un « lieu de découverte, d'échange et de vie » , a ouvert à Bilbao en 2010. Parmi ses autres engagements figure son rôle de Directeur de la création de Yoo (2001–08), une société de promotion immobilière dans laquelle il s'était associé avec le promoteur John Hitchcox et Jade Jagger.

ST. MARTIN'S LANE HOTEL
London, UK, 1999

Opening date: September 1999. Client: Ian Schrager London Ltd.

Set on St. Martin's Lane not far from Trafalgar Square, the first hotel to be opened in London by the American Ian Schrager, in collaboration with the French designer Philippe Starck, is nothing if not a success. Starck's unexpected combinations of giant flower vases, outsized chess pieces, Louis XV-style armchairs, and stools shaped like golden molars combined with Schrager's marketing talent are what is required to bring the rich and the fashionable together in one place. The place is a revamped modernist office building whose façade remains remarkably uncluttered by such inconvenient items as the hotel's name. Clearly, you don't belong in this hotel if you don't know that you have arrived. This is a successful combination of a renovated modernist architecture with Starck's theatrical sense of space and design.

Das in der St. Martin's Lane unweit des Trafalgar Square gelegene, von dem Amerikaner Ian Schrager eröffnete und in Zusammenarbeit mit dem französischen Designer Philippe Starck gestaltete Hotel ist zweifellos ein Erfolg. Starcks ungewöhnliche Kombinationen von riesigen Blumenvasen, überdimensionalen Schachfiguren, Sesseln im Louis-XV-Stil und Stühlen in Form goldener Backenzähne, ergeben zusammen mit Schragers Marketingtalent die erforderlichen Zutaten, um die Hautevolee anzuziehen. Das Haus ist ein renoviertes modernes Bürogebäude, dessen Fassade auffallend frei ist von Banalitäten wie dem Namenszug des Hotels. Alles in allem stellt dieses Projekt eine gelungene Mischung aus moderner Architektur und Starcks theatralischer Auffassung von Raum und Form dar.

En bordure de St. Martin's Lane, non loin de Trafalgar Square, ce premier hôtel ouvert à Londres par l'Américain Ian Schrager en collaboration avec le designer français Philippe Starck est un grand succès. Le bizarre assemblage starckien de vases pour fleurs géants, de pièces d'échec surdimensionnées, de fauteuils de style Louis XV et de tabourets dorés en forme de molaires ainsi que le vigoureux marketing de Schrager correspondent aux attentes d'une clientèle riche et sensible à la mode. Il s'agit en fait de la restructuration d'un immeuble de bureaux moderniste dont la façade se passe de toute enseigne : vous ne méritez pas de descendre ici si vous n'en connaissez pas l'adresse. Combinaison réussie d'architecture moderniste revisitée et d'un sens théâtral de l'espace et du design à la Starck.

The enormous revolving doors on St. Martin's Lane lead to the entrance foyer, which opens out into a bar and restaurant.

Die riesige Drehtür auf der an der St. Martin's Lane gelegenen Gebäudeseite führt in die Hotelhalle, die sich zu einer Bar und einem Restaurant erweitert.

Les énormes portes pivotantes donnant sur St. Martin's Lane conduisent au hall d'entrée qui s'ouvre sur un bar et un restaurant.

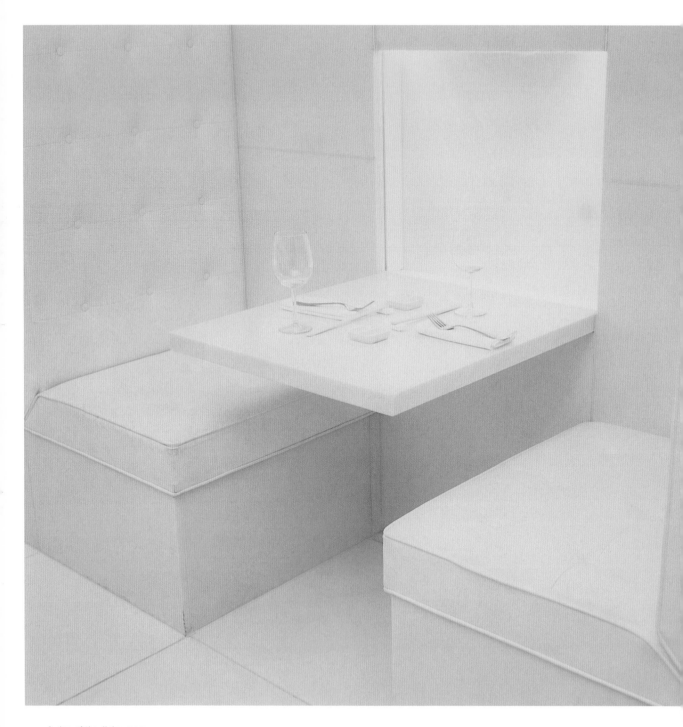

A view of the dining room.

Ansicht des Restaurants.

Vue de la salle à manger.

The ground-level bar, located at the rear of the entrance foyer, features these small vertical tables. Well suited to bar use, they, typically for Philippe Starck, challenge existing furniture typology.

Die Bar an der Rückseite der Hotelhalle ist mit kleinen, auf überproportional langen Beinen stehenden Tischen ausgestattet, die auf eine für Starck charakteristische Weise die bestehende Typologie für Einrichtungsgegenstände in Frage stellt.

Le bar du rez-de-chaussée, situé à l'arrière du hall d'entrée, est équipé de petites tables perchées. Bien adaptées à l'utilisation dans un bar, elles sont fidèles aux principes de Starck qui remet en question la typologie classique du mobilier.

TASCHEN SHOP

Paris, France, 2001

Located near the heart of historic Paris in the Saint-Germain-des-Prés area, the **TASCHEN SHOP** occupies a deep, relatively narrow space on the Rue de Buci. When weather permits, the shop's counters extend out onto the sidewalks of the busy pedestrian street. Called "a stage setting for books," the interior design contrasts an undeniable modernity with bronze surfaces and dark rare wood enveloped in shadows. Affordable books are thus given a prestigious setting where it is quite easy for visitors to browse and choose. A large video screen fills the back wall of the boutique. An identical deep space on the second floor is occupied by the offices of TASCHEN France, with furniture by Jean Nouvel and 28-meter-long computer-generated murals by the artist Albert Oehlen.

Die nahe dem historischen Zentrum von Paris im Viertel Saint-Germain-des-Prés gelegene **TASCHEN-BUCHHANDLUNG** ist in einem langen und relativ schmalen Ladenlokal auf der Rue de Buci untergebracht. Wenn es das Wetter erlaubt, lassen sich die Verkaufstische bis auf den Bürgersteig der belebten Fußgängerzone verlängern. Das „Bühnenbild für Bücher" genannte Design setzt eine unleugbare Modernität in Kontrast zu bronzefarbenen Oberflächen und seltenen, dunklen Hölzern. Dadurch erhalten die preisgünstigen Bücher einen kostbaren Rahmen, in dem die Besucher in Ruhe stöbern und auswählen können. Die Rückwand des Geschäfts wird von einer großen Videoleinwand eingenommen. In einem identisch geschnittenen Raum im Obergeschoss befinden sich die Büros von TASCHEN France, die mit Möbeln von Jean Nouvel und einem 28 m langen, computergenerierten Wandgemälde des Künstlers Albert Oehlen ausgestattet sind.

Située en plein quartier de Saint-Germain-des-Prés, la **BOUTIQUE TASCHEN** occupe un local profond mais assez étroit, rue de Buci. Lorsque le temps le permet, les comptoirs sont installés sur le trottoir de cette rue très fréquentée. « Mise-en-scène pour les livres », l'aménagement intérieur fait contraster dans un esprit indéniablement contemporain des bois exotiques rares, des éléments de bronze et de miroir. Des ouvrages de grande diffusion bénéficient ainsi d'un cadre prestigieux et peuvent être facilement feuilletés par les visiteurs. Un grand écran de télévision remplit le mur du fond. Au premier étage, un espace identique est occupé par les bureaux de TASCHEN France. Son mobilier est de Jean Nouvel et une grande peinture murale à base d'images numériques est signée par l'artiste Albert Oehlen.

The almost unadorned façade of the building was modified several times in the course of design work, due to the rigid attitude of France's historic monuments authorities. Above, the rear of the boutique with its large-scale video screen.

Die fast schmucklose Fassade des Gebäudes wurde aufgrund der strengen Vorschriften des französischen Denkmalamts im Verlauf der Bauarbeiten mehrmals verändert. Der rückwärtige Teil der Buchhandlung mit der großformatigen Videoleinwand (oben).

La façade presque sans ornement a été modifiée à plusieurs reprises pour se plier aux règles strictes de la protection des sites classés. En haut, le fond de la boutique et son grand écran vidéo.

Warm wood tones and subtle lighting together with selected pieces of old furniture give the boutique a luxurious aspect that contrasts with the up-to-date nature of the books themselves.

Die warmen Farbtöne der Hölzer und eine dezente Beleuchtung verleihen dem Geschäft zusammen mit einigen erlesenen Antiquitäten eine exquisite Note, die mit dem modernen Charakter der Bücher selbst kontrastiert.

Les tonalités chaleureuses du bois et l'éclairage subtil se combinent à des meubles de style ancien pour donner à cette boutique une atmosphère luxueuse qui contraste avec la nature très actuelle des livres présentés.

YOSHIO TANIGUCHI

Yoshio Taniguchi & Associates
Edomizaka Mori Building 8F
4-1-40 Toranomon
Minato-ku, Tokyo 105-0001
Japan

Tel: +81 3 3438 1247
Fax: +81 3 3438 1248

YOSHIO TANIGUCHI was born in Tokyo in 1937. He received a bachelor's degree in mechanical engineering from Keio University in 1960 and a M.Arch. degree from the Harvard Graduate School of Design in 1964. He worked in the office Kenzo Tange from 1964 to 1972. He created Taniguchi, Takamiya and Associates in 1975, and Taniguchi and Associates in 1979. His built work includes the Tokyo Sea Life Park, Tokyo (1989); Marugame Genichiro-Inokuma Museum of Contemporary Art and Marugame City Library, Marugame (1991); Toyota Municipal Museum of Art, Toyota City (1995); the Tokyo National Museum Gallery of Horyuji Treasures, Tokyo (1997–99); and the complete renovation and expansion of the Museum of Modern Art (MoMA) in New York. He won the project after being invited in 1997 to participate in the competition along with Wiel Arets, Steven Holl, Rem Koolhaas, Herzog & de Meuron, Toyo Ito, Dominique Perrault, Bernard Tschumi, Rafael Viñoly, and Williams & Tsien (completed 2004). The new MoMA, which has brought him international renown, was Taniguchi's first project realized outside Japan. His Centennial Hall, Kyoto National Museum, was finished in 2006.

YOSHIO TANIGUCHI wurde 1937 in Tokio geboren. 1960 schloss er sein Maschinenbaustudium an der Keio University mit dem Bachelor ab und erwarb 1964 seinen Master of Architecture an der Harvard Graduate School of Design. Von 1964 bis 1972 arbeitete er im Büro von Kenzo Tange. 1975 gründete er Taniguchi, Takamiya and Associates, 1979 Taniguchi and Associates. Das Büro hat u. a. folgende Gebäude realisiert: den Tokyo Sea Life Park in Tokio (1989), das Marugame Genichiro-Inokuma Museum für moderne Kunst und die Stadtbibliothek in Marugame (1991), das städtische Toyota Museum für Kunst in Toyota City (1995) sowie die hier gezeigte Galerie für Horyuji-Schätze im Tokioter Nationalmuseum (1997–99) und die umfassende Sanierung und Erweiterung des Museum of Modern Art in New York, für die Taniguchi 1997 einen eingeladenen Wettbewerb gewonnen hatte, an dem außer ihm Wiel Arets, Steven Holl, Rem Koolhaas, Herzog & de Meuron, Toyo Ito, Dominique Perrault, Bernard Tschumi, Rafael Viñoly und Williams & Tsien teilnahmen (Fertigstellung 2004). Dies war für Taniguchi der erste Auftrag, der außerhalb Japans realisiert wurde, und er macht ihn international bekannt. Taniguchis Hundertjahrhalle des Nationalmuseums in Kioto wurde 2006 fertiggestellt.

Né à Tokyo en 1937, **YOSHIO TANIGUCHI** est diplômé en ingénierie mécanique de l'Université Keio (1960) et Master of Architecture de la Harvard Graduate School of Design (1964). Il a travaillé pour Kenzo Tange de 1964 à 1972 et a créé Taniguchi, Takamiya and Associates en 1975, puis Taniguchi and Associates en 1979. Parmi ses réalisations : le Parc de la vie sous-marine de Tokyo (1989) ; le musée d'Art contemporain et la bibliothèque de la ville de Marugame, Marugame (1991) ; le Musée d'art municipal Toyota, Toyota-City (1995) ; la galerie des Trésors Horuji du Musée national de Tokyo, Tokyo (1997–98) et la rénovation et l'extension du Museum of Modern Art de New York. Il en avait remporté le concours sur invitation face à Wiel Arets, Steven Holl, Rem Koolhaas, Herzog & de Meuron, Toyo Ito, Dominique Perrault, Bernard Tschumi, Rafael Viñoly et Williams & Tsien (achèvement en 2004). Pour Taniguchi il s'agissait de la première commande réalisée hors du Japon et elle fonda sa notoriété internationale. Le Musée national de Kyoto, Centennial Hall, a été achevé en 2006.

TOKYO NATIONAL MUSEUM, GALLERY OF HORYUJI TREASURES

Tokyo, Japan, 1994–99

Planning: 4/1994–3/1995. Construction: 4/1995–3/1999.
Client: Ministry of Education and Ministry of Construction.
Total floor area: 4031 m².

Set in the grounds of the **TOKYO NATIONAL MUSEUM** in Ueno Park in Tokyo, this new structure by Taniguchi was designed to house a number of treasures from the Horyuji Temple in Nara. The building covers an area of 1934 m² and has a total floor area of 4031 m². It is a four-story structure built of reinforced concrete with a steel frame. Inspired by the wooden boxes used to protect precious art objects in Japan, the design includes a high metal canopy, a glazed entrance area and a completely darkened exhibition area in the interior. Open on two sides to the garden environment with a shallow basin marking the entrance area, the building's construction has a jewel-like precision. It is a masterpiece in itself, worthy of one of the finest architects currently working in Japan.

Yoshio Taniguchi entwarf für das **TOKIOTER NATIONALMUSEUM** im Ueno-Park einen Bau zur Präsentation von Kunstwerken, die ursprünglich dem Horyuji-Tempel in Nara gehörten. Die viergeschossige Stahlbetonkonstruktion – ein mit Stahlbeton ummanteltes Stahlskelett – hat eine Grundfläche von 1934 m² und eine Gesamtnutzfläche von 4031 m². Inspiriert von den in Schichten aufgebauten Holzkisten, die im alten Japan zum Schutz kostbarer Kunstgegenstände verwendet wurden, beinhaltet die Gestaltung ein hohes, überhängendes Schutzdach aus Metall, einen verglasten Eingangsbereich und einen vollständig abgedunkelten Ausstellungsbereich. Im Eingangsbereich ist das Gebäude nach zwei Seiten zum umgebenden Garten und einem flachen Wasserbecken hin geöffnet. Mit seinen präzisen und kostbaren Formen kann dieser Bau mit Recht ein Meisterwerk genannt werden, würdig eines der besten japanischen Architekten unserer Tage.

Sur les terrains du **MUSÉE NATIONAL DE TOKYO**, dans le parc Ueno, cette nouvelle réalisation de Taniguchi a été spécialement construite pour recevoir un certain nombre d'œuvres qui se trouvaient à l'origine dans le temple Horyuji de Nara. Pour une surface au sol de 1934 m², le musée dispose de 4031 m² de planchers sur quatre niveaux. Il est en béton armé sur ossature d'acier. Inspiré des boîtes en bois qui servaient à protéger les objets précieux au Japon, il possède un auvent en métal surplombant, une zone d'entrée vitrée entourée d'un bassin et une aire d'exposition centrale sans ouverture. Donnant de deux côtés sur le parc, il a été construit avec une précision d'horloger. Ce chef-d'œuvre est à l'image du travail de Taniguchi, l'un des architectes les plus raffinés travaillant actuellement au Japon.

The extreme rigor and geometric clarity of Taniguchi's architecture is visible in these images of the main approach path to the museum (left) and in the entrance foyer (below).

Der Hauptzugangsweg zum Museum (links) und das Foyer (unten) machen die extreme Strenge und geometrische Klarheit von Taniguchis Baukunst augenfällig.

La rigueur extrême et la pureté géométrique du travail de Taniguchi sont évidentes dans ces vues de l'accès principal du musée (à gauche) et du foyer d'entrée (ci-dessous).

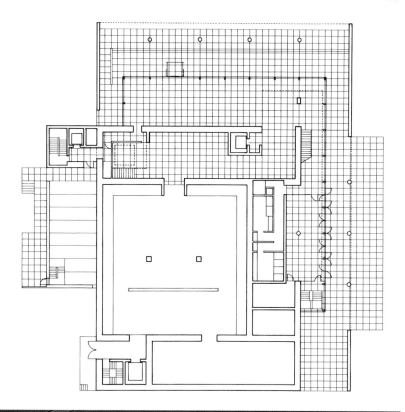

The visitor progresses from the light entrance areas to the almost total darkness of the main exhibition hall, where the extraordinary Buddhist relics of the temple are displayed.

Die Besucher gelangen von dem hellen Eingangsbereich in den abgedunkelten Ausstellungssaal, wo die kostbaren Reliquien des Tempels präsentiert werden.

Partant de la zone d'entrée très lumineuse, le visiteur pénètre dans l'obscurité quasi totale de la principale salle d'exposition où sont présentées d'extraordinaires reliques du temple.

THE MUSEUM OF MODERN ART EXPANSION AND RENOVATION

New York, New York, USA, 2002–04

*Floor area: 24 000 m² (new space). Client: The Trustees of the Museum of Modern Art.
Costs: $ 315 million (construction).*

A mere twenty years after the 1984 expansion of New York's **MUSEUM OF MODERN ART** by Cesar Pelli that created the greenhouse-like rear of the museum and its single place escalators, the institution has reemerged in a surprising new form, laid out, at least in its major components, by Tokyo architect Yoshio Taniguchi. The total budget for the project was 425 million dollars, with construction alone costing 315 million dollars, yet even these figures understate total expenses that rise to 858 million dollars when the costs of MoMA Queens and moving back and forth are added to some acquisitions. Although some say that MoMA lost its original spirit when Pelli added a 55-story residential tower to the premises, the Taniguchi-led expansion creates vast spaces that the curators have clearly had difficulty filling, as is the case in the monumental 33.5-meter-high second-floor atrium. Adding roughly 24 000 m² to the institution, and doubling its available exhibition space, Taniguchi achieved a remarkable degree of refinement and detailing on this project, considering that he was not familiar with American building methods. As early as the schematic design phase, the Museum of Modern Art proposed that Taniguchi work with a firm that had local building experience. Kohn Pedersen Fox (KPF) was selected and ultimately became the executive architect for the project, with Gregory Clement and Steven Rustow heading their effort. Rustow had considerable museum experience, having worked actively on I. M. Pei's Grand Louvre project and in particular the Richelieu Wing phase. KPF was also called to supervise the renovation of the original 1939 building by Phillip Goodwin and Edward Durrell Stone as well as Philip Johnson's 1964 east wing addition. Philip Johnson's 1953 sculpture garden, in an expanded version, emerges as the real center of the new MoMA, where much of the new construction can be admired in a peaceful atmosphere.

Nur 20 Jahre nach der Erweiterung des **MUSEUM OF MODERN ART** durch Cesar Pelli im Jahr 1984 hat sich die Institution in einer überraschenden Form neu erfunden. Pelli hatte das Museum mit einem rückwärtigen wintergartenähnlichen Anbau versehen und es mit Rolltreppen in diesem Bereich ausgestattet. Der anspruchsvolle Entwurf für die neuerliche Erweiterung stammt zum größten Teil von dem Tokioter Architekten Yoshio Taniguchi. Die Kosten für das Projekt beliefen sich auf umgerechnet 353 Millionen Euro, davon waren allein 261 Millionen Euro reine Baukosten. Aber selbst diese hohen Zahlen entsprechen nicht den Gesamtkosten, die etwa 713 Millionen Euro betragen, wenn man den Umzug des MoMA nach Queens und wieder zurück und einige Ankäufe hinzurechnet. Pelli hatte 1984 dem Museum zusätzlich einen 55-geschossigen Wohnturm angefügt (manche meinen, das MoMA hätte dadurch seinen ursprünglichen Charakter verloren). Taniguchi ist es trotzdem gelungen, das Gebäude um Räume mit beträchtlichen Ausmaßen zu erweitern. Offensichtlich hatten die Kuratoren aber einige Probleme, diese zu füllen – deutlich wird dies im 33,5 m hohen monumentalen Atrium im 1. Obergeschoss. Die Erweiterung umfasst 24 000 m² und verdoppelt die bisher vorhandene Ausstellungsfläche. Taniguchi hat einen bemerkenswerten Grad der Verfeinerung und Qualität der Ausführung erreicht und dies, obwohl er mit der amerikanischen Praxis der Bauausführung nicht vertraut war. Schon in der Phase der Entwurfsplanung schlug das Museum of Modern Art Taniguchi vor, mit einem Büro mit Bauerfahrung in den USA zusammenzuarbeiten. Kohn Pedersen Fox (KPF) wurde als Projektpartner ausgewählt und war für die Ausführung zuständig. Gregory Clement und Steven Rustow waren die Projektleiter. Rustow, ein im Museumsbau sehr erfahrener Architekt, hatte vorher im Büro von I. M. Pei an der Erweiterung des Grand Louvre mitgewirkt, und hier besonders am Richelieu-Flügel. KPF wurde auch beauftragt, die Sanierung des ursprünglichen MoMA-Gebäudes von Phillip Goodwin und Edward Durell Stone aus dem Jahr 1939 und des Ostflügels von Philip Johnson aus dem Jahr 1964 zu leiten. Philip Johnsons 1953 geschaffener Skulpturgarten wurde erweitert und entpuppt sich als wahres Zentrum des neuen Museums, von dem aus man einen Großteil des neuen MoMA sehen und in einer friedlichen Atmosphäre bewundern kann.

Vingt ans après l'intervention de Cesar Pelli sur le **MUSEUM OF MODERN ART** de New York, qui avait créé l'extension en forme de serre à l'arrière du musée et posé d'étroits escaliers mécaniques, l'institution connaît aujourd'hui une mutation formelle conçue, pour sa majeure partie, par l'architecte tokyoïte Yoshio Taniguchi. Le budget total de l'opération s'est élevé à 353 millions d'euros, dont 261 pour la seule construction. Cependant, l'investissement s'élèvera à 713 millions lorsque les coûts du MoMA Queens et des différents déménagements auront été intégrés. Si certains ont pu dire que le musée avait déjà perdu son esprit originel lorsque Pelli lui ajouta une tour d'appartements de 55 étages, l'extension de Taniguchi a créé de vastes espaces que les conservateurs semblent avoir quelques difficultés à maîtriser, en particulier les 33,5 m de haut du monumental atrium du premier étage. Tout en ajoutant 24 000 m² et en doublant les espaces d'exposition, Taniguchi a atteint un remarquable niveau de raffinement, surtout quand on sait qu'il n'était pas familier des méthodes de construction américaines. Dès la phase des plans, le MoMA a proposé que l'architecte collabore avec une agence dotée d'une expérience locale. Kohn Pedersen Fox (KPF) fut sélectionnée et finit par devenir l'architecte exécutif de l'ensemble du projet, sous la direction de Gregory Clement et Steven Rustow. Rustow possède une longue expérience des musées puisqu'il a travaillé activement au Grand Louvre de I. M. Pei, en particulier sur l'aile Richelieu. KPF a également été invitée à superviser la rénovation du bâtiment d'origine de Philip Goodwin et Edward Durell Stone (1939) et de l'aile est, ajoutée en 1964 par Philip Johnson. Le Jardin des sculptures de Johnson (1953) est devenu, après agrandissement, le vrai centre du musée, d'où la plus grande partie du nouveau bâtiment peut être admirée dans une atmosphère paisible.

A new building by Taniguchi looks over the slightly extended area of MoMA's Sculpture Garden. Within, design reclaims the place of honor it had in the museum's earlier incarnations.

Das neue Museumsgebäude von Taniguchi überblickt den etwas vergrößerten Skulpturgarten des MoMA. Innen erobert sich die Designabteilung den Rang zurück, den sie früher im Museum hatte.

Le nouveau bâtiment de Taniguchi donne sur le Jardin des sculptures du MoMA, légèrement agrandi. L'intérieur a été totalement repensé, comme lors des précédentes interventions sur ce musée.

Some of the museum space seems to be too large for the art that is exhibited there, and overall, the massive expansion seems to rob MoMA of the intimacy which remained part of its character even after the most recent expansion by Cesar Pelli.

Einige der neuen Museumsräume scheinen zu groß für die in ihnen ausgestellte Kunst zu sein. Insgesamt verliert das MoMA durch die umfangreiche Erweiterung an Intimität, die – auch nach der vorletzten Erweiterung durch Cesar Pelli – einen Teil seines Charmes ausmachte.

Certains volumes sont, semble-t-il, trop grands pour les œuvres qu'ils accueillent. Cette brutale expansion prive peut-être le MoMA de l'intimité qui le caractérisait, même après les dernières interventions de Cesar Pelli.

JYRKI TASA

Jyrki Tasa
Arkkitehdit NRT Oy / Architects NRT Ltd
Kalevankatu 31
00100 Helsinki
Finland

Tel: +358 9 686 6780
Fax: +358 9 685 7588
E-mail: ark.tsto@n-r-t.fi
Web: www.n-r-t.fi

Into House ▶

Born in Turku, Finland, in 1944, **JYRKI TASA** graduated from the Helsinki University of Technology in 1973. He set up an architectural office with Matti Nurmela and Kari Raimoranta in Helsinki the same year. He has been a professor at the University of Oulu since 1988. He has won 20 first prizes in architectural competitions. He won the Finnish State Prize in Architecture and Planning in 1987. His most significant work includes the Malmi Post Office, the Kuhmo Library, the Paavo Nurmi Stadium in Turku, the Into House in Espoo published here, the BE Pop Shopping Center in Pori, and the Moby Dick house. All of these projects are located in Finland.

JYRKI TASA, 1944 im finnischen Turku geboren, schloss 1973 sein Studium an der Technischen Universität Helsinki ab. Im selben Jahr gründete er zusammen mit Matti Nurmela und Kari Raimoranta ein Architekturbüro in Helsinki. Seit 1988 lehrt er außerdem an der Universität von Oulu. Jyrki Tasa ist im Laufe seiner Karriere aus 20 Architekturwettbewerben als Sieger hervorgegangen, und 1987 wurde ihm der Finnische Staatspreis für Architektur und Bauplanung verliehen. Zu seinen wichtigsten, alle in Finnland realisierten Bauten gehören das Postamt in Malmi, die Bibliothek in Kuhmo, das Stadium Paavo Nurmi in Turku, das hier vorgestellte Haus Into in Espoo, das Einkaufszentrum BE Pop in Pori sowie das Haus Moby Dick.

Né en 1944 à Tuku, en Finlande, **JYRKI TASA** est diplômé de l'Université de Technologie d'Helsinki en 1973. Il crée son agence d'architecture avec Matti Nurmela et Kari Raimoranta à Helsinki la même année. Il enseigne à l'Université d'Oulu depuis 1988 et a remporté 20 premiers prix de concours architecturaux. Il a reçu le Prix d'architecture et d'urbanisme de l'État finlandais en 1987. Parmi ses réalisations les plus marquantes, toutes en Finlande : la poste de Malmi, la bibliothèque de Kuhmo, le stade Paavo Nurmi à Turku, la maison Into à Espoo publiée ici, le centre commercial BE Pop à Pori et la maison Moby Dick.

INTO HOUSE

Espoo, Finland, 1997–98

Client: Into Tasa. Floor area: 187 m². Structure: steel tubes and wood. Costs: € 400 000.

This three-level family house is accessible via a walkway at its rear. The relatively closed rear façade contrasts with the open glazed front of the house. Wood paneling and a spectacular suspended spiral staircase animate the interior spaces. With its tilted metal exterior columns, slanted roof and cantilevered main body, this house is dramatic and unexpected. Though it is clearly rooted in modern Finnish architecture, it does not appear to be firmly tied to its own site. The angling of the columns and the cantilevering almost give the impression that the house has just moved from its original location. This kind of imbalance and unexpected design has been seen throughout Tasa's career, as buildings such as the Commercial Center in Pori, Finland (1987–89) show. With a design such as that of the **INTO HOUSE**, Tasa shows his ability to step back from the postmodern tendencies shown in buildings like the Library in Kuhmo (1982–84) while still retaining a degree of fantasy or constructive imbalance.

Der Zugang zu dem auf drei Ebenen angelegten Einfamilienhaus erfolgt über einen Gehweg an der Rückseite des Gebäudes. Die relativ geschlossene rückwärtige Fassade des Hauses bildet einen Kontrast zur offenen, verglasten Vorderfront. Das Interieur beleben die Holztäfelungen und eine auffallende abgehängte Wendeltreppe. Mit den geneigten Außenträgern aus Metall, dem Schrägdach und dem vorspringenden Hauptteil handelt es sich um ein spektakuläres und verblüffendes Gebäude. Wenngleich eindeutig in der modernen finnischen Architektur verwurzelt, scheint es mit seinem eigenen Grund nicht fest verbunden zu sein. Vielmehr entsteht durch die Schräge der Träger und den frei schwebenden Rumpf der Eindruck, als sei das Haus soeben von seinem ursprünglichen Standort hierher gerückt worden. Das Ungleichgewicht und die überraschenden Gestaltungselemente ziehen sich durch die gesamte Karriere von Tasa, so findet man sie auch an Gebäuden wie dem Einkaufszentrum im finnischen Pori (1987–89). In diesem Entwurf des **HAUSES INTO** spiegelt sich die Fähigkeit des Architekten, die postmodernen Vorlieben, wie er sie etwa in seiner Bibliothek in Kuhmo (1982–84) umgesetzt hat, fallen zu lassen und sich dabei dennoch ein hohes Maß an Fantasie und konstruktiver Unausgewogenheit zu bewahren.

On accède à cette maison familiale de trois niveaux par une allée située à l'arrière dont la façade relativement fermée contraste avec la façade avant, ouverte et vitrée. Des lambris de bois et un spectaculaire escalier suspendu en spirale animent les espaces intérieurs. Les colonnes extérieures penchées, le toit incliné et la partie principale en porte-à-faux lui donnent un aspect spectaculaire et inattendu. Bien que nettement enracinée dans l'architecture finlandaise actuelle, elle ne semble pas vraiment liée à son terrain. L'inclinaison des colonnes et le porte-à-faux donnent presque l'impression qu'elle vient de quitter son implantation d'origine. Cette sorte de déséquilibre et de dessin étrange est récurrente dans le travail de Tasa, comme on l'observe déjà dans le Centre commercial de Pori (Finlande, 1987–89). Avec la **MAISON INTO**, Tasa montre sa capacité à évoluer par rapport à ses tendances postmodernes illustrées dans des réalisations comme la bibliothèque de Kuhmo (1982–84), tout en conservant un certain degré de fantaisie ou de déséquilibre constructif.

Left page, the front façade of the house and this page, a side view showing the tilted columns and the large glazed surfaces.

Vorderseite des Hauses (links). Seitenansicht mit den geneigten Stützen und den großflächigen Verglasungen (diese Seite).

À gauche, la façade principale de la maison et, en bas, une vue latérale des colonnes inclinées et des vastes surfaces vitrées.

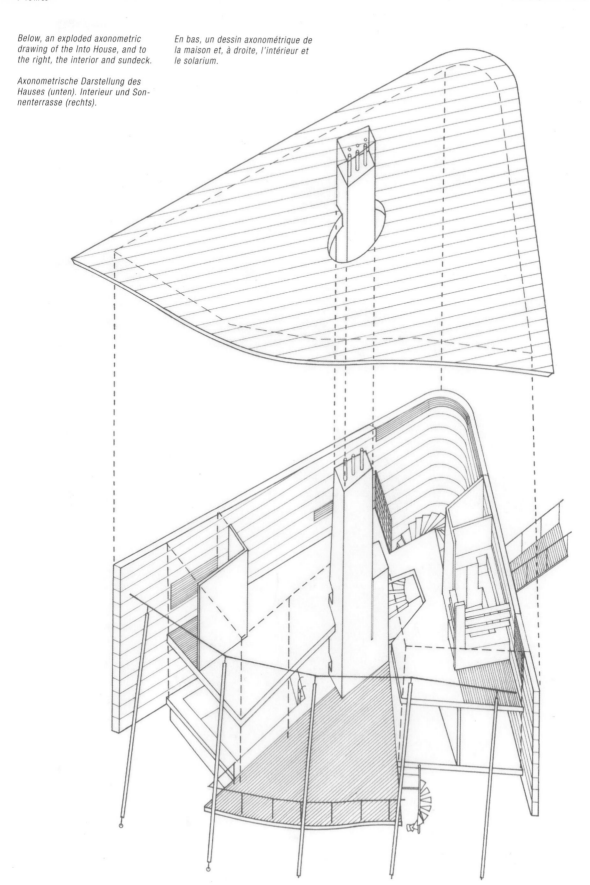

Below, an exploded axonometric
drawing of the Into House, and to
the right, the interior and sundeck.

En bas, un dessin axonométrique de
la maison et, à droite, l'intérieur et
le solarium.

*Axonometrische Darstellung des
Hauses (unten). Interieur und Son-
nenterrasse (rechts).*

TEN ARQUITECTOS

TEN Arquitectos
Cuernavaca 114 P/B
Colonia Condesa
06140 Mexico City DF
Mexico

Tel: +52 55 5211 8004
E-mail: ten@ten-arquitectos.com
Web: www.ten-arquitectos.com

Televisa Services Building ▶

Enrique Norten was born in Mexico City in 1954, and graduated as an architect from the Universidad Iberoamericana there in 1978. He received a master's degree in architecture from Cornell University in 1980. He was partner in Albin y Norten Arquitectos (1981–84) before founding **TEN ARQUITECTOS** in 1986. Bernardo Gómez-Pimienta was born in Brussels in 1961 and studied at the Universidad Anahuac in Mexico City and at Columbia University, New York. He was a partner in TEN Arquitectos from 1987 to 2003. Their work in Mexico includes a Cultural Center, Lindavista (1987–92), a workers' restaurant, San Angel (1993), LE House, Mexico City (1995), and the Museum of Sciences (Mexico City, 1997). Further projects that have earned various awards include the Hotel Habita (2002) and the RR House (2004), both in Mexico City.

Enrique Norten, geboren 1954 in Mexico City, beendete dort 1978 sein Studium an der Universidad Iberoamericana. An der Cornell University erwarb er 1980 den Master of Architecture. Bevor er 1986 **TEN ARQUITECTOS** gründete, war Partner im Büro Albin y Norten (1981–84). Bernardo Gómez-Pimienta, geboren 1961 in Brüssel, studierte an der Universidad Anahuac in Mexico City und an der Columbia University in New York. Von 1987 bis 2003 war er Teilhaber von TEN Arquitectos. Zu ihrem Werk gehören ein Kulturzentrum in Lindavista (1987–92), ein Arbeiterrestaurant in San Angel (1993), das Haus LE (1995) und das Museo de Historia Natural in Mexico City (1997). Zu den mit unterschiedlichen Preisen ausgezeichneten Projekten gehören das Hotel Habita (2002) und das Haus RR (2004, alle Mexico City).

Né à Mexico en 1954, Enrique Norten est architecte diplômé de la Universidad Iberoamericana en 1978. Il obtient un Master of Architecture de la Cornell University en 1980. Après avoir été associé à Albin y Norten Arquitectos (1981–84), il crée **TEN ARQUITECTOS** en 1986. Bernardo Gómez-Pimienta naît à Bruxelles en 1961, et étudie à l'Universidad Anahuac de Mexico et à Columbia University. Il est un des associés de TEN Arquitectos de 1987 à 2003. Leurs réalisations au Mexique comprennent entre autres : un Centre culturel (Lindavista, 1987–92), un restaurant pour travailleurs (San Angel, 1993) et la Maison LE (Mexico, 1995) et le Musée des Sciences (Mexico, 1997). Parmi les projets couronnés de diverses récompenses : l'Hotel Habita (2002) et la Maison RR (2004), tous deux à Mexico.

TELEVISA SERVICES BUILDING

Mexico City, Mexico, 1993–95

Client: Televisa S.A. de C.V.. Floor area: 7500 m². Costs: $ 24 million.

This structure was the recipient of the 1998 Mies van der Rohe Award for Latin American Architecture, given at the Museum of Modern Art in New York. The 7500 m² facility, including parking, offices, an employee dining room, conference rooms, and meeting space, was built using concrete seismic walls and concrete slab supported by steel framing at a cost of $ 24 million. The roof is clad in Alucobond panels. Intended to replace a group of several buildings, in which the same services were housed until 1995, the Televisa Services structure is set on an unusual trapezoidal site. As the architects say, the "soaring aluminum-paneled shell alludes to an industrial vernacular and it also represents a technically expedient method of construction." This "silvery blimp," which houses the employees' dining room, is set on a more weighty black concrete volume where the garage and offices are located.

1998 erhielten TEN Arquitectos für diesen Bau den Mies van der Rohe Award for Latin American Architecture des Museum of Modern Art in New York. Der Komplex aus Parkhaus, Büros, einer Kantine sowie Konferenz- und Sitzungsräumen wurde mit erdbebensicheren Wänden und Betondecken, die von einem Stahlskelett getragen werden, errichtet. Das Dach ist mit Alucobond-Platten gedeckt. Der Bau ersetzt eine Gruppe von Häusern, in denen die Firma bis 1995 untergebracht war, und steht auf einem trapezförmigen Grundstück. Die Architekten erklärten, dass „die aluminiumverkleidete Schale auf regionale Industriebauten verweist und zugleich eine technisch ausgereifte Baumethode darstellt". Der „silbrige Ballon", in dem die Kantine untergebracht ist, wurde auf einen wuchtigen schwarzen „Betonsockel" gesetzt, in dem sich das Parkhaus und die Büros befinden.

Ce bâtiment, édifié pour remplacer une groupe de petits immeubles qui abritaient les mêmes fonctions jusqu'en 1995, a reçu le Prix Mies van der Rohe 1998 pour l'Amérique Latine, remis au Museum of Modern Art de New York. Mesurant 7500 m², et ayant coûté $ 24 millions, il comprend des bureaux, des salles de conférence, des espaces de réunion, un restaurant pour le personnel et des parkings. Construit sur un terrain trapézoïdal, sa structure se compose de murs en béton anti-sismiques et d'une dalle de béton soutenue par une ossature d'acier. L'architecte explique que « la coque recouverte de panneaux d'aluminium est une allusion à l'architecture vernaculaire industrielle et représente également une méthode pratique de construction ». La « bosse argentée » qui abrite le restaurant repose sur un volume de béton noir plus massif dans lequel ont été implantés les bureaux et les parkings.

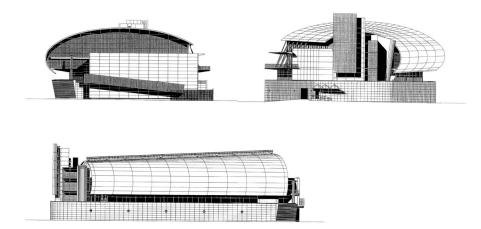

A large open space under the curving aluminum roof is devoted to a dining area.

Ein großer, offener Raum unter dem gewölbten Aluminiumdach wird als Kantine genutzt.

Le vaste espace ouvert sous le toit d'aluminium incurvé est consacré au restaurant d'entreprise.

TEZUKA ARCHITECTS

Tezuka Architects
1-19-9-3F Todoroki
Setagaya
Tokyo 158-0082
Japan

Tel: +81 3 3703 7056
Fax: +81 3 3703 7038
E-mail: tez@sepia.ocn.ne.jp
Web: www.tezuka-arch.com

Matsunoyama Natural Science Museum

TAKAHARU TEZUKA, born in Tokyo in 1964, received his degrees from the Musashi Institute of Technology (1987), and from the University of Pennsylvania (1990). He worked with Richard Rogers Partnership Ltd (1994) and established Tezuka Architects the same year. Born in Kanagawa in 1969, **YUI TEZUKA** was educated at the Musashi Institute of Technology and the Bartlett School of Architecture, University College, London. The practice has completed more than 20 private houses, and won the competition for the Matsunoyama Natural Science Museum in 2000. Since then it has been based in Tokyo. Their work includes the Soejima Hospital; Jyubako House; Shoe Box House; Big Window House; Observatory House; Forest House; Clipping Corner House; Floating House; Engawa House; Houses to Catch the Sky I–III; Saw Roof House; Skylight House; Canopy House; Thin Wall House; Thin Roof House; Anthill House; Step House; Wall-less House; Roof House; Megaphone House; Machiya House; Light Gauge Steel House; and the Wood Deck House.

TAKAHARU TEZUKA, 1964 in Tokio geboren, machte seine Abschlüsse 1987 am Technischen Institut Musashi und 1990 an der University of Pennsylvania. 1994 arbeitete er bei Richard Rogers Partnership Ltd und gründete im selben Jahr Tezuka Architects. **YUI TEZUKA**, geboren 1969 in Kanagawa, studierte ebenfalls am Technischen Institut Musashi und an der Bartlett School of Architecture am University College of London. Das Büro hat mehr als 20 Privathäuser gebaut und 2000 den Wettbewerb für das Naturwissenschaftliche Museum Matsunoyama gewonnen. Seitdem befindet sich das Büro in Tokio. Tezuka Architects haben u. a. folgende Projekte realisiert: das Krankenhaus Soejima, das Jyubako-Haus, das Schuhschachtel-Haus, das Haus „Großes Fenster", das Sternwarten-Haus, das Waldhaus, das Haus „Abgeschnittene Ecke", das schwebende Haus und das Engawa-Haus, ferner die „Fang-den-Himmel-Häuser I–III", das Sägedach-Haus, das Oberlicht-Haus, das Vordach-Haus, das Haus „Dünne Wand", das Haus „Dünnes Dach", das Ameisenhügel-Haus, das Stufen-Haus, das „Haus ohne Wände", das Dach-Haus, das Megafon-Haus, das Machiya-Haus, das „Lichtfühler-Stahlhaus" und das Holzterrassen-Haus.

TAKAHARU TEZUKA, né à Tokyo en 1964, est diplômé de l'Institut de technologie Musashi (1987) et de l'Université de Pennsylvanie (1990). Il a travaillé pour Richard Rogers Partnership Ltd (1994) et fondé l'agence Tezuka Architects la même année. Né à Kanagawa en 1969, **YUI TEZUKA** est diplômé de l'Institut de technologie Musashi et de la Bartlett School of Architecture, University College, Londres. Installée aujourd'hui à Tokyo, l'agence a déjà réalisé l'hôpital de Soejima, Japon (1996) et plus de 20 résidences privées : Jyubako House ; Shoe Box House ; Big Window House ; Observatory House ; Forest House ; Clipping Corner House ; Floating House ; Engawa House ; Houses to Catch the Sky I–III ; Saw Roof House ; Skylight House ; Canopy House ; Thin Wall House ; Thin Roof House ; Anthill House ; Step House ; Wall-less House ; Roof House ; Megaphone House ; Machiya House ; Light Gauge Steel House et la Wood Deck House. Tezuka Architects a remporté le concours pour le Musée des sciences naturelles de Matsunoyama en 2000.

MATSUNOYAMA NATURAL SCIENCE MUSEUM

Matsunoyama, Niigata, Japan, 2002–04

*Floor area: 1248 m². Client: Matsunoyama-machi/Secretariat of Tokamachi Regionwide Area Municipal Corporation.
Costs: € 5.4 million.*

Located approximately 200 km to the north of Tokyo in a region that has the heaviest snowfalls of Japan (up to five meters), the **MATSUNOYAMA NATURAL SCIENCE MUSEUM** was built without firm foundations because the building expands 20 cm in summer. A Corten steel tube designed to resist snow loads of up to 2000 tons meanders over a length of 111 meters, following the topography and allowing visitors to "experience the light and colors under the different depths of snow from 4 m deep to 30 m above the ground." Steel plates 6 mm thick weighing 500 tons were welded in place to the load-bearing steel structure, and four large windows made of 75 mm thick Perspex and located at the turning points in the museum space permit direct observation of life under the snow. A 34-meter-high observation tower, the only element with a normal foundation, completes the project. Tezuka Architects describe the structure as a "submarine, with the tower its periscope," in a willful effort to contrast with the white natural winter landscape.

Das **NATURWISSENSCHAFTLICHE MUSEUM MATSUNOYAMA** liegt etwa 200 km nördlich von Tokio. In dieser Region gibt es die stärksten Schneefälle in Japan – der Schnee kann hier bis zu 5 m hoch liegen. Das Gebäude dehnt sich im Sommer 20 cm aus und hat daher keine festen Fundamente. Eine 111 m lange, mäandrierende Röhre aus Corten-Stahl, die Schneelasten bis 2000 t abfangen kann, folgt der Topografie und ermöglicht es dem Besucher, „das Licht und die Farben unter dem Schnee, der sich hier 4 bis 30 m hoch auftürmt, zu erleben". 6 mm dicke Stahlplatten mit einem Gesamtgewicht von 500 t wurden vor Ort an die tragende Stahlkonstruktion geschweißt. Vier große Fenster mit 75 mm dicken Perspex-Scheiben sind an den Stellen angeordnet, an denen sich die Richtung des Museumsraums ändert. Hier kann das Leben im Schnee direkt beobachtet werden. Ein 34 m hoher Aussichtsturm, der einzige Teil des Museums mit normalen Fundamenten, komplettiert die Anlage. Tezuka Architects beschreiben das Gebäude als „ein U-Boot – mit dem Turm als Periskop". Der Turm stellt dabei einen gewollten Kontrast zur weißen Winterlandschaft her.

Situé à environ 200 km au nord de Tokyo dans une région qui connaît les plus importantes chutes de neige du Japon (jusqu'à 5 m), ce **MUSÉE DES SCIENCES NATURELLES** a été construit sans fondations fixes car il se dilate de 20 cm en été. Il s'agit essentiellement d'un tube en acier Corten conçu pour résister à une charge de neige de 2000 tonnes, qui se fond dans la topographie sur une longueur de 111 m et permet aux visiteurs « de faire l'expérience de la lumière et des couleurs sous différentes épaisseurs de neige, de 4 m de profondeur jusqu'à 30 m au-dessus du niveau du sol ». Les 500 tonnes de tôles d'acier de 6 mm d'épaisseur ont été soudées sur place sur la structure porteuse en acier et quatre grandes baies fermées d'un panneau de Perspex de 75 mm d'épaisseur positionnées aux angles de la structure pour faciliter l'observation directe de la vie sous la neige. Une tour d'observation de 34 m de haut, seul élément à posséder des fondations normales, complète l'ensemble. Tezuka Architects décrit ce musée comme « un sous-marin, dont la tour serait le périscope », volontairement conçu pour contraster avec le paysage hivernal enneigé.

The rusted Corten steel exterior of the museum gives it something of the appearance of a curious industrial artifact, lost in the woods.

Die rostige Fassade aus Corten-Stahl gibt dem Museum etwas von einem sonderbaren industriellen Relikt, das im Wald vergessen wurde.

Sa peau en acier Corten patiné donne au musée l'apparence d'un objet industriel bizarre perdu dans les bois.

A café offers an outside view, while exhibitions concentrate on the unique ecosystems of this region which is prone to very heavy snow in winter.

Das Café bietet einen Ausblick nach draußen. Die Ausstellungen konzentrieren sich auf die einzigartigen Ökosysteme der Region, die im Winter heftigen Schneefällen ausgesetzt ist.

Le café bénéficie d'une vue sur l'extérieur tandis que les expositions se concentrent sur les écosystèmes spécifiques à cette région sujette à d'importantes chutes de neige en hiver.

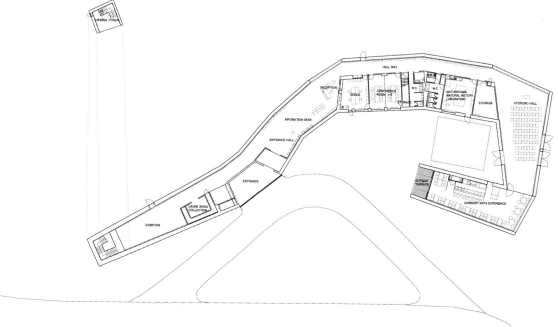

BERNARD TSCHUMI

Bernard Tschumi Architects
227 West 17th Street
New York, New York 10011, USA
Tel: +1 212 807 6340
Fax: +1 212 242 3693

6, rue Beaubourg
75004 Paris, France
Tel: +33 1 5301 9070
Fax: +33 1 5301 9079

E-mail: nyc@tschumi.com
Web: www.tschumi.com

BERNARD TSCHUMI was born in Lausanne, Switzerland, in 1944. He studied in Paris and at the Federal Institute of Technology (ETH), Zurich. He taught at the Architectural Association (AA), London (1970–79), and at Princeton (1976–80). He was the Dean of the Graduate School of Architecture, Planning and Preservation of Columbia University in New York from 1988 to 2003. He opened his own office, Bernard Tschumi Architects (Paris and New York), in 1981. Major projects include: Parc de la Villette, Paris (1982–95); Second Prize in the Kansai International Airport Competition (1988); Video Gallery, Groningen, The Netherlands (1990); Lerner Student Center, Columbia University, New York (1994–99); School of Architecture, Marne-la-Vallée, France (1994–98); and the Interface Flon train station in Lausanne, Switzerland (1988–2001). His recent projects include the Acropolis Museum in Athens (2002–08) and the Vacheron Constantin factory in Geneva (2005).

BERNARD TSCHUMI, geboren 1944 im schweizerischen Lausanne, studierte in Paris und an der Eidgenössischen Technischen Hochschule (ETH) in Zürich. Von 1970 bis 1979 lehrte er an der Architectural Association (AA) in London und von 1976 bis 1980 in Princeton. Von 1988 bis 2003 war er Dekan der Graduate School of Architecture, Planning and Preservation der Columbia University in New York. 1981 gründete Tschumi sein eigenes Büro, Bernard Tschumi Architects, mit Niederlassungen in Paris und New York. Zu seinen wichtigsten Projekten gehören der Parc de la Villette in Paris (1982–95), sein Wettbewerbsbeitrag für den internationalen Flughafen Kansai (1988), für den er den zweiten Preis erhielt, die Videogalerie im niederländischen Groningen (1990), das Lerner Hall Student Center der Columbia University in New York (1994–99), die Architekturschule im französischen Marne-la-Vallée (1994–98) sowie der Bahnhof Interface Flon in Lausanne (1988–2001). Zu seinen neueren Bauten zählen das Akropolismuseum in Athen (2002–08) und die Manufaktur Vacheron Constantin in Genf (2005).

Né à Lausanne, Suisse, en 1944, **BERNARD TSCHUMI** étudie à Paris et à l'Institut Fédéral de technologie de Zurich (ETH). Il enseigne à l'Architectural Association, (Londres, 1970–79), et à Princeton (1976 et 1980). Il est doyen de la Graduate School of Architecture, Planning and Preservation de Columbia University, New York, de 1988 à 2003. Il ouvre son agence, Bernard Tschumi Architects, en 1981 (New York et Paris). Parmi ses principaux projets : le Parc de la Villette (Paris, 1982–95) ; le second prix du concours pour l'aéroport international de Kansaï (1988) ; la Glass Video Gallery (Groningue, Pays-Bas, 1990) ; le Lerner Hall Student Center (Columbia University, New York, 1994–99) et l'École d'Architecture de Marne-la-Vallée, (1994–98) ainsi que la gare d'interconnections du quartier de Flon à Lausanne (Suisse, 1988–2001). Parmi ses travaux les plus récents : le Musée de l'Acropolis à Athènes (2002–08) et la Manufacture Vacheron Constantin à Genève (2005).

LERNER HALL STUDENT CENTER

Columbia University, New York, New York, USA, 1994–99

*Planning: 1994–95. Construction: fall 1996 – summer 1999.
Client: Columbia University. Floor area: 20 903 m². Costs: $ 85 million.*

The $ 85 million 20 903 m² **LERNER HALL STUDENT CENTER** is built (in collaboration with Gruzen Samton Architects) in large part of precast concrete, brick and cast-stone masonry with cast-in-place concrete columns. One of its most surprising features is the bank of ramps set just behind a structural glass wall on the side of the building facing the campus. This skewed space is used incidentally to house some 6000 student mailboxes, but it is also a device to bring students together into a common space, while solving the structural questions related to the uneven terrain of the site. Indeed, the glass façade of the building stands out as being surprisingly different than the opposite (Broadway) side of the building, which had to fit into the plan for the campus alignments and building design of McKim, Mead and White of 1890. As the former Dean of the Columbia School of Architecture, Bernard Tschumi has thus left a lasting mark on the university.

Das für 85 Millionen Dollar in Zusammenarbeit mit Gruzen Samton Architects erbaute, 20 903 m² große **LERNER HALL STUDENT CENTER** besteht überwiegend aus Betonfertigteilen, einer Kombination von Ziegel- und Kunststeinmauerwerk, Aluminium, Glas und vor Ort gegossenen Betonstützen. Um die Unebenheiten des Geländes auf der dem Campus zugewandten Gebäudeseite auszugleichen, wurden im mittleren Bauteil hinter einer Fassade aus Glas Rampen angelegt. Diese verbinden die auf unterschiedlicher Höhe liegenden Geschosse der angrenzenden Bauten, darüber hinaus wird der Bereich hinter der Fassade als Treffpunkt und zur Unterbringung von fast 6000 Briefkästen für die Studenten genutzt. Die Glasfassade unterscheidet sich stark von der am Broadway liegenden Seite des Gebäudes, die sich in den Generalplan für den Campus einfügen musste, den McKim, Mead and White 1890 entwickelt hatte. Damit hat Bernard Tschumi, ehemaliger Dekan der Columbia School of Architecture, eine bleibende Spur an seiner Universität hinterlassen.

Le **LERNER HALL STUDENT CENTER** de 20 903 m² (budget : $ 85 millions) est en grande partie construit (en collaboration avec Gruzen Samton Architects) en éléments de béton préfabriqués, brique et pierre moulée. L'une de ses caractéristiques les plus surprenantes est la succession de rampes implantée juste derrière une façade en verre donnant sur le campus. Cet espace « en biais » sert éventuellement à abriter les quelque 6000 boîtes aux lettres des étudiants, mais correspond aussi à la volonté de réunir les étudiants dans un espace commun tout en résolvant les problèmes de structure posés par un terrain inégal. Cette façade de verre est étonnement différente de celle qui donne sur Broadway contrainte de respecter l'alignement et le plan de masse de McKim, Mead et White de 1890. Ancien doyen de la Columbia School of Architecture, Bernard Tschumi aura laissé une marque durable sur son université.

The architect approached the problem of the difference in levels of the street and campus sides of the building by using a system of inclined ramps.

Der Architekt löste das Problem der unterschiedlichen Höhen von Campus und straßenseitigen Gebäudeteilen durch ein System geneigter Rampen.

L'architecte a traité la différence de niveaux entre la rue et le campus au moyen d'un système de rampes inclinées.

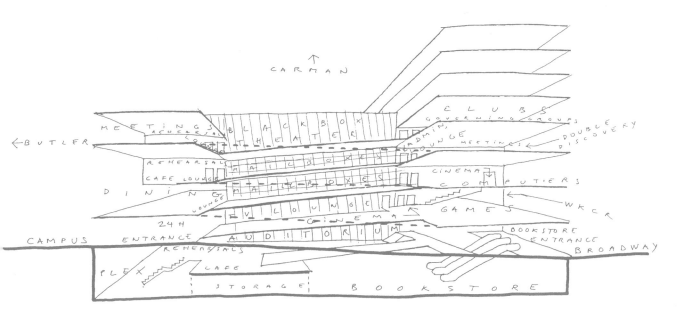

CARMAN

CLUBS

MEETINGS BLACK BOX GOVERNING GROUPS
REHEARS LOUNG THEATER ADMIN LOUNGE DOUBLE
BUTLER MEETINGS DISCOVERY

REHEARSALS MAIL BOXES CINEMA
CAFE LOUNGE MAIL BOXES COMPUTERS
DINING LOUNGE WKCR
LOUNGE LOUNGE GAMES
24H CINEMA BOOKSTORE
CAMPUS ENTRANCE AUDITORIUM ENTRANCE
REHEARSALS BROADWAY
PLEX CAFE
STORAGE BOOKSTORE

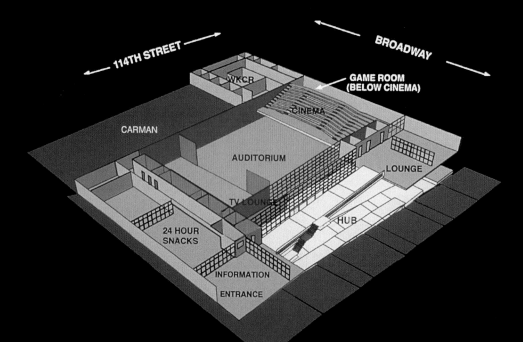

114TH STREET — BROADWAY

WKCR

GAME ROOM
(BELOW CINEMA)

CINEMA

CARMAN

AUDITORIUM

LOUNGE

TV LOUNGE

24 HOUR
SNACKS

HUB

INFORMATION

ENTRANCE

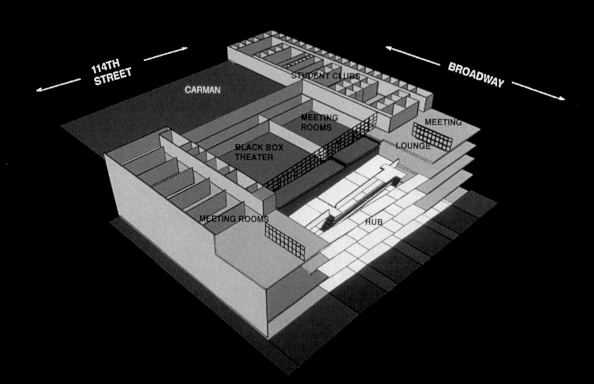

114TH
STREET — BROADWAY

STUDENT CLUBS

CARMAN

MEETING
ROOMS

MEETING

BLACK BOX
THEATER

LOUNGE

MEETING ROOMS

HUB

The tilting of the access ramps gives an unexpected image of a building that is fundamentally very practical and intended for use by large numbers of students.

Die geneigten Erschließungsrampen verleihen dem sehr funktional gestalteten Gebäude, das von einer großen Zahl von Studenten genutzt wird, eine überraschende Note.

L'inclinaison des rampes d'accès donne une image étrange à ce bâtiment très pratique, conçu pour être utilisé par un grand nombre d'étudiants.

JAMES TURRELL

Web: www.rodencrater.com

Roden Crater Project

JAMES TURRELL was born in Los Angeles in 1943. He received a diploma in psychology from Pomona College (1965) and in art from the University of California, Irvine, in 1966. Since that time, he has been responsible for a very large number of exhibitions and installations all over the world. He completed an installation with the architect Tadao Ando on the island of Naoshima in the Inland Sea of Japan in 1999. His interest is in the perception of light in various forms. Although he does not claim to be an architect, he has shown a consistent interest in the use of space in his work, and in particular in the case of the Roden Crater, which he purchased in 1977, of which images are published here. He conceived the lighting of the Pont du Gard near Nîmes in France, and participated in the exhibition "La Beauté" in Avignon (2000).

JAMES TURRELL, geboren 1943 in Los Angeles, erwarb 1965 sein Diplom in Psychologie am Pomona College und 1966 sein Kunstdiplom an der University of California in Irvine. Seither gestaltete er zahlreiche Ausstellungen und Installationen in der ganzen Welt. 1999 führte er zusammen mit dem Architekten Tadao Ando eine Installation auf der Insel Naoshima in der Japanischen Inlandsee aus. Sein besonderes Interesse gilt der Wahrnehmung von Licht in seinen verschiedenen Erscheinungsformen. Obwohl er sich nicht als Architekt definiert, zeugen seine Arbeiten von einer konsequenten Auseinandersetzung mit dem Thema Raum, was sich besonders im Fall des von ihm 1977 erworbenen Geländes Roden Crater und des gleichnamigen Projekts zeigt, das hier vorgestellt wird. Weitere Arbeiten sind das Lichtdesign für die Pont du Gard nahe der französischen Stadt Nîmes sowie ein Beitrag für die Ausstellung „La Beauté" in Avignon (2000).

Né à Los Angeles en 1943, **JAMES TURRELL** est diplômé en psychologie de Pomona College (1965) et en art de l'Université de Californie, Irvine, en 1966. Depuis cette époque, il a beaucoup exposé et monté des expositions dans le monde entier. Il a, entre autres, créé une installation avec l'architecte Tadao Ando sur l'île de Naoshima (Mer intérieure du Japon, 1999). Il s'intéresse à la perception de la lumière sous des formes variées. Bien qu'il ne se prétende pas architecte, il montre un intérêt permanent pour l'utilisation de l'espace, en particulier dans le projet du Roden Crater, volcan acquis en 1977, présenté ici. Il a conçu l'éclairage du Pont du Gard (Nîmes, France) et a participé à l'exposition « La Beauté » en Avignon (2000).

RODEN CRATER PROJECT

near Flagstaff, Arizona, USA, 1977–

Date of purchase: 1977. Site area: 50 000 hectares.

Roden Crater is located about forty miles from Flagstaff, Arizona. The volcano, which has been extinct for 390 000 years, was bought by James Turrell in 1977, and is surrounded by fifty thousand hectares of land that also belongs to the artist. The remnants of some six hundred volcanoes surround the site of Roden Crater. The first phase of the project was completed and opened to the public in July of 2003. The **RODEN CRATER PROJECT** is funded partially by the Dia and Lannan Foundations, as well as a ranch owned by the artist on the site. Turrell has engaged in extensive earthmoving work (several hundred thousand cubic meters of earth have been displaced) to turn the crater into an observatory of celestial phenomena, be they frequent, or rare, such as the lunar solstice that occurs every 18 years (most recently in 2006). The tunnels and rooms within the crater are all intended to bring the visitor into contact with light. "I am trying to make light a physical experience, so when you see light it is no longer illuminating other things, it is *the* thing," says the artist.

Roden Crater liegt circa 65 km von Flagstaff, Arizona, entfernt. 1977 erwarb James Turrell den seit 390 000 Jahren erloschenen Vulkan zusammen mit dem angrenzenden 50 000 ha großen Gelände, auf dem sich die Überreste von etwa 600 weiteren Vulkanen befinden. Die erste Phase des Projekts war im Juli 2003 abgeschlossen. Seither ist das **RODEN CRATER PROJECT** nur eingeschränkt zugänglich für Besucher. Es wird teilweise von der Dia Art Foundation und der Lannan Foundation unterstützt ebenso wie eine auf dem Grundstück liegende Ranch des Künstlers. Turrell ließ umfangreiche Erdarbeiten ausführen, bei denen mehrere Hunderttausend Kubikmeter Erde verschoben wurden, um den Krater in ein Observatorium für Himmelserscheinungen zu verwandeln, seien sie häufig oder selten auftretend, wie die Mondwende, die alle 18 Jahre eintritt (zuletzt 2006). Die im Kraterinneren angelegten Tunnel und Räume sollen die Besucher mit Licht in Kontakt bringen. „Ich versuche, das Licht zu einer physischen Erfahrung zu machen, so dass es nicht mehr dazu dient, etwas anderes zu beleuchten, sondern selbst die Hauptsache ist", so der Künstler.

Roden Crater se trouve à environ 65 km de Flagstaff, en Arizona. Ce volcan, éteint depuis 390 000 ans, a été acheté par James Turrell en 1977 ainsi que les 50 000 hectares de terres qui l'entourent. Le site est marqué par les restes de quelque six cents volcans. La première phase du projet a été achevée et ouverte au public (nombre limité de visiteurs) en juillet 2003. Le **PROJET RODEN CRATER** est financé en partie par les fondations Dia et Lannan, ainsi que le ranch propriété de l'artiste sur le site. Turrell s'est engagé dans d'énormes travaux de terrassement (plusieurs centaines de milliers de m³ ont été déplacés) pour transformer le cratère en un observatoire des phénomènes célestes, fréquents ou rares comme le solstice lunaire qui ne se produit que tous les 18 ans (le dernier a eu lieu en 2006). Les tunnels et salles creusés dans le cratère mettent le visiteur en situation de contact avec la lumière. « J'essaye de faire de la lumière une expérience physique. Lorsque vous voyez la lumière, ce n'est plus seulement un phénomène d'éclairage d'autres choses, c'est la chose même », explique l'artiste.

The visible profile of the volcano has not changed (above, seen from the west), but Turrell has dug profoundly into the mountain to create spaces with openings to the sky (right), one of which is the eye of the crater.

Während das sichtbare Profil des Vulkans unverändert blieb (oben von Westen aus gesehen), hat Turrell tief in den Berg hineingegraben, um Räume zu schaffen, die sich nach oben öffnen (rechte Seite), wobei es sich bei einem dieser Räume um das Zentrum des Kraters handelt.

Le profil visible du volcan n'a pas été modifié (en haut, vue de l'ouest), mais Turrell a fait creuser la montagne en profondeur pour créer des espaces ouverts vers le ciel (à droite), dont l'un est le centre du cratère.

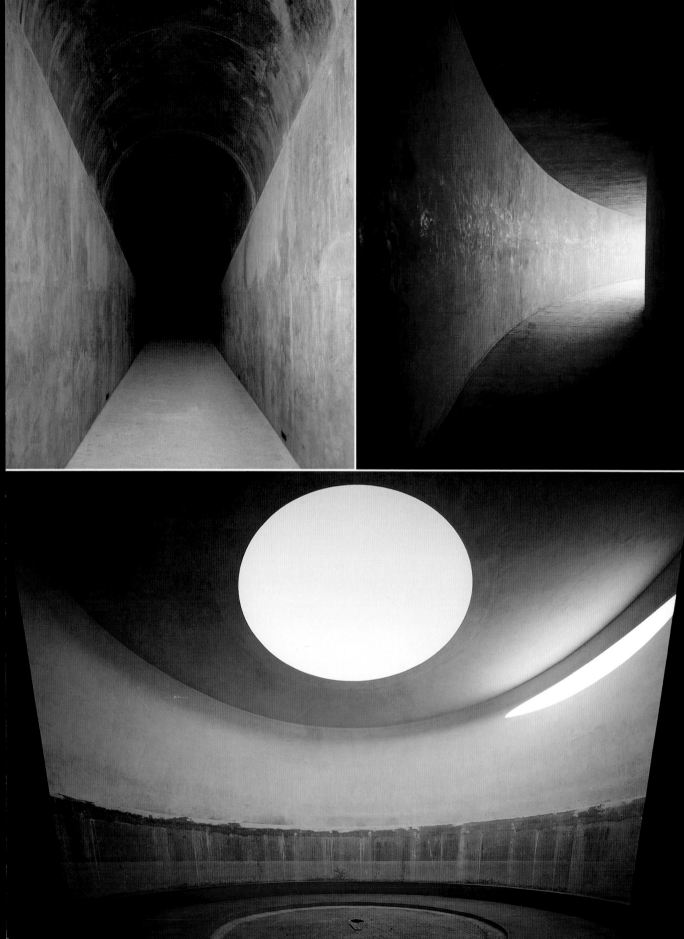

Above left the "Alpha Tunnel" that leads to the East Portal. Below left, the room below the eye of the crater. Above, an access ramp leading to the bowl of the crater.

Der zum Ostportal führende „Alpha Tunnel" (links oben). Der unterhalb des Kraterzentrums liegende Raum (links unten). Eine in den Kraterkessel führende Rampe (oben).

En haut, à gauche, l'« Alpha Tunnel », qui mène à la porte d'entrée Est. En bas, à gauche, la salle sous le centre du cratère. En haut, une rampe d'accès conduit au fond du cratère.

UNSTUDIO

UNStudio
Stadhouderskade 113
1073 AX Amsterdam
The Netherlands

Tel: +31 20 570 2040
Fax: +31 20 570 2041
E-mail: info@unstudio.com
Web: www.unstudio.com

Ben van Berkel was born in Utrecht in 1957 and studied at the Rietveld Academy in Amsterdam and at the Architectural Association (AA) in London, receiving the AA Diploma with honors in 1987. After working briefly in the office of Santiago Calatrava in 1988, he set up his own practice in Amsterdam with Caroline Bos. He has been a visiting professor at Columbia and a visiting lecturer at Princeton (1994). He was a diploma unit master at the AA (1994–95) and at Berlage Institute in Rotterdam. As well as the Erasmus Bridge in Rotterdam (inaugurated in 1996), **UNSTUDIO** has built the Karbouw and ACOM office buildings (1989–93), and the REMU Electricity Station (1989–93), all in Amersfoort; and housing projects and the Aedes East Gallery for Kristin Feireiss in Berlin. Other projects include an extension of the Rijksmuseum Twenthe, Enschede (1992–96); Möbius House, Naarden (1993–98); and Het Valkhof Museum, Nijmegen (1998), all in The Netherlands; a switching station, Innsbruck, Austria (1998–2001); a music theater, Graz, Austria (1998–2007); NMR Laboratory, Utrecht, The Netherlands (2000); Arnhem Station, The Netherlands (1986–2007); VilLA NM, Upstate New York (2000–06); and Mercedes-Benz Museum, Stuttgart (2003–06). UNStudio was also a participant in the competition for the new World Trade Center in New York, in collaboration with Foreign Office Architects, Greg Lynn FORM, Imaginary Forces, Kevin Kennon and Reiser + Umemoto RUR Architecture, under the name of United Architects, and realized "Holiday Home" in 2006.

Ben van Berkel wurde 1957 in Utrecht geboren und studierte an der Rietveld-Akademie in Amsterdam sowie an der Architectural Association (AA) in London, wo er 1987 das Diplom mit Auszeichnung erhielt. Nach einem kurzen Arbeitseinsatz 1988 im Büro von Santiago Calatrava gründete er mit Caroline Bos sein Büro in Amsterdam. Er war Gastprofessor in Columbia und Gastdozent in Princeton (1994). 1994 bis 1995 war er Diploma Unit Master an der AA und am Berlage Institute in Rotterdam. Neben der 1996 eingeweihten Erasmus-Brücke in Rotterdam errichtete **UNSTUDIO** in Amersfoort die Bürobauten für Karbouw und ACOM (1989–93) und das Kraftwerk REMU (1989–1993) sowie in Berlin Wohnungsbauprojekte und die Galerie Aedes East für Kristin Feireiss. Weitere Projekte sind die Erweiterung für das Rijksmuseum Twenthe (Enschede, 1992–96), Haus Möbius (Naarden, 1993–98) sowie das Museum Het Valkhof (Nimwegen, 1998), alle in den Niederlanden, eine Umschaltstation (Innsbruck, 1998–2001), ein Musiktheater (Graz, 1998–2007), das NMR-Labor (Utrecht, 2000), der Bahnhof Arnheim (1986–2007), die VilLA NM (bei New York, 2000–06) sowie das Mercedes-Benz-Museum (Stuttgart, 2003–06). UNStudio beteiligte sich darüber hinaus am Wettbewerb für das neue World Trade Center in New York in Zusammenarbeit mit Foreign Office Architects, Greg Lynn FORM, Imaginary Forces, Kevin Kennon und Reiser + Umemoto RUR Architecture, unter dem Namen United Architects. Außerdem errichtete das Büro 2006 das „Holiday Home".

Ben van Berkel, né à Utrecht en 1957, étudie à la Rietveld Academie d'Amsterdam, ainsi qu'à l'Architectural Association (AA) de Londres, dont il sort diplômé avec mention en 1987. Après avoir brièvement travaillé pour Santiago Calatrava en 1988, il ouvre son agence à Amsterdam, en association avec Caroline Bos. Il a été Professeur invité à la Columbia University, New York, et à Princeton en 1994, et Diploma Unit Master pour l'AA en 1994–95 et pour le Berlage Institute à Rotterdam. En dehors du pont Érasme à Rotterdam (inauguré en 1996), **UNSTUDIO** a construit les immeubles de bureaux Karbouw et ACOM (1989–93), le poste d'électricité REMU (1989–93), le tout à Amersfoort, ainsi que des logements et la galerie Aedes East de Kristin Feireiss à Berlin. Parmi leurs autres projets : l'extension du Rijksmuseum Twenthe, Enschede (1992–96), la maison Möbius, Naarden (1993–98), le musée Het Valkhof, Nimègue (1998), tous au Pays-Bas ; une sous-station à Innsbruck (Autriche, 1998–2001) ; une salle de musique à Graz, Autriche (1998–2007) ; le laboratoire NMR, Utrecht (2000) ; la gare d'Arnhem (Pays-Bas, 1986–2007) ; la villA NM, État de New York (2000–06) et le Mercedes-Benz Museum, Stuttgart (2003–06). UNStudio a participé au concours pour le World Trade Center à New York, en collaboration avec les Foreign Office Architects, Greg Lynn FORM, Imaginary Forces, Kevin Kennon et Reiser + Umemoto RUR Architecture, sous le nom de United Architects, et a réalisé l'installation « Holiday Home » en 2006.

NEUTRON MAGNETIC RESONANCE FACILITIES

Bijvoet University Campus, Utrecht, The Netherlands, 1997–2000

Client: University of Utrecht. Area: 1650 m². Cost: € 3 267 000 (excluding installations).

This laboratory building was designed for the analysis of the structure and behavior of proteins using high-frequency magnetic pulses. The program required the installation of eight spectrometers, a console and a control facility. The presence of high-energy magnetic fields posed specific problems, not only for the machines themselves, which had to be protected against irregularities in their immediate environment, but also for the users of the building. The magnetic fields also disturb computers, credit cards or pacemakers for example. As the architects said, "The magnetic radius shapes structure and surface, directs the program and equipment and affects internal circulation." As it did in the case of the Erasmus Bridge, the philosophy of the firm leads them naturally to projects like this one, that require intensive collaboration with specialists from fields very different from architecture.

Das Laborgebäude wurde für die Analyse der Struktur und des Verhaltens von Proteinen mittels Hochfrequenz-Magnetimpulsen entworfen. Dazu war die Installation von acht Spektralapparaten, einem Bedienungspult und einer Kontrollvorrichtung erforderlich. Hoch energetische Magnetfelder warfen besondere Probleme auf, da nicht nur Maschinen und Geräte vor Störungen geschützt werden mussten, sondern auch die Benutzer des Gebäudes, denn durch Magnetfelder können beispielsweise die Funktion von Computern, Kreditkarten oder Herzschrittmachern beeinträchtigt werden. „Der Magnetradius bestimmt Form und Oberfläche des Gebäudes, das Raumprogramm und die Ausstattung und wirkt sich auf die interne Zirkulation aus", so die Erläuterung der Architekten. Wie bereits bei der Erasmus-Brücke in Rotterdam führt die Philosophie von UNStudio zu Projekten wie diesem, welche die intensive Zusammenarbeit mit Spezialisten aus weit von der Architektur entfernten Bereichen erfordert.

Ce laboratoire se consacre à l'analyse de la structure et du comportement des protéines à partir des résonances magnétiques. Le programme comprenait l'installation de huit spectromètres et d'équipements de contrôle. La présence de champs magnétiques de haute énergie posait des problèmes spécifiques non seulement pour les utilisateurs, qui devaient être protégés, mais également pour les appareillages et les machines aisément perturbés. « Le rayon des ondes magnétiques a joué un rôle dans la détermination des structures et des surfaces, a orienté le programme et les équipements, ainsi que les circulations internes », explique l'architecte. Comme dans le cas du pont Érasme, la philosophie de l'agence s'adapte naturellement à des projets de ce type qui requièrent une collaboration très étroite avec des spécialistes de domaines très particuliers et très éloignés de l'architecture.

The wrapped, interconnected volumes of the NMR facilities are unexpected and yet dictated by the functional requirements of this very particular structure.

Die Gestaltung der miteinander verbundenen, ummantelten Bauteile des Laborgebäudes ist überraschend unkonventionell und dennoch von den funktionalen Erfordernissen dieser speziellen Einrichtung bestimmt.

Les volumes enveloppés et interconnectés du NMR surprennent mais sont dictés par les exigences fonctionnelles de ce bâtiment très particulier.

A thin concrete shell wraps around a steel and glass envelope, enclosing the equipment in an appropriate manner but also creating a contrast between a certain heaviness and a sense of movement. The thin wrappers contain the installations and routing system of the laboratory.

Die innere Hülle aus Stahl und Glas ist von einer dünnen Betonummantelung umgeben, in der die technischen Installationen des Labors untergebracht sind. Diese Konstruktion dient zum einen der Sicherheit und schafft darüber hinaus einen optischen Kontrast zwischen Schwere und Bewegung.

Une fine coque de béton se drape autour d'une enveloppe de verre et d'acier pour enfermer l'outil de recherche tout en générant un contraste entre une certaine pesanteur et un sentiment de mouvement. Les fins enveloppements contiennent les installations et le système de transmission du laboratoire.

An unexpected planar inclination, a glass envelope sitting on top of another one, each feature of the NMR facility attracts attention and alleviates any sense of monotony that might normally arise with such a building. Above, a factory-like interior.

Ungewöhnliche schräge Flächen und zwei aufeinandergesetzte Glashüllen – jedes Gestaltungsmerkmal des NMR-Gebäudes weckt Aufmerksamkeit und verhindert, dass der Eindruck von Monotonie entsteht, der sich häufig bei solchen Zweckbauten einstellt. Ein fabrikähnlicher Innenraum (oben).

Inclinaison surprenante, enveloppes de verre superposées : chaque caractéristique du NMR attire l'attention et allège la monotonie dont ce type de construction est généralement victime. En haut, un style intérieur de type industriel.

MAKOTO SEI WATANABE

Makoto Sei Watanabe
3-6-8-3508 Harumi, Chuo-ku
Tokyo 104-0053
Japan

E-mail: are@makoto-architect.com
Web: www.makoto-architect.com

Iidabashi Subway Station ▶

Born in 1952 in Yokohama, **MAKOTO SEI WATANABE** attended Yokohama National University from which he graduated with a master's degree in architecture in 1976. He worked from 1979 to 1984 in the office of Arata Isozaki before creating his own firm. His first built work, the Aoyama Technical College, Shibuya, Tokyo (1989), created considerable controversy because of its unusual forms, inspired by cartoon graphics. Since then Watanabe has worked more and more with computer-generated designs. His work includes: Chronospace, Minato-ku, Tokyo (1991); Mura-no-Terrace gallery, information office and café, Sakauchi Village, Ibi-gun, Gifu (1995); Fiber Wave, environmental art, Gifu and Tokyo (1995–96); Atlas, housing, Suginami-ku, Tokyo (1996); K-Museum, Koto-ku, Tokyo (1996); and Fiber Wave, environmental art, The Chicago Athenaeum, Chicago (1998). The Iidabashi Subway Station, Tokyo (2000), the Shin Minamata Shinkansen Station (2004), and two stations on the Tsukuba Express Line opened in 2005 show his considerable interest in rail facilities. He has also participated extensively in international exhibitions.

MAKOTO SEI WATANABE, geboren 1952 in Yokohama, studierte an der Staatlichen Universität Yokohama, wo er 1976 seinen Master in Architektur erwarb. 1979 begann er seine Tätigkeit bei Arata Isozaki und gründete 1984 sein eigenes Büro. Sein erster Bau, das Aoyama Technical College in Shibuya-ku, Tokio (1989), rief mit seinen von Cartoonzeichnungen beeinflussten, ungewöhnlichen Formen zahlreiche Kontroversen hervor. Seitdem setzte Watanabe immer stärker auf Computerentwürfe. Zu Watanabes weiteren Arbeiten zählen Chronospace in Minato-ku, Tokio (1991), Mura-no-Terrace, eine Galerie mit Informationszentrum und Café in dem Dorf Sakauchi, Ibi-gun, Gifu (1995), das Environment Fiber Wave in Gifu und Tokio (1995–96), die Wohnanlage Atlas in Suginami-ku und das K-Museum in Koto-ku, Tokio (beide 1996), das Fiber-Wave-Environment für das Chicago Athenaeum (1998) sowie die Iidabashi-U-Bahn-Station in Tokio (2000). Die U-Bahn-Station Shin Minamata Shinkansen (2004) und zwei Stationen der Tsukuba-Express-Linie, die 2005 eröffnet wurden, sind Beleg für Watanabes großes Interesse an Bahnhöfen. Er hat auch an zahlreichen internationalen Ausstellungen teilgenommen.

Né en 1952 à Yokohama, **MAKOTO SEI WATANABÉ** a étudié à l'Université nationale de Yokohama dont il sort diplômé d'architecture en 1976. En 1979, il travaille pour Arata Isozaki et, en 1984, fonde sa propre agence. Sa première réalisation est le Collège technique d'Aoyama construit dans le quartier Shibuya-ku de Tokyo en 1989, qui provoque moult controverses par ses formes insolites inspirées de la bande dessinée. Depuis, Watanabe s'est impliqué de plus en plus dans le design informatique.Parmi ses autres réalisations : Chronospace (Minato-ku, Tokyo, 1991) ; la galerie Mura-no-Terrace, bureau d'information et café à Sakauchi Village (Ibi-gun, Gifu, 1995) ; Fiber Wave, art environnemental (Gifu et Tokyo, 1995–96) ; Atlas, ensemble de logements à Suginami-ku (Tokyo, 1996) et le K Museum (Koto-ku, Tokyo, 1996) ; Fiber Wave, art environnemental, Chicago Athenaeum (Chicago, 1998), et la station de métro d'Iidabashi (2000). La station de métro Shin Minamata (2004) et deux stations de la ligne Tsubuka Express, inaugurées en 2005, sont la preuve de l'intérêt que Watanabe porte aux gares. Il a, en outre, participé à de nombreuses expositions internationales.

IIDABASHI SUBWAY STATION

Tokyo, Japan, 1999–2000

As the architect says, "This is one of the first attempts at deciding the actual form of construction at the will of the computer." For the **IIDABASHI SUBWAY STATION** on Tokyo's Oedo line (opened December 12, 2000), Watanabe installed a computer-generated structure made of green steel pipes, 7.6 centimeters in diameter, forming an interlaced three-dimensional network over the stairs, escalators and platforms of the station. Actually the result of a "dialogue" between Watanabe and the computer program, the design was inspired by the architect's image of the subway network as an overlapping system of tubes, or a "jungle of steel structures," as he says. His intention is to "make visible what is invisible" in the dense urban environment of Tokyo. The "Web Frame" computer program used is based on engineering data and enabled to automatically generate code within the established framework.

„Es handelt sich hier um einen der ersten Versuche, den Computer die eigentliche Form der Konstruktion bestimmen zu lassen", so der Architekt über sein Projekt. Für die Tokioter **U-BAHN-STATION IIDABASHI** der Oedo-Linie, die am 12. Dezember 2000 eröffnet wurde, installierte Watanabe eine computergenerierte Struktur aus grünen Stahlröhren. Mit einem Durchmesser von 7,6 cm erstrecken sie sich als dreidimensionales, miteinander verflochtenes Netzwerk über die Treppen, Rolltreppen und Bahnsteige. Dieses Design war gewissermaßen das Resultat eines „Dialogs" zwischen dem Architekten und dem Computerprogramm und wurde von Watanabes Vorstellung vom U-Bahn-Netz als einem überlappenden System von Röhren oder, wie er es nennt, einem „Dschungel aus Stahlkonstruktionen" inspiriert. Seine Absicht ist, im dicht bebauten Stadtgefüge von Tokio „das Unsichtbare sichtbar zu machen". Das von ihm verwendete Computerprogramm „Web Frame" basiert auf bautechnischen Daten und kann innerhalb einer festgelegten Grundstruktur eine automatische Programmierung vornehmen.

Dans la présentation de son projet, l'architecte précise qu'« il s'agit d'une des premières tentatives de laisser la décision de la forme réelle d'une construction à la bonne volonté d'un ordinateur ». Pour la **STATION DE MÉTRO IIDABASHI** située sur la ligne d'Oedo à Tokyo (ouverte le 12 décembre 2000), Watanabé a réalisé une structure générée par informatique constituée de tuyaux d'acier vert de 7,6 cm de diamètre, formant un réseau tridimensionnel d'entrelacs au-dessus des escaliers, des escalators et des quais. Résultat d'un « dialogue » entre l'architecte et l'ordinateur, le projet lui a été inspiré par sa vision du réseau de métro, système de tubes se chevauchant, ou « jungle de structures d'acier ». Son intention est de « rendre visible ce qui est invisible » dans l'environnement urbain particulièrement dense de Tokyo. Le logiciel d'« ossature de réseau » utilisé fonctionne à partir de données d'ingénierie et génère automatiquement des codes à l'intérieur d'une structure établie.

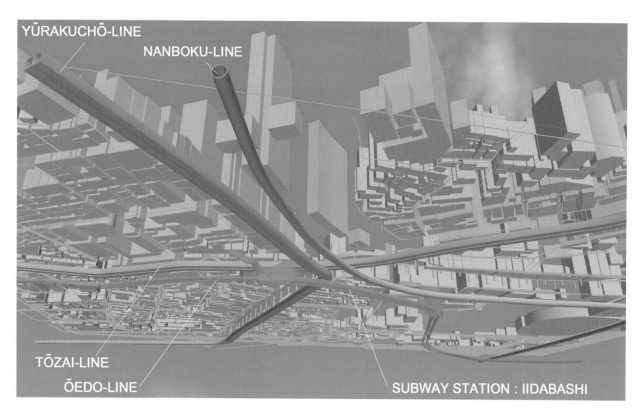

YŪRAKUCHŌ-LINE
NANBOKU-LINE
TŌZAI-LINE
ŌEDO-LINE
SUBWAY STATION : IIDABASHI

Above, a map of the region of Tokyo where the station is located. To the right, the structures designed by Makoto Watanabe visible from the street. This "Wing" houses the ventilation and air-conditioning equipment for the subway station.

Plan des Tokioter Stadtviertels (oben), in dem die Station liegt. Die von der Straße aus sichtbaren, von Makoto Watanabe entworfenen Bauteile (rechte Seite): Hier sind die Belüftungs- und Klimatisierungsvorrichtungen der U-Bahnstation untergebracht.

En haut, carte de la partie de Tokyo où se trouve la station de métro. À droite, les bâtiments de Makoto Watanabé, tels qu'on les voit de la rue. Cette « aile » abrite les installations de ventilation et de climatisation de la station.

Watanabe's theory about this station is even more elaborate than its appearance might lead the visitor to believe. He speaks of the invisible and interconnected web usually unseen by to the travelling public. Here, tunnels within the station.

Watanabes im Zusammenhang mit diesem Projekt entwickelte Gestaltungstheorie ist noch sorgfältiger durchdacht, als es das äußere Erscheinungsbild der Station verrät. So spricht er etwa von dem dicht geknüpften Netz, das für die Passagiere normalerweise unsichtbar bleibt, wie beispielsweise die hier abgebildeten Tunnel.

La théorisation de cette station par Watanabé est encore plus élaborée que son apparence ne pourrait le faire croire. Il parle ainsi de réseaux cachés et interconnectés, habituellement invisibles des voyageurs. Ici, des tunnels de la station.

An architect with a solid reputation for doing the unexpected in his designs, Makoto Sei Watanabe was called on here to deal with the rigorous demands of a system that handles millions of passengers every day. Theory meets reality.

Als Architekt, der den Ruf hat, mit seinen Entwürfen für Überraschungen zu sorgen, wurde Makoto Sei Watanabe beauftragt, sich mit den hohen Anforderungen eines Systems auseinanderzusetzen, das täglich Millionen von Passagieren befördert.

Quand la théorie rencontre la réalité : architecte réputé pour l'originalité de ses réalisations, Makoto Sei Watanabé a été appelé pour répondre aux exigences rigoureuses d'un système qui traite des millions de passagers chaque jour.

Generating Program ∕ WEB FRAME 2000

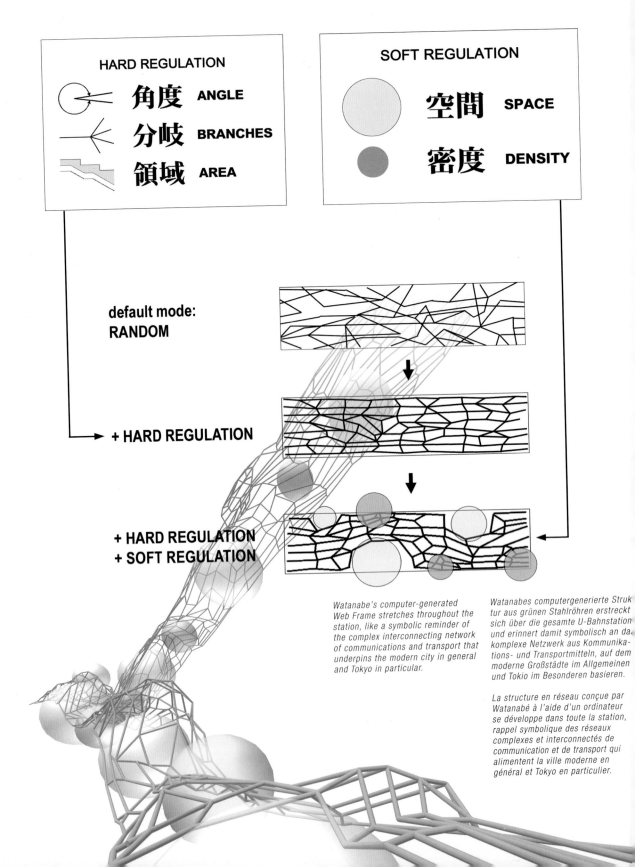

HARD REGULATION

角度 ANGLE

分岐 BRANCHES

領域 AREA

SOFT REGULATION

空間 SPACE

密度 DENSITY

**default mode:
RANDOM**

+ HARD REGULATION

**+ HARD REGULATION
+ SOFT REGULATION**

Watanabe's computer-generated
Web Frame stretches throughout the
station, like a symbolic reminder of
the complex interconnecting network
of communications and transport that
underpins the modern city in general
and Tokyo in particular.

Watanabes computergenerierte Struk
tur aus grünen Stahlröhren erstreckt
sich über die gesamte U-Bahnstation
und erinnert damit symbolisch an da
komplexe Netzwerk aus Kommunika-
tions- und Transportmitteln, auf dem
moderne Großstädte im Allgemeinen
und Tokio im Besonderen basieren.

La structure en réseau conçue par
Watanabé à l'aide d'un ordinateur
se développe dans toute la station,
rappel symbolique des réseaux
complexes et interconnectés de
communication et de transport qui
alimentent la ville moderne en
général et Tokyo en particulier.

TOD WILLIAMS
BILLIE TSIEN ARCHITECTS

Tod Williams Billie Tsien Architects
222 Central Park South
New York, New York 10019
USA

Tel: +1 212 582 2385
Fax: +1 212 245 1984
E-mail: mail@twbta.com
Web: www.twbta.com

TOD WILLIAMS was born in Detroit, Michigan, in 1943. He received his BA (1965) and Master of Fine Arts (1967) degrees from Princeton University. After six years as an associate architect in the office of Richard Meier in New York, he began his own practice in New York in 1974. **BILLIE TSIEN** was born in Ithaca, New York, in 1949. She received her BA at Yale, and her M.Arch. from UCLA (1977). She was a painter and graphic designer (1971–75), cofounding Tod Williams Billie Tsien Architects in 1986. Their built work includes the New College, University of Virginia (Charlottesville, Virginia, 1992); the Neurosciences Institute (La Jolla, California, 1995); the renovation and extension of the Phoenix Art Museum (Arizona,1996; Phase II, 2006); the Cranbrook Natatorium (Bloomfield, Michigan, 1999); and the American Folk Art Museum (New York, New York, 2001). Recent and future work includes the Asia Society Hong Kong Center (Hong Kong, China, 2011); the Barnes Foundation (Philadelphia, Pennsylvania, 2010–12); the Reva and David Logan Center for Creative and Performing Arts, University of Chicago (Chicago, Ilinois, 2012); Orchard Student Residences, Haverford College (Haverford, Pennsylvania, 2012); Tata Consultancy Services Campus (Mumbai, India, Phase I, 2013); Lakeside Center at Prospect Park (Brooklyn, New York, 2014); and the Andlinger Center for Energy and the Environment, Princeton University (Princeton, New Jersey, 2015), all in the USA unless stated otherwise.

TOD WILLIAMS wurde 1943 in Detroit, Michigan, geboren. Er absolvierte einen B. A. (1965) und einen Master of Fine Arts (1967) an der Princeton University. Nach sechs Jahren als Associated Architect im New Yorker Büro von Richard Meier arbeitete er ab 1974 selbstständig. **BILLIE TSIEN** wurde 1949 in Ithaca, New York, geboren. Sie absolvierte einen B. A. in Yale und einen M. Arch. an der UCLA (1977), war als Malerin und Grafikdesignerin tätig (1971–75) und gründete mit Williams 1986 das Büro Tod Williams Billie Tsien Architects. Zu ihren Arbeiten gehören das New College der University of Virginia (Charlottesville, Virginia, 1992), das Neurosciences Institute (La Jolla, Kalifornien, 1995), die Renovierung und Erweiterung des Phoenix Art Museum (Arizona, 1996; 2. Abschnitt 2006), die Cranbrook-Schwimmhalle (Bloomfield, Michigan, 1999) und das American Folk Art Museum (New York, 2001). Jüngere und anstehende Projekte sind das Asia Society Hong Kong Center (Hongkong, 2011), die Barnes Foundation (Philadelphia, Pennsylvania, 2010–12), das Reva and David Logan Center for Creative and Performing Arts, University of Chicago (Chicago, Ilinois, 2012), das Orchard-Studentenwohnheim, Haverford College (Haverford, Pennsylvania, 2012), der Tata Consultancy Services Campus (Mumbai, Indien, 1. Bauabschnitt, 2013), das Lakeside Center im Prospect Park (Brooklyn, New York, 2014), das Andlinger Center for Energy and the Environment, Princeton University (Princeton, New Jersey, 2015).

Né à Détroit, Michigan, en 1943, **TOD WILLIAMS** obtient son B.A. (1965) et son master des beaux-arts (1967) à l'université de Princeton. Après six ans comme architecte associé dans l'agence de Richard Meier à New York, il ouvre sa propre agence à New York en 1974. Née à Ithaca, New York, en 1949, **BILLIE TSIEN** obtient son B.A. à Yale et son M.Arch à l'UCLA (1977). Elle est d'abord peintre et graphiste (1971–75) avant de participer à la fondation de Tod Williams Billie Tsien Architects en 1986. Parmi leurs réalisations, on peut mentionner le New College, université de Virginie (Charlottesville, Virginie, 1992) ; le Neurosciences Institute (La Jolla, Californie, 1995) ; la rénovation et l'extension du Phoenix Art Museum (Arizona, 1996, Phase II, 2006) ; le Cranbrook Natatorium (Bloomfield, Michigan, 1999) et l'American Folk Art Museum (New York, 2001). Parmi leurs projets récents ou futurs, on trouve l'Asia Society Hong Kong Center (Hong Kong, 2011) ; la Fondation Barnes (Philadelphia, 2010–12) ; le Reva and David Logan Center for Creative and Performing Arts, université de Chicago (Chicago, 2012) ; la résidence pour étudiants Orchard, Haverford College (Haverford, Pennsylvanie, 2012) ; Tata Consultancy Services Campus (Bombay, Phase I, 2013) ; le Lakeside Center à Prospect Park (Brooklyn, New York, 2014) ; l'Andlinger Center for Energy and the Environment, université de Princeton (Princeton, New Jersey, 2015).

AMERICAN FOLK ART MUSEUM

New York, New York, USA, 1999–2001

Costs: $ 25 million. Gallery area: 1170 m². Collection: 3500 objects.

Set just next to the Museum of Modern Art on 53rd Street, the **AMERICAN FOLK ART MUSEUM** is an eight-level 3000 m² structure with about 1400 m² of exhibition space. It contains a library, store, cafe and offices as well as the galleries. Although the architects did not design the specific displays for the museum, many of the larger, more significant objects were placed by them. This is in particular true of the public spaces such as the entrance hall and stairwell. As they have in other cases, the architects engaged in a series of rich confrontations of different materials ranging from a green fiberglass screen running along the main stair to the surprising metal façade on 53rd Street. Daylight is brought into the building from the topmost levels, filtering down along slit openings through each floor. Alternating rough finish and polished concrete, they obtain a sensuality in the materials that is unusual in such a building in the heart of Manhattan.

Das **AMERICAN FOLK ART MUSEUM** liegt direkt neben dem Museum of Modern Art an der 53rd Street. Das Gebäude hat acht Stockwerke und 3000 m² Nutz-fläche, von denen circa 1400 m² als Ausstellungsräume dienen, eine Bibliothek, einen Museumsshop, ein Café und Büros. Auch wenn die eigentlichen Ausstellungsräume nicht von den beiden Architekten ausgestaltet wurden, stammen etliche der größeren und signifikanteren Einrichtungsobjekte von ihnen, insbesondere in den öffentlichen Bereichen wie Eingangshalle und Treppenhaus. Wie schon in anderen Bauten haben Williams und Tsien auch hier eine Fülle verschiedener, miteinander kontrastierender Materialien eingesetzt, von einer grünen Glasfaserblende, die entlang der Haupttreppe verläuft, bis zu der auffallenden Metallfassade an der 53rd Street. Das vom Dach-geschoss einfallende Tageslicht dringt durch Fensterschlitze in alle Stockwerke vor. Im Wechsel von roh bearbeiteten Oberflächen und geschliffenem Beton erzielen die Architekten eine Sinnlichkeit in den Materialien, die für ein Gebäude im Herzen Manhattans ungewöhnlich ist.

Juste à côté du Museum of Modern Art sur 53rd Street, le **AMERICAN FOLK ART MUSEUM** (huit niveaux sur 3000 m²) comprend des espaces d'expositions de 1400 m². Le musée possède une bibliothèque, une boutique, un café et des bureaux. Si les architectes n'ont pas conçu la présentation des collections, la plupart des œuvres significatives ont été implantées par eux. C'est en particulier le cas dans les espaces publics comme le hall d'entrée et la cage d'escalier. Comme dans leurs autres réalisations, ils ont organisé une série de confrontations entre divers matériaux allant de l'écran de fibre de verre vert le long de l'escalier principal à la surpre-nante façade métallique sur la rue. La lumière naturelle est canalisée à partir des niveaux supérieurs et se fraye son chemin par des fentes aménagées à chaque niveau. L'alternance de béton poli ou brut crée une sensualité de matériaux inhabituelle dans ce type de bâtiment au cœur de Manhattan.

Adjoining the Museum of Modern Art, the eight-story museum building is just 12 meters wide. Its irregular metal façade gives the building a distinct presence in the street.

Das achtstöckige und nur 12 m breite Museumsgebäude grenzt an das Grundstück des Museum of Modern Art. Durch seine unregelmäßig ge-formte Metallfassade tritt das Gebäu-de im Straßenbild deutlich hervor.

Adjacent au Museum of Modern Art, le bâtiment du musée et ses huit niveaux ne mesure que 12 m de large. Ses façades métalliques irré-gulières lui confèrent une présence urbaine particulière.

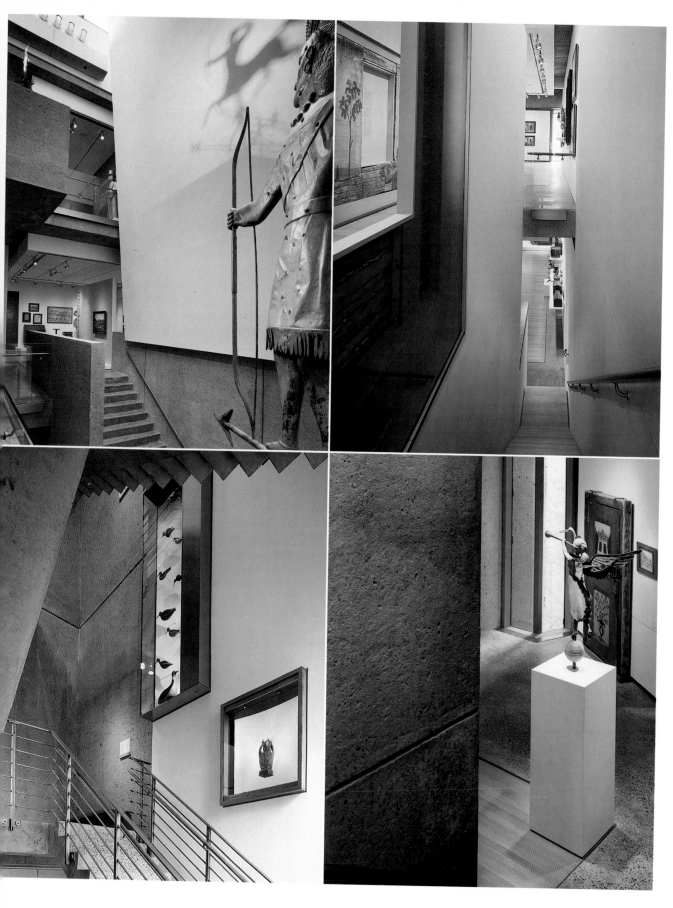

Certain works were placed by the architects including the large weather vane in the form of an American Indian (left page, upper left). The architects' subtle use of surfaces and materials gives a richness to the relatively modest-sized space.

Mehrere Exponate, wie etwa die Wetterfahne in Gestalt eines Indianers (linke Seite, oben links), wurden von den Architekten platziert. Der raffinierte Einsatz von Oberflächen und Materialien bereichert den relativ kleinen Innenraum.

Certaines œuvres ont été mises en place par les architectes dont la girouette en forme d'Indien américain (page de gauche, en haut à gauche). Le recours subtil des architectes au traitement des surfaces et des matériaux confère une certaine richesse aux espaces de petites dimensions.

CARLOS ZAPATA

Carlos Zapata Studio
520 Broadway
New York, New York 10012
USA

Tel: +1 212 966 9292
Fax: +1 212 966 9242
E-mail: mkoff@cz-studio.com
Web: www.cz-studio.com

Quito House ▶

CARLOS ZAPATA obtained his M.Arch. degree from Columbia University and his B.Arch. at the Pratt Institute. Carlos founded his own office in Miami Beach after leaving his position as Design Director and Vice President of Ellerbe Becket/New York. In 1996, Zapata joined Ben Wood to form Wood + Zapata, with offices in Boston and Shanghai; and in 2005, the two offices evolved into separate entities, with Carlos heading Carlos Zapata Studio, headquartered in New York City. The firm's largest completed project to date, the new Soldier Field in Chicago, was completed in 2003. Zapata is also the designer of Miami Airport's new Concourse J, a 15-gate international concourse that opened in fall 2007. Other recent projects include Cooper Square Hotel, a new 148-room luxury hotel in New York City (2008); Bitexco Financial Tower, a 68-story office tower in Ho Chi Minh City, Vietnam (2010); and the Fontainebleau Resorts and Casino, a new 3800-room hotel and casino in Las Vegas (under construction).

CARLOS ZAPATA erwarb seinen Master of Architecture an der Columbia University und seinen Bachelor of Architecture am Pratt Institute in New York. Zapata gründete sein eigenes Büro in Miami Beach, nachdem er seine Stelle als Design Director und Vizepräsident von Ellerbe Becket in New York aufgegeben hatte. 1996 gründete er gemeinsam mit Ben Wood Wood + Zapata mit Büros in Boston und Shanghai. 2005 entwickelten sich aus diesen beiden Standorten unterschiedliche Firmen, von denen Zapata das Carlos Zapata Studio mit Hauptsitz in New York leitet. Das größte bisher realisierte Projekt des Büros ist das neue Stadium Soldier Field in Chicago, das 2003 fertiggestellt wurde. Zapata entwarf auch die Halle J mit 15 Gates am Miami International Airport, die im Herbst 2007 eröffnet wurde. Weitere neuere Projekte sind das Cooper Square Hotel, ein neues Luxushotel in New York City mit 148 Zimmern (2008), der Bitexco Financial Tower, ein 68-geschossiger Büroturm in Ho-Chi-Minh-Stadt in Vietnam (2010), und das Fontainebleau Resorts and Casino, ein neues 3800-Zimmer-Hotel und Kasino in Las Vegas (in Bau).

CARLOS ZAPATA, Bachelor of Architecture du Pratt Institute et Master of Architecture de la Columbia University, a été vice-président de Ellerbe Becket (New York), avant de fonder le Carlos Zapata Design Studio à Miami en 1991. En 1996, il s'associe à Ben Wood pour créer Wood + Zapata, avec une agence à Boston et une à Shanghai. En 2005, les deux agences se séparent, Carlos dirigeant Carlos Zapata Studio au siège de New York. Le plus vaste projet de l'agence est le New Soldier Field (Chicago, 2003). Zapata est aussi l'architecte du Hall J de l'aéroport de Miami, comprenant 15 portes d'embarquement (automne 2007). Parmi ses autres projets : Cooper Square Hotel, un hôtel de luxe de 148 chambres à New York (2008) ; Bitexco Financial Tower, une tour de bureaux de 68 étages, à Hô Chi Minh-Ville, Vietnam (2010) et Fontainebleau Resorts and Casino, un nouvel hôtel-casino de 3 800 chambres à Las Vegas (en construction).

QUITO HOUSE

Miravalle, Quito, Ecuador, 1998–2002

Client: private. Total floor area: 743 m². Costs: not specified.

With its forward leaning façade and surprising terrace, this house would stand out in any environment.

Das mit seiner nach vorn geneigten Fassade und stegartigen Terrasse überraschende Haus würde in jeder Umgebung auffallen.

La façade inclinée vers l'avant et l'étonnante terrasse de cette maison se feraient remarquer dans n'importe quel environnement.

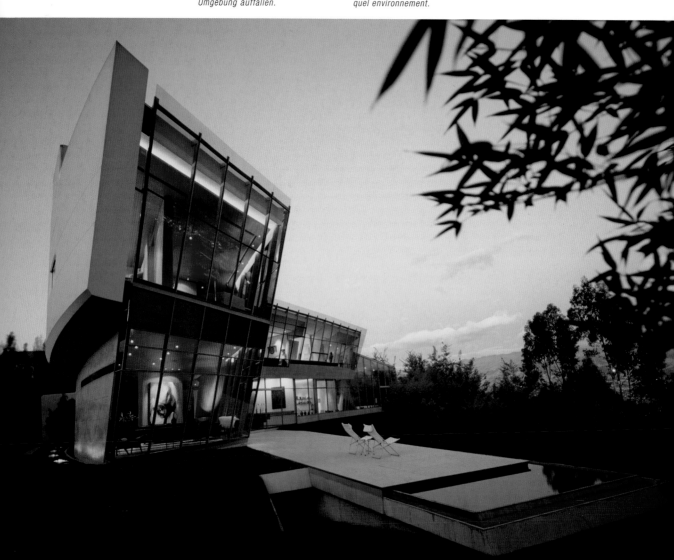

With its cantilevered volume and oblique columns the house appears to be ready to slide backward, or to take off.

Mit seinem auskragenden Baukörper und den schrägen Säulen wirkt das Haus, als würde es gleich nach hinten kippen oder abheben.

Le volume en porte-à-faux et les colonnes obliques donnent l'impression que la maison va glisser vers l'arrière ou s'envoler.

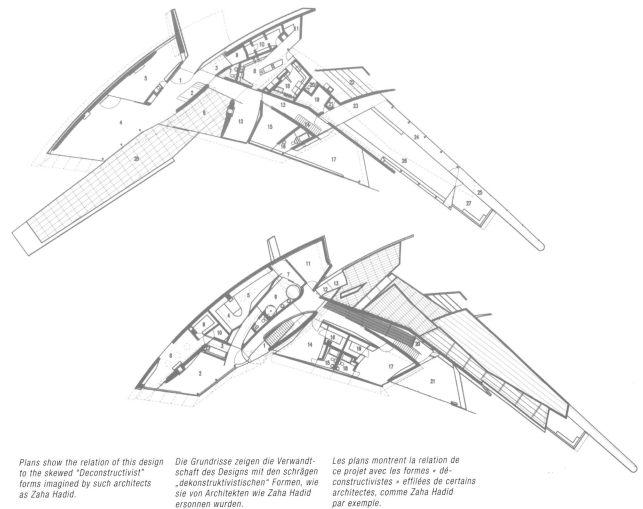

Plans show the relation of this design to the skewed "Deconstructivist" forms imagined by such architects as Zaha Hadid.

Die Grundrisse zeigen die Verwandtschaft des Designs mit den schrägen „dekonstruktivistischen" Formen, wie sie von Architekten wie Zaha Hadid ersonnen wurden.

Les plans montrent la relation de ce projet avec les formes « déconstructivistes » effilées de certains architectes, comme Zaha Hadid par exemple.

Built on an inclined, 5000 m² site very close to Quito with a 180° view of the valley of Miravalle and the Andes Mountains, the 743 m² **QUITO HOUSE** is part of a development with 80 other parcels of land. The main materials are poured-in-place concrete, stucco, glass, granite, zinc, stainless steel, and local wood. The architects write, "the house is an assembly of fluid, energetic, puzzle-like fragments which together fuse with the terrain and accentuate its natural contours. The resulting composition is therefore brought together with a powerful gesture inherent in the terrain itself." Two V-shaped floors are split apart by the main staircase opposite the entrance. The first wing of the first floor contains a living room adjacent to a family room and separated from it by a movable translucent wall. The second wing of the first floor contains a formal dining room, with an informal dining room adjacent to it. A movable wall allows the two dining rooms to become one for special functions. An interior garden next to the main entrance, the guest bathroom, the kitchen area, the laundry with exterior patio, a guest room with bathroom shared by a playroom and storage space are also located here. The children's wing contains two bedrooms with their respective bathrooms. The second wing of the second floor contains the master bedroom, a painter's studio adjacent to it, and the master bathroom adjacent to an open private garden.

Das Wohnhaus hat eine Gesamtnutzfläche von 743 m² und steht auf einem 5000 m² großen, leicht abschüssigen Grundstück nahe Quito mit Aussicht auf das Tal von Miravalle und die umliegenden Berge der Anden. Es ist zusammen mit 80 weiteren Parzellen Teil eines Bauprojekts. Die Baumaterialien für dieses Gebäude sind Gussbeton, Gipsputz, Glas, Granit, Zink, rostfreier Stahl und lokales Holz. Die Architekten über ihren Entwurf: „Das **QUITO-HAUS** ist eine Zusammenstellung fließender, energetischer, puzzleartiger Fragmente, die zusammen mit dem Terrain verschmelzen und dessen natürliche Konturen akzentuieren. Die endgültige Komposition ist folglich aus einer vom Terrain selbst ausgehenden, kraftvollen Geste entstanden." Im Innern bildet die gegenüber dem Eingang liegende Treppe die Trennlinie zwischen den beiden V-förmigen Geschossen. Der vordere Trakt des unteren Stockwerks enthält zwei Wohnbereiche, die sich durch eine durchscheinende Schiebewand voneinander abgrenzen lassen. Im hinteren Trakt befinden sich ein großes und ein kleineres Esszimmer, die sich wiederum durch Öffnen einer Schiebewand für besondere Anlässe zusammenlegen lassen. Ebenfalls in diesem Teil des Hauses liegen ein Wintergarten neben dem Haupteingang, der Küchenbereich, ein Gästezimmer mit Bad, ein Spielzimmer, mehrere Neben- und Versorgungsräume und ein Patio. Der von den Kindern bewohnte Teil enthält zwei Schlafzimmer mit dazugehörigen Badezimmern. Im Obergeschoss sind das Elternschlafzimmer, daran angrenzend ein Maleratelier und ein Badezimmer untergebracht, das sich zu einem kleinen Garten hinaus öffnet.

Construite près de Quito sur un terrain de 5000 m² bénéficiant d'une vue à 180° sur la vallée de Miravalle et les Andes, la **RÉSIDENCE QUITO** de 743 m² fait partie d'un lotissement de 80 parcelles. Les principaux matériaux sont le béton coulé sur place, le stuc, le verre, le granit, le zinc, l'acier inoxydable et le bois de la région. Pour l'architecte : « Cette maison est un assemblage de fragments de puzzle, fluides et énergétiques qui fusionnent avec le terrain et font ressortir son profil naturel. La composition qui en résulte est un geste puissant inhérent au site. » Deux niveaux en V séparés par l'escalier principal s'ouvrent de chaque côté de l'entrée. La première aile du premier niveau contient un séjour adjacent à un salon familial dont il est séparé par un mur translucide. La seconde aile de ce niveau contient une salle à manger de réception et une salle à manger familiale, qu'un cloisonnement mobile permet de réunir en certaines occasions. La même zone comprend également un jardin intérieur près de l'entrée principale, une chambre d'invités, la cuisine, la lingerie et son patio extérieur, une salle de jeux, une salle de bains et un espace de rangement. L'aile des enfants contient deux chambres et leurs salles de bains respectives. La seconde aile du second niveau est occupée par la chambre principale, un atelier de peinture adjacent et la salle de bains principale ouvrant sur un jardin privatif.

The forward tilting glazed façade of the house allows unusual interior spaces to be created with a combination of ample light and a certain amount of protection from the bright sky.

Die vornübergeneigte Glasfassade des Hauses erlaubt eine ungewöhnliche Innenraumgestaltung und bietet sowohl reichlich Tageslicht als auch Schutz vor direkter Sonneneinstrahlung.

La façade vitrée inclinée de la maison permet de créer des volumes intérieurs inhabituels qui combinent un généreux éclairage naturel à un certain degré de protection solaire.

Skewed walls or stairways animate interior spaces and a warm color scheme gives the whole a friendly, open appearance.

Die abgeschrägten Wände und Treppen beleben die Innenräume, während die warme Farbgebung dem Ganzen eine freundliche, offene Note verleiht.

Les murs penchés et les escaliers animent les volumes intérieurs. La coloration chaleureuse confère à l'ensemble un aspect amical et ouvert.

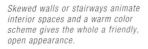

One might imagine a rectilinear modernist design as seen through the deforming effect of a wide-angle lens in the picture above, but it is the architecture itself that leans forward.

Bei der Abbildung könnte es sich um ein durch ein Weitwinkelobjektiv verzerrtes, modernistisches Design handeln, doch es ist die Architektur selbst, die sich vornüberneigt.

On pourrait presque imaginer un projet moderniste déformé par un objectif grand angle : en réalité, c'est la maison elle-même qui se penche en avant.

A swimming pool is largely sheltered by the house and participates in its unusual combination of materials and skewed angles.

Der Swimmingpool ist größtenteils vom Haus geschützt und trägt zu der ungewöhnlichen Kombination von Materialien und schrägen Winkeln bei.

Une piscine participe à l'esprit d'ensemble par un mariage inhabituel de matériaux et les profils des murs et du plafond.

INDEX OF ARCHITECTS / BUILDINGS / PLACES

CREDITS